D1570944

OUR MAN IN MOSCOW

ROBERT A.D. FORD

OUR MAN IN MOSCOW

A diplomat's reflections on the Soviet Union

University of Toronto Press
Toronto Buffalo London

ISBN 0-8020-5805-1

Printed on acid-free paper

Canadian Cataloguing in Publication Data

Ford, R. A. D., 1915–
Our man in Moscow

Includes index.
ISBN 0-8020-5805-1

1. Soviet Union – Politics and government 1945–
2. Soviet Union – Foreign relations – 1945–
3. Soviet Union – Social conditions – 1945–
4. Ford, R. A. D., 1915–
I. Title.

DK274.F67 1989   947.084′2   c88-094432-3

All photographs are from the author's private collection.

This book has been published with the help of grants
from the Canada Council and the Ontario Arts Council
under their block grant programs.

This book is dedicated to the memory of my wife Thereza,
whose love, loyalty, and intelligence
helped me through those many years in the Soviet Union;
and to all those members of the
Canadian foreign service who worked with me,
providing their unstinting support and help,
which made the fulfilment of my task
as head of mission possible.

CONTENTS

PREFACE

Almost forty years ago in Moscow I came across a Russian school primer of the 1900s. One sentence in particular caught my attention: 'The world is large; Russia is great; death is inevitable.' Even if those three thoughts are indisputable, it is difficult to conceive any Western schoolbooks, then or now, juxtaposing them into one sentence for the edification of the young. Yet a Soviet child today would not find the combination surprising.

Russians for centuries have lived and thought in an emotional and logical universe drastically different from ours. The Bolshevik revolution, although ideologically the child of rational Western thought and the inevitable outcome of several centuries of political philosophy, was essentially a Russian affair. Very little that has happened since has altered the dichotomy which exists between Moscow and the West.

The Russians today are conscious of being torn emotionally and politically between their own special view of the universe and a desire to belong to Western civilization. The struggle between Slavophiles and Westerners that has characterized so much of Russian history has not abated. It is not just the inevitable result of occupying an area which touches on Europe, Central Asia, and the Pacific; it is an ill-defined effort to reconcile two worlds in one nation.

It is tempting to agree with Dostoyevsky that 'Russia is a freak of nature and nothing else,' but it would be a tragic mistake to do so. It would be equally tragic to think of it as a vastly powerful and mysterious giant before which one must cringe in fear. The truth lies somewhere in between, and the challenge for the West is to come to terms with this conundrum.

To political pundits, Mikhail Gorbachev's unprecedented Western-oriented style of rapprochement following his ascent to the pinnacle of Soviet power, and the replacement of the old guard in the Kremlin by a more sophisticated generation of leaders, were welcome developments in what had been deteriorating East-West relations. Observers and adversaries allowed themselves some small degree of comfort in seeing an apparent desire to replace the shroud of mystery that had long surrounded the source of Soviet power with a new, translucent cloak fashioned to seem less threatening to the West. If Western strategies, however, regard this unforeseen development as a signal that Russia and Gorbachev are now prepared to deal and be dealt with in Western terms, it would be dangerously misleading.

Gorbachev's predecessors, from Lenin and Stalin to Khrushchev and Brezhnev, were equally adept, each in his own way, at exploiting the advantage of appearing unpredictable in their attempts to further Soviet policies in both internal and foreign affairs. The present leaders as the heirs of Russian history and traditions and of nearly seven decades of Soviet communism carry with them the same historical, political, and ideological baggage that shaped the actions and reactions of each of their predecessors.

To fully understand Russia and Gorbachev today and tomorrow depends on understanding the cause and impact, the success and failure, of those events of the past; the heart-breaking years following the Second World War, the transition from Stalin to Khrushchev, the emergence of Brezhnev, the transformation of the Soviet Union into a truly global power, and the last Brezhnev years, marked by rigid immobilism and a desperate effort to hold on to office.

The nineteenth-century historian Kliuchevski observed that the tsar, through the threat of power, hoped to provoke a spirit of initiative in an oppressed society. He wished the slave, while remaining a slave, to act like a free and fully conscious individual. Similarly, Gorbachev would like to achieve parity with the West through appeals for hard work and increased discipline without diminishing the Soviet system, which appears incapable of meeting the primary requirements of a modern society, except for the creation and maintenance of a formidable military apparatus.

Gorbachev faces the same dilemma as Peter the Great: how to reconcile the creation of a strong, technologically advanced, and efficient infrastructure, which can only result from adequate spiritual or material incentives, with a reaffirmation of the security of the current political system on which the survival of the ruling class depends. Like Peter, the Soviet leaders seem doomed to choose security. This, above all, will be the key element governing the approach the Soviets will take to East-West relations in the years ahead, and in the long run to the problem of economic and social restructuring.

I spent nearly twenty-one years in the Soviet Union as a Canadian diplomat over a period extending from 1946 to 1980. In this book I have attempted to take advantage of this unique experience to illuminate, if only fitfully, the phenomenon which is Russia and with which we have to live if we are all of us to survive. I have tried to make this neither a simple diplomatic memoir nor an academic study of Soviet affairs. But inevitably it deals primarily with politics, since I spent the major part of my time preoccupied with political and economic problems when dealing with senior Soviet officials. However, since I spoke Russian I was also able to make some contact with a cross-section of Soviet society – artists, writers, musicians, administrators, farmers, and ordinary citizens. And as a translator of Russian poetry into English I had an unusual access, within the limits of a closed society, to the Soviet intelligentsia.

As far as conditions permitted, I also travelled outside Moscow. I tried to see as much as possible of a country twice as big as Canada – to make use of my visits to Siberia, Central Asia, Ukraine, the Caucasus, and Old Russia to analyse internal and economic developments, from the immediate post-war period to the end of the Brezhnev era and the rise to power of Mikhail Gorbachev.

What I hope differentiates this from other books on the subject is that special perspective. I am the only Western diplomat who knew and dealt with all the Soviet leaders from the end of the war; I have had a chance at close range to understand and judge Soviet actions on the international scene and in domestic affairs and at the same time I have come to appreciate the sacrifices and suffering of a talented people in the toils of a basically alien and oppressive ideology and system.

I am grateful to the Social Sciences and Humanities Research Council of Canada, and to a Canadian friend who prefers to remain anonymous, for generous help in the preparation of this book. I also wish to thank William Heine and Cheryl Hamilton for their most useful advice and assistance, and Diane Mew for her skilful editing.

PART ONE

In Stalin's Shadow
and After

1

Life under Stalin

My first exposure to the Soviet Union came in the fall of 1946. I had joined the Canadian foreign service in the summer of 1940 after completing my master's degree in history at Cornell University, where I had begun to learn Russian in order to continue my studies in French-Russian relations. My first posting, however, was to Brazil. A year later my personal record caught up with me and a message came transferring me to the new Canadian mission to the Soviet Union in the wartime capital of Kuibishev. But at that moment I was deep in the Brazilian interior and my ambassador replied that he refused to agree to the transfer.

I appeared doomed not to use my hard-won Russian. Three years later, in 1945, I was again appointed to the embassy, by then back in Moscow; but this, too, was delayed by the disclosure by Igor Gouzenko of the vast Soviet spy ring in Canada. Instead I was sent to the First General Assembly of the United Nations in London in January 1946 and then stayed on in the Canadian High Commission while waiting to see whether relations with the Soviet Union would be severed.

This enforced delay had one great compensation. At the opening reception in the House of Lords given by Clement Attlee to the delegates to the General Assembly I overhead an attractive member of the Brazilian delegation making amusing remarks about the Canadians. I could not resist the temptation of turning and saying in Portuguese that the latter was not a secret language. This led inevitably to marriage. And so, when I was finally ordered to proceed to Moscow in September 1946, I had a companion who would share with me the subsequent twenty-one years of trials, tribulations, and excitement in the Soviet Union.

Neither of us seemed very likely candidates to become the longest-serving Western diplomats in the Soviet Union: Thereza, from Rio de Janeiro, a graduate of Columbia University; and I, sixth-generation Canadian on my father's side, American Yankee on my mother's. But somehow it worked out well. We survived, we even enjoyed the challenge, and managed over those years to maintain a reasonably balanced judgment of the Soviet Union.

We sailed from London in a small Soviet ship that took eight days through the North Sea, the Kiel Canal, Stockholm, Helsinki, and finally Leningrad. That sad and magnificent city was emerging from its terrible ordeal, a city which has no compare, sharing the best of Western Europe and of old Muscovy and its Byzantine past. It was a stunning approach for a young second secretary to a world which I was to come to know as thoroughly as a foreigner could over a period of thirty-five years, from the Gulf of Finland to the Crimea, Central Asia and the Caucasus, Siberia and the Pacific.

In 1946 the Soviet Union, even for a diplomat, was an uncomfortable place to be – uncomfortable physically, emotionally, and politically. There could be no real preparation for first exposure to the Soviet reality. Russia was, and still is today, a country which effectively defies classification, as the Russian philosopher Peter Chaadaev said: 'a whole separate world.' In the post-war years one had to contend with the lingering and usually dangerously wrong sentiments connected with the wartime alliance which at almost every level of Western society had created strong illusions – about the Soviet leadership, its intentions toward the West, the nature of the Stalinist system, and even about its military and economic strength. But it did not take long in the winter of 1946–7 to dispel whatever misapprehensions still existed on any of these scores.

We had to base our judgments on only two cities, Leningrad and Moscow, the rest of the country being inaccessible. While the Leningraders had suffered appallingly from the nine-hundred-day siege, and the suburbs which had been in the line of fire had been badly damaged, the city itself had not been subjected to massive aerial bombardment and the profile of one of the great cities of Europe was intact and delicately beautiful. Moscow also had not suffered seriously from air raids. Compared to London, for example, it had escaped unscathed. But the years of neglect had taken their toll and, never a beautiful city, it looked singularly dowdy and unattractive, except for its inner core and the incomparable Kremlin.

With the exception of the United States, France, and Britain, most of the embassies were crowded into small compounds. Ours was no exception. It was a late nineteenth-century building, built by two brothers, rich merchants; and, as usual in Russian palaces and mansions, more attention had been paid to elaborate reception rooms than bedrooms and the comforts we would consider normal. Even Nicholas II preferred sleeping on a couch in his library to the Western-style comfort to which he certainly had access.

The ambassador occupied the top floor, the chancery part of the ground floor, with the military attaché, his sergeant, and our clerical staff in a small building in the courtyard. My wife and I shared a flat on the ground floor with the third secretary and his wife. The garden had been turned into a vegetable plot, and part of the garage served as a root house to store potatoes, cabbage, and turnips during the long winter. But even in these primitive conditions, with very little more than basic rations, and without much chance of importing from abroad, we were very happy, as indeed were most of the foreign colony, many of whom were still housed in the Hotel National, the wives supplementing the meagre restaurant fare by cooking on bunsen burners in their bathrooms.

The embassy was located on a narrow, cobble-stoned street with the mellifluous name, Starokonyushenny Pereulok, which unfortunately translates into Old Stables Lane. But it ran through the Arbat, an old but centrally located district which still had preserved some of its pre-revolutionary charm. If ever we felt depressed at our lack of amenities, we needed only to stroll around it to see how poorly even the better-off Russians lived. Moscow since the revolution had doubled in size but there had been practically no new housing put up in the twenties and thirties except for a few prestige apartment houses for Party officials. Nothing, of course, had been done during the war, and the housing situation was acute. In fact it remained so until Khrushchev took over and launched a program for fast, cheap housing.

In 1946 it was not difficult to peer into curtainless windows and see the appalling overcrowding. It is hard to imagine how the post-war baby boom could have taken place in those conditions. Although there were very few contacts with Russians, we did visit a few Russian apartments. I can still see vividly the entrance to a former upper-middle class apartment building which, like all the others, had not been painted for thirty years. The elevator was permanently stuck about four feet off the floor level, a broken chair in it, and all covered with almost impenetrable dust. Our host was a middle-aged lady, the daughter of an admiral, who gave Russian lessons. Her 'apartment' was one room which she had just heard would shortly be subdivided. Her great problem was how to crowd the few precious relics of her past into half the space.

The problem of living space was thrust dramatically on us when we discovered that our Greek-Russian furnace-man had launched a lawsuit against another occupant of his apartment building. In the communal kitchen every occupant had the right to a certain space on the table, and lines were drawn on it to determine each person's rights. Two of the occupants gave birth to a baby and on the grounds of greater need arbitrarily redrew the lines adjusting the table space in their favour. Our Greek resisted and the matter was taken to court. He lost.

If every inch of living space was fought over, so was every gram of food. That winter was exceptionally severe and the country was once again on the verge of famine. It was not unusual to see some poor devil offering a couple of cubes of sugar for sale, and, as it always had done in the past, the city attracted starving peasants hoping desperately for help.

One day I came upon our Russian messenger, a young man of about twenty-five, who had lost an arm in the war, eating his lunch. It consisted of a piece of bread and hot water. This, it turned out, was his usual midday meal, which we at once improved on. But he seemed to think it not extraordinary. Nor did the population as a whole. So used were the Russians to suffering, death, and disaster, they seemed to be satisfied just to have survived.

Nor did they manifest in any way dissatisfaction with the obvious inequalities. They accepted that we as foreigners should live better than they. But they also accepted that the government and Party officials should have more. This was not only a basic assumption on the part of the average Russian, it was acknowledged officially by the ration system. Even in the embassy, ration cards were distributed by the Soviet government strictly according to rank. The ambassador got the biggest ration, his wife slightly less; then the counsellor, the military attaché, me, the third secretary, and the clerical staff. I once asked a Soviet official how they could justify this. We had just come from England where everyone got exactly the same rations. He looked at me in astonishment. He found it unbelievable that officials whose service to the state was important should get the same rations as an ordinary person. He found it unjust, irrational, and in the long run inefficient.

What I came to realize with the years as the usual Russian combination of cockiness, distrust, and lack of self-confidence was particularly manifest that winter. The war had been won, Eastern Europe was in their grip, the West seemed bemused. But the Soviet leaders knew better than we, who could only guess, how weak the economy was, how uncertain the mood of the country, and how far they could go in reimposing the tightest kind of controls after the relative relaxation of the war years.

In 1946–7 we Westerners in Moscow generally were baffled at the refusal of the Soviet authorities to permit us to see for ourselves the extent of the damage the Germans had inflicted on areas they had occupied. We argued that, once the West knew from first-hand accounts how badly the Russian and Ukrainian peoples had suffered, there would be great sympathy in the West for them and help would be forthcoming.

The Russians never argued with us; they simply rejected every request to travel in these areas on the grounds that neither transportation nor accommodation was adequate. But to themselves they probably justified these refusals on the grounds that Western sympathy would be short-lived and probably not manifested in a practical way; that our governments would be encouraged to take a strong line politically against the Soviet Union when the extent of the damage to its economy became known; and finally, Western help was not wanted anyway because it would help to perpetuate memories of wartime aid and make it more difficult for the Soviet authorities to maintain control of populations already automatically suspect because they had been occupied.

Few events brought home more clearly to the Western public the unchanged attitude of the Soviets than the case of Igor Gouzenko, the code clerk in the Soviet embassy in Ottawa, who defected in the fall of 1945, bringing with him indisputable evidence of widespread Soviet espionage activities master-minded by the secret service agents in the embassy. The Gouzenko affair, which had delayed my arrival in Moscow by a whole year, was still causing repercussions in our embassy. The counsellor was withdrawn, and the ambassador, Dana Wilgress, who had been absent from the spring of 1946, returned only briefly in March 1947 for the Four Power Conference on Germany. He departed immediately afterwards, leaving me unexpectedly in charge.

The Moscow conference of the Big Four was an exercise in complete futility, but it did finally convince the West that Stalin had no intention of continuing any further the illusion of a Western-Soviet alliance. It needed only the brutal frankness of Foreign Minister Vyacheslav Molotov to drive the lesson home. While Molotov with his inexorable rigidity was a revelation to many in the West, Ernest Bevin, the then British foreign secretary, provided his own rude shocks to the Russians. On one occasion Bevin was goaded beyond endurance by Molotov's constant harping on the welfare of the working people as represented by the Soviet leaders. He stopped Molotov in mid-stream, placed his heavy workman's hands on the table, and challenged Molotov to do the same in order to show who represented the workers. Molotov, with his carefully manicured hands that had never seen a day's manual work, was overcome with confusion and dropped the subject.

But even so, Bevin could not give up his hope that there must be some way in which the two 'socialist' regimes could co-operate. And when he left Moscow by the military train for Berlin, I recall his suddenly seizing Andrei Vishinsky, who had been designated to see him off, by the arm. Forming a circle of British and Soviet officials in the Byelorussia railway station, he began singing 'For He's a Jolly Good Fellow,' to the dismay of the dreadful Vishinsky –

surely the last person in the world to be so addressed, with the shadow of the terror trials over which he had presided looming over him.

As the Soviet grip on Eastern Europe tightened, so did the grip over their own people. Even in 1946–7, the few Russians we saw, outside of the officials with whom we dealt, hardly bothered to conceal the panic which had beset the Party as the Germans approached Moscow in the winter of 1941–2. Those who had an excuse to leave did so, and those who had to stay often burnt their Party cards and tried to conceal their allegiances. When the danger passed the faithful returned and those who had remained were all immediately under suspicion. Did they stay because secretly they hoped for a German victory? This was the question and it came later to be posed to everyone who had by force majeure remained in the vast territories conquered by the Nazis, and even to those soldiers made prisoner of war, often as a result of bureaucratic or tactical blunders by an officer caste weakened by Stalin's purges of the late thirties.

In addition to this paranoiac suspicion of over half the population, Stalin was worried by the concessions which the exigencies of the struggle had wrung from him: the revival of the Orthodox Church, the playing down of Marxist ideology and a revival of Russian national feeling, the dangerous notion in the minds of the people that fascism was the only enemy and Western capitalists were friends and allies, vague promises that the horrors of the thirties would disappear and the government would concentrate on building a better, happier, and more liberal society.

To implement these promises after the war would have seriously endangered the Soviet system in the best of circumstances. But conditions were, on the contrary, very difficult. The problem of reconstructing whole cities – Minsk, Kiev, Kharkov, to mention only three – and vast industrial areas that had been devastated, particularly in Ukraine, was immense by any standard. The rejection of American aid meant it had to be done by the primitive tools the Russians had at their disposal, and often in territories seething with dissent such as Ukraine, or those only recently incorporated forcibly into the Soviet Union, such as Moldavia, Estonia, Latvia, Lithuania, and Finnish Karelia. Then there was the problem of occupying militarily most of Eastern and Central Europe and of dealing with the troops inevitably disaffected by exposure to vastly higher standards of living than anything they had ever seen before.

In spite of all this, the Russian spirit was so high at the end of the war, and the enthusiasm engendered by what they, the Russian people, had accomplished, that they could, in my opinion, have been inspired to accomplish the great task of reconstruction without risking the overthrow of the regime. But Stalin, in his maniacal isolation in the Kremlin, distrustful as much of his own people as of the outside world, could only see one way to handle it – by a redoubling of the terror by which he had crushed his enemies, supposed and real, decimated the hierarchy of the Communist Party, and cowed the people into total submission.

The foreigners in Moscow were of course aware of the enormities of the concentration camp system. And, in spite of the bureaucratic efforts to keep us confined to Moscow, there was the occasional glimpse of a cattle car jammed with detainees starting on its agonizing journey to Magadan, or of prisoners – occasionally German, more often Russian or Ukrainian – toiling on projects such as road-building. And, a supreme irony, we even saw a group of prisoners in Leningrad repairing Smolny, the headquarters of Lenin in 1917.

It was difficult at times to live in relative comfort and freedom in Moscow, and to be polite and diplomatic with the Soviet officials we had to deal with, when we knew or guessed what was still happening to so many innocent people, punished often for no greater crime than to be a Lithuanian or a Ukrainian, or to have had the misfortune to become a prisoner of the Germans. For Stalin this in itself was a crime. It did not even require some innocuous expression of dissatisfaction, as in the case of Alexander Solzhenitsyn, to be condemned to a decade in the labour camps of northern Siberia.

During that period it became impossible to meet any Russian intellectuals, as the Soviet press and the activities of the police increasingly warned against the dangers of association with foreigners. Sergei Prokoviev was one of the few intellectuals permitted some leeway in limited contacts with foreigners – unlike Dmitri

Shostakovich, who practically never was seen except occasionally as a mere shadow at the back of a box in the Conservatory of Music.

Naturally the Soviets exploited Prokoviev's prestige as a composer and his great reputation in the West for their own purposes. He was tolerated because of the immense popularity of the ballets 'Cinderella' and 'Romeo and Juliet,' for which he wrote the music. The nostalgia of the West, and the past, filled a great emotional need for the average Russian in those days and the choice of classical themes permitted the avoidance of ideological pitfalls. And it was 'Romeo and Juliet' that the Soviets often served up for gala occasions. At one of these, during the intermission, my wife commented in French that the ballet was indifferent but it was the superb music which held it together. The man standing with his back to her turned, bowed, and said: 'Je suis Prokoviev, Madame. Je vous remercie.' After that, we met the composer and his Spanish-French wife occasionally, and their pleasure in talking with someone from outside and in French and English was obvious. But they did not dare come to the embassy, and when we returned to Moscow in 1951 they were inaccessible. Prokoviev's death in March 1953 went almost unnoticed in the concentration on the passing of Stalin.

It was frustrating for all the foreigners who had a liking for Russian literature to find it impossible to meet such great writers as Boris Pasternak and Anna Akhmatova, or even indeed to find their works in Russian. By the fall of 1946 this isolation of the writers had become official doctrine through the launching of a series of decrees, the aim of which was to repress the few signs of liberalism that had appeared in Soviet literature during the war. The tough party boss of Leningrad, Andrei Zhdanov, was given the task of organizing the attack of the intelligentsia. The renewed repression of the arts was to be the pattern for the following eight years, and became generally known as the Zhdanovshchina.

Very few were spared in the violent attacks on poets, novelists, historians, philosophers, dramatists, composers, musicians. The main sins were 'cosmopolitanism' and 'formalism' and under these rubrics the slightest deviation from socialist realism meant at the least expulsion from the Writers' Union, at the worst disappearance into the great maw of the concentration camps.

In retrospect it seems nearly miraculous that Pasternak managed to survive those last dreadful years. He kept his head down, continued his marvellous translations of Shakespeare, probably the best interpretations of the bard in any foreign language, but made no effort to write what was required of him, nor to publish what he knew at that time was unpublishable. And yet in his quiet cottage in the writers' colony of Peredelkino, which I came to know well twenty years later through my acquaintance with the poet Andrei Voznesensky, Pasternak gradually evolved *Doctor Zhivago* and the marvellous poems which were to be his final literary, political, and philosophical testament to the world.

Akhmatova fared far worse. Her poetry had always been suspect because of its very nature; its personal flavour, its fragility, its message of a private view of the universe, its elegance, all contrasting too sharply with the collectivized world of post-war Stalinism. It was not enough that lyric poets did not write verse which 'helped to construct socialism'; Stalin and Zhdanov considered that any poetry which escaped ideological classification was *ipso facto* subversive. Thus the great poets Marina Tsvetaeva and Osip Mandelshtam and so many others were silenced. Tsvetaeva, like Essenin and Mayakovsky before her, killed herself during the last years of the war, and Mandelshtam disappeared in a concentration camp, prophetically fulfilling his comment on the system: 'Russia is the only place where poetry is really important. They'll kill people for it here.'

For the leaders of the Soviet Union in 1946 there was no way in which personal poetry could be fitted into their concept of society. It did not contribute to the building of communism; worse, by portraying a personal world outside the collective universe, it could be considered anti-Soviet. Thus Akhmatova was denounced publicly in the press, in specially convoked meetings, by her colleagues in the literary world, as a dangerous parasite. Her books were withdrawn from circulation and she was expelled from the Writers' Union, which meant depriving her of any opportunity to earn a living. She had already lost her husband and son in the Gulag. Only the generosity of courageous friends kept her alive.

At the time it seemed puzzling that an apparently inoffensive poet should take the brunt of the attack of literature, and I wrote down in my notebook, à propos of Akhmatova, the lines of Paul Eluard:

> Si l'homme doit mourir avant d'avoir son heure,
> Il faut que les poètes meurent les premiers.
> (If man must die before his hour,
> The poets must be the first to die).

The composers also began to come under strong attack, in particular Prokoviev and Shostakovich. Prokoviev managed to take this in his stride, but Shostakovich, by nature a highly sensitive and retiring person, was brought close to a nervous breakdown by the denunciation of some of his best music, and by the efforts of Stalinist members of the Composers' Union to force him to write the kind of music they thought the construction of a communist society required.

Most Soviet citizens were sufficiently adept at reading the meanings of pronouncements in the press to interpret the attacks on the intelligentsia for 'cosmopolitanism' as a warning to avoid contact with foreigners. But to make absolutely sure that there was no misunderstanding, two decrees, in June 1947 and in January 1948, spelled it out in detail.

The decree of 1947, entitled 'On Liability for Divulging State Secrets and for Losing Documents Containing State Secrets,' provided for the most severe penalties even for accidental contraventions of the decree. After listing in great detail the nature of information the revelation of which could get you twenty years in a forced labour camp, it ended up with a generalized clause stating that classified information included 'any other measures in the field of foreign policy and foreign trade not contained in officially published data.' This decree clearly made talking to foreigners too dangerous for consideration even by highly placed officials. As a result, even talks at the Foreign Ministry with officials authorized to discuss foreign problems were usually confined to the strictest formality.

As if this were not clear enough, the second decree of January 1948 prescribed that only the Ministry of Foreign Affairs was authorized to deal with officials of foreign states. Whatever doubts any Soviet citizens might have had about the nature of their relations with foreigners was now crystal clear. The last illusion, if any still existed, about the wartime alliance was thus firmly dispelled. And the press quickly developed the theme that it was anti-Soviet to adopt an attitude other than suspicion and hostility towards countries, and their representatives on the spot, supposedly dedicated to the destruction of communism. This in turn called for greater awareness of the need for vigilance against spies and potential spies in their midst.

The NKVD increasingly ignored public opinion in the West in operating against Western embassies. The last wisps of allied co-operation were blown away as almost every mission experienced direct actions against its staff or against local Russian employees. The American embassy had more than its share of the sudden disappearance of local staff, including Alexander Dolgin who twenty-five years later, after an almost miraculous escape from the world of the 'camps,' wrote his extraordinary memoirs *An American in the Gulag*. And when the Brazilian embassy was removed, one of its local employees, Victor Louis, was sent to Siberia, out of which he emerged again after the death of Stalin to become a correspondent of the *London Evening News* and a skilful disinformation agent of the KGB.

The Greek ambassador, Dmitrios Politis, had married a Russian girl, a trapeze artist in the Moscow circus. When he became dean of the diplomatic corps she automatically became doyenne. But this did not save her when he was transferred to another post. She was refused an exit visa and the day after he left Moscow she was arrested.

Many embassies had the problem of wartime marriages. In some cases exit visas had been granted to the Russian wives. In many others the husbands had had to depart leaving their wives behind. Some took refuge in their husbands' embassies, others kept up a tenacious relationship with foreigners until they lost their courage and disappeared from view.

The Latin American missions in particular had serious difficulties, usually over marriages, over various restrictions, or hypersensitivity to Soviet criticism. Chile, Colombia, and Uruguay all withdrew their missions for a combination of these factors. The

Brazilian government took offence at an extremely insulting editorial in *Pravda* and broke off diplomatic relations. However, the government of Colonel Peron in Argentina had sensed some kind of affinity with the Soviet Union and at about the same time sent an enormous mission to Moscow which the Russians found flattering, puzzling, and somewhat embarrassing, since accommodation that the Argentines considered consonant with their Spanish pride was almost non-existent. In fact, most of them left after a few frustating months in seedy hotels.

In some ways Canadians found it easier to adapt to life in Russia than many other foreigners. The vastness of the country, twice the size of Canada, which is the second biggest in the world, and the long, hard winters did not bother us. The landscape of Old Russia was jarringly similar to that of Ontario and Quebec and living and surviving in our harsh northern climate gave us a certain feeling of sympathy for the Russians, so dissimilar to us in other respects.

After fourteen months in Moscow, my government transferred me to London. We prepared to leave Moscow with mixed feelings. Life there had been very difficult materially, and even more of a strain pyschologically. Apart from the particular problems of Canadian-Soviet relations and the constant menace of retaliation for our outspoken action against the Soviet spy ring in Canada, the revelations of which did much to open eyes in the West to the illusions under which Western governments had tended to operate in dealing with Moscow, there was the more general and agonizing atmosphere of increasingly open and brutal oppression by Stalin against his own people.

In early November 1947 I turned over my mission to my successor John Holmes. We started back the way we had come: by the Red Arrow to Leningrad, affording a glimpse of that great city preparing to celebrate the anniversary of the revolution; then on a tiny twelve-hundred-ton ship, seized in the way of reparations from Finland, through the Gulf of Finland to a Helsinki already shivering in the first grip of northern winter; to Stockholm, marvellously intact and prosperous after Moscow and Leningrad; and then through the Kiel Canal into the North Sea. A frightening gale struck us half way to the Thames and it took three days to make the crossing, three days during which the Russian crew, unused to the ship and, I had the impression, even the sea, almost disappeared, leaving the handful of passengers to look after themselves. It was a weary, but thankful, boatload that finally disembarked at Greenwich. We turned our back for a while on what Louis de Robien has called 'Toute la Russie avec son charme morbide, ses contrastes et son incohérence.' It was clearly not an incomprehensible mystery. What it was loomed only vaguely, although with overwhelming importance in my mind; it would take many more years for its shape to begin to become clear.

In March 1951 I returned to Moscow as chargé d'affaires en pied. With the Korean War raging and relations tense, the prospects of the war spreading to involve the Soviet Union and the Western Allies directly seemed far from impossible.

We chose to travel by train from Paris via Prague and Warsaw. Prague was sullen and brooding after the 1948 coup but still physically beautiful, particularly under a fresh layer of snow. Warsaw, by contrast, carried the horrifying impact of a person rising from the dead. Out of the rubble of almost total destruction, the old city, the Stari Miesta, the church where Chopin's heart lies, and some of the government buildings were emerging again. It was hard to believe that a new city could be built on the ashes of the old. But the Poles had courageously decided to reject the idea of moving the capital to another spot and instead were starting again from scratch. Poland demanded Warsaw and, in spite of all the odds, the Poles were determined to give it to her. We were to see Warsaw again several times in the next few years and every time I was filled with admiration for the way the Poles stubbornly worked at what seemed in March 1951 like an almost impossible task.

From Warsaw to Moscow took almost three days, involving a long stop at the new frontier of Brest-Litovsk while the under-carriages of the coaches were changed to the Russian broad gauge. The railway tracks had been completely destroyed and rebuilt but most of the small towns and villages we passed were only just stirring out of the devastation of the war.

Moscow itself in those three and a half years was little changed except for the five skyscrapers and the new university which Stalin had decreed. It was typical that, entirely ignoring the overwhelming need for housing, he had decided to allocate the few resources available at that time to the construction of buildings intended almost solely for the glorification of his regime. Probably deciding that Moscow needed skyscrapers to make it more modern, he failed to understand that the purpose of a high-rise building is to make the most economical use of expensive real estate. His skyscrapers were intended to adorn the horizons of Moscow. The city is built on concentric circles radiating out from the Kremlin, and it was on one of these outer rings, the Sadovaya Circle, that these high-rise buildings were placed, at considerable distances from each other. The only exception was the university, located on the Lenin Hills. But while the skyscraper concept in what was then open country was questionable, the need for a new university was uncontrovertible. Elsewhere, too, although the mass of the population seemed to be ignored, a considerable amount of prestige building was going on, and an effort was being made to modernize the main thoroughfares such as Gorky Street, Leningrad Chaussée, and Kaluga Chaussée.

The old Arbat was unchanged, although during the summer the cobble-stones in our street were torn up and macadam put down. In the embassy all our small staff was still crowded into the compound, as was now the case with most of the other Western missions, which had in the intervening years been given more or less adequate housing. But most of the embassies, including our own, still supplied their own heat and were not equipped with hot water. To take a bath we had to light a wood fire in the bathroom; the smell of burning birch still lingers in my memory, connected, it must be added, to the growing apprehension that one day the whole ancient building would go up in flames.

In 1951, the average accommodation for a Russian family was one room of five metres by four. One Russian we encountered occupied with his wife, two children aged twelve and five, and the inevitable babushka, a room smaller than our bedroom. In addition, they were entitled to the use of a gas stove and a place at the communal kitchen table. They considered themselves lucky in that their building was fairly central and had a communal bathroom.

Most of the houses were in a very bad state of repair although an effort was made to keep the façades of those facing main streets reasonably neat. But even in these houses the courtyards were generally in an appalling state. The city government had no funds available for repair (there is no Russian word for 'maintenance' and it obviously is not a concept engrained in the Russian character). Money for the repair of the main corridors and exteriors of apartment buildings came from the rent money administered by the street supervisor who usually established his own priorities.

Even in those difficult days there seemed to be a good deal of apartment exchange going on, often based on the judicial distribution of bribes. The dachas or log huts were still a feature of Moscow itself and it was only in the summer of 1952 that a whole block of shacks in central Moscow facing the new Sovietskaya Hotel was pulled down and symbolically turned into a parking lot for the ZIL limousines of the upper stratum of society.

The stratification of society, already noticeable in 1946-7, had become even more marked. Society appeared to be settling down along definable lines. Apart from the very small group at the top of the pyramid living a life apart, so well described by Svetlana Stalina, a new bourgeoisie was rapidly growing up, consisting of senior bureaucrats, officers, industrial and business 'managers,' intellectuals, and artists. They lived relatively well and even in those days were obviously determined to hang on to what they had won and if possible pass it on to their children.

There was a vast gap between their standard of living and that of the urban proletariat. Their life was hard and monotonous but they were beginning to receive some material rewards in the way of a small increase in consumer goods, as compared with 1946. But this increase was severely limited by the demands of heavy industry and rearmament. Even so, their standard was vastly greater than that of the rural population whose economic status seemed fixed at an abysmally low level.

In 1951 fees for admittance to secondary schools and to universities became standard practice. While these fees were very low and there were many scholarships, and once admitted to university a student received a stipend, nevertheless the barriers were sufficiently high to prevent the average student from a poor family acquiring the advantages of higher education. The aim seemed at least partly to oblige the ordinary student to enter the labour force; the result was inevitably the building up over the years of a new educated class able and eager to pass its privileges on to their children.

One had to admit that in this unfair distribution of wealth, the basic poverty had to be taken into account. There was clearly not enough of everything to go around and reconstruction, building the basis of an industrial society, and massive rearmament took first priority. Any attempt to impose an equitable egalitarian system would have been impossible even if human nature had not asserted itself. Therefore, the pragmatic solution of rationing facilities and commodities according to position and money was inevitable and the theory was easily fitted to the fact: 'egalitarianism is a left-wing deviation.'

If Moscow appeared on the whole outwardly little changed from 1946, this was highly deceptive. There was a definitive shift in the direction of hostility to the West. The Communist coup in Czechoslovakia, the defection of Tito, the Berlin blockade, the Marshall Plan, the creation of NATO, and the Korean War had all created a situation in which the Soviet authorities found themselves psychologically isolated, and their economy and military resources overstrained. One result was the reimposition and rapid growth of Stalinist terror in the intervening years. The last remnants of courtesy toward their erstwhile allies had completely disappeared and the attitude of hostility on the part of Soviet government officials and the press, though remarkably very seldom on the part of the average Russian, was pointed. In addition, the fear of sudden and unexplained arrest had returned to dominate the country. Fear was something almost tactile.

Many years later I asked the poet Evgenny Evtushenko if he had written his famous poem 'Fear' as a vivid reminder of the frightening Stalin years or as a political document for the future. Evtushenko said it was a bit of both. He recalled those awesome years as a teenager and the feeling of fear and uncertainty that reigned in every household so that the poem was indeed a picture of that period. As he put it, 'Fear floated like a shadow everywhere, / Penetrating every floor.' It was written, he said, during the

Khrushchev thaw, and indeed it could only have been written then, and it reflected the apprehension that the terror might come back. So it was also a political message to alert his readers to the need for awareness of what happened in the past and which must never be allowed again.

In these circumstances, the winter of 1951–2, and indeed the whole of 1952, was a period of intense strain on the Soviet people, both physically and morally, and this was reflected in the Western diplomatic corps. Our isolation from the officials and intellectuals, and only superficial contact with the average Russian, forced us into a solidarity we might not otherwise have felt. But many members of the small Western community found the constant pressures and frustrations, and the ever-present surveillance, more than they could bear. More than one member of our group had to be evacuated urgently to avoid a nervous breakdown.

There was a remarkable constellation of brilliant ambassadors at that time. Manlio Brosio of Italy, later to become ambassador to Britain, the United States, and France and secretary-general of NATO; Louis Joxe of France, later a key member of de Gaulle's cabinet; Sarvapal Radakrishna, ambassador of India, fellow of All Souls College, Oxford, one of the leading philosophers of his time and later president of India; and George Kennan.

Kennan's stay was brief and ended disastrously but, typically, it left an indelible mark. He is one of the most engaging men I have ever met, and one of the most remarkable brains. His deep understanding of the Russian people and the Russian psyche is unrivalled. But he was not a good ambassador. He was too deeply involved emotionally with the fate of Russia, and his approach was too convoluted, too intellectual, to permit him to arrive at balanced conclusions.

In those years Stalin very seldom received foreign dignitaries, rarely an ambassador, and only appeared in public on the May Day or 7 November parade, a remote figure atop the mausoleum of Lenin on Red Square. Very occasionally we would catch a glimpse of him as he sped through the old Arbat on the way to or from his dacha in the country. Then all traffic froze as the cavalcade passed down what everyone called 'The Route.' But once I had a chance to observe him close up, at the annual party meeting in the Bolshoi

Theatre on 6 November 1952. He looked very much his years and he fidgeted and squirmed a good deal. His hair, while still thick in front, was thinning at the back and a large bald spot showed. He looked thoroughly bored and cynical about the whole perform- ance. He laughed uproariously, however, at rather feeble jokes about the Americans. During the concert, Stalin appeared indiffer- ent to the young ballerina Maya Plisetskaya, applauded a men's chorus singing a bellicose song about 'Stalin's Hawks,' and was vaguely interested in a group of twenty-two violinists, among them to my astonishment the great David Oistrakh. Many years later I reminded Oistrakh of this. He looked uncomfortable and said that when you received an order from Stalin to play, you played.

But for most of the time, and for all but a handful of Russians all the time, Stalin was a terrifying and remote figure. His relationship to what went on in the country was no more properly understood than was the relationship of the tsar to government and society before the revolution.

The few steps towards relaxation taken by Stalin during the war were extracted from him reluctantly and were quickly abandoned afterwards. And it is not certain that Stalinism could have survived without the discipline, the terror, the sacrifices, and the massive indoctrination he imposed on the Russian people. But in addition, there was something in the character of Stalin himself, of the Russian people and their history, which made the dreadful regime which he epitomized almost inevitable, and made it in any case almost certain that Stalin would revert to it in its purest form as soon as the restrictions imposed by wartime necessities were lifted. As Valery Grossman wrote in 1963: 'What hope is there for Russia if even her greatest prophets cannot tell freedom from slavery? What hope is there for Russia if her greatest geniuses see the bright and gentle beauty of her soul made manifest in her submissive acceptance of slavery? What hope is there for Russia if Lenin, who transformed her most, did not destroy but strengthened the tie between Russia's progress and Russia's slavery? When will Russia ever be free? Perhaps never.'

2

The Post-Stalin Era
and the
Yugoslav Experience

The tensions in Moscow became almost intolerable with the arrest, in January 1953, of a number of Kremlin doctors charged with plotting to murder leading military personalities at the instigation of Israeli, American, and British intelligence. Six of the doctors were Jewish and almost immediately signs of anti-semitism, never very far below the surface, began to appear. In February diplomatic relations were severed with Israel, and its delegation, which since its opening five years earlier had been an inspiration for Soviet Jewry and a thorn in the flesh of the Soviets, was closed.

There was an almost tangible feeling of fear in the air and rumours of a new purge were rampant. As if to confuse even more, Stalin chose this moment to break a long period of isolation and in quick succession received the French, Argentine, and Indian ambassadors, all of whom reported him in apparent good health and spirits.

It was a complete surprise, therefore, when a communiqué was issued in the early morning of 4 March reporting that Stalin had suffered a cerebral haemorrhage on the night of 1–2 March. Since information on the health and activities of the Vozhd (Great Leader, as he was commonly called) was never divulged, and this announcement was accompanied by a call on all Soviet citizens to 'display the greatest unity, solidarity, fortitude of spirit and vigilance,' and to rally round the Central Committee of the Party and the Soviet government, it was plain that the end was near.

In the small hours of the morning of Friday, 6 March, Radio Moscow asked its listeners to tune in for an important announcement in fifteen minutes. The interval passed in silence and the announcer then asked the listeners to tune in in ten minutes, then twenty minutes, and so on. It was a few minutes after four in the morning when a lugubrious voice announced the death of Stalin at 9:50 p.m. the previous night.

By sunrise that same day the city was already covered with black-bordered red flags and when the newspapers appeared at noon their pages were bordered with black. The main news was the announcement of the composition of the funeral commission, the death certificate, and the third and last medical bulletin from four o'clock the previous morning. In the centre of the city preparations were under way for Stalin's lying-in-state. The militia and paramilitary troops took over the area in the guise of controlling security for the funeral. All vehicular traffic was re-routed outside this forbidden sector which was quickly sealed off by police cordons and barricades at every intersection. Nevertheless, these activities attracted crowds who quickly started to congregate on the fringes of the closed zone. As the numbers grew, police and army cordons were reinforced to keep the people at bay. At four in the afternoon the Dom Soyuzov (Trade Union House) next to the Bolshoi Theatre, where Stalin was laid in state, was opened to receive the homage of the people. A long queue had already formed stretching up Pushkin Street as far as the Sadovaya Circle. Pushkin Street is rather narrow and was probably selected because it permitted the army and police to control the crowd more easily.

The atmosphere of the queues was strangely mixed. Sometimes it seemed more that of a holiday than a funeral, although occasionally one saw signs of real grief. One of our staff from the embassy encountered in the queue the Russian wife of a foreign correspondent who had been prevented for years from leaving the Soviet Union. She seemed genuinely shocked and tearful over the death of the man responsible for her fate. Very often, however, the crowd openly jeered and heckled the mounted police and showed a sudden and remarkable lack of fear. Around the Dom Soyuzov and inside the guards were all drawn from the elite troops of the NKVD who stood quite immobile and inscrutable with only their sharp eyes moving up and down the people in the queue.

The funeral itself took place on 9 March. The previous day I had been designated to represent the Canadian government and the following morning at 2:30 a.m. I was informed by the chief of protocol that I was expected to be at the Dom Soyuzov at 8:50 a.m.; 9 March was a typical grey Russian winter day. The temperature was well below zero fahrenheit but we fortunately escaped the thirty below temperatures of a week earlier.

The centre of the city presented an extraordinary sight. In a great circle extending around the Kremlin were concentric lines of barricades consisting of double or occasional triple lines of trucks parked end to end and blocking the streets leading to the centre of the city except for a narrow passage for official cars. Troops and NKVD militia guarded the entrances. Within the barricades the streets were completely deserted except for the police and soldiers. I had the feeling that the buildings had been emptied. Certainly the windows overlooking the Manezhnaya Square, Revolution Square, and Mokhovaya had been boarded up.

Two security checks were made before I reached the Dom Soyuzov and another extremely thorough one inside the building. This dignified classical structure was now hardly recognizable. All the rooms we passed through had been stripped bare and were full of plainclothes police. The beautiful Hall of Columns where the body of Stalin lay in state had been made hideous by the addition of red and black drapes over the usual mustard-coloured plush curtains.

The bier was at one end of the hall at a slight elevation, slightly tilted at the head. An enormous red flag draped in black covered almost half the wall behind the coffin, which was rather small, covered in orange-red cotton sateen, pleated and frilled. Around it was an almost tropical mass of potted palms and wreaths made of artificial flowers. The body itself was covered up to the waist with the repulsive sateen, but his chest, hands, and face were visible. His medals and decorations were displayed at his feet on individual small red cushions. There were no candles but very strong lights. A large orchestra played Tchaikovsky and Chopin, interlarded with hymns to Stalin sung by a choir. The whole effect was one of appalling vulgarity.

The foreign diplomatic representatives were ranged in a semi-circle on one side of the room not far from the coffin. After about an hour of silent watching the foreign communist delegations appeared: the secretaries of the French, Italian, and Spanish Communist parties and all the East European leaders trooped in and were ranged in another semicircle. Then came the Soviet marshals and admirals.

Shortly after ten o'clock the members of the new Presidium filed into the hall and took their place at the foot of the bier. As the new first secretary and prime minister, Georgi Malenkov stood in front; in the first line behind him were Lavrenti Beria, Nikita Khrushchev, the Chinese prime minister Chou En-lai, Marshal Voroshilov, and Molotov. Malenkov stood with his back to the bier, looking singularly unattractive and sour. The only personal note was Svetlana Alliluyeva, Stalin's daughter, who briefly embraced her father.

At a nod from Khrushchev, who was in charge of the funeral arrangements, the marshals removed Stalin's medals which they later carried in the procession. Soldiers placed the lid on the coffin. It consisted of a wooden frame covered in red with a covering of plexiglass over the face and hands looking like a blister on a fighter plane. His marshal's cap lay on the lid.

The coffin was removed from the dais and carried by members of the Presidium from the hall, Malenkov and Beria in the lead. At the door it was transferred to a horse-drawn gun carriage. Preceding the coffin were the marshals and admirals, followed by the Presidium, the foreign communist dignitaries, and the diplomatic representatives. The long cold route by foot to Red Square passed between triple rows of soldiers. The streets were completely deserted and one had the eerie feeling of participating in a parade without spectators.

Inside the hall we had been forced to remain standing in our heavy overcoats for well over two and a half hours in eighty degree temperature. It was unnerving to be suddenly plunged into weather eighty or ninety degrees lower. Some, in fact, did not survive. The Czech party leader, Klement Gottwald, for example, caught a chill and died a few days later. On the whole, however, we were lucky when we recalled that Lenin's funeral in 1924 took eight hours at thirty-four below fahrenheit.

On reaching Lenin's mausoleum the coffin was placed on a stand facing it. By some mysterious process the word LENIN carved in stone had been removed overnight and LENIN-STALIN substituted. The key members of the Presidium climbed on the top of the mausoleum accompanied by the leading foreign communists. After some milling around, the diplomatic representatives were also invited to ascend the tomb and were ranged on the platforms on each side of the Presidium from which we had a magnificent, though bitterly cold, view of the proceedings. I do not think any Western representatives have ever since stood on Lenin's tomb.

Khrushchev opened the proceedings and invited Malenkov to give the eulogy of the departed leader, followed by Beria and Molotov. The latter was the only one who expressed any emotion and his words occasionally brought tears to the eyes of the audience. He looked old, ill, and depressed; Khrushchev like a busy-body; Malenkov pasty, pallid, fat, unattractive; Beria like a reformed gangster. They all seemed small and unimportant, perhaps because of the overwhelming shadow of their mentor.

At the end of the speeches the Presidium descended from the mausoleum and followed the coffin down into the vault to the accompaniment of a thirty-gun salute. This was followed by a military parade and fly-past, after which the Presidium and foreign communists once again descended into the mausoleum and then disappeared into the Kremlin through the private passageway provided for this purpose.

The diplomats were invited to view the remains and we in turn descended into the vault. Lenin lay in his traditional place under his glass covering. Beside him, but not under glass, Stalin had been placed. We passed within a foot or two of him and it was extraordinary to gaze at the visage of the man who only a week before had been the most powerful dictator in the history of the world and who, only four months before, we had seen at this same place review the armed might of the Soviet Union. And in all this pomp and circumstance there was one very Russian and very incongruous note. Just inside Lenin's tomb a little table with a green baize cover had been set up with glasses and bottles of mineral water.

At the end of this unique day I reflected that somehow it had all seemed an anticlimax. We had been looking forward for so long to the departure of this dreadful figure it was inevitable that no matter what happened it would seem inadequate. But it seemed unjust and improper that the man who had been responsible for the loss of more lives than any single person since Genghis Khan should go quietly to his grave on the spot where he had so often celebrated his triumphs.

Thinking about the implications of the unexpected removal of the terrible incubus that had weighed on Russia and the world, I remembered a sentence from Marcel Proust's *La Fugitive*: 'When you find yourself at the edge of the abyss and it seems that God has abandoned you, no longer do you hesitate in expecting a miracle from Him.' The world had lived so long under the menacing shadow of the monstrous figure of Stalin, it was hard at first to adjust to the fact that he was gone, the miracle had happened. The true miracle indeed only came three years later in the form of Khrushchev's consolidation of power and his reversal of the worst aspects of Stalinist terror. But already within a few weeks of the funeral one could feel cautious tremors of hope that life would improve, that the terror would evaporate, that perhaps even some of the inmates of the camps – those who had survived – might reappear.

At the beginning there was little sign of the thaw. Even Ilya Ehrenburg's first effort at glorifying Stalin after the days of March was as bad as any of the poems of praise lavished on the Vozhd when he was alive. His novel epitomizing the changes that were to come, *The Thaw*, only appeared much later. But somehow we felt that a thaw was on the way. There were little signs: an advertisement at Lomonsov University for a lecture on the popular poet of the twenties, Evgenny Essenin, on which someone had pencilled 'And why not Blok?' The Russian wives of some foreign correspondents and others who had waited for years with patient courage were suddenly given exit visas. The travel regulations for foreigners were slightly liberalized. More significant, all reference to the doctors' plot disappeared, and with it the anti-semitic campaign. In an atmosphere of almost total secrecy one studied these little signs and, with the average Russian, dared to hope things would get better.

Taking advantage of this relative relaxation, I travelled by train to Georgia in early June 1953. What was immediately notable there, and in Ukraine which I visited a few weeks later, was the strength of local nationalism. The two republics are very different. The Georgians are racially, historically, and linguistically distinct from the Russians, and their country is a spectacularly rugged mountain land with a Mediterranean touch. But Ukraine is a country which in every way overlaps with Russia, linguistically, historically, racially, and even geographically, and Ukrainian nationalism is an extremely complicated and emotional problem.

My visit to Kharkov, Poltava, and Kiev was a depressing experience, partly because I had the impression of a people who had almost gone through too much: the First World War, revolution and civil war, division between Poland, Czechoslovakia, Romania, and the Soviet Union, the dreadful decimation of the peasants in the thirties in the collectivization of agriculture, which fell particularly hard on the rural population of Ukraine; then the Second World War with the destruction of Kiev and the devastation of Kharkov, Odessa, the Crimea, Zaporozhe, and the Don Basin. The appalling human losses from the conflict were followed by Stalin's paranoiac striking-out after the war at the almost defenceless Ukrainians, because they had been occupied and because in despair many of them followed Bandura into the misguided venture of supporting the Germans against the Russian Bolsheviks.

Kiev and Kharkov were in the slow process of reconstruction, but the people were depressed and cowed. Ukrainian national feeling had survived but it seemed apparent in 1953 that the Russians were determined first to try to reduce the Ukrainian language and culture to a folkloric role, and, second, never to permit Ukrainian nationalism to become a threat to Great Russian domination. In fact it should be recalled that nearly all of the so-called Ukrainians who reached positions of importance in the Soviet hierarchy were generally not Ukrainian in the linguistic or racial sense but were simply born and brought up there, like Khrushchev, Brezhnev, Polyansky, Kirilenko, or else 'converted' Ukrainians like Nikolai Podgorny who, in spite of a lingering Ukrainian accent, had become totally identified with Russia.

We were accustomed to the poor standard of living in Moscow, and to the primitive state of the villages and small towns in the Moscow area. I expected something more from the richest agricultural provinces of the Soviet Union, but on the contrary, the situation was even worse. In the middle of August no meat, fruit, or salads were to be obtained in the markets and often not even in the better restaurants. Even making concessions to wartime damage, the primitive state of the villages and even Kharkov and Kiev, except for the 'show' centres, was dreadful. And as soon as one left the main highway one was into the black mud which helped to deter the Nazis. Pre-war maps, even a detailed Soviet map of 1940, showed no paved road between Kiev and Kharkov, the third and fourth largest cities of the Soviet Union. The road we travelled in 1953 existed because German engineers built it to supply their troops, and German prisoners of war rebuilt it after the war.

The villages and farms looked little changed from pictures of centuries before and, in spite of some signs of mechanization, peasants in some places had appropriated one-half of the asphalt surfaced highway to serve as a primitive winnowing ground for their own meagre share of the wheat harvest.

After seeing the state of the economy at first hand it was no surprise therefore when Malenkov in late August of that year presented to the Supreme Soviet a plan for the rapid development of the food and consumer industries, accompanied by cuts in taxes and prices.

He was right in recognizing that the economy and the society needed vigorous action. But his methods alarmed his colleagues who were afraid he was trying to secure total power by demagogic methods, and by what appeared to be an effort to downgrade the Party apparatus; the army men feared a cut in their budget, and even those members of the hierarchy who recognized the dire straits in which the economy was foundering believed tough disciplinary action was required, not a relaxation of tension. Although Khrushchev knew that a vigorous program was required to improve the food and light industry sectors of the economy, he chose to use the occasion to start a campaign to destroy Malenkov. He delivered a long exposé of the shortcomings of Soviet agriculture, for the first time quoting accurate figures of the catastrophic state of the farm economy. It was clear to the foreign observers in Moscow that Malenkov had thrown down the gauntlet and Khrushchev had picked it up, although in an area that seemed to us rather improbable. But the gradual replacement through the rest of 1953 and the beginning of 1954 of Malenkov supporters in key positions by Khrushchev men offered more solid proof that a real struggle for power was taking place.

In the meantime Malenkov had made several small remarks and gestures which demonstrated a wish to improve relations with the Western powers. For example, Molotov, now foreign minister again, suddenly requested me to call on him and almost wordlessly handed over a request for the appointment of a Soviet ambassador to Canada. I was followed in by the chargés d'affaires of Yugoslavia and Greece, with the same request, indicating that the Soviet government wished to restore full diplomatic relations with these three countries with which for a number of years relations had been strained, for differing but valid reasons. In the case of Canada, it was the aftermath of the Gouzenko spy affair; for Yugoslavia the rupture between Tito and the Soviets; and in the case of Greece, the civil war.

An original and entertaining demonstration that the atmosphere was changing took place on 7 November at the annual reception given by the Soviet government to celebrate their national day. The usual austere military parade and 'voluntary' walk-past of the populace took place in the morning in Red Square. In the evening the heads of mission were invited to a reception in the former merchant's mansion, Spiridonovka, the usual site for the rare manifestations of Soviet amiability towards their foreign guests. This elaborate palace was completed just before the First World War and reflected the prevailing taste of the Moscow nouveaux riches. Each of the vast rooms was decorated in a different style: Renaissance, Louis Seize, Napoleonic, Austrian baroque. But it all held together in a curiously Russo-Byzantine way and made a fitting background for the elaborately unreal receptions the Soviets felt obliged occasionally to give for the diplomatic corps or foreign guests. The Soviet officials in their black and gold diplomatic uniforms and the Western diplomats in white tie and tails seemed to blend perfectly into the absurd décor.

At these functions senior Soviet functionaries had never appeared. But this time most of the Presidium with the exception of Malenkov and Khrushchev were present. Molotov was official host and with him was his wife, returned not very long before from exile in Siberia. Molotov always impressed me as the archetype of the old Bolshevik to whom nothing could be more important than the Party. If he had been arrested in the purges he would undoubtedly have admitted guilt to anything Stalin wanted if he felt this would serve the cause. His behaviour revealed much of the communist mentality, but one wondered what the relations between him and his wife could be. He had seen Stalin send her to Siberia simply because she was a Jew and her presence in the Kremlin disturbed him in his anti-semitic drive, yet Molotov continued to serve Stalin, and eventually welcomed her back to Moscow almost as if nothing had happened in the intervening years.

The leading Soviets present, Molotov, Kaganovich, Anastas Mikoyan, Nikolai Bulganin, and M.G. Pervukhin, as well as Walter Ulbricht, then deputy premier of the German Democratic Republic, sat together at a table while the rest of us stood. At a certain moment the chief of protocol was sent to fetch a small group of ambassadors: Charles Bohlen, who in April had taken over the American embassy, Sir William Hayter, the British ambassador, Louis Joxe of France, the Chinese ambassador, and the Argentine and Burmese ambassadors, clearly to add two neutrals. Almost immediately toasts and speeches to peace and international understanding, and even to the Western allies, began to be exchanged, and the atmosphere became extraordinarily relaxed.

Apart from being a clear signal to the West that the Soviet leaders had decided to change at least their attitude if not immediately their policies, the evening afforded a glimpse of the real side of these men who, segregated from the outside world for so long, had assumed an excessively sinister aspect. They were obviously human, although one could hardly forget that no doubt a few months before they had sat down with Beria in equally convivial gatherings before they decided on his elimination.

Mikoyan was undoubtedly the recognized wit of the group. He drank a great deal but never lost control of himself. He was quick and clever but with a nasty turn of mind. Molotov as usual was serious, plodding, and heavy. I had the impression he would have liked to be as articulate as Mikoyan and was jealous of the Armenian's quickness of wit. Kaganovich looked and acted like a peasant. He had enormous hands which he used to reinforce a point. He was vulgar, humorous in a heavy-handed way, sentimental. He drank and talked a great deal, insisting that he was a plain man who knew nothing but the feeling of the common man. His speeches were almost hysterical on the subject of war and one felt he was probably honest in his feelings.

It is curious in retrospect that Malenkov himself lacked the qualities of survival in view of the school of inner Kremlin politics in which he was brought up. He had the intelligence and the grasp of world affairs, of the changing nature of international relations, and of the deficiencies in the Soviet economic system to have made a great leader. It is possible he could have introduced the internal innovations of Khrushchev with less fanfare, and started on the road to détente with the West without the latter's often dangerous flamboyance. But he lacked the human touch, contact with his own people, and understanding of the degree of revulsion in the country against Stalinism. His temporary alliance with Beria and the NKVD made it impossible in the long run to withstand the skilful campaign of Khrushchev to ease him out of power.

Shortly after the 7 November celebration I was informed that the government had agreed to the appointment of a Soviet ambassador to Ottawa and that we would reciprocate by sending an ambassador to Moscow. In March 1954 I returned to Ottawa to become head of the European Division in the External Affairs Ministry.

Just as I was leaving, some of the first manifestations of the thaw appeared, perhaps the most important being the first poetry by Boris Pasternak to be published in several decades. They were some of the poems which eventually formed an annex to *Doctor Zhivago* and they were included in an otherwise routine issue of the literary magazine *Znamya*. Although rumours were already circulating in the literary world about Pasternak's novel, its real and, as far as the Soviet authorities were concerned, subversive nature was not appreciated. But the poems themselves with their extraordinary images and fresh new forms were a revelation to the average literate Russian deadened for two decades by the sterile claptrap of socialist realism.

The following poem from *Zhivago* in my translation may appear totally inoffensive, but this type of poetry had been unacceptable to the Stalinists because it did not positively contribute to the construction of communism and because, expressing private emotions, it tended to encourage individualism as opposed to 'collective thinking.'

White Night

Far in the past, dimly it comes back to me,
A house on the Petersburg quay,
You – a student from Kursk, daughter
Of a poor merchant from the steppes.

You were lovely, with so many admirers,
Both of us were beautiful that white night,
We found a place on your windowsill
And looked down on your far skyscrapers.

The morning touched with the first
Tremor the street lamps, like
Butterflies of gas. So, quietly, I talked
To you as if you were asleep.

We embraced, we kissed, and I
Felt shy with the true secret,
As the panorama of Petersburg, from
The Neva banks spread out before us.

There, far off in the misty distance
Of this night of Spring-like whiteness
The nightingales with glorious thunder
Announced the frontiers of Summer.

With a crazy abandon, traffic roared through
The streets. The voice of a little bird
Far off awakened rapture and confusion
In the depths of a charmed thicket.

Disguised as a barefoot wanderer
The night slipped along the garden fence,
And left on our windowsill the trace
Of a conversation overheard.

In the echoes of an overheard conversation,
In the garden, in the startled shadows,
The branches of the apple and cherry trees
Were decked out in the colour of whitewash.

And the trees, white ghosts, pressed
Like a multitude into the street,
The signs of farewell of the white
Nights ... having seen so much.

After the long and dreadful night of Stalinism the appearance of these marvellous poems was a kind of literary and human miracle. Indeed the very survival of Pasternak was a miracle. So many of his fellow poets had disappeared into the camps, leaving only the hint of what great poetry was lost to mankind. It was hard to believe he had not only survived, but survived with his spirit intact. As another great writer, Alexander Zinoviev, said two decades later: 'Moya dusha, moya krepost – My soul is my fortress.'

The following decade saw me constantly engaged in Soviet affairs but from the periphery. The three years in Ottawa were devoted very much to dealing with Canadian-Soviet relations, for at that time the European Division in External Affairs included all of Europe, Africa, and the Middle East. It required analysing and interpreting the emergence of Nikita Khrushchev as paramount leader of the Soviet Union, and determining Canada's stake in the gradually improving atmosphere. Canada in fact took the lead in breaking the ice through exchanges of trade and fisheries delegations, and the visit to Russia of Lester B. Pearson, then minister of external affairs.

Much of this painstaking work came apart with the bloody suppression of the Hungarian revolt by the Soviets in the fall of 1956, and was further complicated by the Egyptian-Israeli conflict, armed intervention by Britain and France, and the danger of

Soviet interference on behalf of Egypt. When the dust settled a bit I was sent to New York to help out in the second half of the marathon General Assembly of the United Nations.

I wanted and needed a complete change of pace, but was somewhat taken aback when I was offered Colombia. After only brief reflection, I accepted. From my four rewarding years in Brazil and the extensive travelling I had done in Uruguay, Argentina, Paraguay, Bolivia, Peru, Ecuador, Panama, and later Mexico and Central America, I was eager to know more of Latin America. I felt Canadians had neglected that area and had failed to recognize its importance for us. The Colombians did not make the mistake in reverse, and there was an almost embarrassing response to a lecture I gave in Spanish at the University of the Andes, entitled 'Canada, pais americano.'

The 'Athens of America,' as Bogotá liked to call itself, had a remarkably high percentage of literate people. My arrival coincided with the publication of my first book of poetry, *A Window on the North*, which won the Governor General's award. It helped me at least to open a window on Canada.

But even there I could not escape the Soviet Union. Apart from being frequently asked by Ottawa to comment on Soviet developments, Colombia was suffering from the aftermath of a civil war which had taken at least one hundred thousand lives and ended in military rule. It had started in 1948 with the Communist-inspired uprising called the 'Bogotaça,' the forerunner of Fidel Castro's revolt in Cuba. It exploited the misery of those who were at the bottom of the social scale and which today partly explains, though it can never justify, the ease with which the drug dealers can enlist the collaboration of the impoverished peasantry in cultivating coca.

But our stay in the Andes was short-lived and in December 1958 we were moved to Yugoslavia, which was an ideal spot from which to observe East-West relations. Belgrade, two years after the Soviet invasion of Hungary, was still nervous about Soviet intentions.

The Yugoslavs were never quite sure, even twelve years after the break with Moscow, if Khrushchev might not try to exploit the manifest divisions – national, social, economic, and ideological – which existed in that loose confederation. Keeping it together in spite of the immense problems involved in reconstructing the country after the devastating German occupation and civil war, resisting the constant pressure from the Soviet bloc, and trying to find a way out of its isolation between East and West, was a remarkable feat of politics and statecraft. Lawrence Durrell, who had been press attaché in the British embassy, considered Yugoslavia a comic-opera Balkan place with no redeeming features. But he found a wonderfully apt description for communism, which he called 'a deviation of an infinite sadness.' I had no hesitation in applying that description to the Soviet Union. But the Yugoslavs managed to combine the Slav and Mediterranean in a way which made their peculiar slapdash kind of communism tolerable.

Belgrade seemed immediately familiar, in part because of the language, in part the communist system. The city is very Slavic in temperament, but the Yugoslavs have achieved a wonderful balance of Russian imagination and melancholy with a sufficient southern element to make them one of the most attractive of European peoples. Perhaps this also helped to differentiate considerably the Yugoslav form of communism from the Soviet model.

It was inevitable that I should compare the two, with Tito's Yugoslavia obviously coming out on top. Almost immediately the relatively relaxed nature of society was apparent. We could travel where we liked and profited from it to explore in the next two and a half years Old Serbia, Bosnia and Herzegovina, Dalmatia, Montenegro, Croatia, Slovenia, the Banat, the Albanian enclaves, each marvellously different, vital, still often picturesque, alive.

There was no question, of course, that any active opposition to the government would be put down with force, and before 1948 Yugoslavia had been the most violently anti-West and pro-Soviet of the communist regimes in Eastern Europe. I had already met Tito when he visited Moscow in 1947 and, while impressed by his bearing and personality, had noted that his speeches and policies were indistinguishable from that of Stalin. If any doubts remained about the basic toughness of the regime, one had only to look at the prison of Sremska Mitrovica, not far from Belgrade, and think of Milovan Djilas who was incarcerated there for his book *The New Class*.

The new class in Yugoslavia was in fact only too obvious,

particularly to one who knew Moscow. Not that the evolution towards new and hereditary privileges and wealth was not taking place in the Soviet Union; but the speed with which it had happened in Yugoslavia shocked the more orthodox communists and the tougher partisans who had shared the unbelievable hardships of the long struggle against Hitler.

Finding jobs for many of these guerrilla leaders, who could not be fitted easily into the new society, was a problem. But this was not the case with the many wartime associates of Tito, who came from educated, often wealthy, families, and had served with distinction in the war. They fitted easily into the regime and with them, in sharp contrast to the Soviets, one could develop friendly and profitable relations, and have discussions on questions of policy or ideology undreamed of in Moscow.

Nevertheless, Belgrade was still in many ways an eccentric Balkan capital and we could never be sure what unusual happening might take place. We were exposed to this almost immediately after our arrival when we negotiated the exchange of our very inadequate modern villa for a house in Uzicka not far from Tito's residence. It was inhabited by a member of the hierarchy who had had a series of heart attacks and was advised to slow down. He wished a smaller house, and therefore we arranged to exchange residences.

The first night in the new house I discovered in a compartment in the bedroom a loaded Luger pistol which I sent back the following day with my visiting card. Then we also discovered a system of wires and alarms which connected with Tito's residence and were intended apparently to alert the key members of the regime in the event of trouble. Having them dismantled was a more delicate matter but was finally accomplished without anyone losing face.

During the Nazi occupation the house had been the residence of the head of the Gestapo. The Yugoslav official who had exchanged it with us had remarked that he hoped we would have better luck in it because he was convinced it had become demonized during the war. In fact nothing seemed to work properly. The water supply would suddenly stop with no apparent explanation and the electricity would be cut off although the rest of the area was unaffected. Indeed, shortly after moving in we gave a dinner party and to make the entry of blazing crêpes suzettes effective the cook turned off the lights. My reaction was 'they're at it again,' but the chief of protocol at once blamed it on the eccentric electrical system of Belgrade. There were so many unexplained incidents my wife had recourse to an ancient Catholic tradition. She called in the local priest who found it not unusual to be asked to exorcise the house. By a liberal sprinkling of incense and the use of prayers intended to expel the demons, we were able to cleanse the premises and had no further trouble.

A short time later my security officer said to me: 'I think we have a problem.' We did. My predecessor had warned one of the Canadian members of our staff employed as a guard about being seen in the company of a woman who managed the Select Bar. He agreed to see her no more but was then caught with her at night when he was on duty in the chancery. I agreed he had to go, but then the problems began. A week after his departure to Canada the woman appeared with a licence proving he had married her. Since she was suspected of being a police informer as well as the local madam, she hardly seemed to qualify as an immigrant. But our immigration regulations permitted her to join her husband provided she could pass the medicals which, to everyone's astonishment, she did. She left and a few days later Protocol called in one of my staff to say that she had absconded with the profits of the Select Bar. The dinars never were recovered and the Select Bar went out of business.

This was in the best tradition of Lawrence Durrell's Yugoslavia. The writer found funny the ostentation of Tito and the new class. I found it understandable in view of their basic feeling of uncertainty about themselves and the privations of the guerrilla war, but also slightly sad. Tito himself maintained a manner of living reminiscent of an oriental potentate. His clothes were of the best quality, although slightly flamboyant, and in 1959 he was listed as one of the world's ten best-dressed men. His self-designed marshal's uniforms were magnificent. He was never seen without a diamond ring, the origin of which is typical. In Moscow in the thirties, as a Yugoslav communist, he earned some extra money by translating and spent his earnings on the diamond ring. I once remarked to him that Stalin's police were not very acute, otherwise they would have had deep suspicions of a communist sufficiently original to spend his money on diamonds. He just laughed.

Tito normally lived in a palatial villa in Belgrade. The White Palace, the former residence of the Regent Paul, was used for official receptions. He also maintained a large country house twenty kilometres from Belgrade, and a hunting lodge in Karadjordjevo in the Voijvodina. The former royal villas in Bled, Split, and Montenegro, and houses in Dubrovnik and Ohrid were also used by him from time to time. Already in 1959 the island of Brioni had been turned into a private reserve where he spent more and more of his time. When he travelled to Africa and Asia it was on a magnificent scale, with a private yacht, two supply ships, and two DC-6B airplanes. When the Emperor of Ethiopia made a state visit he toured Slovenia with Tito in the latter's custom-built Rolls-Royce. At Bled he entertained Haile Selassie with a ball and a fireworks display while an orchestra was rowed up and down the lake in specially constructed barges.

Tito and his lieutenants always justified this display on the grounds that it was necessary to impress the Yugoslav people and, more important, the rest of the world with the strength and prosperity of the country. But it was hard at times to reconcile this extravagance with the aid freely given by the United States and other Western countries.

When I arrived in Belgrade Tito was absent on one of these ostentatious three-month-long trips through the Middle East and Asia. But he received me shortly after his return. He was then sixty-seven and remarkably fit. In fact I saw him often over the next few years, and whether it was an exacting official visit, or a hunting party in the Voijvodina which lasted nearly all night, he seldom betrayed a sign of his age.

This was a period of relatively good relations with the West, and, concomitantly, strained relations with the Soviet Union. Tito had not quite recovered from the shock of the Hungarian revolt and Soviet intervention which had brought Soviet troops to the borders of Yugoslavia. Above all, he had not forgotten Soviet duplicity over the disappearance of Imre Nagy. The Hungarian leader had sought asylum in the Yugoslav embassy in Budapest and had been turned over to the Soviets in return for a guarantee of his personal security. He was at once taken to the Soviet Union and presumably executed.

For their part, the Soviets credited the independent line taken by Tito with contributing to the forces of nationalism in Eastern Europe, and had retreated from the policy of rapprochement tried out by Khrushchev in 1955 which had, in any case, been treated with considerable reserve by Tito. It was extraordinary, in fact, that Khrushchev should have so badly misjudged Tito to think that the latter could be easily lured back into the Soviet fold by a personal visit and a few polite words. The experience of Tito in surviving the difficult years of exile in Moscow in the thirties, of inspiring and leading a devoted band of partisans under the Nazi occupation, and of holding together in the chaos of post-war Yugoslavia all the disparate groups which make up this remarkable country, had formed a tough, suspicious, brilliant, and ambitious man who could not be fooled by mere words. A communist he was, but a Yugoslav nationalist above everything else.

Since the mid-fifties Tito had been searching for a way to end the isolation of Yugoslavia. His solution was the non-aligned movement, and the skill with which he built it up into a political force of considerable importance in the world helped to give Yugoslavia an importance it did not objectively merit, and to turn it from a poor Balkan outcast into an influential country. It was a stroke of genius on Tito's part to 'invent' non-alignment, for he was the prime mover. He took the inchoate idea behind the Five Principles of the Bandung conference of 1955 and turned them into a practical body of political thought.

While Tito was cultivating friends in the newly independent countries of Africa and Asia, the crucial factor in his decision to press for the formation of a movement or bloc of non-aligned countries was the gradual exclusion of Yugoslavia from what could then still be called the world communist movement. In January 1959, the Twenty-First Congress of the Communist Party of the Soviet Union took place. Yugoslavia was not invited, not even with observer status. In November the representatives of eighty-one communist parties met in Moscow and proceeded to read the Yugoslav League of Communists out of the movement.

It was therefore necessary for a small country posing a constant ideological threat to the Soviet bloc (though rather less than was imagined by the Russians) to secure the widest political support possible. While Tito assiduously cultivated good political and economic relations with the West he could never be sure when the crunch came just how far his NATO friends would go in supporting a maverick communist against a Soviet attempt to overthrow him.

For the Yugoslavs the development of a bloc of non-aligned countries must have seemed logical and inevitable. As good Marxists they considered the former colonial territories as the most reasonable field for expansion; they seemed the part of the world most likely to accept their social ideas, the most sympathetic to the picture of a small country attempting to maintain its independence. Economically, the Yugoslavs hoped to unload some of their rather second-rate, but cheap, manufactured goods in Asia and Africa, and in this they were quite successful. Politically, at first it appealed to the Yugoslavs as a way out of isolation; but it developed into a means of dissuading the Soviet Union from attacking Yugoslavia on the grounds that Moscow would hesitate to alienate the non-aligned countries by a hostile act. And finally, the Yugoslavs hoped that non-alignment, if properly organized, would add to their international prestige, particularly in the United Nations, as indeed it did.

Inevitably, the question arose among the Yugoslav politicians and intellectuals – and they were an inquiring, able, and stimulating lot – as to whether the position of Yugoslavia, poised between East and West, merited the evolution of a new type of Marxist ideology to meet the circumstances. The arguments were conducted even at the top. At one of Tito's regular hunting parties I found myself with Vladimir Rankovic, then vice-president and the leading contender for the succession to Tito. He embarked on an examination of the advantages and disadvantages of trying to develop their own special interpretation of communism into an ideology, an ideology he implied that might have some appeal to the newly independent countries, which were inclined to reject capitalism but were repelled by Soviet communism. If this was ever seriously considered – and given Yugoslav conceit it is possible – in the long run Tito could not bring himself to cut the final umbilical cord with Moscow which this would have meant. No specific Yugoslav interpretation of communism was in fact ever developed.

But Tito did set out to put some order in non-alignment and organized the first summit meeting in Belgrade in September 1961. This was a remarkable tour de force. Although it accomplished nothing very concrete, it did demonstrate to both of the big blocs the amount of political influence Tito could muster. It led to the practice of greater consultation among the non-aligned nations and greater co-ordination of their policies in the United Nations.

If the value of non-alignment was apparent to Yugoslavia, it was not so obvious to us. With only minor deviations the Yugoslavs followed the Soviet line in most important issues in foreign affairs: disarmament, cessation of nuclear tests, the German peace treaty, Berlin, the Congo, colonial questions in general. It was never very clear either to what extent the Yugoslavs used their influence with the often impressionable and inexperienced leaders of newly independent countries to adopt Marxist internal policies and to support Soviet foreign policy goals.

Although it was difficult at times to distinguish between gratuitous support for Soviet positions and actions genuinely calculated to strengthen Belgrade, there was hardly any doubt that in general an independent Yugoslavia was of great value to the West. The assertion of independence from Moscow in 1948 set in train a series of developments which made questionable the basis on which the world communist movement had previously functioned: synonymity of the interests of communism and the state interests of the Soviet Union; the unchallenged ideological and strategic control of every party by Moscow; and the slavish copying of all Soviet methods. The Yugoslav rejection of these assumptions had an unsettling effect in Eastern Europe, and it proved of considerable interest to the Chinese as they felt their way towards a position of equality in the Sino-Soviet bloc.

An independent Yugoslavia was and still is a major obstacle to Soviet domination of Southeast Europe. It was the withdrawal of Yugoslav support after 1948 which led to the collapse of the communist attempt to take over Greece. The defection of Yugoslavia led to the geographical separation of Albania from the Soviet bloc, then its break with Moscow, its turning to China for assistance and eventually its almost total isolation as it became disillusioned with China in turn. Yugoslav independence reduced Soviet pressure on Austria and Italy and it denied to the Russians direct access to the Adriatic. Finally, Yugoslav activities in the non-aligned world afforded the new countries an ostensibly acceptable left-wing alternative to the Soviet Union and reduced the latter's possibilities for mischief-making in the third world.

John Foster Dulles had been inclined to regard non-alignment with great suspicion, and his attitude was not dissimilar to that of the Russians: if you are not for me, you are against me. But by 1961 the new administration in Washington was taking a more flexible view of the third world and the appointment of George Kennan to Belgrade confirmed it. None of his future staff knew him and they nervously sought my opinion of the great eccentric. I said he was one of the most brilliant men I knew but highly emotional. He would either love or detest Tito and this would be an important determinant in his attitude.

In fact Kennan was seduced by Tito but believed the reverse had also happened. The secret of Tito's survival was that he had remained as tough and unseduceable as when he was a guerrilla leader. Kennan thought that Tito would adopt a policy of strict non-alignment at the first summit meeting in 1961. When on the third day Tito rose to make his major speech, which came down firmly in favour of the Soviets with regard to Germany and nuclear testing, Kennan was like a man whose mistress had deceived him. Tito's line was indeed disappointing but it was hardly unexpected.

When I left Yugoslavia in 1961 Tito and his wife Jovanka, a handsome but solidly built woman of considerable charm, invited us in an unusual gesture towards a Western diplomat to a final weekend on the island of Brioni to say goodbye. This idyllic spot, just off the coast of Istria which had been ceded to Yugoslavia by Italy after the war, had become one of Tito's favourite retreats. Here in the beautiful white villa he had constructed, he would retire to rest or to confer with his closest friends and collaborators.

We stayed in a rest-house at one end of the island, but spent a considerable time with the presidential pair. Tito was at the height of his power and prestige and his constant support and companion, Jovanka, was always at his side, as she had been since their days together in the resistance movement against the Germans. I met them both again on frequent occasions after I left Belgrade – in Cairo, in Helsinki, and in Moscow – and Jovanka was always with him. Thus when he came alone on an official visit to the Soviet Union in August 1977, I could not help remarking to him on her absence. His reply was sharp and evasive and it was then that it came to light that she had been dismissed in disgrace. No one knows for certain what happened or why. The Balkan tradition dies hard.

Tito was the last survivor of the wartime heroes and one of the most influential figures of the succeeding decades whose importance has yet fully to be assessed. Without him it is doubtful whether the numerous mutually inimical ethnic groups that make up the South Slav federation could have remained united in one country. And his early and determined rejection of Soviet leadership was crucial in the weakening of communist doctrine, Soviet control of world communism, and the Soviet strategic situation in Europe, as well as in the rise in national feeling in Eastern Europe. Yugoslavia remains a key element in future developments. If it continues on the course laid down by Tito, it will constitute a factor of stability in Europe. If disputes over communist doctrine and nationalist quarrels arise again in the future, its situation between East and West will make it a potential cause of conflict. But the Yugoslavs have shown themselves remarkably astute and realistic in the post-war years.

3

The Impact of
Khrushchev

In the spring of 1961 John Diefenbaker appointed me ambassador to the United Arab Republic, alias Egypt: the union collapsed shortly after my official visit to its second capital, Damascus, in September of that year.

Gamal Abdul Nasser, when I came to Cairo, was basking in the limelight of a leading role in the non-aligned movement, and of having allegedly defeated the British-French-Israeli armies in the 1956 war. Canada enjoyed reasonably good relations with Egypt, even though Nasser had underlying suspicions about our relationship with Britain and our support for Israel. But Lester Pearson's initiatives which brought the war to an end helped to compensate for this.

As in Yugoslavia, the Soviet Union was a major preoccupation. Nasser routinely denounced the Western powers and proclaimed his political and military solidarity with Moscow. He claimed authorship of 'Arab socialism,' and accepted Russian economic and technological aid to build the Aswan Dam. Hence much of my time was spent in trying to determine what Soviet aid and influence meant in concrete terms for the West – grossly exaggerated as I thought then and ephemeral as it turned out in the long run.

I was not particularly surprised, therefore, to be informed late in 1963 that I had been appointed ambassador to the Soviet Union.

After Belgrade and Cairo it seemed a logical move. So much so that, when I made my farewell call on Nasser, he remarked that my predecessor, Arnold Smith, had also gone to Moscow, as had my Danish and Dutch colleagues. He wondered if there was a pattern of thinking there on the part of Western governments. It looked ominous to him.

It was twenty-five above in Cairo and twenty-five below in Moscow when we returned to the Soviet Union early in January 1964, to a country the spirit of which had changed considerably in the decade of our absence, and to a Soviet leader who was a very different man from the first secretary of the Party struggling to reach the top against ferocious opposition a decade before when I had last seen him.

Dostoyevsky wrote in *The Possessed*:

A really great people can never accept a secondary part in the history of Humanity nor even one of the first; but will have the first part. A nation which loses this belief ceases to be a nation. But there is only one truth, and therefore only a single one out of the nations can have the true God, even though other nations may have great gods of their own. Only one nation is 'god-bearing'; that's the Russian people.

Nikita Khrushchev probably never read that passage, although he was largely responsible for the rehabilitation of the writer. But as a good Russian he seemed instinctively to feel and act in the spirit enshrined in Dostoyevsky. From his famous 'we will bury you' remark, to his prediction that the Soviet Union would overtake the United States in economic achievements by 1975, he was motivated by the passionate belief that Communist Russia was unique, could be the first nation in the world, and, in spite of the evidence, would surpass the major Western powers.

I had not met Khrushchev when he was one of the most faithful supporters of Stalin, nor in 1953, when he was still fighting his way to the top. In February 1956 word had seeped out through various sources of his denunciation of Stalin in his 'secret speech' at the end of the Twentieth Congress of the CPSU. Although the Soviets never published the text, the authenticity of the versions that reached the West have never been denied. And almost immediately the destruction of the Stalin cult began. While the West pondered what it meant, its effect was devastating inside the Soviet Union, in the Eastern European countries, and in the communist parties of the West, particularly in France and Italy where the orthodox had for a generation denied the awful truths about Stalin, now publicly admitted by his closest henchmen.

We will never know what the motives of Khrushchev were in unleashing this dangerous campaign, and his memoirs do little to explain. Although he was already well on the way to becoming the undisputed leader, he still had to have at least the tacit support of the Presidium and the Central Committee. People such as Malenkov, Molotov, and Kaganovich must have objected to the destruction of the Stalin myth, and others must have feared the consequences for themselves and for the system. But Khrushchev was undoubtedly the leading force in tearing down the image of the Vozhd and for it he brought to bear all his formidable energy and talents of persuasion.

There were two main reasons for the decision to demystify Stalin. First was the tremendous feeling, above all among the upper echelons of the Communist Party, that steps had to be taken to prevent ever again the revival of one-man rule by terror, and this could only be assured if the truth about Stalin were known. Second was the belief that the Soviet Union could not hope to modernize its society and economy until the system by which Stalin had dominated the country was thoroughly discredited.

This involved very great risks, not only to the former close associates of Stalin, but also to the thousands of mindless Party bureaucrats who had been brought up in the Stalinist method and who were neither able nor wanted to change. The traumatic shock the revelation about Stalin caused throughout the country continued to reverberate for years and I could still feel it two decades later in Moscow.

Physically Moscow was beginning to change. The priority Khrushchev had given to housing, combined with his impatience to get things done, had resulted in the mushrooming of countless drab blocks of apartment buildings. To save money, all but a few prestige buildings were a uniform five storeys, without elevators, and built to the same style from prefabricated units. Perhaps the creation of these instant slums (the Russians called them 'Khrush-chobi,' a pun on the word 'Trushchobi,' meaning tenements) was the only way in which the desperate housing shortage could be overcome in a short time, but the result was deadly monotony and very poor quality.

Our street, Old Stables Lane in the Arbat, was unchanged, but 'The Route' had become fairly quiet with the construction parallel to it of a six-lane avenue leading from the Smolensk Highway to the Kremlin. Modern new buildings flanked it in an obvious attempt to inject some kind of modernity into the city, part of Khrushchev's plan which resulted in the planting in the heart of the Kremlin of an ultra modern concert and conference hall and, near Red Square, the monstrous six-thousand-bed Hotel Rossiya.

Adjoining the New Arbat are the Norwegian embassy and a small, delightful chapel. Khrushchev gave orders for both to be pulled down as inconsistent with the plan of modernization. The Norwegian ambassador invited Khrushchev to tea on the eve of his official visit to Oslo, and convinced him that the lovely old embassy building should be preserved. The chapel was also saved by his fall later that year.

People were better dressed and there were more consumer goods in the shops but the material changes were largely marginal and hardly comparable to the vast improvement which had taken place in the real standard of living in most Western countries in that decade.

The important change was one that was hard to measure – the disappearance of fear. It was hard to measure because the dissidents had not yet appeared on the scene nor the Jewish emigration movement. The police were still everywhere and the embassy was as carefully guarded as before. The normal number of KGB efforts to penetrate the embassy and suborn some of the staff which had taken place over the preceding years was ample proof that their methods had not altered.

But what was missing was the almost palpable sense of terror which had clung to the country in the days of Stalin and which needed Khrushchev's 'secret speech' in 1956 to dissipate. It was Stalin's use of irrational and unpredictable terror, which could, without apparent reason, strike at anyone, that had gripped the whole population, from the hierarchy to the simplest worker, in a paroxysm of fear. By 1964 this had disappeared. It was still the tightest of totalitarian police states but Soviet citizens who followed instructions and did not oppose the system were reasonably sure of being unmolested. Khrushchev had effectively dismantled the Gulag Archipelago and no one wanted it reinstated, above all the Party itself which had proportionately suffered even more than the rest of the population from Stalin's arbitrary use of terror. Nor were the administrators and technicians responsible for trying to modernize the economy eager to revive a system of slave labour which was desperately inefficient. Nor obviously were the intelligentsia.

But by January 1964 de-Stalinization was slowing down. At the Twenty-Second Party Congress in 1961 Khrushchev brought the denunciation of Stalin and Stalinism out into the open, publicly listing crimes against the Soviet people perpetrated not only by Stalin himself but by Molotov, Malenkov, Kaganovich, and Voroshilov as well. The day after his revelations, the mausoleum on Red Square reverted solely to Lenin, proving that, when they want to, Soviet workers can do a good job. Overnight the inscription chiselled into the stone and the façade were changed back to the original form, and a deep grave was dug near the Kremlin wall for Stalin's remains. Stalingrad, of course, became Volgograd. Khrushchev followed up the denunciation of Stalin with permission to publish Solzhenitsyn's *A Day in the Life of Ivan Denisovich* in 1962 and a brief flowering of Russian literature followed. But Khrushchev himself, having deliberately and effectively encouraged the campaign to expose Stalin's crimes, had begun to realize the risks he and the Party ran by permitting 'liberalization' to go too far and too fast.

Although the brakes were already being put on, the atmosphere was heady, compared with ten years before. It was still possible at small parties to meet poets such as Bulat Okhudjava and Simeon Kirsanov, writers such as Valery Aksionov and Yuri Neghibin, although they were very soon to become more cautious in their contacts with foreigners. More remarkable was the ease with which Soviet officials came to the embassy. The rules soon became apparent. If there was an official excuse they would come, but not otherwise. For example, if I gave a reception for a delegation from the cinema industry, which was going officially to Canada, then all the requisite people – directors, writers, actors and actresses from the Soviet industry – would turn up. But if you invited any of them two weeks later to the embassy, 'as friends,' then there was no chance of their accepting.

Still, it was encouraging to be able to meet Russians and have reasonable and friendly exchanges of views with them. At times, indeed, the Soviet eagerness to come to the embassy if there were the slightest official pretext became almost overwhelming. The strain on our resourcefulness in entertaining all these unexpected Russians prompted my wife to sigh once, 'Oh for the days when they hated us.'

The shabby charm of the Old Arbat remained, although already the Moscow City soviet was busy pulling down old buildings in a frantic effort to modernize one of the more sought-after residential areas in the inner city. Our embassy had remained untouched except for being painted battleship grey. After a fight with the ubiquitous UPDK (the organization with which foreigners had to deal to get anything from an apartment to shampooing rugs), we succeeded in changing it to the traditional Russian yellow and white, which added considerably to the colourfulness of the street.

Inside, the residence had changed little but the inevitable expansion of staff had required the construction of an addition to the chancery. But there was now hot water and the heating had been linked up to the city system. This meant our Greek-Russian janitors and furnace-men had gone, but the end result was hardly an improvement. When I complained about the cold, UPDK explained that the pipes were seventy years old and could be changed but it would take eight months!

The danger of fire seemed to have been reduced by the installation of a hot-water system but it overlooked the human element. Coming home from a Kremlin reception in early spring, we found the whole street blocked off by police and firemen who dramatically escorted us through to the fire at the Canadian embassy. It turned out fortunately to be a blaze in one of the buildings in the compound. The Hungarian-born wife of one of our guards in a fit of Magyar pique had set fire to her apartment.

The Canadian wives were a heroic lot, having to live in uncomfortable flats in shoddy apartment buildings, excluded largely from local contacts, struggling with a difficult language, avoiding the constant probing of the KGB, educating their children in an alien environment, and simply running a household. While we lived in more secure and better accommodation in the embassy compound, my wife had to cope with most of these problems, as well as the inevitable social responsibilities of an ambassador's wife. There was an almost endless round of receptions, luncheons, dinners which, though often boring and trivial, were an essential part of the job of exchanging information and ideas. It was, in any case, as my wife put it, a cutlet-for-cutlet affair.

In addition she had to deal with a staff which at one point consisted of an Egyptian cook, a Russian maid, a Portuguese butler, and a Finnish housekeeper whose main job seemed to be largely to keep the others from murdering one another and to scout the city in the hope of finding some fresh produce. Her exclamation after a successful expedition became legendary: 'Madame, I find fresh on the ulitsa polski eggs.' Translated, that meant that a rare shipment of eggs had arrived from Poland and were for sale in street kiosks.

But there was no way we could fulfil our representational duties by living off the land. This required careful planning to get the necessary supplies from Helsinki. If the Russians ever felt humiliated by the fact that the diplomatic corps had to rely on imports of almost everything except caviar and vodka from tiny Finland, they never showed it.

Then there were the numerous visitors, ministers, government officials, businessmen, artists, casual travellers, most of whose wives needed a helping hand. But the occasion into which my wife poured her most loving care was the annual Christmas party for the Canadian children, which helped to cheer up the melancholy Moscow winter.

The Russia of 1964 was marked by the unique personality of Khrushchev (or Nikita Sergeyevich, as everybody called him) as that of 1952 had been impressed by the terrible Georgian. He was a combination of peasant shrewdness and mistrust, and almost limitless physical energy, with a curiosity about everything new or different and an overbearing confidence in his brains and ability. It was that overconfidence which in the end betrayed him.

By the time we arrived, the sheer enormity of the task of running his immense country had begun to limit his public appearances, but he still insisted on having the entire roster of ambassadors turn up at the airport for each visiting head of state or government and entertaining them at lavish receptions in the Kremlin. Shortly after our arrival we met him for the first time at a reception for Fidel Castro. Khrushchev came bouncily along the room greeting guests. I was introduced as the new Canadian ambassador.

He looked me over and said: 'You don't look like a Canadian. Oh, of course, you must be French Canadian.'

I replied that I was a Canadian of pure Scottish-English stock. He looked puzzled and my wife, whose rather extravagant hat had attracted his eye, intervened.

'He's really Georgian,' she said, pointing to my dark hair and mustache. Khrushchev roared his appreciation and after that usually referred to me as the Georgian.

One had to be constantly on one's toes because it was impossible to tell when he would appear. One night we went to see the Cambodian national ballet and to our astonishment, and even more to that of the Cambodian ambassador, Khrushchev appeared with a bored-looking Presidium in tow. Another time, I had a hunch he would come to the Bulgarian national day so I turned up very early, to find Khrushchev already there furiously lecturing a visiting delegation of Bulgarian pig farmers on how to raise pigs. 'Corn,' he was saying, 'is the answer. Go to Iowa, that's where they know how to raise pigs.' The Bulgarians were not amused.

A few years later I became very good friends with the poet Andrei Voznesensky, who gave me an account of a run-in with Khrushchev in 1963 which illustrates graphically the crudeness but basic humanity of the man. I had noticed in Voznesensky's dacha in Peredelkino a large photograph of himself addressing a conference of intellectuals with Khrushchev just behind him standing and shaking his fist. Seeing my fascination with the photo Voznesensky told me the story.

After several attempts by Khrushchev to put the brakes on the cultural 'liberalism' which he had himself launched, he decided to convene a conference of all the leading intellectuals in the new Palace of Congresses in the Kremlin. It lasted three days and was attended throughout by all members of the Presidium. The first two days consisted of a long series of speeches by tame writers and artists, filled with fulsome praises of Khrushchev and including frequent attacks on the 'decadent, deviationist' work of Voznesensky and of Aksionov, the playwright and son of Natalia Ginsberg, who spent sixteen years in concentration camps and subsequently wrote a remarkable account of her experience, *Into the Whirlwind*, needless to say never published in Russia.

On the last day Khrushchev said he wanted to see this person who was frequently attacked and to hear what he had to say. Voznesensky, dressed in a black roll-neck sweater, came to the lectern and began defending his liberal position in poetry. At once Khrushchev interrupted him but Voznesensky could not see who it was and, never dreaming it was Khrushchev, said into the microphone: 'Please stop interrupting and let me speak.' Khrushchev stopped and Voznesensky continued talking. A few minutes later Khrushchev intervened again to attack him as an imperialist, a spokesman for capitalism, and so on.

Voznesensky then turned around to see who was talking and was astounded to see it was Khrushchev. The latter, apparently impressed by Voznesensky's young baby face said: 'Well, all right, go on, tell us something.' He continued but Khrushchev again interrupted, shouting: 'Shelepin has a passport ready for you to go abroad.' Alexander Shelepin, who was then head of the KGB, jumped up and shouted: 'Yes, it' s all ready. And anyway, what do you mean by coming here dressed like a beatnik?' Khrushchev, obviously having no idea what a beatnik was, added: 'Yes, you're just a beatnik-agent.'

At this point Voznesensky, genuinely frightened, overturned the glass of water on the reading stand and got down on his hands and knees to recover it. Khrushchev said impatiently: 'Oh, never mind that. Go ahead and let's hear some of your poetry.' He recited several poems, and although interrupted by comments from Khrushchev, the latter let him finish, then leaned down from the podium, took the poet by the hand and said: 'Go ahead and work, young man.'

Voznesensky detailed another incident at the conference which well illustrates Khrushchev's muddle-headed approach to the arts. The only person who applauded when Voznesensky finished reading his poetry was a painter, Golitsin, a member in good standing of the Union of Artists and a producer of totally conformist 'socialist-realist' landscapes. Khrushchev was furious and demanded that this 'agent' should come forward.

Khrushchev asked why he had applauded Voznesensky. Golitsin replied that he liked his poetry. 'What other poets do you like?' Khrushchev asked. 'Mayakovsky,' Golitsin replied and launched into a recital of verses of the darling of the establishment. Finally Khrushchev had to stop him, saying he did not want to hear anything more from this abstract painter. Golitsin replied that on the contrary he hated abstract painting and was a socialist-realist artist at which Khrushchev gave up and angrily told him to go back to his seat.

Khrushchev then demanded that Aksionov show himself. The latter was frightened out of his wits and as soon as he got to the podium drew from his pocket a piece of paper and read a short statement thanking the first secretary for having released his mother from the concentration camp and having saved his father from imprisonment. Khrushchev seemed only to have taken in the words 'father' and 'concentration camp' and furiously demanded if he had come there to seek revenge. Aksionov innocently asked why he should want revenge for an act of mercy at which point Khrushchev gave up on Aksionov as well and ordered him off the platform.

Voznesensky was snubbed by everyone when he left the hall and fully expected that he would be expelled from the Writers' Union and probably arrested. He therefore went to stay with some relatives in a little town in Latvia hoping if he kept out of sight the storm would pass. In fact nothing happened to him and it is typical of Khrushchev that he seldom ventured beyond words in his diatribes, which he unleashed without either understanding what the new writers and artists had to say, or what it could lead to. He was therefore in the last few years of his regime struggling in his clumsy way with a phenomenon for which he was totally unprepared.

As a postscript to this, just two months before he died Khrushchev sent a message to Voznesensky. He apologized sincerely for his attack on the poet, explaining that there were very many things which he had not understood.

Khrushchev was a man too much in a hurry, and with too little knowledge and preparation, and possibly too much power, to take the right decisions to solve his country's manifold problems. By 1964 his experiments in the Party structure, in the administration, and in agriculture were already creating doubts and fears in the minds of the Party faithful. Nevertheless, at the beginning of 1964 he seemed almost unassailable, and his power practically unlimited both in the administration and in the Party where, judiciously using the general revulsion over the crimes of Stalin, he had quickly moved his own men into positions of authority at almost every level.

At the same time resentment against him personally and against many of his policies had been slowly welling up. One of the sources of his power had been the support of the military which he both used and controlled. Inexplicably he suddenly announced a cut in the military budget and a reduction in the armed forces of one million two hundred thousand men, at the same time reducing the pensions of those retired. His excuse was the need for manpower in industry and in agriculture. But it caused extreme resentment and meant that the army could not be counted on when the coup was eventually mounted against Khrushchev.

The manpower to be released was hardly needed in agriculture. A staggering 27 per cent of the labour force was at work on the farms compared to less that 5 per cent in the United States and Canada. But an already enormously inefficient system had been further complicated by an extraordinary decree whereby Khrushchev divided the functions in the Party structure into a Central Committee for industry and another for agriculture and applied this division down to the lowest level of activity. In the confusion and rivalries which arose out of this 'reform,' agriculture and industry both suffered, and Party members, particularly in the central organization, felt that through the dual system of reporting, both directly to Khrushchev, the latter's supreme power was increased at their expense.

And yet Khrushchev had made startling gains in farm production in his ten years in office. In 1953 grain production was 36 million tons, two-and-a-half million tons less than in 1940. In 1956 it had increased to 125 million of which 16 million came from the so-called Virgin Lands of northern Kazakhstan which he opened up largely to wheat cultivation. I took an intense interest in this project because of the visit of the first deputy minister of agriculture, Vladimir Matskevich, to Canada in 1955. He had outlined their plans to us and confided that he had been sent to study the Canadian experience because climatic and other conditions in the Palliser Triangle area of Saskatchewan and Alberta were almost identical with northern Kazakhstan.

It should have been obvious that these rolling grasslands in a northern climate, with irregular rainfall, had to be opened up with care. The Canadian experiment had been a costly one. The prairie at first produced unheard-of crops of best-quality wheat. But wind erosion, excessive and careless exploitation, and occasional droughts almost turned it into a dustbowl until agricultural science, careful study, and common sense produced rules by which this ecologically sensitive area could be made to produce fine wheat on a regular basis.

The shock brigades of Russian and Ukrainian youths sent out to the Virgin Lands by Khrushchev had astounding success in producing wheat, with the result that the orders from the Kremlin, ignoring the advice of the experts, demanded greater amounts every year. The inevitable result came in 1963 when drought throughout most of the country, compounded by over-planting in the Virgin Lands, produced a harvest not sufficient to feed the population. For the first time the Soviet government had to buy grain abroad, paying for it mostly through the unloading of gold stores.

The harvest in 1964, however, was a good one and we were permitted a look at the Virgin Lands, up until then terra incognita to most foreigners. Lord Thomson of Fleet was largely responsible. He had developed a good personal rapport with Khrushchev, his Canadian origin possibly making it easier for Nikita Sergeyevich to understand. In early August 1964 he was invited to Moscow to discuss with Khrushchev a plan dear to both of them, a biography of the Soviet leader to be written by staffers of the *Sunday Times*. Lord Thomson, who came to lunch with us, told me it had all been agreed and two of his best reporters would be attached to Khrushchev for an unspecified period of time to talk to him about his early life, his way of work, and so on. This extraordinary project, of course, came to nothing with the overthrow of its main protagonist.

In the middle of Lord Thomson's talks with Khrushchev he was suddenly invited to go to Kazakhstan with him to see for himself that the farms had recovered from the 1963 disaster. Lord Thomson accepted and after the visit urged Khrushchev to invite some of the ambassadors to have a look for themselves. As a result the representatives of the main grain-growing countries were flown out to Tselinagrad (literally 'Virgin City') at the end of August and taken through the whole area in Khrushchev's private train. The trip had the aura of a grand-ducal progress with the train stopping from time to time in the middle of vast prairies of grain while we descended to receive the traditional bread and salt from the local peasantry.

Few Westerners since then have had as good an opportunity to study this remote area, which is and will continue to be vital in the overall world production of grain. What was immediately obvious was that it had bounced back from the disaster of 1963, and we inadvertently saw photographs showing dust storms which almost completely hid even farm buildings. In fact the Virgin Lands did produce a crop of some twelve million tons that year.

It was a gigantic enterprise, no mean feat in a largely unpopulated area as big as Britain and Ireland, to settle and farm it in a decade, lay out a communications network, build a chain of elevators, and supply the population with the basic amenities. Tselinagrad, formerly the old tsarist garrison town of Akmolinsk, had become a city of one hundred and fifty thousand and smaller centres were going up. Everything was slipshod and had an air of temporary accommodation, but it functioned.

As we travelled through the farms and talked to officials and farmers the drawbacks became more apparent. There was no lack of well-informed agronomists – I met no less than twenty-six – who had studied the Canadian experience, who knew what had to be done to meet the challenge of periodic drought, thin soil, wind erosion, and a dangerously short growing season. But there was little they could do to resist the tremendous pressure from Khrushchev to squeeze every drop of grain from the area. As a result, very little land was left fallow even though the experts recommended as much as 50 per cent; nothing was done to protect the top soil from wind erosion; too much attention was paid to chemical fertilizers; care of the machinery was perfunctory; and finally, the elevators were stationed at one-hundred-kilometre intervals (sixteen in Canada) so that the wastage in getting the grain to the silos was enormous. At one of the biggest collective farms, many of whose agronomists had been to Western Canada, I was told that they all knew what had to be done to prevent the area turning into a dustbowl but their recommendations were invariably ignored by Moscow in its constant demand for more grain.

All the same, it was clear that the Virgin Lands had become a new and vital element in Soviet society. There would be occasional disasters, but its wheat production would be an invaluable aid to overall grain production. And perhaps just as important, a previously almost empty region, bordering on China, had been populated with 'whites.' Previously it had been the traditional grazing lands for the nomad Kazakhs whose loyalty in a contest with China the Russians could never be sure of. Now they had been swamped by the Russian and Ukrainian settlers, so that a 'European' bulwark had been put on the very frontiers of the Chinese empire.

The only sufferers, if one excludes the poor devils who were sent there from their native Russia or Ukraine to settle this inhospitable land, were the Kazakhs who not only had been largely driven from the steppe country but had become a minority in their own republic. The arrogance of the Russians to their native peoples became apparent in the arrangements for the trip. The only Kazakhs we saw were waiters in the restaurants and the 'foreign minister' and 'deputy foreign minister' of the Kazakh Republic, imported from Alma-Ata for the occasion. I usually shared a car with the deputy foreign minister. Once the Russian director of a collective farm asked to ride with us. He introduced himself and asked the Kazakh who he was. The reaction to the answer was one of astounded disbelief, after which he paid no more attention to him except for the occasional puzzled glance.

The Virgin Lands project has had its ups and down, but it has served a number of Soviet aims. It has on an average added ten to fifteen million tons of grain to the total harvest every year. It has expanded the frontiers of 'European Russia' into a vast area of Central Asia, thus counterbalancing the growing population of Kazakhs, Uzbeks, and other Soviets of Asian origin. And with its peopling by Europeans, it has opened up the possibilities for moving the industrial frontier further east and exploiting otherwise unprofitable mineral and energy resources.

Meanwhile resentment against the arbitrary and often insensitive 'reforms' of Khrushchev was growing in a vital area, that of the Party rank and file. One reform, applicable to all Party bodies from raion (or county) committees right up to the Central Committee, made it obligatory for one-third of all members of each committee to be replaced at each election, with the exception of the first secretary and 'experienced Party workers of special merit.' Theoretically this was a very useful innovation, intended to force new blood into very stodgy bodies, but in practice it sapped the authority of the Party secretaries and committee members. It struck at the financial remuneration of the party workers as well and created a feeling of insecurity at almost every level, including the Central Committee. It is a measure of the distance power had placed Khrushchev from reality that he failed to realize that this measure would deprive him of the support in the Party which had proved indispensable to him before in combating an anti-Khrushchev majority in the Presidium.

Problems had also arisen in foreign affairs, above all over the question of relations with China. In February 1964, Mikhail Suslov presented a report on China, which Khrushchev referred to on frequent occasions, including an unforgettable moment at a meeting in the Kremlin Palace of Congresses in honour of Lenin's birthday. Clearly bored by the reading of a long and detailed ideological report, Khrushchev suddenly put down his text and said: 'And now, comrades, I am going to speak from the heart,' launching into an emotional and clearly spontaneous attack on the

Chinese leadership. This was the only time I ever saw a Soviet spokesman depart from his text, and it evoked a real and emotional reaction from his audience.

Relations with China had been deteriorating rapidly since Khrushchev's visit to the United States in 1959 and his trip to Peking immediately afterwards in a disastrously unsuccessful effort to persuade Mao Tse-tung that an understanding with Washington was a necessary prerequisite to peaceful coexistence in a nuclear world. Mao believed this was betrayal of the cause, that Khrushchev was giving in to 'nuclear blackmail,' and that the communist powers, China anyway, could survive a nuclear holocaust. For years afterwards this callous Chinese view was repeated by the Russians as a justification for disregarding the Chinese arguments against the policy of peaceful coexistence.

But there was, of course, much more to the quarrel than a doctrinal dispute over relations with the United States. Khrushchev was a peasant and a boor, albeit an often amusing and delightful one, and he had no hesitation in telling Mao and his colleagues how and where they went wrong in internal and foreign policies. It must have been exasperating for Khrushchev to see the way the Chinese were misusing Soviet economic and military aid. From the Chinese point of view, the Soviets' refusal to give China nuclear weapons' technology, and their failure to support Peking against the United States in the Quemoy crisis or in the frontier quarrel with India, in spite of immediate and unqualified Chinese support for Russia in its Hungarian crisis in 1956, must all have been very hard to swallow.

Added to this was the personal antipathy between Mao and Khrushchev. There has seldom, if ever, been any real comprehension between the Chinese and the Russians and no ideological coating could disguise this for long. Mao accepted tacitly the leading position of Stalin in the world communist movement because he was the undisputed leader of the largest communist country, who had been instrumental in winning the war which had helped to bring the Chinese communists to power, and for whom Mao had great personal respect. But on the death of Stalin, Mao expected the Russians to accept *him* as the oldest and most experienced communist leader and head of the biggest Communist Party in the world. He had no respect for Khrushchev as leader and even less for him as a man. It was rumoured in Moscow that Mao disdained him because he was an uneducated peasant, he did not know how to eat properly, and above all because he smelled bad. Khrushchev indeed was of lowly origin and his manners were distinctly uncouth, but hardly something one would expect another communist to reproach him with. After a visit to China ten years later I realized that the Chinese communist leaders were more fastidious than their Russian counterparts and hardly troubled to conceal their contempt for them.

In April 1964 Khrushchev celebrated his seventieth birthday with some fanfare but on a reasonably restrained note compared to the effusive adulation poured on Stalin when he reached this landmark in 1949. Having seen a good deal of Khrushchev in the preceding week, particularly at receptions connected with the visit of the Polish party secretary, Wladislaw Gomulka, I noted at the time that he seemed in good spirits and excellent physical shape. At the Kremlin he was extraordinarily ebullient and spoke extemporaneously, mostly about the inequities of Mao Tse-tung, with a fire and emotion which evoked an immediate response from his audience. This very earthy, very Russian, very nationalistic and practical approach clearly appealed.

Khrushchev still dominated all the other members of the hierarchy in prestige, authority, and personality. Only Leonid Brezhnev stood out from the crowd. All the others remained in the background, although it was not the same kind of anonymity that surrounded Stalin, which was one of fear. The Presidium seemed to exude a compound of respect for Khrushchev's positions combined with an acceptance of his general popularity among the people, although already increasingly tart anti-Khrushchev jokes were beginning to circulate.

By the summer, however, I was beginning to feel some doubts about the ability of Khrushchev to survive the increasingly acute crises in internal Party and economic matters and failures in international affairs. Brezhnev and Podgorny seemed to have been designated to the succession, but it was not working very well and on 15 July 1964, Khrushchev proposed, and the Supreme Soviet ratified, that Mikoyan should take over the largely honorific post of president (chairman of the Presidium of the Supreme Soviet), so that Brezhnev could 'concentrate on his activities' in the Secretariat. There seemed little doubt that Khrushchev had chosen his crown prince. And this was probably his fatal error, because by it he identified a person around whom opposition could coalesce. It was an error which Brezhnev himself never forgot during his long years in power.

The dramatic events of 15–16 October are too well known to bear repetition in detail. Khrushchev, holidaying in Sochi, was summoned back to Moscow to find the entire Presidium aligned against him and had no choice but to accept the inevitable – retirement 'due to age and ill health.' The takeover was extraordinarily smooth and painless. Brezhnev became first secretary of the Party, Kosygin prime minister, and Mikoyan remained as president. The only immediate casualty was Khrushchev's son-in-law Adjhubei, who was removed from the editorship of *Izvestia*. Later changes came as Mikoyan was replaced by Podgorny and the head of the propaganda department in the Central Committee, Leonid Ilichev, was removed to a safer spot as a deputy foreign minister. The people of Moscow took the changes in their usual phlegmatic way. This was a matter between 'them' and did not affect 'us.'

There was, and still is, speculation over the reasons for the palace coup and for the timing, which at first glance seemed highly inauspicious. The week of the coup coincided with the official visit of President Dorticos of Cuba and the planned return to earth of the first space flight of three cosmonauts. But there was probably in fact only a very limited time available for the plotters. It had to take place when Khrushchev was absent from Moscow and it had to be done quickly – before the 15 November plenum on agriculture which Khrushchev had summoned, before the 15 December meeting of Communist parties, and before he could make his visit to West Germany.

The speed and efficiency of the operation were the result of the complete isolation of Khrushchev in the Presidium and the erosion of his support in the Party as a whole. We knew from several sources that Mikoyan was the only one whose loyalty to the cabal was in doubt. Subsequently it became known that he was not present at the Presidium meeting of 11 October at which the decision to proceed was taken, and when he joined the Presidium two days later he at first opposed the ouster of Khrushchev but came around when he saw he was isolated.

The basic reason for the coup, and the only one which made it possible, was the personal resentment which had grown up among members of the hierarchy at the bullying, overbearing behaviour of Khrushchev. The editorial of *Pravda* on 17 October put it in its usual opaque style when it said that 'Hare-brained schemes, premature conclusions, hasty and unrealistic decisions and actions, vainglory, windbagging, administration by fiat, unwillingness to take account of the findings of science and practical experiences – all are alien to a Leninist Party' which, it went on, cannot tolerate bureaucratic methods and single-personality decisions.

Khrushchev represented a Russian era which by 1964 was well and truly over. Just as Stalin represented the period of Sturm und Drang of modern Russia, Khrushchev represented to a remarkable degree the hopes, aspirations, and failings of the Russian peasant come to power. But as the Soviet Union became a great country, his image became dated and most Russians of the ruling class knew it and were increasingly embarrassed and ashamed of his unfashionable appearance and peasant vulgarity. The men who engineered his fall were more sophisticated, more bourgeois, more aware of the shortcomings of their country, more anxious to appear part of the civilized Western world.

But the disappearance of Khrushchev removed one of the most exciting personalities of the post-war period. Moscow became a much duller place without his ebullient though unpredictable presence and that of Nina Petrovna, his very human, earthy, practical wife.

The legacy of Khrushchev is vast. He exposed the Stalinist terror and destroyed the empire of the concentration camps. He unleashed an unprecedented few years of literary creativity. He began the slow, laborious path to constructing a new and more civilized relationship between the Western powers and the Soviet Union, and above all the United States. He attacked the problem of agriculture, he attempted to decentralize the economy, and gradually shifted priorities in the allocation of limited resources to the long-neglected consumer goods industry. In the last year of his reign he was beginning to experiment with radical new economic ideas not only of Soviet but of Polish, Hungarian, and even Yugoslav origin.

Although Khrushchev's approach to internal, Party, and foreign problems was always contained within the limits of his Marxist ideology, he brought to bear on them an empiric approach. But none of them was really capable of solution unless he was prepared to break out of the ideological strait-jacket, and nothing in his upbringing or background permitted him to do this. Hence he threshed around in an often frantic manner in an attempt to find a way to lift the monstrous burdens left by Stalin, but with only partial success. Certainly he himself often held back or retreated from many positions he had adopted when he recognized the dangers they represented for the Party, above all in the question of de-Stalinization.

In his relations with the West, Khrushchev must be given full credit for the decision to withdraw from Austria and Porkalla-Ud in Finland and start the process towards normalization of relations with West Germany and the other NATO countries. It would be idle to speculate on the possible course of developments in Soviet-American relations if the u-2 incident had not aborted the promise inherent in his visit to the United States in 1959. It seemed to have a traumatic effect on his thinking, leading to the Cuban and Berlin crises, but no Soviet leader since Khrushchev has dealt so recklessly with American power.

After his removal from office, he disappeared with incredible speed from Soviet records. Anyone who knew nothing of Soviet history and arrived in the Soviet Union in November 1964 would be mystified as to who had ruled Russia in the preceding decade, or indeed during the Stalin era. It is one of the paradoxes of the Soviet system that there is no way of accommodating into the hagiography rulers who have erred.

Khrushchev was left in peace and obscurity, living in an apartment only a few steps from the Canadian embassy, under discreet but very effective surveillance. Because of my physical proximity I was asked to help two important visitors to see him: Shirley Temple Black and Richard Nixon. Shirley Temple and her husband were on a private visit to the Soviet Union, and she wished to see Khrushchev, who had made a great impression on her when he visited Hollywood in 1959. In fact, she showed me his visiting card on which he had scribbled a few lines urging her to come to Russia.

Richard Nixon, at that time out of power, was visiting Finland together with Joey Smallwood, Premier of Newfoundland, in connection with a joint Fenno-Newfoundland Power Board. While waiting in Helsinki for completion of the contract, Nixon suggested they visit Russia. And, never averse to publicity, he decided to try to see the man with whom in 1958, as Eisenhower's vice-president, he had had the famous 'kitchen debate' over the merits and demerits of communism and capitalism. Turned back at the door of Khrushchev's apartment building, they had come to the Canadian embassy to seek my help in getting access to him. I do not think I fully succeeded in convincing them or Shirley Temple that their request was impossible since Khrushchev had become a non-person. Nixon and Smallwood returned in any case to the apartment and again were turned away by the police.

The non-person died peacefully on 11 September 1971. Two days later a laconic statement in *Pravda* said that former pensioner Nikita Khrushchev had passed away. I was by then the longest serving ambassador in Moscow and therefore dean of the diplomatic corps. As such, tongue-in-cheek, I asked the chief of protocol if I was expected to do anything to honour the former prime minister. The query filled him with consternation and he promised to look into the matter. The reply came twenty-four hours later and was simply: 'You should be guided by the announcement in *Pravda*.' Nevertheless, I wrote a personal letter to Nina Petrovna and a few months later received a very gracious acknowledgment, an unusual event in the Soviet Union, where letters are seldom, if ever, answered.

Khrushchev was denied a niche in the Kremlin wall, where so many of his lesser colleagues are buried. Having declared him heretical and non-existent, presumably it would have been inconsistent to recognize him in death. So he lies inconspicuously in a grave in the Novidevichi Monastery, not far from the last resting place of Chekhov. His monument, an abstract sculpture, was made by Ernst Neizvestny, who subsequently emigrated to the West, and designed the illustrations for my book *Dostoyevsky and Other Poems*.

Pasternak is quoted by Olga Ivinskaya as saying: 'For so long we were ruled over by a madman and a murderer – and now by a fool and a pig. The madman had his occasional flights of fancy, he had an intuitional feeling for certain things, despite all his wild obscurantism. Now we are ruled over by mediocrities.' Pasternak had valid reasons for hating Khrushchev, but his judgment in this case was very wrong. No matter what the final verdict on him, Khrushchev was no mediocrity.

4

Brezhnev Takes Control

The fifty-eight-year-old Leonid Brezhnev who supplanted Khrushchev in 1964 was a very different figure from the ill and wasting leader with whom the West became familiar in the last seven years of his reign. The long eighteen-year rulership of Brezhnev can indeed be divided into two parts: from October 1964 until 1975, when he was a clever and energetic head of his country; and from 1975 when sickness slowly transformed him into another person until his death in 1982. His infirmity in the later years inevitably has distorted our concept of him and overshadowed the accomplishments of his first decade in office.

One of the reasons for the fall of Khrushchev was the increasingly dictatorial and arbitrary nature of his rule, and the erratic nature of his policies. He had his great successes, but he governed too much by intuition, imposing new policies without adequate preparation and abandoning them for something else with equal ease. His colleagues also resented the 'nekulturni' image of Soviet man which he projected abroad. Brezhnev and his supporters were careful to avoid these faults. They tried with some success to present the image of well-dressed, sober, cultured, rational, and dedicated men. It was difficult to imagine any of them ever thumping the table with a shoe. But at the same time they had difficulty in their public appearances keeping the attention of their audiences in any other way. They were able, and in the case of Kosygin even brilliant, but they lacked charisma and imagination.

In 1964 Brezhnev was a heavily good-looking man, invariably impeccably dressed, but faced from the beginning with a reputation for mediocrity, if not stupidity. Certainly he lacked the charisma of Lenin, Stalin, or Khrushchev, but his competence, his political flair, and his sound common sense were indisputable. He could hardly have been mediocre to survive as head of the Soviet Communist Party for eighteen years. Born in 1906 and brought up in a steel town in the Dnieper industrial region of Ukraine of poor working stock, he was old enough when the First World War broke out that it and the bloodshed of the revolution left a vivid impact on him. Like many of his generation who joined the Communist Party, he was given a summary technical engineering education in the thirties. Promotion inside the Party apparatus followed rapidly with the need to replace the many loyal Party workers who were liquidated by Stalin in the great purges of the thirties. In the Second World War Brezhnev became a political commissar in the Red Army, a role which was later blurred in the heroic accounts of his alleged exploits as a combat officer. However, like Khrushchev before him, he did see action in the campaigns in the northern Caucasus and Ukraine. When the time came in the mid-seventies to refurbish Brezhnev's image, numerous books appeared glorifying his role as a soldier, including an account allegedly written by him of the battle of Malaya Zemlya.

There was never any doubt about the toughness of Brezhnev, and he was to be ruthless in getting rid of colleagues who might appear to be opponents or potential opponents, although he dealt with them in a relatively benign fashion. He had the astuteness to move slowly and cautiously to build up a political system which made his personal position almost unassailable. He cultivated good relations with the military and, by accepting the rank of marshal of the Soviet Union, identified himself personally with the army class. This was easy for him to do as he glorified in his wartime action and it was easy to get a conversation going with him by referring to a campaign in which he had participated.

He moved quickly to place men loyal to him in key positions in the Secretariat, the Presidium (which he renamed the Politburo), the Central Committee, and the Party apparatus as a whole. Many of these men were officials who had originated in the Dnieper area or had worked with him in Moldavia or the Virgin Lands. The old crony system became an integral part of his means of survival as the Dnieper Mafia infiltrated the corridors of power. Ideology he left largely in the hands of Mikhail Suslov. Their rigidly conservative views coincided, but Brezhnev was bored with the intricacies of Marxist-Leninist doctrine and he was happy to have Suslov defend its purity and evolve orthodox explanations for specific political acts.

Brezhnev had clearly studied the reasons why Khrushchev had proved easy to eliminate and he was determined to avoid those errors. He himself had worked his way into a position of key importance partly by self-effacement, so that he was not considered a danger to either Khrushchev or his colleagues. Brezhnev also saw the dangers inherent in identifying his heir apparent and, until the aberration in his final years of trying to promote Chernenko, he successfully stuck to this principle.

He was quick to sense criticism or opposition to himself or his policies and to remove anyone whom he considered a real or potential contender for the crown. This helped to consolidate his position; but it also deprived the government of many talented officials, most of them younger and more dynamic than Brezhnev, and reduced the intellectual level of the Politburo. Instead he built around him a solid group of men of at least his own age who shared his cautious, conservative, and limited view of the world and the Soviet Union, whose positions depended on the survival of the leader. This system, while successful in preserving Brezhnev and his colleagues, inevitably ended up as the sclerotic combination which ruled the Soviet Union for the last four or five years of the Brezhnev era.

Brezhnev had many very human features. He was inordinately vain – about his personal appearance, about his literary abilities, about his role in the war, and his role as a world statesman. He could not resist toys and gadgets and above all foreign cars, for which he had a passion. When he appeared in his marshal's uniform, his chest was completely covered in medals. At first he resisted an effort to create a new 'cult of personality' (the current joke explained this on the grounds that you could not have a cult of personality if you had no personality!), but eventually succumbed to it, partly because his colleagues believed their leader had to be built up as a figure of respect, partly because he himself enjoyed it.

His human weaknesses often led him to favour or protect friends and relatives. He was either unaware of some of the more flagrant examples of nepotism and corruption, or else his family loyalties outweighed his scruples. The most amusing illustration of this, which I can vouch for as authentic, concerned his favourite daughter who was wedded, in the first of a series of marriages, to one of the lesser lights in the Moscow circus. The husband's crucial, though not very spectacular, role was that of the anchorman in a gymnastic team. During the visit of the circus to Western Europe in 1966, he acquired a Mercedes automobile and apparently drove it back with no problem to Moscow. A few weeks later he turned up at the West German embassy to inquire if they could tell him how to maintenance it. The ambassador, who had no idea that this was the son-in-law of Brezhnev, gave permission and the gymnast became a weekly visitor to the embassy garage, striking up a friendship with the ambassador's driver, an ex-tank sergeant and a Mercedes mechanic.

Then, in the summer of 1967, the circus went on a major tour of Canada and the United States. Before he left, the son-in-law had another request. Could he leave his Mercedes in the embassy garage while he was away? It was the only safe place in Moscow. Even if he was ready to pay the exorbitant price of putting his car in a closed garage (and it was not sure he would be able to find one), he would certainly find all the movable parts gone when he got back. The ambassador again agreed. And when the circus returned to Moscow, the son-in-law picked up his Mercedes and invited the ambassador's driver to have dinner with him and his wife. It was only then that it was discovered who the circus peformer's wife was. We found it diverting that the son-in-law of the most important man in the Soviet Union would quite unbashedly use the facilities of the embassy of the hated West Germans to maintain his prized possession, a Mercedes car. It also demonstrated as early as 1967 how great was the abuse of power and privilege.

Brezhnev's horror at the destruction in human lives and

property occasioned by the Second World War was, I think, very genuine, as was his determination to prevent another holocaust. Almost every conversation I had with him, and every meeting with him which I attended, was marked by some reference to the useless destructiveness of war and the need never to forget what had happened in the past. While he was not averse to using such references to impress foreign visitors, there was never any doubt in my mind that his feelings were real. Certainly they played a role in his later search for an understanding with the United States, although they never altered his basic policy of making the Soviet Union so strong no other power would ever again be in a position to attack it.

Brezhnev, in the first years of his leadership, had an intuitive sense of what the country wanted. The Russians had welcomed the disappearance of the Georgian tyrant who had terrorized them, and the relaxed peasant style of Khrushchev. The educated classes, whether or not members of the Party, however, had become embarrassed by the Khrushchev image presented of the Soviet Union, and were disturbed by his eccentricities. Brezhnev recognized that they, and the country as a whole, badly wanted a conservative leader who at the same time would be respected abroad. They were fed up with fireworks, and Brezhnev gave them a feeling of respectability and solidity. They wanted an end to internal experimentation and foreign adventures. And Brezhnev reassured them on both scores, although at the cost of appearing dull and mediocre.

One of the difficulties with the new leadership was its inability, apparent from Brezhnev's very first policy speech, to take new initiatives to meet the numerous and acknowledged economic problems or to find ideological or material incentives to inspire greater effort on the part of the people. The one exception was the repeal of the 'unfounded measures' imposed on the private agriculture sector by Khrushchev in 1956. This was to have a significant effect in increasing farm productivity in succeeding years.

Brezhnev in fact recognized the legitimacy of private farm plots and encouraged the raising of livestock by individuals. It was a clear acknowledgment of the value of the private sector in providing agricultural produce in general and ideologically it marked a step back from the 'collective ideal,' although this aim had not been abandoned. This step was interpreted generally as an indication of greater flexibility and pragmatism in approaching the problems afflicting the Soviet economy. Nevertheless, we foreign observers maintained what proved to be a healthy scepticism about the distance down this road the Soviet leaders would dare to venture.

A few days later I learned from a Soviet source that one of the factors leading to the decision to overthrow Khrushchev was a plenum on agriculture which he had planned for late November and at which he intended to introduce yet another vast reorganization of agriculture, including further encroachments on the private farm holdings. Kosygin was said to have opposed the scheme because of the effect on the economy of so many shifts in policy. At any rate the Party activists, after the fall of Khrushchev, were out in force explaining to the farm population that he had been planning to liquidate the private plots.

Another change, this time in the Party structure, came soon after. The November 1962 plenum had divided the Party vertically into industrial and agricultural wings. This 'tinkering with the administrative structure,' as Brezhnev described it, and the dislocation it had caused in the Party apparatus down to the raion or county level, was generally believed to have caused considerable resentment among the 'apparatchiks' and was one of the major criticisms of Khrushchev. The latter's aim had apparently been to involve the Party directly in management at the local level by injecting centrally controlled Party committees into production control; to stimulate production by the direct intervention of activists; and to provide him with the means of limiting the authority of his opponents and of rewarding his supporters at the regional level by manipulating power-divided committees.

The apparatchiks obviously found much of this most unwelcome. There was a good deal of evidence, some of it dating from mid-1963, which suggested that obstruction and delays in carrying out Khrushchev's scheme had prevented its implementation. The reversal of this plan by the 1964 plenum was a clear indication that

Brezhnev intended to restore Party loyalty and to reassure the Party ideologues and rank and file members that he would pay heed to their wishes and needs as a first priority. Following the plenum, elections were announced for reunified committees on the 'territorial production principle' in December. Personnel changes in the Central Committee pointed to a rapid and complete reversion to the top priority given to 'Partiinost,' which might be translated as 'the Party above all.'

This is not to say that the Party under Khrushchev had in fact suffered a serious diminution of authority, but the growing emphasis on science and technology and empirical judgments of success had created grounds for concern in the Party apparatus that traditional values were being eroded. The changes immediately introduced by Brezhnev were clearly intended on the one hand to reassert Party supremacy as against the state bureaucracy and technocratic forces generally, and on the other to reinforce his power over the cadres.

One of the questions which preoccupied foreign observers was the attitude Brezhnev and his colleagues would take towards the intelligentsia. There was little to go on from official pronouncements. The press published the usual well-worn platitudes extolling the merits of 'socialist realism' and the need to apply 'the principles of partisanship and kinship with the people' in all aspects of art. But at the same time the charlatan T.D. Lysenko, whose anti-intellectual dogmas in the field of genetics and agricultural science flourished under Khrushchev, was strongly attacked, and the scientists he had exiled to Novosibirsk for opposing his opinions were permitted to publish the results of the research they had carried out in exile.

The poet Joseph Brodsky, imprisoned for 'parasitism,' was released, as well as Olga Ivinskaya, the friend and subsequently memorialist of Pasternak. The 1965 program for the magazine *Yunost* gave prominent place to such 'formalist' poets as Bella Akhmadulina, Andrei Voznesensky, and Evgenny Evtushenko. In *Sovietskaya Kultura* an argument raged over the role of conventionality or formalism in art. One contributor, Vladimir Dobin, went so far as to assert the 'inseparability in art of conventionality and actuality.' This does not appear a very startling statement but it is one which a few months earlier would have sufficed, in Dobin's own words, to have its originator branded a heretic and 'subjected to administrative penalties.' But the argument is interesting as an example of the kind of nit-picking that went on, reminiscent of medieval theologians; and, as in the middle ages, the penalty for deviation was severe.

Another important change in the ideological field was the transfer and downgrading of Leonid Ilichev from the Secretariat in Moscow in 1965. His rigid and often inept actions as Khrushchev's cultural tsar had made too many foes, but his administrative ability saved him from disgrace and he was demoted to the position of a deputy minister of foreign affairs, where his unbending tactics were to serve in good stead later when he was appointed to head the Soviet delegation to the endless negotiations with China on border problems.

The new government displayed a combination of caution mixed with faint traces of liberalism. It appeared likely that the few positive signs reflected more a move by the 'liberals' to push the bounds of socialist realism outwards rather than a really new policy on the part of the leadership – a classical manoeuvre by the Soviet intelligentsia. But I thought at the time the chances not very great that a more accommodating policy in the arts might evolve, and the most that might be hoped for was a retention of the basic gains made since 1956.

In the more general sphere of ideology, the new leadership moved quickly to reassert the policy of the 'state of the whole people,' as an ideological rebuff to the Chinese but with some elaborations to distinguish it from the dogma evolved by Khrushchev and publicized in 1961. The argument basically was that class antagonism had ended in the Soviet Union with the disappearance of the exploiting classes and that therefore the dictatorship of the proletariat was no longer necessary. Stalin was said to have preserved dictatorship contrary to historical need by alleging the existence of internal enemies, and so on. At the same time Khrushchev had used this doctrine to accuse the Chinese of perpetuating the dictatorship of the proletariat in the same way as Stalin through Mao's personality cult.

In December 1964 the Communist Party reiterated the policy of the state of the whole people. It accused certain unnamed people of maintaining the dictatorship of the proletariat when its internal tasks were solved, of wanting to retain the mechanism of class suppression and using it not against their enemies but against the allies of the proletariat. *Pravda* declared that after the abolition of the exploiting classes, the class struggle continued against criminals, idlers, and people of 'private ownership mentality.' But it construed this as a struggle against capitalist survivals 'which in content, scale and methods presents to the working class an absolutely different task from the class struggle and by no means justifies retaining its dictatorship.' It claimed this was bourgeois and revisionist propaganda, which holds that the personality cult is born of the dictatorship of the proletariat. In fact it was a distortion 'which became possible only under definite historical conditions.' Then, openly attacking the Chinese, *Pravda* claimed that to oppose the state of the whole people was to oppose the construction of the new society, to attempt to return to Stalinism.

This was one of the few efforts during the entire Brezhnev period to produce any new ideas in the ideological sphere. They were in fact a restatement of the Khrushchev theses and were elaborated in a way that could only be construed in Peking as an attack on Chinese communist party theory and practice. They had no effect on the mass of the Soviet people, who cared practically nothing for nuances of ideology, or, so far as one could make out, on Party members or the intelligentsia. Whether the system was called dictatorship of the proletariat or the state of the whole people made no difference to their lives or their thinking and altered absolutely nothing. Nevertheless, the overriding importance of ideology demanded that the question be argued at great and sterile length.

Early in December 1964 I had my first meeting with Alexei Kosygin in his capacity of chairman of the Council of Ministers. While most of the interview concerned Canadian-Soviet relations, at that moment when the political scene was just beginning to stir after a period of some quiescence, we also discussed foreign affairs – but without much success. He was tense and nervous, and unwilling to expend his undoubted intellectual talents. In fact his outline of the foreign policy of the new government was singularly uninspiring. He stressed its continuity not only with Khrushchev, whom he never mentioned by name, but with 'great Lenin.' He only departed from his text to remark that the Chinese, insisting on the disturbing doctrine of the inevitability of war, clearly rejected peaceful coexistence. He counselled the West to reflect on this and to work for the avoidance of war.

A few days later, at a meeting of the Supreme Soviet, Kosygin offered a fairly explicit olive branch to the United States. It seemed likely that the dissolution of hopes for an agreement with the Chinese had led the Soviets to think more seriously about the desirability of improved relations with Washington. In addition, one of the first priorities of the government was the economy; so to concentrate on its improvement, some lowering of tension with the United States seemed desirable in spite of the political and ideological obstacles represented by American involvement in Vietnam.

President Johnson's State of the Union message in January 1965 contained a general statement favouring better relations with the Soviet Union, contacts at all levels, and a curiously off-hand invitation to the Soviet leaders to come to the United States. *Pravda* welcomed the possibility of exchanges of visits, to which Johnson responded warmly with the implication that a meeting was in the offing. In fact, there were no grounds for this optimism, and no secret meeting between the Soviet ambassador in Washington, Anatoly Dobrynin, and the president, as had been rumoured, to prepare the ground. As was so often the case, public diplomacy bore little relationship to the facts. It was to be another two and a half years before Kosygin met Johnson at Glassboro, in the first tentative step towards American-Soviet détente, which was quickly aborted by the Soviet intervention in Czechoslovakia and thus effectively postponed until 1972.

In any case, the new leaders in the Kremlin were more concerned with the economy. This preoccupation continued throughout the Brezhnev-Kosygin era without producing any visible improvement. The problems that have since become familiar were already evident in 1965: a slowing rate of growth, under-utilization of capital investments, slow growth in labour productivity, insufficient application of technology, inability to reduce labour costs, poor quality of consumer goods and their distribution, and agricultural failures. Nevertheless, the economic figures at the end of 1965 looked very good in retrospect; there was an increase in industrial production of 8.9 per cent over 1964 and of 5 per cent in labour productivity.

Still, the situation was sufficiently unsatisfactory to prompt the introduction of economic reforms in September 1965, which were identified with Kosygin. When Khrushchev was ousted Kosygin was sixty, but he had already been in or near the centre of power since the war. In those days access to the top leaders was relatively easy, so that I had frequent opportunities to assess their personalities and abilities. Although born in the country, Kosygin made his career in Leningrad and he demonstrated the urbanity and culture that always separated the natives of the most western of Russian cities from the rest. He had a formidable intelligence, an extraordinary capacity for work (he once told me he frequently worked sixteen hours a day), and an amazing memory and ability to absorb a brief, even on subjects with which he could not be expected to be familiar. On economic and technical subjects he was frighteningly well informed.

He had became a deputy chairman of the RSFSR Council of Ministers at the age of thirty-six and chairman at thirty-nine. He was made a full member of Stalin's Presidium at forty-two and managed to survive until the death of the Vozhd, although the evidence indicates that his position was very precarious in 1952. In spite of his usually gloomy and dour appearance, he could be amusing and very human. His devotion to his wife, who died in the mid-sixties, and his daughter Ludmilla, who was married to German Gvishiani, the brilliant Georgian deputy chairman of the State Committee on Science and Technology, was obvious and real. He was more open to new ideas, particularly in the economics sphere, than others of his generation, but this was very relative. His loyalty to the Communist Party and communist ideology was total and I never detected on his part the slightest deviation from the principal aim of all the leaders – which was to guard, strengthen, and preserve the position of total power of the Communist Party in the country.

Hence the so-called Kosygin economic reform of 1965 must be

treated with great reserve. Kosygin was intelligent enough to recognize the dilemma. The Soviet economy since 1945 had grown by leaps and bounds. At the same time the military machine had come within striking distance of equalling that of the United States, helped by an extraordinary concentration of talent, including Andrei Sakharov, in the production of nuclear weapons and space technology. While not downgrading this achievement, the reason for this spectacular growth was simple. The point of departure was so low and the natural and human resources available so great the advance was bound to be rapid. And the application of totalitarian methods proved effective in healing the wounds of war and increasing the production of the basic products needed for the creation of an industrialized economy, above all steel, coal, oil, gas, electric power, railways, internal waterways, and so on. By 1965 Soviet indices in these items were comparable to u.s. production.

But by this time these items were no longer the criteria by which one necessarily judged the strength of a country's economy. It was clear to me that Kosygin, and the other leaders to a lesser extent, was beginning to realize that brute strength, while clearly necessary, was not enough; what really counted was quality. The importance of electronics had changed the nature of the ball game. Khrushchev's boast of catching up with the United States was no longer relevant. The Soviets had caught up, but in the meantime the rules had changed.

Kosygin seemed to have become aware in 1965 that the heavily centralized economic bureaucracy that had produced spectacular achievements in heavy industry was no longer fully applicable to a more sophisticated economy. It was feasible to issue instructions from the Kremlin which would result in the production of the requisite number of steel rails, but it was not so easy to produce, say, women's girdles in the same way.

The economic system was almost totally dependent on the concept of producing units, irrespective of cost, in accordance with a five-year plan, modified and elaborated in yearly plans determined by specialists in Moscow, who were in turn guided by political decisions that often bore little relationship to economic realities. Factory managers thus became little more that administrators, since every item of their production was laid down by

Moscow to the last detail. The price of the finished product was not tied to the cost of production. Sometimes it was put well beneath cost if the item was considered desirable to public morale; in other cases it was vastly inflated because the product was not considered essential and a lower price would have caused an immediate and acute shortage.

Since the number and supply of workers was also determined by Moscow, and the manager had no control over his raw supplies, the chances of exercising initiative were not great. This equally applied to the workers, who were paid a low salary which was practically never related to productivity and who had no incentive to work harder than was absolutely necessary. Since the system also made the concept of unemployment unacceptable, it was almost impossible to fire a worker, and very often an enterprise was forced to hire more employees than it could use.

In spite of some tinkering, this system was still functioning, if that is the correct expression to apply to the Soviet Union, when the Brezhnev era ended. In 1980, for example, a scientific journal in Moscow published complaints concerning oil exploration in Siberia. The enterprise charged with drilling for oil was allotted a fixed sum of money and expected to produce a fixed quota of wells drilled. As a result, to meet the quota, the line of least resistance dictated the drilling of wells near established bases. These were mostly dry but it did not matter since they qualified as part of the plan.

Similarly, even in the winter of 1979–80 sudden shortages occurred in the Moscow shops. One Russian explained to me the disappearance of detergents. The factory producing the containers had not received the plastic from the plastics factory, which in turn had been unable to find means to ship the plastic. Since shipping depended on another enterprise, which in turn had its own quotas and priorities, none of the factories concerned was able to operate properly.

Kosygin approached the economic problem in two ways. First, recognizing the need to improve the technological quality of Soviet products, he replaced the amiable but uninspiring chairman of the State Committee on Science and Technology, Konstantin Rudnev, by one of the leading personalities in the special world of the

Academy of Science, Vladimir Kirillin, a highly respected, sophisticated, and able man who remained in the job, and indeed as a deputy prime minister, until January 1980.

His second step was to endorse some aspects of economic reform which had become identified with Yevsei Liberman, a professor of economics at Kharkov University, and which bears some resemblance to the Gorbachev reforms. While maintaining all of the basic concepts of a communist economy, Liberman proposed to cut through much of the underbush of bureaucratic controls by extensive decentralization and by essentially introducing the key elements of a market economy. Profitability would become the major factor in determining the success of a plant and managers would be given considerable leeway in determining wages, conditions of work, and other incentives. They would also deal directly with the other enterprises in securing their raw materials and equipment, and would have an important voice in designing the product and in marketing it.

In August 1964 Khrushchev had cautiously approved the introduction of 'Libermanism' in two textile plants, the Mayak and the Bolshevika. A year later Kosygin ordered the experiment be extended to other plants; but it was now so surrounded by provisos and hampered by new regulations that it was unlikely to succeed. Whether he was forced to compromise by other members of the Politburo who were suspicious of any experimentation, or whether he himself was unable to break through his innate communist conservatism, the 'reform' was entrusted to ministers and managers who had been in the same position for years and who had been trained to obey, not to think. And at the same time that tentative moves were being made to give more initiative to plant managers, the central control of Moscow was tightened.

It is a highly debatable proposition that the majority of the Russian people want freedom, freedom of almost any kind. As Alexander Zinoviev, the philosopher who came to the West in 1978, said on arriving in Munich: 'The Soviet system is eminently suitable for the Soviet people. So far as the average citizen is concerned, he has his bread and his vodka, he need not pay doctor's bills, he is told that housing is virtually free (which it is not), work is guaranteed, he is not expected to work too hard, and he has learned to live without freedom. If elections were held tomorrow, no doubt he would wish to keep the present regime in power.'

It is not surprising, therefore, that the Liberman experiment was met with scepticism if not outright opposition — by most plant managers, who were neither prepared intellectually for the challenge nor happy to run the risk of innovation; by the bureaucrats of Gosplan (the State Planning Organization) in Moscow, who saw some of their immense authority being eroded; by the Communist Party officials, who believed the scheme threatened their own duplicating role in the economy; and even by the workers, who feared they would have to work harder for the same pay. Fifteen years later the Central Committee was still issuing decrees as an answer to the continuing problems of the economy, calling on Party workers to redouble their supervision of plants and factories to make sure the plans were fulfilled.

Without the enthusiastic co-operation of the entire bureaucracy and the administrative machine, without an ideologically unequivocal endorsement by the Party, and above all without the clear support of Brezhnev, who was never enthusiastic about the reform, it was never likely to develop into a viable alternative. Already, in October 1965, the sceptics must have had their doubts reinforced by the fact that the textile industry in the first year of Libermanism had suffered a 3 per cent decline in production.

Libermanism was never given a chance and never could have worked without a clear-cut decision to introduce a market economy and establish a direct relationship between the price of a product and its cost. It tottered along for another two and a half years until the experiment in 'liberal' communism in Czechoslovakia finally killed it.

The Twenty-Third Congress met on 26 April 1966, and was almost immediately dubbed by the average Russian the ten days that did not shake the world. In contrast to the sparkle and originality of the Khrushchev era, it was marked by monumental dullness and the endless repetition of stale slogans. I heard afterwards that there had been considerable division of opinion about revising Soviet history to incorporate reference to Stalin in a balanced way, but it was not possible to reach a conclusion because of the fear that it might herald a reversion to Stalinist methods. There was no question, of course, of rehabilitating Khrushchev.

Collective leadership was confirmed by the Party, although Brezhnev, who had changed his title from first secretary back to general secretary – the designation used by Lenin and Stalin – was clearly its leading member. But on this, his first opportunity to inspire, he demonstrated clearly that he lacked charisma. In general, the congress tried to give the impression of a stable, confident, and mature leadership, intended to reassure their own people and the outside world that there would be no further palace coups, no repetition of the procedure by which Khrushchev had been abruptly and secretly ousted. While trying thus to reassure, the congress was preoccupied with the problem of ideology and of instilling the proper Marxist feeling of dedication among the rank and file, particularly the youth. But no effort was made to send out a stirring call to the youth or the country as a whole, no material incentives were dangled before them.

It was quite apparent to foreign observers that the young were disenchanted and far more interested in a career than in ideology, and that there had been a gradual erosion of influence of the Party on young intellectuals. (In Russia the term 'intelligentsia' was applied to almost everyone who had a higher education.) The Party had no real answer except to make it clear that no criticism of the regime would be tolerated, while reassuring them that a return to Stalinist repression was not in the offing. But in a curious way, the dull and temporizing congress of 1966 accurately mirrored the evolving Soviet society and the mood of the people, who seemed satisfied with something approaching normalcy. The leadership appeared equally pleased with the results and settled down to the mundane tasks of gradually improving the standard of living.

There is always an underlying need in a country like Russia for a great and dominant personality, but Brezhnev was proving that, with luck, the system could survive without one. In 1967 the leadership was undoubtedly collective, depending in part on the fact that Brezhnev as head of the Party and Kosygin as head of the administration complemented each other nicely. Indeed, since the fall of Khrushchev there had been only three important personnel changes; Mikoyan had been retired in April 1966 and replaced in the largely ceremonial position of president by Nikolai Podgorny, who was at the same time removed from the Secretariat along with Alexander Shelepin. A position in the Secretariat and the Politburo had always been considered essential for advancement to the summit, so the lateral promotion of Podgorny removed him from the running. Shelepin had had too much power in his hands, being the only youthful Politburo member who was also in the Secretariat, and Brezhnev was clearly cutting him down to size.

Dominating the economic scene during the first few years of the Brezhnev era was the strain of maintaining and improving the enormous war machine. Brezhnev was already aware of the potential political power that the military could exercise – not as a class or political grouping but as a force that could determine the outcome of an internal political crisis as it did in the 'anti-Party' attempt to oust Khrushchev in 1957. Partly because he fancied himself as a soldier, and partly because he was astute enough to recognize the need to bolster his relatively shaky position, Brezhnev catered to the armed forces in many ways. He flattered the generals and marshals, he increased the privileges and perks of the officer class, but above all he authorized almost endless spending on research and development, on the remarkable building of a world-wide surface and submarine fleet, and by the maintenance of a huge standing army.

Brezhnev would probably have preferred to find some means of reducing or stabilizing this drain on the economy, but the Vietnam war and tense relations with both China and the United States made it difficult to justify. An effort was made to improve relations with both countries. In February 1965 Kosygin visited Hanoi, Pyongyang, and Peking. But Mao interpreted the tour as an attempt by Moscow to stir up trouble in China's backyard and relations continued to deteriorate until they broke into active hostility on the Ussuri River in 1969.

Brezhnev sensed that it was impossible to reconcile a desire for détente with the United States and their support for Communist Vietnam. And the bombing of Hanoi at the precise moment that Kosygin was visiting it convinced the Soviet leaders that they would have to postpone the idea of a rapprochement with the West until the time was more propitious. This included détente with West

Germany which Khrushchev had been toying with before his fall. It had to wait for the advent to power of Willy Brandt for Ostpolitik to take on a measure of reality.

But France was not so tightly bound to the exigencies of Soviet-American relations. On the contrary, in the spring of 1966 de Gaulle seemed determined both to distance France from NATO and particularly the Americans, and to restore warmth to Franco-Soviet relations. He therefore organized an official visit to the Soviet Union as part of a carefully planned strategy to enhance French influence in the world and to implement his long-term policy of making France an independent force in global affairs. De Gaulle was not the first Western statesman to visit Moscow. Two British prime ministers, the Conservative Harold Macmillan and the Labour leader Harold Wilson, had come to Moscow, but in both cases one had the impression that the visits were not carefully planned components of British policy. Wilson, for example, came in the early spring of 1966, and displayed a singular lack of understanding of the Russians. He insisted he was coming as one socialist to another for a simple working visit and therefore wished a minimum of fanfare – no guards of honour, official banquets, and so on. The Russians, who love panoply and for whom pomp and circumstance are a necessary part of life, were deeply offended and gave Wilson very casual treatment.

De Gaulle, on the other hand, not only insisted on all the honours, he invented new ones. He was the king of the French and therefore had to be lodged in the Kremlin. After recovering from their shock, the Russians were enchanted and quickly restored some of the imperial chambers for him. And when de Gaulle received the heads of diplomatic missions, he insisted that this had to be in his official residence, and so for the first time this ceremony took place in the Vladimir Hall, one of the ornate but splendid historic rooms of the original Kremlin Palace.

De Gaulle was at his best on this occasion, towering over most of the assembly, superbly imperial against the tsarist background. It was in this atmosphere that I was astounded to have the general ask me for news of Quebec. The provincial elections had just taken place and the Liberal leader, Jean Lesage, had been defeated by the Union Nationale under the relatively unknown Daniel Johnson.

De Gaulle wanted to know how his good friend Lesage could have been defeated, and expressed considerable suspicion about the French credentials of someone called Johnson. He ended up by sending his warm greetings to the federal prime minister, Lester Pearson. Ironically only about a year later he was to embrace Johnson and insult Pearson and the federal government by his cry of 'Vive le Québec libre' from the balcony of the city hall in Montreal. Perhaps he was preparing himself for this moment when he unexpectedly insisted on addressing the public from the balcony of Moscow city hall, to a surprised audience of passers-by who, naturally, understood not a word of French, although de Gaulle in his meticulous way had learned enough Russian to be able to deliver a few well-pronounced and elegant sentences on his arrival in Moscow.

The author in 1957 with his first book of poetry, for which he won the
Governor General's Award

First meeting with President Tito of Yugoslavia, January 1959

The author in 1962

With the Patriarch of the Serbian Orthodox Church, Belgrade, 1960

With Tito and his wife Jovanka on the island of Brioni; the presidential pair bid
farewell to the Fords, May 1961

Presentation of letters of credence to President Nasser,
Cairo, June 1961

Visiting the Canadian contingent of the United Nations Expeditionary Force at
Gaza, 1962

left With Thereza at the Canadian embassy, Cairo, 1962

An informal moment with Deputy Prime Minister Dmitri Polyansky during the
Soviet tour of Canada, 1966

At the artists' colony at Peredelkino:
the author and Thereza with Lili Brik outside her dacha

With the Soviet poet Andrei Voznesensky, Moscow, 1972

Photograph of Andrei Voznesensky with dedication to the author

Moscow tour of the Montreal company, Le Théatre du nouveau monde: the
author and Soviet deputy minister of culture with members of the company

The mayor of London, Ontario, presents the author with
the freedom of the city, 1965

Centennial year:
celebrating on 1 July 1967 at the Canadian embassy in Moscow

The author and Thereza with Nina Kandinsky, Moscow, 1975

PART TWO

The Russian Face to the West

5

Canada and Russia: An Uneasy Relationship

The development of more relaxed East-West relations began with the signing of the Anti-Ballistic Missile Treaty between the United States and the Soviet Union in 1963, which was followed by a thaw in British-Soviet relations and a determined effort by General de Gaulle to improve French relations with the Soviet Union.

The Canadian contribution had been modest. The field of manoeuvre for secondary players in a game primarily between Moscow and Washington was, and still is, strictly limited. But in the 1960s the Vietnam war had created an impasse which made any substantial change in the frigid relations between the superpowers highly unlikely. At the same time it caused uneasiness among America's allies, particularly when some of them sensed that the Soviet leaders wished for a less confrontational relationship.

There are four main factors that must always be taken into consideration in Canada's relations with the Soviet Union: our security, which is almost identical with that of the United States; trade, particularly in grains; the overwhelming economic and political importance of our relationship with the United States; and the fact that an important part of our population is of Jewish, Ukrainian, Russian, or East European origin and therefore deeply interested in what happens in the Soviet Union.

In spite of the geographical distance and the fact that Canadians and Russians never fought each other directly (except for the small Canadian intervention in the civil war in Siberia in 1917–18), Canadian-Soviet relations since 1945 have been constantly subjected to crisis. The revelation of Soviet duplicity in the Gouzenko spy affair in 1945 dissipated the illusions of many, by no means all of them communist sympathizers, who believed that the wartime alliance could be extended into mutual co-operation in peacetime.

During the time I spent in Russia as chargé d'affaires I knew I could count on the full support of Lester Pearson, then External Affairs minister. And when I returned to Ottawa in 1954, he insisted on my devoting the first two or three months there preparing an analysis of the Soviet Union after Stalin and the implications for Canada and the West. My report became one of the key documents in Canada-Soviet relations over the next decade. As the official primarily responsible for organizing his visit to the Soviet Union in 1956 I was in continuous contact with him. His policy in developing relations with Russia and Eastern Europe was always realistic and far-sighted and never touched with exaggerated ideological opinions. Prime Minister Louis St Laurent was not an expert on international affairs and was quite happy to leave this to a man whose knowledge and experience were extensive and sound.

It was John Diefenbaker who appointed me ambassador to Russia shortly before the Liberals under Lester Pearson returned to power in 1963. One of the first communications I received from the new government was from Paul Martin, who had become External Affairs minister, confirming the appointment, which he said also had the enthusiastic support of Pearson. I thus knew that when I returned to Moscow in January 1964 I had the approval and understanding of the new government. I was going to need it, since at that time Canadian-Soviet relations were not very cordial.

The Soviets were invariably quick to take offence at almost any article in the Canadian press which they considered insulting to their national pride. And they followed with keen attention the ethnic, particularly the Ukrainian, papers in Canada for anything they considered to be anti-Soviet activity. The usual form of reaction was to summon me to the Foreign Ministry for a dressing down, especially if any member of Parliament or minister had in any way been associated. My reply was usually a patient lecture on the nature of our democratic society and of our free press, and the impossibility, even if it were considered desirable, for the government to control the lawful activities of legitimate societies and of the press. These explanations were usually received with total incomprehension.

Early in 1964 our military attaché was accused of espionage. He was in any case on the point of leaving, so no expulsion took place. The following year, the naval attaché was the target of accusations. In Canada, the Spencer and Munsinger espionage cases of 1965 and the innuendoes connected with them involving the Soviet embassy aroused the ire of the Soviets. The strength of the attack in the Soviet press on the Canadian government even required a special call on Anastas Mikoyan, who was at that time president, to ascertain the genuineness of Soviet indignation and to attempt to assuage this.

Nevertheless, from various remarks made to me in 1965 and early in 1966 by Soviet officials and members of the Politburo, I concluded that the Soviets would respond favourably to any overture from Canada. I felt that Canada had an interest in improving relations with the Soviet Union at a time when the United States was not in a position to do so, provided that we kept always in mind that such relations could never be strictly bilateral, but trilateral.

I had returned to Canada in June 1965 to receive the freedom of the city of London, Ontario, and an honorary degree of Doctor of Letters from the University of Western Ontario. Prime Minister Pearson then asked me to stay on in Ottawa for several months as acting deputy under-secretary of external affairs. He continued to be deeply interested in the Canadian relationship with the Soviet Union and frequently invited me to discuss developments. He proved particularly receptive to my argument that the maintenance of Canadian independence from the United States was easier to achieve in a period of relaxed international relations than in one of tension, when there was a tendency in Washington to require its allies to close ranks in the face of a Soviet threat. The government decided therefore to move cautiously forward.

Two events occurred to make the effort to improve relations

worthwhile. First there was the prospect of a crop failure in the Soviet Union in 1966, which coincided with the expiry of the Canadian-Soviet trade agreement. The Canadian minister of trade and commerce, Robert Winters, decided to head his delegation to the talks aimed at renewing the agreement. The negotiations were curious in the extreme. The Soviet grain-trading agency Export-khleb had let it be known that they might be in the market for wheat. So Bill McNamara, head of the Canadian Wheat Board, whose antennae were acutely tuned to signals from Moscow, at once joined the Canadian party in Moscow.

For the first few days the Russians spoke vaguely of buying small quantities of grain; then suddenly, in an abruptly called evening meeting, they announced they wished to sign an agreement to buy nine million tons of wheat over a three-year period. Since our experts had not detected indications that the harvest was going to be that bad, we were astounded not only at the size of the offer but its extension over a period of three years. No contract of this magnitude had yet been proferred to any country by the Soviets.

Our delegation was even more shocked by the announcement from the Soviet side the following morning of a withdrawal of the offer and accusations against the Wheat Board of misinterpreting the original proposal. This was quite unjustified since the relations between the Wheat Board and Exportkhleb had been, and continue to be, extraordinarily frank, friendly, and honest. The delegation was baffled by this move. I suggested that it probably sprang from sudden doubts higher up. The Soviets never liked to admit the real reason for any move and therefore, to conceal their embarrassment for having gone too fast, put the blame on the other side.

After a sleepless night, the delegation was summoned once again to a meeting twenty-four hours later to be greeted by a smiling group of Russians who proceeded to sign the original contract as if nothing had happened. They came to regret it. The crops in the following years were fairly good and the Soviets, hard-pressed for foreign currency as always, asked for a deferment of the succeeding years of the contract to which the Wheat Board quickly agreed, rightly reasoning that it was better to maintain the special relationship with Exportkhleb than insist on the latter buying wheat it did not need.

Ten years later, through an indiscretion by a senior Soviet official, I came upon the explanation. Apparently a mistake had been made by the Russians in typing up and translating the contract, and it was only after it had been agreed and initialed that the Soviets realized it should have read one million tons of wheat a year for three years. When I expressed scepticism, I was assured the story was true; in any event, shortly after the contract was signed the director of Exportkhleb was demoted and sent into exile as agricultural attaché in Beirut.

Canada's policy proved a wise one; the Soviets frequently reiterated that, with or without an accord, they would come first to Canada for wheat. When the United States in 1974 signed an agreement by which the Soviet Union guaranteed to buy a minimum of six million tons of wheat and other grains per year, I had initial doubts about the ability of Canada to compete. But the Soviets have never failed to purchase large quantities of grain from Canada.

Although the Soviet press never mentioned the purchase of wheat from Canada, or any other country, it quickly became known. Since they bought mostly durum hard wheat, the Russians came to associate white bread with Canadian wheat, assuaging their national pride by saying that Canadians grew the best wheat, but Russians made the best bread, a claim which is not far from the truth. When a Soviet delegation visited a bakery in Winnipeg, they were horrified to find that large amounts of chemicals were used in producing bread.

The other event that helped improved Canadian-Soviet relations was a long overdue invitation to the Supreme Soviet to send a parliamentary delegation to Canada to repay the visit made by Canadian parliamentarians a few years before. This is not normally an earth-shattering event. But during the previous winter I had met and talked on several occasions with Dmitri Polyansky, then one of the youngest and ablest members of the Politburo, its agriculture expert and first deputy prime minister. At forty-nine, he seemed the coming man in the Politburo and heir apparent to

Kosygin as prime minister. I had the impression he would accept an invitation to visit Canada to improve agricultural ties between the two countries and I was authorized to extend it. The Soviet response was to make him head of the delegation.

The group arrived in Ottawa in late June 1966. The visit had a remarkable parallel with that of another parliamentary delegation in 1983 headed by Mikhail Gorbachev. Both appeared to have the double aim of improving Soviet-Canadian relations and of giving younger members of the hierarchy some exposure to the Western world. This was less necessary in the case of Polyansky, who had already been premier of the Russian Federated Soviet Socialist Republic and as such had exchanged visits with Nelson Rockefeller, governor of New York.

Energetic, curious, ambitious, extrovert, Polyansky aroused great interest wherever he went. In turn, he demonstrated an almost Khrushchevian desire to find out about any Canadian practices that might have some practical, technological application to the Soviet system. He was fascinated by the new Ford Motor Company plant at Oakville and wondered aloud whether the Soviet government had not made a mistake in inviting Fiat to build a plant on the Volga to make the Lada, the Soviet version of the Fiat. He was at first totally unbelieving of the way in which huge farms in the West could produce wheat with little more than a handful of workers. But when he came to accept that the farms he saw were not model farms especially arranged to bamboozle him (the Potemkin experience dies hard in the Russian mind), he began issuing instructions to his agricultural experts to take note of everything they saw.

The main results of the visit were to consolidate the Canadian inside track in the Soviet wheat trade, which has been invaluable to the prairie economy; to arouse the interest of the Soviet leaders in Canada as an important country of the capitalist world, not just an adjunct of the United States; and to begin the slow process toward détente in East-West relations.

But these goals were not easily achieved, and there were several incidents which almost caused the visit to end in disaster. At a luncheon given by his Canadian hosts, Polyansky made an attack on the United States for its actions in Vietnam which aroused a storm of protest, not necessarily for what he said (it differed not greatly from what Lester Pearson had said at Temple University the year before), but because a Russian had said it in Canada. The following day on the plane to Winnipeg, I tried to explain to Polyansky the reasons why it was not acceptable for him to say the things Pearson could. It was obvious the Soviets had made a major miscalculation. The speech had been written in Moscow, and had not even been cleared with the Soviet ambassador to Canada. It illustrated the extent of misunderstanding between peoples, which is one of the fundamental problems in East-West relations.

The next near disaster came when Polyansky announced that he had to return to Moscow a day earlier, thus eliminating an official dinner organized by the Canadian government. When I told Polyansky this in Vancouver, he interpreted it as an insult. Arriving unexpectedly (I was in shirtsleeves and my wife was in the bath) at my hotel room with his entire entourage in tow, he announced that because of this affront, he would go home immediately. I called Ottawa and after a painful night of negotiations, the prime minister agreed to give an informal dinner at his Sussex Drive residence on the last day of the visit. I informed Polyansky the next morning, and honour was saved. The fault had been entirely Russian and the first temptation was to let them go home. But as so often in dealing with the Russians, it was essential to resist the obvious retort, be patient, be adjustable, and wait for results.

The dinner at Sussex Drive was fascinating. Polyansky was obsessed by the idea of West German revanchism tied to American aggressiveness as illustrated by Vietnam. And his suggestions for Canada were to follow the lead of General de Gaulle and leave the military side of the NATO alliance. Lester Pearson tried to explain how Canadians found the Americans good people, good neighbours, good friends, and good allies even if we did not always agree with them. But we also wanted good relations with our northern neighbour, a statement Polyansky seemed to find naïve, since he was convinced the Americans would do their best to prevent it.

In a later conversation with Polyansky, he admitted that the Soviet leaders did not always comprehend what went on in Washington nor indeed the complexities of Canadian relations with the United States, which is not surprising in view of their own history of domination of smaller neighbours.

I do not think the Russians ever did figure out exactly how to classify Canada. We never fitted in easily into any of their preconceived categories. They became convinced in the long run that most Canadians wanted to take a line independent of the United States, but were prevented by big financial interests in combination with professional anti-Soviet elements; and they were certain that when the chips were down, Washington would always prevent Canada from any important deviation from American policies. They simply could not accept that on the whole it was Soviet policies which threatened or seemed to threaten the Western alliance and that our participation in NATO and our close and natural friendship with the United States corresponded with Canadian national interests.

The Polyansky visit had some odd aspects. His entourage included not only interpreters and secretaries, but a political counsellor, an agricultural counsellor who later became deputy minister of agriculture and advocate at court when it came to Soviet-Canadian agricultural disputes, a doctor, and a bodyguard. We had some trouble with the RCMP over the bodyguard because they objected to him toting his own pistol; our police also thought that they were sufficiently efficient to provide all the protection necessary. They were indeed efficient in providing the Russians with the psychological assurance that they were not going to be assassinated or attacked by a raging mob of Ukrainians. But it soon became apparent that the bodyguard's duties were not only to protect the first deputy prime minister, but also to keep tabs on his activities. He was in fact the only person to whom Polyansky showed a measure of deference. It is interesting to note that Gorbachev, when he visited Canada in 1983, was accompanied by almost exactly the same entourage except that he had *two* bodyguards.

The Soviet delegation was nervous about the reaction of Ukrainian groups in Canada. In reality, they had nothing to worry about and they were pleasantly surprised when the Ukrainian-Canadian mayor of Winnipeg made his speech of welcome in both Ukrainian and English. They were also taken aback when John

Diefenbaker, then leader of the opposition, on whom Polyansky called, addressed him with a few words of Ukrainian, which were certainly more understandable than his French. Diefenbaker told me later he had picked up a little of the language as a boy in a small town in Saskatchewan where almost half the population was of Ukrainian origin.

Apart from Niagara Falls, which was included at the specific request of Polyansky and which from then on became a must for any Soviet delegation to Canada, the Russians were particularly excited by the reception in Medicine Hat, which they called 'Vrachobnaya Shlyapa' (literally Medical Hat). They were met by some twenty leading members of the local community on horseback and in cowboy hats. It was a wonder that the mounted cavalcade got back into town safely as most of them had not been on a horse for twenty years or so. Medicine Hat was indeed spectacular for the Russians, since it included not only the cowboys, but a steak dinner with pieces of meat so huge the Russians didn't know what to do with them, a barbecue breakfast with cowboy songs, and a visit to the Fort McLeod stampede. All of this fitted in with their preconceived notion of Canada and obviously put the right touch on the visit.

In September 1966 messages were transmitted to Alexei Kosygin from Prime Minister Pearson expressing a wish to expand and develop relations following on the successful visit of Polyansky to Canada, and from the governor general, Georges Vanier, to President Podgorny inviting him, along with other heads of state, to the celebrations of the centennial of Confederation in 1967. Podgorny, when he accepted the invitation, elaborated to me at some length on the possibility for closer and more profitable relations with Canada. The atmosphere seemed right to do something concrete, and the government decided to respond to an outstanding invitation by the foreign minister, Andrei Gromyko, for the secretary of state for external affairs, Paul Martin, to visit the Soviet Union in November of 1966.

The Russians made Martin's visit an occasion to stress the importance they wished to attach to their relations with Canada. In addition to the normal talks with Gromyko and a courtesy call on

Polyansky, Martin was also received by Prime Minister Kosygin and President Podgorny. Then at the very last moment on the last day of the official visit in Moscow, we were informed that Brezhnev would receive him in his office at seven o'clock that evening. This was a highly unusual gesture which impressed the Russians as much as it did the Canadians and was clearly intended to indicate that their interest in Canada was genuine.

Brezhnev made it quite clear that the Soviets were interested in Canada because of our independent line in foreign policy, our experience in agriculture in climatic conditions almost identical with those of Russia, and our rapid progress as an industrial power. After the meeting with Brezhnev in the impersonal office he occupied in the austere, grey building of the Party Central Committee, a senior Soviet diplomat said to me that he had noticed one of the characteristics of Canadians was to downplay their achievements. The Russians had come to the conclusion that Canada now occupied the sixth and maybe even the fifth place in order of importance among the industrialized countries. When I queried him on this, he ticked them off: United States, Japan, West Germany, France, Britain, Canada, Italy. He added that some of their experts would even put Canada ahead of Britain.

Brezhnev kept us at the Central Committee headquarters for more than an hour. Gromyko's dinner had been called for 7 p.m. and we eventually arrived at 8:30. Gromyko obviously considered this perfectly normal and our Russian hosts thought we had been given a very special accolade. Unfortunately, the three days of intensive work, including evening sessions at the ballet, had taken their toll on Martin. At the end of the dinner, Groymko made a very serious and considered speech about Soviet foreign policy and how his government viewed Canada. Without a prepared text, Martin had to improvise. He was always a master of obfuscation, but this time his remarks completely bewildered the Russian translator, who looked at me in despair. I shrugged my shoulders and to my surprise and secret delight, he gave up trying to translate the Martinese and turned it into a series of universal clichés. Only those few in the room who understood both English and Russian appreciated the performance.

In substantive terms, nothing much came out of the Martin visit, except agreement to study ways and means of improving our mutual trade and of making more productive the existing programs for scientific, cultural, and academic exchanges. A disquieting amount of time was spent on the question of Vietnam, partly because of the obsession of the Canadian government at that time with seeking to find a way out of the imbroglio, and partly because the Russians were determined to judge the United States harshly and clearly wanted a message to go back to Washington. Our efforts to convince the Russians to use their influence with North Vietnam to be more flexible in its response to American attempts to reach a compromise were totally rejected. The Russians considered reasonable and justified the North Vietnamese demand for a total withdrawal of American troops before any negotiations could commence. In fact, in the end we found ourselves in the position of explaining the Americans to the Russians, while assuring them that we were not acting as their messengers.

The next stage in the gradual development of détente occurred during the Canadian centennial year of 1967. The Soviet government was determined to show the flag on the North American continent both by taking part in Expo 67 in Montreal and by sending a high-level delegation. Plans were being made on both sides for President Podgorny to attend, but the outbreak of the Six-Day War between Israel and the Arabs and the pro-Israeli views of the Canadian government and public were used by the Soviets as a pretext to decline. His place was taken by Dmitri Polyansky.

The Soviet pavilion at Expo was enormous. Its design was impressive rather than elegant, and put up by a firm of Italian contractors. There was a long and rancorous debate within the Soviet government about this, the more patriotic wishing to entrust the construction to Soviet workers, the more realistic recognizing the impracticality of this course. It was also contructed in such a way that it could be dismantled and returned to the Soviet Union, where it was eventually reassembled as one of the buildings in Moscow's permanent exhibition park.

The Soviet presence was also enhanced by the attendance, in addition to Polyansky, of the presidents of all the constituent republics, two vice-presidents, twelve prime ministers of the republics, fourteen members of the republican Supreme Soviets, twenty-five managers of important industries, twenty-five important scientists or academicians, twenty-two important party officials, thirty-three federal ministers, fifty-six deputy ministers, seventy-five republican ministers, fourteen deputy ministers of the republics, forty senior functionaries, nine leading journalists and twenty-six mayors, including the mayor of Moscow.

Soviet participation in the cultural side of Expo was little short of overpowering. The Bolshoi Opera made its first North American appearance, and numerous ballet stars, singers, and other performers, the Red Army Choir, the Moscow Circus, and various folklore groups performed. Each republic fêted its special day, usually in the presence of its president or prime minister. Soviet tourist groups were also permitted to visit Expo and usually Ottawa, Toronto, and Niagara Falls. While membership in these groups was obviously considered a form of reward for good behaviour, one official told me that Expo was considered 'the school of the world' and specialists visiting it were expected to study and report anything new they saw in their field of expertise.

Altogether some six thousand Soviet citizens visited Canada during that summer. Since I accompanied Polyansky and his high-powered delegation, I could see that they were impressed by the efficiency and comfort of our big cities. For the first time, large numbers of Russians, including an important cross-section of the ruling hierarchy, were exposed to a new and very different way of life. While it is doubtful that they absorbed very many ideological lessons, it is likely that at least some ideas penetrated to them. And it was equally important in the expansion of Canadian-Soviet relations. For many key Soviet personalities, Canada became the only Western country they knew. In the years to come this undoubtedly created a favourable climate of opinion; it served to increase their estimate of the position of Canada in the world and its economic strength and potential.

Dmitri Polyansky's program followed the lines of most of the foreign dignitaries who represented their countries at the Centennial celebrations: an official reception in Ottawa, an official visit to Expo, and a trip to one of the provinces. Because of his tight schedule, Polyansky chose Quebec, and the premier of the province gave him a formal banquet in Montreal. His encounter with Daniel Johnson was anticipated with some trepidation by Canadian officials because of the recent catastrophic visit of de Gaulle.

It was not surprising, therefore, to hear Johnson in his speech touch on the aspirations of Quebec for a new role in the world. What was surprising was the context in which he put it. At some length he explained that he would like to see Quebec have the same position in the Canadian confederation as Ukraine had in the Soviet Union. I was sitting next to the minister of justice, Jean-Jacques Bertrand. I told him the premier was badly misinformed and that even the worst enemy of Quebec would not wish on it the fate of Ukraine. Officially it had the status of a republic with all the visible signs of independence: its own language, flag, constitution, foreign ministry, and a seat in the United Nations through a fluke of history, the San Francisco compromise on the United Nations Charter in 1945. But in practice it was an integral part of the Soviet Union, firmly under the thumb of the central government which had not the slightest compunction in suppressing any sign of Ukrainian nationalist or religious feeling. Bertrand took this all in, said it was clear the analogy was wrong, and right after the banquet told Johnson.

Polyansky, with the example of de Gaulle before him, studiously ignored these remarks in his public reply. Later Johnson called on him in his hotel room. Polyansky told him he would be happy to supply documentation on the Soviet constitution but the premier should understand that in practice his country was a strongly centralized administration. Clearly the Soviets did not want to get involved in the Quebec-Ottawa dispute; yet it would have been easy, if they had wished, to stir up more trouble.

Their attitude to the Canadian confederation has nearly always been correct, not out of love for Canada but out of carefully calculated self-interest. Always considering the United States as their main opponent, it followed that anything which increased the strength of America was detrimental to the Soviet Union. Therefore it was in the Soviet interest to encourage the existence of a strong, stable, and united Canada. If Canada fragmented, the

Soviets calculated that what remained would not be able to withstand for long the tremendous pull of the American colossus.

Until 1967 they had given little thought to the idea of Quebec independence. The consulate they established in Montreal was intended primarily to serve trade, consular, and shipping interests and had little contact with the Quebec government. The rise of French-Canadian nationalism took them by surprise, and, when the Soviet Institute for United States Studies was expanded in 1972 to include Canada, they had great difficulty in finding any scholars or officials who knew French or indeed anything at all about Quebec.

Since then, the Soviets have paid much more attention to the question of Canadian unity. But the Quebec branch of the USSR–Canada Friendship Society, a communist-front organization, active, well organized and unwaveringly pro-Moscow, was more interested in the economic problems of Quebec than the linguistic or nationalistic disputes. The society, the Communist Party of Canada, and the Soviet government have all maintained a discreet distance from the basic problem of Quebec separatism.

In the early 1970s it appeared that the Quebec government was on the verge of opening a commercial delegation in Moscow. The project indeed had been under discussion with Soviet officials for at least a year and a request for office space and living accommodations had been made as early as the summer of 1971. In 1972 Quebec sent a three-man delegation to Moscow, ostensibly for commercial negotiations. The main practical aim was to engage the Russians in part of the James Bay project and to secure licensing for the construction of Soviet turbines. This appeared to come straight out of talks between Premier Robert Bourassa and Alexei Kosygin in Montreal the year before. Bourassa's conseiller spécial, Bernard Desrochers, told me that the Russians had encouraged them in this project, and I gathered he had been in Moscow two years before, without of course calling at the embassy. As soon as the office was established, Bourassa planned to make an official visit to the Soviet Union for the formal opening ceremony.

While the commercial office might have had the primary intention of promoting trade, it was clear to me that it would inevitably play a political role and become a kind of unofficial

Quebec representation in the Soviet Union. It could be used as a hostage for Canadian government behaviour in the matter of political activities of émigré groups in Canada, particularly the Ukrainians and Balts. The Russians always maintained it was within Ottawa's power to control anti-Soviet activities of these groups, and I was concerned that a Quebec office in Moscow could be used by the Soviets in a political way damaging to Canadian unity if they chose to put pressure on Canada to keep the émigré groups in line.

In the long run nothing came of this project, perhaps because the Russians did not join in the James Bay enterprise, perhaps because Bourassa got cold feet about the political implications of a Quebec office in Moscow. Whether or not the Soviets really encouraged the idea is impossible to tell, but I noted after the election of the Parti Québécois that the Soviet press and officials maintained an extraordinary degree of caution with regard to the question of Quebec-Ottawa relations. Even when another Quebec commercial delegation visited Moscow in September 1977, it was treated simply as yet another possible Canadian source of useful technology and with no political overtones.

What seemed to interest the Soviets more than Quebec separatism were the economic and social problems in Canada and signs of weakness in the Canadian economy. These were naturally interpreted in Marxist ideological terms, and one article in *Pravda* decided that the election of the Parti Québécois in 1976 was less a vote for separatism than a workers' protest against the Liberal government and its social and economic policies. It concluded that separatism was not in the interests of the Canadian workers and speculated it was very hard to see how the PQ could achieve independence for Quebec since the United States would not view favourably the birth of a new sovereign state on its northern borders. The article described the Liberal and Conservative parties as bourgeois and the PQ as petit-bourgeois, a fine distinction which put it somewhat closer to the 'exploited proletariat' than the 'exploiting bourgeoisie.'

Only once did the Soviet authorities waver in their refusal to get involved in the Canadian problem and that was the direct result of John Diefenbaker's interest in Ukraine. Having been brought up in an area heavily populated by Ukrainians, he inevitably absorbed some of their pride in their history and culture, and their prejudices against the Russians. Once in power, in 1957, he toyed with the idea of openly supporting the concept of Ukrainian independence, and at the same time of moving in the United Nations to take away the seats allotted to the Ukrainian and Byelorussian republics as purely fictitious countries. The Soviets got wind of this and made it privately but unmistakably clear that they would raise the question of Quebec independence if Diefenbaker persisted in this course. He quickly desisted.

The strong Soviet feelings about Ukraine came violently to the surface on the occasion of the fiftieth anniversary of the Soviet Union, also in 1967. They have always watched with intense interest the activities of the Ukrainians in Canada, since they represent the largest concentration of people of Ukrainian origin outside the Soviet Union. Most Ukrainian Canadians are descendants of settlers who came to Canada well before the revolution and many of them from those parts of Ukraine which were then under the control of Austria. Many are only distantly interested in the policies of Ukraine, but they have a continuing and legitimate interest in the history and culture of their ancestors. If they are required to take sides, they are mostly anti-Russian and anti-Soviet.

During all my years in the Soviet Union, I had to be on the receiving end of regular Soviet protests about the anti-Soviet activities of Ukrainian nationalists in Canada. The last was lodged in February 1980, over a speech by Flora MacDonald, secretary of state for external affairs, linking in a very general way the Soviet takeover of Ukraine in 1918 with the invasion of Afghanistan. But the most impassioned remonstration occurred in November 1967 and was sparked by demonstrations of exceptional size and length outside the Soviet embassy in Ottawa on 7 November, the fiftieth anniversary of the revolution. What irked the Soviets particularly was the presence of one of the leaders of the emigré Ukrainian Bandera group, Stetsko, who was normally resident in West Germany. This was sufficient cause to accuse the Canadian government of complicity and it was several months before the emotion generated by this affair wore off.

The Soviet government at regular intervals reminded us of the fact that Canada did not legally recognize the incorporation of the Baltic states into the Soviet Union, and protested about the continued inclusion of Estonian, Latvian, and Lithuanian consuls in the official diplomatic list of the Department of External Affairs. Together with the diplomats of many NATO countries, we did not make visits, official or private, to any of the three Baltic republics. The moral reasons for this policy were clear, and it obviously had useful domestic implications. Nevertheless, since the Baltic states were unlikely to have an independent existence for a long time to come, it is questionable whether we made the life of these small but remarkable peoples more tolerable by treating them as pariahs.

The invasion of Czechoslovakia in August 1968 put an abrupt halt on the part of most Western countries to the effort at improving relations with the Soviet Union. But it soon became apparent that the Czech experiment in liberal communism was over, that there was no way Soviet control could be reversed, and that sanctions against Moscow would be useless. The Czech affront had to be swallowed as part of the price of coexistence with the Soviet giant.

In the middle of the crisis over Czechoslovakia, I had received a message from John Diefenbaker, then the leader of the opposition, to inform me that his brother Elmer was arriving in Moscow. I knew Elmer already; he was a plain and modest druggist from Prince Albert, Saskatchewan, with no political pretensions whatsoever, but a penchant for foreign travel. He was part of a group touring Eastern Europe, including Russia, which had been caught in Prague when the invasion took place. All but two on the tour decided to go home, but Elmer and a female chiropractor from Brooklyn were not inclined to let a Russian invasion interfere with a trip they had already paid for, and they came on together to Moscow. Elmer was given cordial treatment by the Russians, but he spent most of his time explaining to his bewildered hosts that he had no sentimental ties to the lady from Brooklyn who, suddenly terrified by the sight of Russia, never left his side. I also had some difficulty in convincing the Soviets that Elmer's trip had no political significance and that he had continued it solely because he had already paid for it.

In the wake of the Czech crisis, life had to go on, and

considerable efforts were made to increase Canadian-Soviet trade and cultural, scientific, and technological exchanges. The Royal Winnipeg Ballet staged an extraordinarily successful tour in November and December of 1968, their fresh, competent style and originality bringing gasps of astonishment and pleasure from the Soviet audiences. I was surprised to find the Russian prima ballerina Maya Plisetskaya at the performance of 'Aimez-vous Bach?' Obviously the technical skill of the Canadians was inferior to that of the Bolshoi Ballet, but what enchanted her and most of the audience was the freshness of approach. The ballet starts with a lesson in classical exercises in a ballet school to the music of Bach, but when the teacher takes a break, the students turn it into a rock session to jazzed-up Bach. This was a delight for Soviet spectators and artists, nourished strictly on the classics.

Plisetskaya, with whom my wife and I had become friends, told us later that she and most of the Bolshoi stars constantly argued with the cultural bureaucrats that innovation in the ballet was not inconsistent with socialist realism. Artists grew stale, and the public became bored, with the constant repetition of the classics. She said she had cited the Winnipeg Ballet as an example, but added with an expressive movement of her graceful arms that naturally the ideologues could not understand what she was talking about. It was just the idea of change that terrified them.

Negotiations also continued with the Academy of Sciences and the head of its committee dealing with scientific and technological exchanges with foreign countries, German Gvishiani. This extraordinarily talented and able Georgian had been given the task of trying to acquire legitimately as much technological know-how as possible from developed industrial societies in the West. The exposure of so many Soviet specialists to Canadian expertise during their visits in 1967 had aroused the interest of Gvishiani's committee in Canada as a potential alternative source of North American technology. He made it quite clear in all my talks with him that his committee was operating on a strictly pragmatic basis and he constantly and not very subtlely reminded me that should relations improve with the United States, their interest in Canada would be limited to technology adapted to Arctic conditions.

Indeed, I needed no reminder from Gvishiani, or anyone else, to bring home to me the delicate role of any ambassador from the West in Moscow during those years. The task of a Canadian ambassador, in particular, was different in many respects from that in an allied or neutral country. Living in a highly restricted, usually unfriendly, frequently hostile country, but one the policies and developments of which were of vital importance to Canada and the West, meant concentrating a very high proportion of one's time on political work, analyses of Soviet intentions, and the defence of Canadian interests. Apart from the constant effort to study and interpret Soviet developments, it required attempting on every occasion that presented itself to explain Western policies, and to listen patiently to often patently untruthful justifications of Soviet policy at every level.

There was inevitably much less in the way of public relations and social activities, but every opportunity was seized to present Canada as a solid member of NATO, an important economic power, with an increasingly rich cultural life, and striving constantly to construct reasonable and mutually useful relations with the Soviet Union. And as relations improved, there were more frequent artistic and intellectual exchanges which presented occasions for more agreeable contacts with the Russians.

The artistic life in Moscow, and in Leningrad, Kiev, and many of the smaller republican capitals, was intense, although often stultifying because of the insistence on 'socialist realism,' which excluded everything but the most timid experimentation, but fortunately encompassed the classics of music, ballet, and theatre. The opera, ballet, and theatre were a delight, though there came a time when it seemed impossible to digest one more performance of 'Swan Lake.' In fact it was this artistic frustration that drove so many performers to defect.

The music was equally fine, with artists such as David and Igor Oistrakh, the pianists Emil Gilels and Svlatislav Richter, the conductor Kondrashin, and the magnificent cellist Mstislav Rostropovich and his wife and opera star, Galina Vishnevskaya.

Contact with Soviet citizens was normally very difficult, but I had the opportunity, through my own poetry and my translations of Russian verse, to know Russian poets such as Andrei Voznesensky, Evgenny Evtushenko, Bella Akhmadulina, Bulat Okuzhava, Simeon Kirsanov, Konstantin Simonov, Robert Rozhdestvensky, and the legendary Lili Brik, sister of Elsa Triolet and the great love of the poet of the revolution, Vladimir Mayakovsky. Many a relaxed and fascinating Sunday was passed in her dacha at Peredelkino, next door to that of Boris Pasternak.

All my writer and artist acquaintances lived a precarious existence, pushing as much as they could against the limits of the system, often overwhelmed by the ennui of the late Brezhnev era, and hoping eventually something would happen to open up the horizons. Nor was this confined to the intellectuals. Many of the younger members of the Party and above all the economists, administrators, and engineers were aware of the economic and social problems which were building up. They were all anxious to end the stagnation of the later Brezhnev rule. As far back as 1975 some Party officials with a first-hand knowledge of the West had hinted to me that changes were required.

These contacts gave an intellectual stimulus to what might have become a highly sterile existence of exchanging speculation on developments in Soviet official policies with diplomatic colleagues or trying to read between the lines of *Pravda*. My task as ambassador became more complicated when I became dean of the diplomatic corps late in 1971. In Catholic countries the dean is traditionally the ambassador of the Holy See. But in others, including Canada and the Soviet Union, the dean is simply the ambassador with the longest time in the country to which he is accredited. The position, while facilitating official contacts with the top Soviets, carried with it many excessively boring duties, such as giving a reception for every departing ambassador, and making a speech extolling his personal qualities and the marvels of the country he represented, a task often calling for great ingenuity when it concerned the ambassador of some remote African or Asian nation.

It also meant standing up to the Soviet authorities at various times when the latter introduced regulations which affected the whole diplomatic corps and to which a majority objected. Since there were sub-groupings, such as the Latin Americans, the Africans, the Arabs, the Islamic countries, the Commonwealth, NATO, and the Warsaw Pact, each one with its own head, it was very seldom that I could get the unanimous consent to represent them vis-à-vis the foreign ministry. On only two occasions did I succeed in acting in the name of all of them and that was on the seventieth birthday of President Podgorny when I was received in the Kremlin to present the best wishes of the corps, and after Brezhnev became chairman of the Supreme Soviet when I made a speech on behalf of the corps congratulating him on his assumption of this honour.

When a very difficult question arose in which I could not hope to get the agreement of the communists and many of the non-aligned ambassadors who were afraid of offending the Russians, I simply acted on behalf of a rather vague majority. Some of the issues which had to be taken up concerned complaints about police harassment of visitors to embassies, complicated and unrealistic currency regulations, and on one occasion a long-running battle with the bureaucracy over an attempt to force the embassies to pay the salaries of the local employees directly to an agency of the Soviet government. We objected on the grounds that it was bad enough having to hire employees who were obviously agents of the Soviet government, but at least we might have the option of controlling them in some small way through the payment of their salaries and the distribution of perquisites.

As a Canadian I had close ties with members of the Commonwealth and the francophone African states, who were often miserable, confused, and ignored by the Russians and the more important members of the diplomatic corps. Inevitably as dean I had the unenviable job of receiving their complaints about their treatment by the Soviets. They seemed to prefer talking over their problems with me rather than with the Foreign Ministry. Some of these problems were funny, some sad.

Usually it was a bitter complaint about the racism of the Russians. While most of them were given adequate housing, the Russians made practically no attempt to make them happy or to soften a little the impact of the long Russian winter on them. One of the continuing complaints was over Lumumba University, which had been set up by the Russians as an offshoot of Moscow University to absorb the influx of African students which pro-Soviet and neutral governments sent to the Soviet Union so that they might get a

'socialist' education. (Most of them left convinced rightists.) However, by the 1970s, Lumumba University had become strictly the
second-rate branch of Moscow University, almost entirely inhabited by blacks, whereas the European and North American students
were always sent to Moscow University. I do not know whether the
Russians were aware of the extent of the feeling of the African
representatives in Moscow on this score. But in their complaints to
me, it was clear that it rankled. What also rankled was the number
of incidents of attacks on Russian girls who were bold enough to go
out with black students.

My wife was also called constantly by the wives of black
ambassadors, to complain about their solitary lives and their
complete isolation. But occasionally the help sought from her was
slightly different. One day the wife of the ambassador of Gabon,
who had been in Moscow for about a year, asked to see my wife
about a problem which had arisen in her embassy. She was a
Christian, but the ambassador was a Moslem. They had lived
happily in Moscow for a year with her five daughters. Then her
husband decided to bring his second wife from Gabon. The
problem was that the second wife was younger and had six sons,
and the ambassador's wife was afraid her husband would want to
take wife number two to the official functions. Could we issue
invitations spelling out her maiden name, so that wife number two
could not, according to protocol, accompany the ambassador?
That was no problem, and she went away happy.

On another occasion the ambassador of Sierra Leone called on
me on what he described as a matter of the greatest urgency and
importance. His president had for years been trying to get himself
invited to the Soviet Union; the Russians had finally agreed and
proposed a visit at the end of January. I said: Congratulations, but
what is the problem? The ambassador replied that his president
was an old man (forty-nine), and to come in January was tanta-
mount to condemning him to death. He would never survive
Moscow in January. What he wanted from me was my opinion as to
whether this was being done deliberately by the Russians to kill his
president, or whether it was just a matter of ignorance. I was
tempted to conclude that it was an outright provocation, but
instead I reminded him that twenty-five million Canadians lived in

a climate harsher than that of Moscow, and it would probably not occur to us that a visit to Ottawa in January was necessarily a sentence of death. I advised him to accept the invitation but to propose other dates. This he did, but it took the Russians so long to come up with a new date that the president, losing his patience, went to China instead.

Probably the most amusing but also revealing story concerned the ambassador of Chad. I received notice that he had died, and I proceeded to the embassy to extend my condolences and sign their book. A week later the head of the Islamic group, the ambassador of Morocco, called on me to ask my advice on a protocol matter. All the Arab, African, and Moslem ambassadors had gone to the airport to pay their last respects to the body of their colleague before it was shipped off to N'Djamena. In the first place, there was no Soviet representative at the airport and he wanted to know what the procedure was. I replied that in the past the body of an ambassador would have been sent home on a cruiser, but that was hardly practical from Moscow to N'Djamena. They were, of course, quite justified in complaining about a breach of protocol that no Soviet official was present. The Moroccan ambassador also wanted to know if it was correct that the Russians should have attempted to get the poor Chadians to pay in hard currency for the transport of the body, which travelled on Aeroflot. I suggested normal procedure would have been for the Russians to extend the courtesy of transporting the body at their own expense.

These complaints, however, were minor compared to the principal one. An official of the Chadian embassy had gone on board the aircraft to accompany the body to N'Djamena. But when he arrived, there was no body. A search had been made at every stop en route, but it could not be found. Finally, it was discovered placed up against a wall in the hot sun at Moscow airport. It had simply been forgotten. As dean I protested to the Soviets, but they simply shrugged it off as one of the perils of air travel.

Incidents such as these, perhaps of no great moment in the international field, made up much of the day-to-day work as dean. Still, hardly a week went by without some event of importance. And, in spite of the cramped and difficult conditions, I had the knowledge that my work and increasing expertise did have some relevance to Canadian and indeed Western security and interests.

Life in the Soviet Union was not all hard political work. We took every opportunity that presented itself to travel – to Siberia, Georgia, Armenia, Abhazia, Central Asia, southern Russia, Ukraine, Byelorussia, the Pskov and Leningrad areas, and, of course, Central and Old Russia. These excursions were essential for a proper understanding of the multicultural society of the Soviet Union; and one needs to travel the seven thousand five hundred kilometres from Moscow to the Pacific – preferably on the Trans-Siberian Railway and in winter – really to grasp the immense complexity of a country twice the size of Canada.

6

Groping toward Détente

In April 1968 the Liberal party had elected Pierre Trudeau leader when Lester Pearson stepped down. I had first known the new prime minister in 1952 when he unexpectedly turned up in Moscow at a mysterious economic conference organized by the Soviets and attended mostly by representatives of communist front organizations. He spent a month in Moscow and quickly became disenchanted with Russian hotel food and lodging and, I suspect, bored with the conference, which indulged in ritual Marxist condemnations of Western capitalist imperialism. More and more time was spent with us in the embassy, where I introduced him to the pleasures of Russian caviar. Nor did he hesitate to accompany my wife and myself to Easter mass in the impromptu chapel of the American embassy.

I was in London, Ontario, for the funeral of my father when the Liberal leadership changed hands. I came to Ottawa for consultations with the Department of External Affairs and had dinner with the new prime minister. Although Trudeau barely bothered to conceal his dislike and suspicion of External Affairs, this never affected our relationship, on my part of respect and admiration for his considerable intellect, his original thinking, and his refusal to be bound by accepted wisdom on almost any subject. Over the following years, in spite of occasional differences of opinion on

Soviet developments, I could always see him on my frequent trips to Ottawa, for general consultations, to discuss some new crisis, or even infrequently some promising opening in Canadian-Soviet relations.

As Trudeau moved to concentrate policy on foreign affairs in the hands of the Prime Minister's Office and the Privy Council Office, I often found myself in the odd position of having to inform External Affairs officials, even the under-secretary, of Trudeau's thinking about East-West relations. The blame was by no means entirely Trudeau's. External Affairs was late in accepting the idea that a new era had arrived and that Trudeau was not Lester Pearson. He had his own ideas about world affairs and intended to apply them. The easy relationship between External Affairs and a prime minister who had come up out of the ranks of the foreign service officers was over but it took the bureaucracy a long time to realize it.

During my first conversation with Trudeau in April 1968 he made it clear that he intended to visit the Soviet Union. When I mentioned this to Marcel Cadieux, then under-secretary, he dismissed it out of hand, since he believed there were higher priorities. Although at times I had the feeling of having two masters, in fact the guidelines and instructions I received from External Affairs and the new minister, Mitchell Sharp, were always compatible with what the prime minister wanted – as indeed they had to be.

The Russians quickly showed signs of interest in the new Canadian leader. In July of 1969 the deputy foreign minister, Valery Kuznetsov, talked to me at some length about their appreciation of the foreign policy that General de Gaulle had developed for France, implying that they hoped Canada could develop a similar policy in North America. He told me that our new prime minister had aroused a great deal of interest amongst the Soviet leadership because of his unique intellectual capacities, his originality of spirit, and the feeling he gave of wishing to break through the barriers of the past. Kuznetsov was certain that, if the prime minister could visit the Soviet Union, he would have a great personal success and also provide the same kind of stimulus to the development of our relations as de Gaulle had done in the case of France.

I suspected the new Soviet interest in Canada had also been stimulated by Trudeau's attitude to NATO. I had been asked to be co-chairman with our ambassador to Belgium, Paul Tremblay, of an interdepartmental committee to re-examine Canadian relations with Europe. Work on the committee meant spending a good deal of time in Ottawa during the winter of 1968–9, particularly as it required extensive consultations with National Defence, Trade and Commerce, and other government departments as well as ministers, members of the opposition, and outside experts.

Trudeau made it perfectly clear that he hoped our recommendation would be for a downgrading of Europe in the Canadian perspective, and a complete withdrawal of Canadian troops in Europe. There was even a considerable sentiment among some ministers, although not, I think, shared by Trudeau, in favour of a semi-neutralist foreign policy for Canada along the lines of that of Sweden. Some members seemed to have the illusion that we could greatly reduce our defence budget and transfer the money saved to new social welfare programs. I argued that the money saved would be a pittance compared to the cost of a large social welfare program. If we wished to adopt neutralism à la Suède, then we would have to be prepared to spend ten times what we did already on defence, unless of course we wished to give up all pretensions of being a truly independent country and rely totally on the United States for the defence of Canada.

The recommendations of the committee in favour of enhanced trade and cultural relations with Western Europe and the maintenance of the existing Canadian commitment in Europe were not received with much enthusiasm by the government, which in any case went ahead with a 50 per cent reduction in the Canadian contingent in NATO command Europe. But at least the committee played some role in preventing a complete withdrawal, which would have disastrously weakened Canada's voice in Western councils.

In the summer of 1969 an invitation was extended to the Soviet minister of foreign affairs, Andrei Gromyko, to visit Canada. Since Canada was the first NATO country to break ranks in the ineffective political boycott of the Russians in response to Czechoslovakia, he replied with an immediate affirmative. This was one of the few occasions when I saw Gromyko let down his defences and show what he really meant: surprise and delight.

The visit took place from 1 to 3 October and provided Gromyko with his first look at Canada. He was a bit baffled when, at the airport, he was greeted by demonstrators shouting 'Down with the new tsars.' When I explained that they were a pro-Mao Trotskyite group of singular unimportance, he was simply mystified. He was even more baffled when a meeting with government officials had to be transferred from the Parliament Centre Block to another site because of a demonstration by a large group of strikers, displaying banners reading: 'Down with the lousy Canadian Government.' He obviously thought we ran things very sloppily.

The talks with external affairs minister Mitchell Sharp and with the prime minister were cordial and constructive, concentrating on ways of exchanging information on northern development, wheat, trade, and other specific matters. The stress was on the fact that Russia and Canada as neighbours carried the obligation to maintain good relations on a basis of mutual respect and through informative co-operation. The visit was important to the Soviets to show that the invasion of Czechoslovakia was on the way to being forgotten, to open further access to Canadian, and therefore North American, technology, and to give the Soviets an opportunity to extend personally to the prime minister an official invitation to visit the Soviet Union.

The overwhelming importance of the u.s.-Soviet relationship was evident throughout Gromyko's visit. I sat next to him at the official luncheon and the only question that interested him was Nixon's State of the Union address in February and the president's assertion that he wished to move from the era of confrontation to one of co-operation. Gromyko found it hard to reconcile this with the old Nixon and his hard-line anti-Soviet rhetoric. I said I thought Nixon meant what he said, but Gromyko kept coming back to it, obviously wondering if it were not a trap. Even after tea with Governor General Roland Michener (which with all the vice-regal trappings at Rideau Hall dazzled Gromyko), he again returned to the question of Nixon and the possibility of real change.

Typically, before issuing the formal invitation the Soviets had discreetly ascertained in advance that Trudeau was prepared to come to Russia. Preparations soon began for the visit in October 1970. The attention the Soviets gave to it was apparent in the fact that Trudeau's program was equivalent to that of a head of state. All his wishes were met almost immediately, including scheduling a visit to the Arctic city of Norilsk, in an area of Siberia completely forbidden to foreigners. In the meantime, however, the FLQ crisis arose in Quebec, culminating in the kidnapping of labour minister Pierre Laporte and James Cross, the British trade commissioner in Montreal. A few days before the visit was due to take place, I received an urgent signal to see Chairman Kosygin and deliver a personal message saying that the visit would have to be postponed because of the murder of Laporte by the terrorists and the subsequent confused and potentially dangerous situation in Quebec.

Knowing the Soviet tendency to look beyond the obvious for some devious explanation, I stressed to Kosygin that the postponement was due entirely to an internal Canadian problem which made it impossible for the prime minister to leave the country at that time. Kosygin accepted the explanation at its face value, though with regret, and at once proposed alternate dates. But later the deputy foreign minister expressed scepticism about our explanation for the postponement and sought the hand of Washington, implying that our recent recognition of Peking plus the visit to Moscow was too much for our big neighbour. Although most Soviet officials came to realize that the Quebec crisis was sufficient to justify postponing the visit, they could never understand what they considered to be Trudeau's over-reaction. Send in the troops, yes, but not on the basis of a few terrorists. Perhaps they had sound information to support their view that there never had been a dangerous, certainly not a potentially revolutionary, situation in Quebec. Or else they were simply unable at a distance to take an objective view. I confess that, from Moscow, Quebec did not appear on the verge of revolt.

New dates were soon fixed for the prime minister's visit in May 1971, but it took on a distinctly different turn when two months before he was due to arrive, he married Margaret Sinclair. The program remained basically the same in the minds of the Soviets, but it was clear to us at the embassy that it would be in a way a honeymoon for the Trudeaus and some provision would have to be made to prevent a twenty-one-year-old bride from going off the deep end as a result of exposure to the ineffable boredom of Soviet official functions. It was not easy. Margaret evinced little enthusiasm for attending even the functions expressly laid on for her, such as a visit to the Bolshoi Ballet School, and her dismay at having to sit through lengthy official ceremonies and banquets was all too apparent. It turned out as well that she was feeling poorly. My wife discovered after a couple of days that Margaret was pregnant and had not had the courage to tell her husband yet. However, despite his young bride's distaste for a Russian honeymoon, Trudeau's visit was one of the most successful I saw in my many years in Moscow. The Russians were determined to make it a success from the very start and this was the essential ingredient. The prime minister was equally determined to make it work, and even Margaret, in spite of a few tantrums, made her own contribution.

The official host was Alexei Kosygin, chairman of the Council of Ministers and thus the equivalent of prime minister. Trudeau had two long sessions with Kosygin, one two-hour session with Leonid Brezhnev, and a meeting with President Podgorny. While all the major issues of the day were discussed either in the formal talks or in various receptions, the most important political elements were the Canadian-Soviet Protocol on Consultations, and an umbrella agreement on economic co-operation, drafts of both of which were presented to me by Gromyko a fortnight before the visit began. The agreement on economic co-operation was too complicated to complete during the prime minister's visit, but the government decided to proceed with the idea of the protocol. The Soviet draft was clearly based on the French-Soviet protocol signed by presidents Pompidou and Podgorny in October 1970. It seemed to proceed directly from the Soviet idea that Canada could play a role somewhat akin to that of France. We presented a counter-draft which toned down some of the sections which were more appropriate to great power consultations and added parts more purely Canadian in content. It was signed by the prime minister and Chairman Kosygin on 19 May.

The prime minister stressed at the time that he did not believe the protocol was in any way incompatible with Canadian membership in NATO or NORAD or with our traditional alliances. The Russians on their side repeatedly stated that they accepted this and that they did not wish to interfere with our friendship and co-operation with other countries – reassurances which we took with a grain of salt. In a meeting with Trudeau, Brezhnev expressed the view that the protocol was important politically because it would open the way to a rapid improvement in Canadian-Soviet relations, and even more significant, it would be welcomed by everyone who favoured the search for détente. In his words, 'future historians will remember those who drew up and signed this document.'

The protocol caused us some problems with our allies, particularly with the United States. My relations with the American ambassador, Jacob Beam, cooled considerably, since we did not inform the Americans in advance of our intentions. I argued at the time that we should do so but was overruled. Several years later Trudeau admitted to me that it would have been preferable to advise Washington even if it had been only a day before.

American irritation over the protocol was increased by a remark made by Trudeau at his press conference at the conclusion of the Moscow portion of the visit. In reply to a question as to the reason for signing the protocol, he said that it had been prompted in part because the Canadian identity was endangered by the 'overwhelming presence' of the United States from a cultural, economic 'and perhaps even military point of view.' I was immediately subjected to intense questioning by American and other allied officials about the significance of the remark, above all the reference to the American military presence as a threat to Canadian identity. What angered the Americans was that it had been made in Moscow, and the Soviets were unabashedly delighted. I do not think Trudeau intended to suggest that Canada felt threatened by the United States and was therefore seeking a better relationship with the Soviet Union to balance American might. I am certain it was simply a slip of the tongue. But I am equally certain that it was a psychological lapse, since it reflected a deep-seated distrust of the United States and a friendly feeling toward the Soviet Union on the part of the prime minister.

In the circumstances, the United States government's reaction to this provocative remark and the signature of the protocol was very mild and American press comments were cool and objective. The *Washington Post* saw it as part of Canada's drive for the expression of a distinctive national personality, although it added that it was hard for an American to imagine what Trudeau had had in mind when he hinted that living next to the United States involved certain unspecified military perils. The *New York Times*, in a very perceptive editorial, saw no cause for alarm and viewed it as a logical extension of Canada's efforts to diversify and expand its foreign contacts and of a piece with the recent establishment of diplomatic relations between Canada and the People's Republic of China. And it ended by asking: 'Who can say that this added communicative channel may not prove valuable at times in the context of over-all East-West relations despite Canada's disclaimer of any intermediary role? If the agreement makes the United States less inclined to take Canada for granted and more sensitive to Canada's concern for protecting the Arctic and avoiding American domination, it will be all to the good.'

The Soviet enthusiasm for the protocol was hard to explain. It had some temporary significance as an indication of improved relations between our two countries, and served to demonstrate a diplomatic victory on the part of the Soviet leadership. But a Protocol on Consultations between a lesser power such as Canada and a superpower can only have content if there is political will on both sides to use it. And if there was a political will in May 1971, it evaporated in both Moscow and Ottawa in the years to come. On one or two occasions when we wished to utilize the protocol for political consultations there was very little reaction on the Russian side, and when the Russians might have made use of it – for example to advise the Canadian government in advance of their reasons for intervening in Afghanistan – they clearly could not or would not do so.

Trudeau's two-hour conversation with Brezhnev, who was at that time still in very good form with no signs of any particular mental or physical strain, although he smoked constantly, dealt with the generalities of Canadian-Soviet relations. In retrospect it is of interest because of what he had to say about the United States. He complained he was sometimes depicted in the West as a hard-liner, but in fact exactly the contrary was true. He was a very realistic man, which he had to be if he was to improve the living standards in his own country and also follow a strong foreign policy. He then indulged in a rambling but quite emotional description of the experiences of the Soviet peoples in the last war. But now, he said, we are living in a very new and very difficult age. In the past, history remembered those people who had conquered or who had tried to conquer the world. In more recent times, statesmen seemed to be remembered either as rabid reactionaries, or as realists who wanted good relations between countries and peoples. 'I and my colleagues want to go down in history as realists.'

Brezhnev said the Soviet Union had to find a way to go about reducing tension with the West. He referred to good Soviet relations with countries such as Sweden, Finland, and Afghanistan, two of them monarchies. He said he had very good personal relations with the leaders of all three countries, a statement that sounds ominous in retrospect. He then stated categorically: 'We want good relations with the United States.' After a few words about how impressed he was with the importance of public opinion in the United States, particularly in its criticism of the war in Vietnam, he said people would not believe false leaders and would force governments to adopt policies leading to good relations with other countries. 'I am a humanist and a democrat and I am ready to sign with the Prime Minister a treaty of peace and I will do one with the United States. I would be happy to attach my signature to such a treaty.'

While one always had to be sceptical about Soviet pronouncements on peace, the prime minister became convinced that, whatever Brezhnev's ultimate aim in seeking détente, he had already firmly determined to seek an improvement in relations with the United States. At that moment the intensification of the war in Vietnam and the strained relations between Washington and Moscow made this seem improbable. But the conversation with Brezhnev was significant evidence that he hoped for a change of direction.

The visit in Moscow ended upon an unusually upbeat note. There had been the usual formal evenings such as a performance in the Bolshoi Opera House and a Kremlin banquet, and I had been asked what the Trudeaus would like to do on the third night. In view of Margaret's youth I suggested a dinner with a gypsy orchestra. This caused considerable problems since Kosygin would have to be host and the presence of gypsies, it was feared, would strike altogether too frivolous a note for the austere head of government. It is a measure of the Soviet desire to please that he was persuaded to accept and a very agreeable supper was organized in a restaurant surrounded by birch trees in a forest not far from Moscow. It was delightful to see how the stony face of Kosygin gradually relaxed under the influence of the gypsy music, which he confessed he had never heard before. It was on this pleasant note that the prime ministerial party then left on a week's tour to Kiev, Tashkent, Norilsk, Murmansk, and Leningrad. The visits to the two Arctic towns had been requested by Canada in order to stress the importance we attached to our relationship across the North Pole and our desire to develop exchanges of expertise, technology, and knowledge about our two Arctic regions. The Arctic Circle city of Norilsk, with a population of one hundred thousand, is important for its nickel mining and industry. Although the temperature in late May was minus four degrees and it snowed, our reception was tumultuous, with what seemed the entire population lining the streets and waving Canadian flags. Since this was the first official visit by a Western leader to the Soviet Arctic, the warmth of the reception and the indefatigable curiosity about the outside world were to be expected. Norilsk is a considerable tour de force. It was no mean feat to construct a city of its size in conditions comparable to Inuvik in the Canadian Arctic. But, as Trudeau perceptively remarked, one-tenth of the population would probably have sufficed in another society where the mania for 'gigantism' did not reign.

After a stop-over in Murmansk came the final visit to Leningrad. While largely touristic, it also stressed the northern connection, including the Leningrad-Montreal sea link provided at that time by the more or less regular service of the Soviet liner *Alexandr Pushkin*. The visit to Leningrad again ended on a jovial note with a performance in the old Imperial Opera House, followed by dinner in a cavernous restaurant with a deafening band, where an unusual and highly embarrassing breach of security took place. Most of the

Russians in the restaurant had no idea who the distinguished guests were and suddenly a hefty blonde came up to Trudeau and practically lifted him to his feet and whisked him off to the dance floor, to the horror of the deputy prime minister and the security detail, who I noticed subsequently led the dancing partner off, presumably for a detailed interrogation.

In my experience, only three foreign visitors – Nixon, de Gaulle, and Pompidou – were given the lavish treatment accorded to Prime Minister Trudeau in terms of the amount of time spent with him by all the most important Soviet leaders and the top officials in the provincial capitals. And every effort was made to meet his wishes on the twelve-day trip. It did succeed in putting Canada on the map in a vast part of the country, and the treatment in the press and in public speeches of Canada as a friendly country with problems similar to their own and disposed to co-operate in an amical spirit to solve them helped to weaken the traditional dogma of a hostile and united capitalist world threatening Soviet socialist achievements.

The visit marked an important watershed in the evolution of Canada's position in the world and in its international outlook and image. It impressed on Canadians and foreigners the idea of Canada looking beyond the traditional North Atlantic triangle and being capable of treating on a basis of equality with the other superpower without in any way diminishing our role in NATO. Indeed, it strengthened it as our importance on the international scene increased.

In the mid-summer of 1971 the prime minister sent me instructions to invite Kosygin on a return visit to Canada in October. The Soviets were taken aback because of the speed with which the Canadian government wished to organize the return visit, but their delight was manifest in an immediate acceptance. Trudeau himself later confessed it had been a mistake to invite Kosygin back so quickly because this was at once interpreted by the Russians as an indication that the Canadian government wished to go much further in developing relations with them than in fact it did. To underline the importance that the Russians attached to the visit, Kosygin insisted that it be of a reasonable length and include cities across Canada and that it be restricted to Canada alone. I saw him in the Kremlin twice before the visit and it was clear that he had devoted a good deal of personal attention to the detailed planning.

I also had a long talk with the deputy editor-in-chief of *Pravda*, who speculated that the Kosygin visit would be 'big news,' particularly in the United States where the reaction would be most interesting. He was certain that the timing of the Kosygin visit to Canada would lead the Americans to conclude it was connected with the projected Nixon visit to Peking. As Soviet officials pondered the connection between the Kosygin visit and relations with the United States there was even an intriguing attempt to find out if Nixon might try to take the opportunity of the Kosygin visit to Canada to meet him, possibly on the border. The Russians did not follow this up, however, and it would have been totally inappropriate, even if the Americans had been interested. I thought at the time that the sudden Sino-American rapprochement was one of the reasons why the Russians were quick to accept the Canadian invitation, although I made it perfectly clear on every occasion that there was no connection in our minds whatsoever.

During that summer and early fall there was a good deal of speculation that Kosygin's position was slipping and that he was shortly to be removed from the Politburo. It was prompted by over-zealousness on the part of some of the Kremlinologists in Washington and London and in the American and British embassies in Moscow who had made a classical deduction from the traditional signs in the Soviet press pointing to possible disgrace. I was in the difficult position of being certain the Soviet government would not have accepted the invitation to Kosygin if he were about to fall into disgrace, but unable to explain to my American, British, and other colleagues why I disagreed since we did not want a premature leakage of news on the impending visit.

This took place in mid-October amid the splendours of the Canadian autumn. Although we share the same climate with the Russians, their fall is one of overcast skies and drizzle so that the leaves turn a rather muddy brown. The Gatineau Hills in their brilliant red were a revelation to the Soviet party. The talks themselves and the official entertainment in Ottawa went according to the book. A dramatic incident which almost disrupted the visit resulted indirectly from the fine weather: it was so splendid that Kosygin decided to walk with Trudeau from Parliament Hill to his apartments in the Château Laurier. This departure from the itinerary permitted an angry Hungarian refugee to attempt, fortunately unsuccessfully, to attack Kosygin. Ruffled but unhurt, Kosygin reacted with considerable calm.

We were uncertain how the visit to Montreal would go, in particular how the totally different personalities of Alexei Kosygin and Quebec Premier Robert Bourassa would mesh. To my astonishment, they found the common ground of economics and became engrossed in such topics as the James Bay power project and adjustment to the economic problems caused by recent Nixonian financial measures which had hurt Canadian trade. Incidentally, it was interesting to see how astounded the Russians were at the size of our two-way trade with the United States and the high percentage of manufactured goods Canada exported to the United States. Kosygin confessed that he had believed we exported only raw materials.

After a brief visit to Vancouver, the party headed for Edmonton, which the Russians immediately dubbed the Canadian Novosibirsk, the metropolis of Siberia. Kosygin was intrigued partly because of the personality of Premier Peter Lougheed who had been introduced to him as a typical Big Canadian Capitalist, and partly because of his interest in the problems of a large city in the far north. But the highlight for the Russians and probably the most successful part of the entire trip in many ways was the induction of Alexei Kosygin into an Indian tribe by an Indian chief and Indian princess in native dress. His entourage was startled, as I was, to see the dour number two of the Soviet hierarchy calmly squat on the floor in his new headdress to smoke the pipe of peace. But he was obviously delighted with this colourful custom.

The visit ended with an official reception in Toronto, including a session with the Canadian Manufacturers' Association. It was coloured by typical misjudgment on the part of Margaret Trudeau, who had decided to turn up in Toronto for the final lap. Kosygin's hostess was his daughter Ludmilla, a cultured and very conservative Russian. In spite of my wife's attempt to dissuade her, Margaret took Ludmilla to a restricted movie which contained sexually explicit scenes. After half an hour, Ludmilla' s distaste and embarrassment overcame her desire not to offend her hostess and she got up and left – to the disappointment of Margaret who was obviously enjoying it.

Nevertheless, Kosygin seemed fond of Margaret and frequently asked after her in later years, although her subsequent behaviour and her 'memoirs' baffled and shocked him. I recall once visiting the deputy foreign minister on some matter and noticed Margaret's first book in a German translation prominently displayed on his desk. He clearly wanted me to know that he was doing his Canadian homework. (The only foreign language he spoke was German.) But at the end of the meeting he asked me if it was an essential piece of reading. I gave him a categorical 'no' and he looked relieved.

The Soviets were highly gratified by the Kosygin visit and from a practical point of view it soon opened up new horizons. An agreement was signed to set up a joint commission to cover cultural, academic, scientific, and technical exchanges of experts and ideas. The Canadian government was particularly interested in trying to promote a greater exchange of information about northern and Arctic affairs. We were eager to find out more about the Soviet treatment of their Eskimos and their techniques in building on permafrost. Although Jean Chrétien, then minister of northern affairs, visited the Soviet Union and particularly the north, and Soviet experts returned to Canada, it was extremely difficult to have a meeting of minds. One of the problems lay in the fact that what we called Northern Affairs was the responsibility in Russia of a deputy prime minister, who was in charge of Gosstroi, a huge administrative apparatus responsible for all the major construction projects in the country, including Siberia. Gosstroi, in turn, had no interest whatsoever in any exchanges with Canada except in practical domains such as construction techniques in severe climatic conditions. This in turn was further complicated by the fact that much of the labour provided for Gosstroi's projects in Siberia came from prisoners. Almost the only concrete result of our efforts in the Arctic was our gift of a herd of musk oxen to the Soviet government. I objected strongly on the grounds that we should have got something from the Russians in return, which we never did. And it was only by making a very considerable fuss that there was even an acknowledgment of the gift in the Soviet press.

While the Russians never failed to stress the new era which had arrived in our political relations, Kosygin, whom I saw quite frequently, always concentrated on pragmatic things. For example, in April 1972 he talked only of big projects we could undertake together, such as one involving Canadian paper-making equipment and Soviet hydro-electric equipment, joint oil and gas pipelines, high voltage transmission lines, and joint projects in northern transportation and construction. During a visit to Canada, deputy prime minister Nikolai Tikhonov, who later became prime minister after the death of Kosygin, was impressed by the Canadian developer Robert Campeau and tried to get us to put pressure on him to come to the Soviet Union to discuss techniques for the rapid construction of small prefabricated houses. It was clear they wanted them for new settlements in the north. Nothing came of this, and so many other projects, because we could never combine the methods of operation of Canadian private enterprise and the enormously cumbersome Soviet bureaucracy. Any project was further complicated by the need to fit it into the Soviet five-year plans, which meant making decisions years in advance.

The Soviet experience with the Olivetti typewriter was a good example of this. Kosygin visited an Olivetti plant in Italy and decided that a certain model was what they needed; so eventually an agreement was signed for the assembly of this machine in Russia. Three years passed with no progress and the Italians thought the project had been abandoned when suddenly they were informed that everything had been cleared and they could proceed. Olivetti then suggested that, after three years, that particular model was a little out of date and they had a new one which would much better suit Soviet purposes. The Soviets threw up their hands in horror and said it had to be the older model or nothing because to change the specifications would require going through the entire process all over again of getting it cleared through the bureaucracy. So it was the old model that was sold.

In the mean time, Soviet-American relations moved into a different phase of enthusiastic co-operation and this was reflected on the Canadian-Soviet commercial front. The Russians continued to maintain an interest in trade with Canada, but it was clear that their fascination with the huge turned their attention inevitably to the United States. In addition, many projects which might have developed from Canada, often involving the Canadian subsidiaries of American firms, had to be abandoned when the mother companies thought there was an opportunity to do more business by dealing directly with the Soviets. Canadian trade in grain, however, was never seriously affected, even when the Americans moved into the market in an important way. The Soviet promises that they would always look first to Canada were not broken and the trade in wheat from the Canadian Pacific ports to the Soviet Far East remained an important element in commercial relations.

There was a joint interest in preventing slippage in the development of a solid basis of Canadian-Soviet relations; this would have been normal after the Nixon visit to Moscow in 1972 turned Soviet attention to the United States. The visit of Mitchell Sharp, in November 1973, was therefore utilized by both countries to maintain the momentum. Sharp not only had a long meeting with Andrei Gromyko, but a session with President Podgorny and an unusual call on Kosygin in his villa in Pitsunda on the Black Sea. The government, having contributed a good deal to creating an atmosphere propitious to East-West détente, did not want Canadian interests to be neglected in the light of the u.s.-Soviet summits. And the Russians on their side did not want to appear to be concentrating exclusively on the other superpower at the expense of smaller countries.

Indeed in this context, shortly after the meeting in 1975 convened by French President Valery Giscard d'Estaing at Rambouillet of the five major capitalist countries, subsequently transformed into the annual Group of Seven summits including Canada and Italy, a high Soviet official told me they found it peculiar that Canada had been excluded in the beginning since the Soviets considered Canada a major economic power, as important as Britain and more influential than Italy. The official cited figures of our GNP and our role in world trade as arguments that Canada should have been invited to Rambouillet. He was certain we had been vetoed by the Americans, although it was actually Giscard d'Estaing who opposed Canadian participation, fearing a strengthening of the North American, Anglo-Saxon element and greatly misjudging the French element in Canada and our independence of action of Washington.

It was hockey that helped to keep interest in Canada high. Shortly after the war the Russians adopted Canadian ice hockey. They are good natural sportsmen, they have the same climate to produce skaters, and they have the money and organization to produce good players. For years the Canadian Amateur Hockey Association sent its annual winning team to Russia as a kind of prize. From 1960 on, the competition was getting tougher and our amateurs were being increasingly clobbered by the Soviet teams. When the Drummondville Bulldogs suffered a humiliating series of defeats, the Russians said they were no longer interested in playing hockey with Canada except against our best. But our best were professionals and the Soviets were afraid of losing their official amateur status if they played against National Hockey League teams. The Soviets knew as well as I did that Soviet hockey players were professionals in every sense of the word, but they had set their sights on winning the Olympics and did not wish to prejudice their status. (They hardly needed to bother since the International Olympic Committee consistently applied the traditional rules about professionalism to Canadians and accepted without demur Soviet attestations that their players were amateurs.)

After protracted and difficult negotiations a formula was finally worked out which permitted a crack Soviet team to meet a Canadian team chosen from NHL players. The resulting series in September 1972, in Canada and in Moscow, was a masterpiece of skill and suspense, and raised Soviet interest in the game to fever pitch. Brezhnev and half of the Politburo attended nearly every game and it was estimated that millions of people watched it on television. I missed the first game as I was on an official visit to Georgia, but everywhere I went people clapped when they caught sight of the Canadian flag, and at the official dinner in Tbilisi my guests installed a TV set so that we could follow the game.

The series was not without its tense moments. Some three thousand Canadian fans had come over to Moscow for the games. On the first night they stood and sang lustily when 'O Canada' was played. When the Soviet national anthem was played, the audience was mute. The words, a poem of praise to Stalin, dated from the days of the Vozhd and had been scrapped. The Soviets were so humiliated they got to work and in a few months produced new words. The police were very nervous, expecting the worst, but the Canadian fans were remarkably well behaved except for one unfortunate individual who got drunk and broke up the National Hotel bar. When he woke up he was behind prison bars where he stayed until the evening of the last game, when an officer appeared, told him to get his things, and escorted him to a police car and armed militiamen. He was convinced it was the first stop on the way to Siberia and the Russians offered no explanation until they arrived at the arena, and with big smiles escorted him to his seat.

From then on, hockey and Canada were synonymous, although all too often it gave rise to disputes. The need to win on the Soviet side was overwhelming. It became a question of national pride and Soviet victories were hailed as proof of the superiority of the system. On one occasion, my wife became so angry when the person sitting below her in the arena crowed happily over a Soviet lead that she bonked him on the head with her handbag. It turned out to be the deputy minister of foreign trade, who fortunately took it in good spirits. Indeed, he used to recount the incident years later in a light-hearted way.

In the spring of 1975 a dispute arose about over-fishing of capelin and herring by the Soviet fishing fleet off the Nova Scotia and Newfoundland coasts in contravention of international agreements assigning quotas and fishing areas to the major fishing countries. This had aroused considerable resentment in Canada, particularly as Canadian fishermen had limited their activities in accordance with international agreements intended to avoid the destruction of the diminishing sources of fish. I made a number of strong interventions with the Ministry of Fisheries and the Foreign Ministry, both of which seemed convinced they could ignore the problem. It was a shock to the Soviets, therefore, when the government decided to close all Canadian ports to Soviet vessels. This was a highly effective response: most of the Soviet fleet could not operate for very long so far from their own ports without taking on water, food, and fuel and putting in for repairs.

After the first stunned reaction by the Soviets, the minister of fisheries told me it was possible to avoid a collision course, and all could be worked out between experts. At the same time, the Foreign Ministry rejected all the evidence of Soviet misbehaviour and accused us of discrimination and anti-Sovietism. As usual in dealing with the Russians, they never admitted that they were in the wrong, but in fact shortly afterward they agreed to a meeting of experts in Ottawa at which a compromise very satisfactory from the Canadian point of view was worked out. The move that broke the logjam was a meeting in Helsinki in 1975 between Prime Minister Trudeau and Leonid Brezhnev at the conference to sign the Final Act of the Helsinki documents, when the two leaders agreed that the dispute should not be permitted to drag on further and complicate the otherwise good relations between Canada and the Soviet Union.

From the fisheries dispute until 1979, relations in all areas developed normally, with exchange visits in every field of activity and a slow increase in trade. This was given official recognition by the Soviets in a speech by Brezhnev in 1976 when for the first time he elevated Canada to the company of the United States, France, West Germany, Britain, Italy, and Japan as important countries in the Soviet perspective. This may appear a frivolous way to judge developments, but our 'promotion' was frequently commented on by Soviet officials, who took it as a cue to the way to treat the Canadian embassy.

In addition to the federal government, several provincial governments, particularly the prairie provinces, began to show interest in increasing trade with the Russians. Saskatchewan Premier Alan Blakeney and Alberta Premier Peter Lougheed both went to Moscow for trade talks. But the most unorthodox trip was that of Manitoba's Ed Schreyer, who as head of a New Democratic Party government, and apparently labouring under the illusion that the Soviet communists looked favourably on social democracy, was anxious to visit the Soviet Union, but went about it in a very odd way. Without approaching the federal government, he negotiated directly with the Soviet embassy in Ottawa to get an invitation to visit Russia as chairman of Manitoba Hydro, which was interested in purchasing Soviet turbines designed to generate electricity from slow-moving rivers like the Nelson. After six months in which he got nowhere, he finally asked the federal government for help and we arranged his visit. I advised him to come as premier, but he insisted he wanted to come simply as chairman of Manitoba Hydro. As a result, the Russians, who attach great importance to pomp and ceremony, were considerably miffed and gave him the second-class treatment to which they considered the chairman of Manitoba Hydro was entitled. It was also a rather strange visit inasmuch as Schreyer insisted on treating the Soviets as fellow socialists and putting himself in the position of negotiating with the Russians for the purchase of turbines they were dying to sell.

The Canadian federal election of November 1972, which returned a minority Liberal government, was a surprise and a disappointment to the Russians. Kosygin did not go so far as to suggest that there was an anti-Soviet conspiracy, but he was obviously puzzled as to what had prompted the Liberal slide. I assured him that the reasons for the Conservative gains lay entirely in internal problems and that Canadian policy toward the Soviet Union had played no role in the election. To reassure the Russians, Prime Minister Trudeau sent a letter to Kosygin stating that the policy of developing better relations with the Soviet Union would not be altered and that, so far as he could make out, there was no likelihood that the other principal parties in Canada would demand any change. His letter was received with visible relief and satisfaction by the Soviet authorities. In fact for the next few years there was no variation in Canadian policy and there seemed to be almost universal acceptance in Canada of the need for a more stable relationship with the Soviet Union. The Russians were, of course, relieved when the Trudeau government was re-elected with a large majority in 1974. Although the flurry of high-level political visits was over, the practice of exchanging messages continued during the next five years of the Liberal government, and proved a very useful way of keeping the momentum in Soviet-Canadian relations going. This period had its ups and downs, the downs being inevitable given the Soviet system and the determination of the Soviets to continue to utilize the KGB in an aggressive way even when relations were good.

Soviet disappointment at the Conservative victory in 1979 was slightly tempered by their resentment over the expulsion some six months earlier by the Trudeau government of thirteen members of the Soviet missions in Canada for espionage. They watched with very considerable care the installation of the government of Joe Clark. They reserved their judgment until November 1979, and the throne speech, when *Pravda* ventured on a first cautious judgment that the Soviets saw no unpleasant surprises in a Conservative government, nor on the other hand, much to cheer about. With the usual Marxist gloss, it painted a picture of big capitalism with the collusion of American imperialism attempting to reverse the nationalist gains of the Liberal period. It was sceptical about the ability of the Conservatives to resist the pressure of the 'Pentagon and NATO militarists,' but it added a note of hope that the Conservatives would look for solutions to Canada's economic and social problems beyond its traditional partners. The puzzlement of the Russians was compounded by the fact that they could find nothing in the throne speech to throw light on future Canadian foreign policy.

Nevertheless, the Russians were quite correct with the Conservative government and Brezhnev sent a letter to Prime Minister Clark, the primary aim of which seemed to establish some more direct contact with the new government. The Russians did not expect a very active foreign policy from the Conservative government, which was in a minority in the House of Commons and which had been out of power for some sixteen years. They were, however, pleased with the appointment of Flora MacDonald to External Affairs and responded quickly to an indication that she wished to visit the Soviet Union to repay the Gromyko visit of several years before. She intrigued and puzzled the Russians who frequently asked me what was meant by the term 'red Tory.' We were in the process of working out details of her visit to Moscow when a no-confidence vote in the House of Commons brought down the Conservative government and precipitated new elections. The visit would not have taken place in any event because of the invasion of

Afghanistan and the strong reaction of the Canadian government to it which led to an abrupt souring of relations. It was further complicated by the expulsion of additional members of the Soviet embassy in Ottawa and the inevitable retaliation by the Soviets.

It was therefore with intense relief that the Soviets greeted the return of the Liberal government in February 1980, and they noted with great interest an off-the-cuff remark by Trudeau that he wanted good relations with both superpowers. They were a little anxious that he might not stay the course in view of his statement a few months earlier that he intended to leave politics. They need not have been alarmed. A week after the elections, I was back in Ottawa and when my wife reminded Trudeau of his statement, he said with a smile, 'Yes, my dear, but I wasn't in power at that time.' The Soviets were in any case sufficiently realistic to know that the measures taken by Canada as a result of the invasion of Afghanistan could not be quickly dismantled. But they did have the hope, which proved to be justified, that the Liberal government would try to maintain a certain measure of balance in its relations with the Soviet Union.

Although the evolution of Canadian relations with the Soviet Union started seriously in 1966, it is obvious that the course they took in the following decade and a half depended very largely on Pierre Trudeau. This cultured, fascinating, and determined man put his imprint in a large way on Canadian foreign policy, and above all on Canadians' perspective of their country. At the heart of his political philosophy lay his belief that the Soviet Union had to be brought into the mainstream of world politics, that Canada had a unique opportunity to help in this process, and that the end result would benefit Canada as well as the Western community of nations.

Trudeau's rebellion against the well-to-do Catholic bourgeois milieu of French Montreal in which he had been raised led him almost inevitably into exploring forbidden political fruit. As a young man in the worst years of the cold war, he went to Yugoslavia before the split with Moscow, to Stalin's Russia, to China. Whether this fascination for the communist world was due to more than a symbolic nose-thumbing at the capitalist West is hard to tell. I never detected any great interest in Marxism or doctrinal intricacies. But he was fascinated by the Soviet Union and the Russians, and a rapprochement with Moscow became a top priority in his foreign policy as soon as he became prime minister in 1968. From then on he did all he could, within the limits of his office, to develop and preserve a special relationship with Brezhnev, Kosygin, and the other Soviet leaders. Whenever he was presented with irrefutable evidence of Soviet wrongdoing, as in the case of the thirteen Soviet spies expelled from Canada in 1978, he did not hesitate to take the necessary actions, while at the same time trying to preserve the essence of the relationship.

He delighted, of course, in tantalizing his colleagues. He would refuse to see the foreign minister of Turkey, for example, but find time to have the Russian poet Andrei Voznesensky for lunch. And he did not hesitate at grave moments in East-West relations to slip out of his Sussex Drive residence on foot and drop in on the Soviet ambassador. No reports were ever made on these peculiar rendez-vous and what passed between him and the ambassador remains secret. But the ambassador was Alexander Yakovlev, a confidant of Gorbachev who later became one of the leading members of the Politburo.

When Trudeau returned to power in 1980, he re-examined the Conservative government's decision to boycott the Olympic Games to be held in Moscow that summer. He and some of his cabinet were not entirely happy with the situation, but accepted the fact that the decision could not be reversed. In the succeeding years there could be little movement in East-West relations because of immobilism in Moscow and the initial hard line of the Reagan administration in Washington. But as soon as the flicker of an opportunity appeared he launched his 'peace mission' which took him to Moscow, East Berlin, and Prague in a well-intentioned but totally futile effort to lessen tensions. It was doomed to failure because there was no one in Moscow to talk to at that time (since first Andropov and then Chernenko were dying), and because of suspicion in Washington about Trudeau and his motives. There is always only a very minor role for third parties to play in East-West relations, even if the time is right. And when the time is right the superpowers prefer to handle their relations without interference.

Canadian-Soviet relations can never be treated as a strictly bilateral affair. It has to be a Canadian–United States–Soviet Union triangle. The major error of Trudeau was to ignore this. He was probably no more anti-American than many Canadian nationalists of the sixties and seventies. And in those days if you were an outspoken defender of the Canadian national identity, you ended up almost inevitably anti-American. Trudeau was both a Canadian nationalist and an advocate of good relations with the Russians and the end result was deep distrust of him in Washington. And this in turn reduced his value as an interlocutor. The Russians are highly realistic. They welcomed what Trudeau did, for Soviet national interests, but they recognized that his usefulness in the big superpower game was strictly limited.

The Russians were, and still are, interested in Canada as an important and technically advanced North American power struggling with many of the problems they themselves face. They seem to like and to a certain extent admire Canadians as people while puzzled by our ambivalent position in the world. They feel vaguely that Canadians share something with them, that we are big and rich enough to bother with, but not strong and aggressive enough to threaten them, and that just possibly we might have the answers to some of the technical problems which they themselves are unable to solve.

But underlying this, as a constant factor in their attitude to Canada during my sixteen years as ambassador, was the hope of detaching us a little from American influence, which only became a possibility in Soviet calculations when a broad body of public opinion grew up in Canada in favour of distancing Canada from the United States. The fact that the aim of Canadian nationalists in trying to diminish dependence on the United Sates was not the same as the Soviet hope of detaching Canada from its American ally is immaterial. When Moscow saw a chance to drive a small wedge they seized the opportunity, even though they had few illusions about how far this could or should be exploited. I was never under any illusion about the importance of Canada in Soviet thinking. The relationship with the United States was the overriding consideration of the Soviets and one way or another Canada had to be fitted into this calculation.

7

Living with the KGB

No matter how good Western intentions, there were at least two sets of problems which constantly created obstacles to good relations with the Soviet Union: the activities of the KGB and the Soviet treatment of its dissidents. The first constituted an incessant and at times intolerable interference in the affairs of other countries. The second was such a flagrant violation of the political and religious rights of groups and individuals that it evoked an angry response in the West either by people who had special ties to those persecuted, such as Jews, Ukrainians, and Lithuanian Catholics, or by the public in general, revolted by the treatment of individual protesters. Canada was no exception and our relations with the Soviet Union in the seventies were often set back by revelations of KGB machinations or by some particularly unpalatable attack on human rights. The Soviet acceptance of the Helsinki Act in 1975 only served to accentuate the glaring contrast between the solemn engagements the Russians had undertaken and their actual performance.

The contest between the embassy and the Soviet police organizations – the uniformed militia and the KGB, or Committee for State Security, which encompassed intelligence and counter-intelligence activities in Russia and abroad – never ceased during all the years I was in Moscow. The state of Canadian-Soviet relations seldom altered the situation. The police were just as aggressively active when euphoria reigned as when relations were strained. Seldom a month passed without some evidence of their unceasing efforts to penetrate the embassy's defences or to suborn the Canadian-based staff. These efforts also frequently extended to Canadian tourists. And, of course, the activities in Canada of the KGB and the GRU, the military intelligence agency, continued unabated.

The protection of our embassy was a first priority. We were assigned five Canadian guards, two of whom were always on duty during the day and one at night. Outside the embassy, the Russian militia patrolled at all times. There was never less than two policemen on duty, ostensibly to protect the embassy against enraged Soviet citizens, but in fact primarily to survey our activities and to prevent ordinary Soviet citizens from entering. The zeal of the policemen was at times exasperating, and many Canadian tourists complained bitterly about being prevented from entering their own embassy. Whenever possible, the Canadian guards attempted to make sure that legitimate visitors were permitted in. On one occasion, a diplomatic incident occurred when the Italian ambassador, a mild-mannered man who spoke some Russian, decided to walk over from his embassy, which was not far away, to call on me. When the Soviet policemen stopped him, he spoke to them in Russian, at which point he was abruptly and forcibly turned away. I had great pleasure in using this incident to make a formal protest against the excesses of the police in providing 'protection'.

Nevertheless, on a number of occasions, unauthorized Soviet civilians managed to slip by the militia. The most dramatic incident involved a private in uniform. I was alerted immediately to the fact that he was inside the embassy and we attempted to find out what he wanted. He was from an infantry regiment stationed in Soviet Central Asia and was in Moscow on leave. He claimed to have read about Canada and it sounded like a country he would like to live in. He had used a week of his leave studying access to the embassy and he waited until the Soviet militiaman at the chancery entrance had strolled down the street for a cigarette with his comrade to dash across the street and into the embassy. Within twenty minutes of his arrival, I had a call from the Soviet chief of protocol asking me to return the man and informing me that they had information he was a fanatic who was trying to assassinate me. In the mean time, both ends of the street were blocked off by military vehicles and a dozen or so militia stood guard ouside the embassy. We had long discussions by telephone with the Soviet authorities and tried to convince them that the man seemed to be genuinely innocent and perhaps slightly unbalanced. When after twenty-four hours, the guard had not been lifted and the case seemed absolutely hopeless since there was no possible way that the Russians would permit a soldier in uniform who had taken refuge in an 'imperialist' embassy to leave the country, we had no alternative but to persuade him to give himself up.

On another occasion, a Soviet citizen half-entered the embassy before the militia realized what was happening and tackled him at the door. A scuffle ensued with one of our guards, but the man was dragged off to the militia box on the corner. This time again we protested about the prevention of free entry to the premises and again were informed the police were acting on our behalf because the man was seriously ill and needed hospitalization. Mark Gayn, the highly respected *Toronto Star* correspondent, who spoke Russian, was also the victim several times of the militia blockade. We frequently raised this question with the Soviets after the signing of the Helsinki Agreement in the context of the free movement of persons, but needless to say got nowhere.

The Russians made a special effort to bug every important embassy in Moscow, even the communist embassies. In 1964 the Romanian embassy moved out of the old palace they had occupied into a building they put up themselves. The palace was then transferred to a newly established third world country. The new occupants found to their astonishment that it had been thoroughly bugged some time before, an eavesdropping system clearly directed against the Soviet's slightly recalcitrant communist allies, the Romanians. In the case of the Canadian embassy, to counteract Soviet activities we constructed a room containing special facilities which permitted us to discuss particularly sensitive questions without fear of being overheard. Since perforce we were obliged to spend a fair amount of our working time in the 'safe room,' our government was persuaded to send a photo-mural of the Canadian woods in autumn which helped prevent claustrophobia and was the envy of some of our less imaginative NATO partners.

Despite our precautions, in January 1976 the Soviets almost succeeded in placing an 'ear' in the embassy. For nearly a year and a half we had been requesting the authorities to repaint the outside of the embassy, to no avail. Suddenly, I was recalled to Ottawa for consultations. The day after my departure, the Soviets announced that they were ready to paint, although the temperature was twenty below. And indeed they turned up the following day with scaffolding and set to work with a will. Fortunately, a member of the staff well acquainted with listening devices was suspicious of the length of time it took them to paint outside my office, a corner room with windows on two sides. The moment the scaffolding was removed, he proceeded to tear out the walls around the windows and discovered a listening device of extraordinary sophistication which would never have been detected under ordinary circumstances since there was nothing on the wall to hint at its existence. The one hole was about the size of a pin. Naturally, it was removed and examined.

Some months later, I suggested that we should not let the Russians get away with an action of this sort in a period in which our relations were supposed to be good. I therefore called on the head of the Canadian department in the Soviet Ministry of Foreign Affairs and produced photographs of the device and said that we found it difficult to understand how the Soviets could indulge in this anti-Canadian activity at a time when they wanted better relations. My interlocutor, totally impassive, examined the photographs, said he knew nothing about it, and if any such things had been implanted in my office, it must have been done by another power unfriendly both to Canada and to the Soviet Union. Some time later, my minister-counsellor was called in to the Soviet official's office and told they had made exhaustive inquiries concerning the matter and could give categorical assurance that no Soviet organization or agency whatsoever had any part in that action. When the official was asked how, in that case, the 'action' could have been carried out, the answer was simply that it was a matter for the Canadians themselves to sort out.

This exchange illustrated the old Russian system known as

Vranye. Vranye is a form of lying, quite distinct from the normal lie (*lyozh*). When an individual is placed in an embarrassing position, instead of admitting the truth, he responds by an elaborate and usually obvious mistruth. Russian protocol requires that the other person, instead of denouncing him as a shamefaced liar, reply by another half-truth. In this way, both sides know what the facts are, but face is saved. This tradition cropped up frequently in life in Russia, not only on official occasions, but also in ordinary circumstances. It was sometimes amusing, more often exasperating, occasionally so imaginative as to fit Leonid Andreyev's description of it as an art form. The most extravagant example that I encountered was a lyrical description of the Palace of Congress in Moscow given to me in Rio in 1945 by a Soviet diplomat. I knew the palace existed only in architectural drawings, and in fact has never been built because the site chosen for it beside the Moskva River was too sandy, but it would have spoiled the fun to puncture his fantasy.

Some forms of KGB harassment took a more amusing turn. The embassy of Zaire was headed by a gentleman called Futu who, as the chief of an important tribe in his country, was not inclined to be pushed around by the Russians. On one occasion the latter asked him to send his car for a week to a Soviet garage in accordance with Soviet regulations 'for a check-up.' When it came back, Futu's staff examined it carefully and found a listening device in the back seat. Instead of protesting, Futu persuaded his government to invite the Soviet ambassador in Kinshasa 'in accordance with government regulations' to submit his car for a week's check-up. The Zairians, of course, did nothing to the car and then returned it to the embassy. Then they watched with great amusement as the Russians went mad taking the car apart in an effort to find the bug. On another occasion, the winter came early in Moscow, but the city council only turned on the central heating on 15 October when winter was supposed officially to start. Zairian protests got nowhere, so they simply turned off the electricity and the water in the Soviet embassy in Kinshasa. This became known as 'le système Futu' and was the great envy of other embassies in Moscow, whose governments, like Canada's, were not so able to play diplomatic tit for tat.

The most dangerous aspect of KGB activities was the attempt to entrap or suborn Canadian members of the staff. The military attachés were the most exposed and not a single year went by without an incident involving one or other of the three forces represented in Moscow. Sometimes it was a pure case of entrapment and the invention of accusations. On other occasions the KGB utilized the most flimsy of evidence to accuse our attachés of espionage. Naturally, the tough action the Canadian government took against spies operating out of the Soviet embassy in Ottawa evoked a response in Moscow in the form of retaliation. When these activities in Canada were exposed, however, the Soviet reaction and retaliation were more restrained if Canadian-Soviet relations were good or if there was something they wanted from us, either in the form of trade or politics. Thus when the Canadian government expelled thirteen members of the Soviet embassy for espionage in February 1978, almost decimating the embassy at the time, we expected a very strong reaction on the part of the Soviets. The Russians, in a rare show of restraint, refrained from expelling a member of the Canadian embassy, although they did cancel a number of high-level meetings and visits.

What the Soviets had not anticipated was that two years later three more members of the Soviet embassy would be ordered out of Canada. Their expulsion was based on convincing evidence of continuing activities by agents working out of the embassy, including cases where the Soviets were utilizing Canada to spy on third countries. It was not a propitious moment in our relations, coming immediately after the Soviet invasion of Afghanistan and the strong Canadian reaction to it. This time the Russians reacted violently. Within a week, I was called to the Soviet foreign office and told that as a result of 'campaigns in Canada to discredit officials of the Soviet Embassy in Ottawa and because for many years the Canadian embassy in Moscow had been utilized as a base for intelligence activities in favour of a third power,' the Soviet government declared it could no longer tolerate the presence in Russia of the air attaché at the embassy, and demanded his departure.

When the three Soviet officials were expelled, the Canadian government had advised the Soviet authorities that any unjustified retaliation against the Canadian embassy would result in retaliation in turn by the Canadian government. The Soviet Foreign Ministry gave me to understand that it would not tolerate 'such blackmail' and hinted darkly about information they had concerning the espionage activities of the air attaché and other members of the embassy staff. Flora MacDonald, who was then secretary of state for external affairs, had her Scottish blood boiling at that point. She refused to back down, and expelled another member of the Soviet staff in retaliation for the Soviet retaliation. At this point, I was beginning to calculate how many members of the embassy were going to be withdrawn and how to reorganize the work with reduced staff.

The reaction came in a totally unexpected way and startled the diplomatic community as well as our own embassy. Instead of demanding the withdrawal of further Canadian personnel, the Soviets withdrew twenty members of the locally engaged staff. Because of the expense of living in Moscow and the extreme shortage of housing and office space, all the Western embassies in Moscow employed large numbers of Soviet personnel in such jobs as telephone operators, translators, commercial assistants, drivers, maids, and so on. All of these Russians were supplied by the ubiquitous UPDK, the organization for the service of foreigners. This organization, which depended on the Foreign Ministry and was guided by the KGB, was the only organization through which embassies in Moscow could find Russian staff. Naturally, the workers were all obliged to report on our activities; we treated them courteously and kindly, but guardedly, always keeping in mind their obligations to the secret police.

Nevertheless, they played an essential role in the embassy and the withdrawal of twenty of them, out of about thirty-five, caused us enormous troubles. If it had not been so annoying, it would have been amusing to see the ingenious way in which the operation was carried out. One worker would come and say his mother was dying in Stavropol and he had to leave to be with her. Another would say that her little sister needed her help in Leningrad, and yet another that he'd been offered a better job at twice the pay. The unkindest cut of all was when the Soviet staff in my home were withdrawn – in tears, it should be added. While we didn't starve without a cook, it became almost impossible to carry on our normal, social-political functions without staff. Hosting numerous such functions was obligatory for the dean of the diplomatic corps in Moscow, which I had become in 1971.

When we protested to the Soviets and asked them to provide replacements for those who had been removed, they quoted the new constitution which said it was the employee's right to leave his or her employment at any time for any reason – a marvellous piece of gobbledegook, since not only was it a fact that no Soviet employee in any branch of Soviet activity could change his job, but it was well known that it was impossible for foreign embassies to go into the labour market. The Soviets replied that as there was no unemployment in Russia, it would be very difficult to find appropriate candidates, who might not in any case want to work at the Canadian embassy in view of the hostile anti-Soviet campaign in Canada.

I took the matter up with the Foreign Ministry and added that as dean of the diplomatic corps, I had to report that the Soviet action had been very badly received by all missions. The Foreign Ministry official then looked quite happy and said: 'Good. I am glad they have got the point.' He then asked me if I knew how many Russian employees there were in the American embassy: over one hundred. He suggested the Americans should think about it. (Obviously they didn't, since the removal of the Soviet staff from their embassy six years later appeared to come as a complete surprise to Washington.) He then said we could employ our own people. When I replied there was obviously no accommodation in Moscow for thirty-five Canadians, he replied with another of the mendacities which contributed to the irritation of dealing with the Russians, that accommodation would be no problem. In fact, it would have been a very serious one for our embassy and for most others if we had to fill all those jobs with Canadian staff. The expense would have been prohibitive and the morale problems of so many Canadians, unaccustomed to living abroad and in the unfamiliar and hostile atmosphere of Moscow, would have been enormous. However, after the Liberal victory in the elections of February 1980, the atmosphere changed again and one by one, new employees suddenly appeared, provided by the UPDK. That particular incident was over.

During my entire stay in Moscow, the Soviets kept up constant pressure on the Canadian staff in an effort to find out some weak spot. Most of them stood firm, but inevitably there were a few who permitted themselves to be ensnared. The bait was either sex or greed. Since Soviet women were on the whole not a particularly attractive lot, it always amazed me that they could be used as a lure. But some fell in the trap, fortunately without any dire consequences. It was a common tactic of the KGB: even one of my British colleagues admitted years after his retirement that he had had an affair with a Russian maid.

On another occasion a Latin American ambassador was confronted by the KGB with photographs of himself in bed with a Russian woman. They threatened to show them to his wife if he refused to co-operate. He simply laughed and said: 'You would do me a favour if you did. My wife thinks I am impotent.'

The KGB did not confine its use of women agents to members of the embassy. One of their most successful operations was against a senior official of one of the Protestant churches of Canada on a naive trip to Russia to preach religious fraternity and peace. Already in Moscow he had come under the charms of his interpreter. When he went to Central Asia, a local official of the Orthodox Church invited him to a picnic in the countryside and asked if he could bring his sister along. The sister turned out to be the interpreter from Moscow. At the appropriate moment, the official disappeared, the interpreter took off her clothes and two militiamen jumped out of nearby bushes and arrested him for attempted rape, complete with photographs. He was released after a few days and returned to Moscow with a threat of dire consequences to his career if he did not co-operate. Fortunately, he had the good sense when he returned to Canada to tell his superiors what had happened, thus destroying the possibility of blackmail.

Attempts were also made to suborn Canadian students, businessmen, or journalists, with remarkably little success. But the major effort of the KGB was against the support personnel of the embassy, the loyal, indispensable and on the whole competent staff who provided the administrative infrastructure – the guards, secretaries, communicators, clerks, non-commissioned officers, and so on. They were particularly vulnerable because they were less likely than career officers to have experience in living abroad under strange and difficult circumstances, and less likely to profit from the rich cultural fare that Moscow provided. In addition, they were not protected by the cover, flimsy though it might be, of diplomatic passports.

The ambassador's residence occupied the second floor of one part of the chancery. All the staff, with the exception of the minister-counsellor who occupied a small and ancient house in the compound, lived in several apartment blocks provided by the Soviet authorities for housing foreigners. We had succeeded in putting at least three or four Canadian families in the same block to give them a sense of community and to facilitate transportation to and from the embassy. And a considerable effort was made to provide each apartment with modern household appliances and Canadian furniture. But once outside the apartment they entered the shoddy world of Soviet construction: elevators that often stalled, peeling plaster, and decrepit entrances. Beyond, at every possible entrance to the apartment blocks, were the ubiquitous police, recording every move and preventing unauthorized persons from entering.

Of course, there were always some who either thought they could beat the police system, or who ignored the consequences. There was the temptation to make money in the black market where roubles could be acquired at a more favourable rate than in the bank. One or two were trapped but not activated by the KGB until they were sent back to Canada or to other posts. Usually this came to light through Soviet defectors. However, others who felt the trap closing on them were sufficiently aware of the dangers to come to me, admit their mistake, and leave before it was too late. Getting them out of Moscow before the Soviet bureaucracy realized what we were doing was often an agonizing operation.

For those who did not have the courage to do so, the results were sad. The best-known case was that of John Watkins, chargé d'affaires from 1949 to 1951, who returned as ambassador in 1954.

Watkins was an admirable scholar, author of the best English translation of *Madame Bovary*, translator of the Icelandic sagas, and an acknowledged expert on old Norse literature. Unfortunately, he was a homosexual in the days when this was considered reprehensible. The KGB found it easy to entrap him and enrolled him as an active collaborator. Word of his involvement came through Soviet defectors, by which time Watkins had retired from the public service. He submitted voluntarily to questioning by the RCMP, but died shortly afterwards of a heart attack. He had in fact suffered for several years from a heart condition. Watkins was a sad case, but I do not think he was a spy for the KGB in the sense of transmitting documents or information. He was probably used rather as an agent of influence, which he was in a position to be when he became an assistant under-secretary of state. But full knowledge of his secret died with him.

I was never subjected to any direct attack by the KGB, but as with several other Western ambassadors, I was the object of not very subtle efforts at disinformation, usually by members of the Soviet Academy of Sciences who had no formal excuse for easy association with foreign diplomats. 'Disinformation' basically took the form of messages which seemed plausible, but whose purpose was to sow confusion. If we knew what was really going on, it was often useful to have this disinformation because it could be reconstructed to add to our overall picture of a Soviet effort in some particular field.

My KGB 'contact' was Anatoli Gorsky, alias Gromov, who in the sixties went under the name of Professor Nikitin. He had been the Soviet case officer of the British spies Philby, Burgess, and Maclean, and of John Watkins. He was also the agent who attempted before my arrival in Moscow to suborn an officer of the Canadian embassy. The way in which I met Nikitin was typical of the KGB. The Brazilian ambassador, who had strong leftist leanings, was asked by Nikitin to invite me to dinner with him. After dinner, the ambassador discreetly withdrew and the point of the contact became clear. It was shortly after Pierre Trudeau had become prime minister and Nikitin's task was to find out obliquely if Trudeau would accept an invitation to visit the Soviet Union. This could have been done just as easily through a member of the

Foreign Ministry, but the Russians obviously did not want a rebuff, and in their typical Byzantine fashion preferred the less direct approach.

External Affairs instructed me to keep up the contact and I met Nikitin on regular occasions after that. Most of the time it seemed to be a straight case of disinformation, but there were a few other times in which genuine messages, concerning possible Soviet reactions if the Canadian government took certain steps, were passed along. And on one occasion there was an even stranger operation. The Soviets somehow discovered that I was a close personal friend of the Canadian detective-story writer Ross Macdonald, whose real name was Kenneth Millar and with whom I went to university. The Soviets had decided to launch the 'socially conscious' detective story on the Soviet market and hoped to start with Dashiell Hammett and Ross Macdonald. Although they had not signed the international copyright convention, they wished to have a tacit agreement from Macdonald. Instead of approaching the embassy through the Ministry of Culture or the Federation of Writers, they decided to do it through the KGB. I passed the messages on to Macdonald, who gave his permission and received in return a token number of roubles. Shortly thereafter, *Blue City*, one of the early novels (set in an unidentified city which in fact is London, Ontario, and dedicated to me), and *The Moving Target* were published in Russian.

I used the Nikitin channel and some others, in turn, to pass on some disinformation of my own. One such operation was carried out by my wife. We gave a dinner in honour of the deputy foreign minister, Valery Kuznetsov, who later became first vice-president of the Supreme Soviet. My wife, in the course of the conversation, told him that she had heard a story that Lin Piao, the vice-president of China, who had just been killed in an airplane accident, had in fact been assassinated by Mao because he had been sleeping with Mao's wife. Kuznetsov looked at her steadily for a full minute and then said: 'We have no such information.' About a month later, Moscow radio was broadcasting in its foreign language services (we first heard it, curiously enough in Portuguese) that Lin Piao had been assassinated by Mao because he was having an affair with

Mao's wife. The story was a total invention on the part of my wife who simply wanted to startle Kuznetsov.

On several occasions, in a more practical way, my wife and I would discuss some problem, usually in the official car which was certainly bugged, so that the information would get back to the Soviets, in the hope that the problem would be resolved. Occasionally, when we had failed to get the Soviet authorities to act on certain matters, we would discuss counter measures that I could recommend to Ottawa. This method often produced the right results.

One form of police harassment which was particularly irritating was the interpretation and arbitrary manipulation of the regulations concerning travel outside Moscow. In 1966 they were modified marginally. Advance notice to the Soviet authorities of travel intentions in those parts of the country not forbidden to foreigners was reduced from forty-eight to twenty-four hours and permission was granted to travel by car to some of the 'villes d'art' in the Moscow region outside the forty-kilometre zone. It had been particularly exasperating to have to travel to the beautiful town of Suzdal, which was in an open area, by train and at night, because it passed through a forbidden zone on the outskirts of Moscow. The travel regulations were all rather pointless since if we travelled by plane or train, we had to buy our tickets through a state organization, and if by car, our Russian drivers knew what we were doing.

I had a constant struggle with the Soviet authorities in my efforts to push back and civilize a little bit these barbarous regulations. But the results were not always very satisfactory. At one point, in the course of an official visit to Leningrad, I requested permission to travel some twenty kilometres outside the free area, along the Gulf of Finland, to the town of Lomonosov where I wished to visit the Menshikov palace and other monuments of classical Russian architecture. Lomonosov, unfortunately, is located almost directly opposite the island fortress of Kronstadt, an important naval base in the Gulf of Finland and in a forbidden zone. But the Foreign Ministry made an exception and when I arrived in Leningrad a member of the Leningrad Soviet presented me with a printed program which included a visit to Lomonosov. At the appointed time, a protocol officer met me and, in the official car with a Russian driver, we set out on our journey. We had scarcely arrived in Lomonosov when the car was surrounded by police, and my wife and I were ordered to go to the police station for having broken the regulations concerning entry to a military zone. The protocol officer was speechless with fright and indignation. I naturally refused to budge and for the next two hours the confrontation continued. We sat glaring at each other. Finally with great embarrassment, authorization arrived to permit us a quick look at the palace and an escort back to Leningrad. Incidents of this sort took place frequently, especially with the military attachés.

My wife became adept at outfacing the Russians. Once she went to a concert in the Palace of Congresses with the wife of a visiting official. Coming out they started to cross the almost trafficless street to where their car was parked. A militiaman stopped them and said they had to go about half a kilometre on foot to a place where they were allowed to cross. She refused and soon found herself confronted by half a dozen policemen, to the consternation of her friend. She simply said in Russian: 'You obviously don't know who I am. I am the mistress of Leonid Ilitch [Brezhnev], and you had better get out of my way.' They hesitated, clearly baffled, but decided not to take a chance that she was right, and quickly let them go.

Some members of the staff found it quite impossible to live in an atmosphere compounded of physical discomfort, shortages of almost everything, a language with which they could not cope, a totally alien culture, and above all the ever-present and unavoidable police surveillance. My wife and I found it possible to adjust to all this by an awareness of what the surveillance was and how to circumvent it. But it did require a long experience of the country and I felt a good deal of sympathy for many of the staff who came unprepared for a fairly brief tour of duty and who could hardly wait to leave. Fortunately, the case was not often repeated of one officer whose wife did not even unpack her suitcases for the first six months of their stay in the desperate hope that something would happen to have her husband transferred to another post.

Communications with the outside world were not easy. To

telephone abroad, one had to go to the central telephone station and place a call from there, although by the mid-1960s the situation improved and it was possible to do this from the embassy. Conversations were often difficult because of the strain put on the line by the censors who were listening in. Inn the mid-1970s direct dialing was introduced but was abandoned after a while because of the possibilities this gave for private citizens to telephone directly abroad.

For confidential communications, we relied on secret cypher messages sent very rapidly by leased line. In the early sixties our cyphers had been acquired by the KGB through a Canadian code clerk who had been recruited by a Soviet girl-friend. We were not alone, as they also succeeded in obtaining the Japanese and Swedish cyphers at the same time. By the mid-sixties, however, we had an unbreakable cypher system and messages were coded and decoded in a totally sound-proofed room. The line could have been interrupted by the Russians if they wanted, but they knew it would have invited immediate retaliation by the Canadian authorities against their embassy in Ottawa. Mail came in normally once a week with a courier who operated out of London. While fairly slow, at least it was sure.

One of the few occasions on which we were able to baffle the KGB occurred during the 1972 hockey games between Canada and Russia when three thousand Canadian fans descended on Moscow. The police had no idea of what to expect. One Soviet official said to me that it was the largest single group of foreigners ever to come to the country without guns in their hands. They were certain we had numerous intelligence agents infiltrated among the hockey buffs. At any rate they took no chances and surveilled them with care.

There was only one incident, involving a prominent Canadian, Edgar Bronfman Jr, and it was handled in a particularly Soviet way. I received an urgent call to receive a senior Soviet official, who turned up with two unidentified individuals who were clearly KGB. After much skirmishing they came to the point. Bronfman had been distributing skull caps and religious material at the Moscow synagogue. If he continued, the police would be obliged to arrest him. They were taking the unusual step of advising me because they knew he was a friend of mine and since they knew he was invited to the embassy for lunch that day I could perhaps talk to him. Otherwise the happy atmosphere of the games would be ruined. I strongly objected officially to this KGB offensive, but did speak to Bronfman and he, somewhat shaken, desisted.

Another problem with the KGB involved the issuance of visas for members of the Soviet embassy in Ottawa, the consulate general in Montreal, and occasionally visiting delegations. In view of the past history of these missions we had decided to limit the size of their personnel, a quota which was deeply resented by the Soviets but fully justified in view of the percentage of employees who were professional KGB or GRU agents. But the result was a constant effort to foist these agents on us as legitimate diplomats and an equally stubborn refusal by Canada to accept any of those identified as KGB. This became slightly embarrassing when Vladimir Suslov was appointed head of the Second European Department which dealt with Canada in the Foreign Ministry. He had served for many years in the Soviet delegation to the United Nations in New York, had been identified as KGB, and was so listed in John Barron's book KGB, published in 1974. There was only one sensible solution and that was to decide that Suslov had been co-opted by the KGB in New York, that he was not a professional agent, and that in any case it would have been totally counter-productive to treat him as an agent.

This problem also arose in 1975 in an intense form when it became clear that two key officials in the Soviet Olympic Games, S.S. Pavlov and Alexander Gresko, were both KGB. Soviet participation in the 1976 Olympics in Montreal was, of course, very important but we were reluctant to admit these two individuals. We did refuse a visa in 1975 to Pavlov, but with the greatest of reluctance granted one to Gresko. The deputy foreign minister was scathing in the conversation I had with him over Pavlov, in which he alternated between belittling our counter-intelligence service as 'mere children,' ridiculing the idea that the Soviets would ever use people as senior as Pavlov for espionage purposes, and refusing to accept our right to dictate the composition of Soviet delegations. I insisted on the right to do so and suggested it might be possible out of two hundred and sixty million Russians to find a few who were not publicly identified as spies. My case had been undercut, unfortunately, by Prime Minister Trudeau who, in one of his more eccentric gestures, had received Gresko on his visit to Ottawa.

A quota on Soviet missions in Canada was maintained as one way of controlling the KGB, and as a means of bargaining for better conditions for the Canadian embassy in Moscow and for Canadian journalists who at one time numbered three: the representatives of CBC, the Canadian Press, and the *Toronto Telegram*, although all except the CBC disappeared as the expenses involved and the difficulties in reporting news grew. Peter Worthington, later editor of the *Toronto Sun*, had particular difficulty with the Soviet authorities and was constantly accused of writing libellous and inflammatory stories. He was not averse to provoking the Soviets. The embassy had a hockey team which played various Soviet ministries and Worthington insisted on wearing a sweater with the number 007.

But this soon turned into something deadly serious involving his official translator, Olga Farmakovskaya. She had managed to get permission to go on a Soviet cruise ship in the Mediterranean, jumped ship in Beirut, and asked for political asylum in Canada. It turned out that her husband was a lieutenant-colonel in the KGB and the latter reacted strongly. Worthington himself left before he could be expelled, but this did not prevent the Soviets from levelling accusations against him, the *Telegram*, and the embassy for complicity in the defection. This continued to rankle with the Russians, particularly as Worthington wasn't entirely innocent, and his successor was approached by the KGB with offers of cash to build up a case against Worthington and Farmakovskaya; and by the Press Department with threats of retaliation if he wrote 'anti-Soviet' articles, by which they meant concentrating his reporting on the seamier side of life in the Soviet Union.

Another difficult case involved a Canadian citizen of Russian origin, Mrs Asta Sokov, who on a visit to relatives made the mistake of attempting to smuggle jewellery and antiques out of the country and was arrested at Moscow airport. After six months' detention in Lefortovo prison, she was convicted and sentenced to eight years' imprisonment. I made frequent and strong pleas for leniency and finally in November she was released and permitted to return home, a distinctly chastened woman. The arrest and severe sentence for a minor charge were clearly intended by the police to discourage visitors in the future from attempting to circumvent Soviet regulations.

The minuscule Canadian Communist Party seemed to have an importance to the Russians out of all proportion to its significance. It did not seem to be used directly by the KGB, the Russians presumably having learned a lesson from the Gouzenko affair in 1945 when Sam Carr, then the only Communist member of the federal House of Commons, was exposed as being directly involved in nuclear espionage on behalf of the Russians. The party itself had no influence on the Canadian political scene and yet the CPSU spent a good deal of rare hard currency in supporting the Canadian communists. The answer seemed to lie in the party's mere existence. Being small, weak, and otherwise unimportant, it was totally dependent on Moscow and therefore could be counted on to support the Soviet line on any given subject. This was then reported back duly from the *Canadian Tribune*, the newspaper of the Canadian Communist Party, and published in the Soviet press, giving the impression that an important Canadian political party supported the Soviet Union.

This inflated view of the Canadian Communist Party was brought home to me when I was visiting the Crimea. Looking for the former palace of Prince Yusupov, we came across a vast park and a monumental gate which was closed. We had stopped to investigate when police suddenly appeared and told us to move on. Then, catching sight of the Canadian flag on the car, the police officer remarked: 'Your great leader has just been here.' Somewhat mystified, I could not quite believe that Pierre Trudeau, unpredictable as he often was, could have slipped unperceived into the Crimea. It was only later that I discovered that the palace had become a resort for leaders of friendly communist parties and that the person in question was William Kashtan, head of the Canadian Communist Party.

8

The Struggle for Human Rights

Russia has always been to a greater or lesser degree a police state, which justified its reliance on repressive measures as necessary to protect the homeland from the threat from abroad and the threat from within. In the Brezhnev era, in spite of the enormous increase in the military strength of the state, the concept of an alleged foreign threat, and its concomitant, a siege mentality, still existed. The heritage of slightly greater tolerance under Khrushchev had created the illusion among many that a measure of change was possible. Brezhnev was at heart a conformist but not a Stalinist. If repression during his rule seemed tougher, it was because the outside world was more aware of the activities of the dissidents. The response of the authorities was somewhat more sophisticated than in the past, but from the start of the Brezhnev regime there was little doubt that dissent of any kind would be crushed. And for this, a powerful KGB and militia were essential.

Human rights as we conceive them and the Soviet system are almost totally incompatible. Religion was, inevitably, anathema to the official dogma. While tolerated if the practitioners are sufficiently docile, it was savagely persecuted if it appeared a threat to the state. Nationalism also runs counter to the ideology, as communism is supposed to have replaced old-fashioned national aspirations. In practice, this meant nationalism on the part of the lesser groups, in particular the Balts, Ukrainians and Caucasians, whereas Russian nationalism was encouraged in order to reinforce the interests of the state and the party. Any musical, literary, or artistic manifestation which did not correspond to the official doctrine of socialist realism led to severe penalties. Any political opposition or even criticism of the system or the party was automatically subject to persecution because it was interpreted as rejection of a system which allegedly meets the requirements of all citizens.

In practice, this meant that persecution of human rights in the Soviet Union was total. There are many countries where political dissidents are persecuted, Chile for example; there are others where religious minorities are attacked, such as Iran; there are some where national minorities are suppressed, as in Iraq or Turkey. But there are few outside the communist world where *every* form of dissent is subject to active and continuing repression.

It often seemed odd to me that a state which had been in existence for over sixty years, had survived the most severe tests, and possessed probably the most powerful system of control and police ever developed, should be frightened of a few weak and unorganized critical voices. The answer was briefly that the Soviet leaders could not envisage criticism as anything but treason, nor permit even the slightest fissure in the edifice of power and privilege they had built up.

It was curious, therefore, that the Soviets accepted the Helsinki Final Act in August 1975, since it was clear that the articles on human rights could never be applied by them, nor have they been. These clauses were the price Moscow had to pay for what the Russians considered a legalization of the frontiers in central Europe and for strengthening détente with the West which was already beginning to falter. The Soviets also gambled that détente was sufficiently important to the West that we would not press them too hard on the issue of human rights. But they gravely miscalculated.

We did not hear very much in the West about dissent until Brezhnev came to power. All but the very bravest critics of the regime had been thoroughly cowed by the total terror of Stalin, and it was only under the relatively more relaxed rule of Khrushchev that various kinds of dissent began to stir to life. They only really surfaced in 1965, perhaps because it took a decade for the timid exponents of opposition to venture into action. Khrushchev, if he had remained in power, would probably have acted in no different way than Brezhnev in crushing dissent. He had used slightly more liberal tactics for his own purposes but, as he showed in the suppression of Hungary in 1956, he would have had no hesitation in destroying any opposition if he felt it endangered the regime.

There exists considerable confusion in the West about the nature of internal opposition to the Soviets because of the tendency to call it a dissident movement. There is not and never was such a thing as 'a movement,' and dissent involved only a tiny number of people divided into as many as a dozen different groupings and tendencies, of which the most numerous and, after 1970 the most active and successful, was formed by Jewish activists. They constituted a special category because while made up largely of Jews who wished to emigrate for religious or personal reasons, there were among them a number of political activists, particularly among the refuseniks, those whose exit visas had been refused and who were inevitably forced into opposition.

The establishment of the state of Israel, and more graphically the establishment of an Israeli legation headed by Golda Meir in Moscow in 1948, opened the eyes of Soviet Jewry to the Zionist alternative. Stalin recognized the state of Israel and established diplomatic relations primarily with the aim of hastening the process of disintegration of Western influence, which he thought would result from injecting an alien presence into the Arab world. In this he was undoubtedly right, but he miscalculated the effect on what he had every reason to think were the cowed and semi-assimilated Jews of the Soviet Union.

This new Jewish awareness of an alternative homeland in Israel was met by growing Soviet suspicion of anyone who looked beyond the frontiers of the Soviet Union for support or comfort. There was, of course, no question under Khrushchev of mass emigration of Jews to Israel, or indeed of anyone else. To apply for permission to leave the communist 'paradise' was in itself an act of treason and few had the courage or foolhardiness to take this suicidal step. Yet one of the contradictions in the Soviet system is that a small trickle of Soviet Jews, even during and after the 1967 war, was permitted to leave.

The Soviets officially proclaimed a Russian 'homeland' for the Jews in 1934, but it was a cruel joke: Birobidzhan, the Jewish Autonomous Oblast, some thirty-six thousand square kilometres of swamp and forest on the Amur River in a bleak area of southern Siberia, on the Chinese frontier. When it was first offered to the Jews in 1928 as a place for colonization, it contained only a small population, mostly Korean, Kazakh, and Tungu. Ironically, one of the reasons given for the choice of Birobidzhan was to strengthen the defences of the Soviet Union against a potential enemy in Asia. But its remote location, its harsh climate and lack of any resources made it unlikely to appeal to many Jews as a practical alternative to Palestine. The Soviet intention of creating a Siberian ghetto was clear from the anti-Zionist propaganda which accompanied the proclamation of the 'homeland.'

Perhaps as many as fifty thousand Jews actually went to Birobidzhan before the war, but most of them managed to leave. After the war, the Jewish Anti-Fascist Committee in Moscow was active in trying to arrange immigration to Birobidzhan and in the period 1946–8 some six thousand Jews arrived. But in 1948, with the creation of Israel, the authorities closed down all Jewish institutions and immigration ended. The last available statistics in 1959 showed that there were 14,269 Jews, or 8.8 per cent of the population of the area. When I passed through the small town of Birobidzhan in February 1967, the only trace of Jewishness was a rather pathetic sign in Hebrew on the railway platform.

The wars of 1967 and 1973, particularly the Six-Day War, inevitably had an impact on the plight of Jews in the Soviet Union. The government's aim for many years had been to detach Soviet Jews from their religion and above all their attachment to the extra-national element, Zionism. They were prepared to accept in the Party and even in non-political positions of responsibility only those Jews who were prepared to renounce their religion and their national feeling. The Six-Day War retarded such assimilation by enhancing Jewish pride and their national and religious feeling of identification with Israel, even though nearly all the Soviet Jews I met were also thoroughly steeped in Russian history and literature. Thus the government felt bound to increase its attack on Zionism and interpreted almost any sign of Jewish interest in Israel as support for Zionism. This quickly led to an increase in covert anti-semitism: the decline in admittance of Jews to institutions of higher learning, the closing of doors in many professions, ostracism by Russians.

As a result, interest in emigration became more marked, in many cases not out of religious conviction but out of despair that as Jews they were going to be denied a share of the future in Russia. And behind that was the never very distant memory of the tsarist pogroms and the anti-Jewish obsession of Stalin. It is doubtful that very many Soviet Jews would have risked demanding the right to emigrate had it not been for the Six-Day War, the attention paid to the problem abroad, the courage of the individual dissidents who first demanded the strict observance of the Soviet constitution guaranteeing the freedom to emigrate, and the gradual evolution of the Soviet system away from Stalinism.

The demands of the Soviet Jews to emigrate to Israel were on the surface easier to meet than those of other nationalities. To accede to the demands of the Baltic nationalists or the Ukrainians would have meant agreeing to the weakening or dismembering of the Soviet state. But to accede to the Jewish aims meant creating an uncomfortable precedent for other discontented elements in the country. And the Jewish demands to emigrate raised in an uncomfortable way the whole question of human rights in the Soviet Union.

The problem became ultimately linked to that of détente. Almost fourteen thousand Jews were allowed to emigrate in 1971, although the Soviet authorities played down the actual numbers. It seems likely that the principal reason for the relatively large number of emigrants that year was to fend off international pressure. But of crucial importance, of course, was the improvement in U.S.-Soviet relations in 1972 in which Jewish emigration became the key element. Without détente, it is difficult to imagine that the Soviets would have allowed the considerable emigration that took place in the succeeding years.

The Soviet tactic was to combine strong deterrents intended to discourage applications for exit visas with a trickle of emigrants, carefully screened so that a very high proportion came from rural areas and provincial cities rather than the large cities where the highly educated Jews were concentrated. The procedure for emigrating became humiliating, often dangerous, and expensive (in 1971, for example, the cost of an exit visa was four hundred roubles plus five hundred roubles for withdrawal of Soviet citizenship – this at a time when the average monthly wage was one hundred and thirty roubles). The applicant usually was dismissed from his job and then persecuted for parasitism because he was not working. Police harassment and interrogations were often the case, with public trials frequent in order to discourage others. The more famous cases over the years were those of the poet Joseph Brodsky, accused of parasitism, Edvard Kusnetsov, who attempted to hijack a plane to escape, and Anatoli Shcharansky, accused of espionage.

Shcharansky's 1978 trial in Moscow was given considerable publicity, obviously to act as a warning. The prosecutor frequently referred to the dangers for Soviet citizens of the 'influence of Western centres of ideological subversion and special services' which camouflaged their real intentions by calling them defence of human rights, 'vividly demonstrated by the case of Shcharansky.' Shcharansky made a moving rebuttal in his own defence and a plea for Soviet Jews, and insisted that the trial was pure theatre. He was sentenced to thirteen years for treason.

On the last day of the trial, a courageous group of nearly one hundred supporters gathered outside the courthouse, Shcharansky's mother read to the Western press a letter to President Jimmy Carter thanking him for his help and appealing for assistance to see her son before his imprisonment. Andrei Sakharov and his wife also appeared and attempted to get Shcharansky's mother into the courthouse, resulting in the unusual spectacle for Moscow of a minor roughhouse with the militia. When the crowd was told of the length of Shcharansky's prison term, they broke into song – the national anthem of Israel. Brodsky and Kuznetsov were eventually released and expelled, the former to become the 1987 Nobel Prize winner for literature, and even Shcharansky was finally permitted to leave.

How to help the Soviet Jews has been an ongoing concern for

Western governments. I always advised a general policy of focusing attention on the situation of Soviet Jewry in hopes of modifying Soviet persecution. Whenever possible, we intervened in cases of dissidents or refuseniks to plead for clemency on the grounds that a large segment of our population was legitimately interested in the fate of the arrested people and that their release would remove an obstacle to good relations between our countries. The Soviets inevitably replied by rejecting this argument and accusing us of meddling in their internal affairs. But seldom did these démarches damage our political relations and they probably had some beneficial long-term effect on the plight of Jewish dissidents.

The anti-semitism of the average Russian in almost every position in life is deeply ingrained and even many of the assimilated Jews were reluctant to admit that they were of Jewish origin. In Khabarovsk, in the dead of the Siberian winter, a senior member of the city council, who had regaled us for several days with inflated economic statistics and boasting about Soviet achievements, suddenly blurted out that he was Jewish and begged for real information about Israel and about the life of Jews in Canada. Alexander Barshai, the brilliant conductor of the Barshai Chamber Orchestra, made no secret to me of his ambitions to go to Israel. But most of the extraordinary musicians who were the jewel of the Moscow musical firmament, such as Emil Gilels, Leonid Kogan and the Oistrakhs, father and son, were not disposed to talk of their problem.

Those few Jewish intellectuals I met who were prepared to talk were agonizing examples of the dilemma of the Jews. Nearly all would have preferred to stay in the Soviet Union and be loyal citizens in an intellectual atmosphere to which they were accustomed, if the Soviet authorities had made it possible. But increasingly over the years it became apparent that it was not going to be feasible to reconcile the basic elements of their faith and serve the state. And this was not even possible for most of those who would have liked to assimilate, or who were not practising Jews, because of the deep-seated Russian prejudice against them.

The visible evidence of the drama could be seen every day: at the Dutch embassy where the long line of emigrants awaited their

Israeli visas, the length of the line a sure indication of the varying attitude of the Soviet government; and at the Moscow synagogue where, in spite of constant provocation and harassment, the faithful still came to pray. The other visible evidence came in the form of the show trials of Jewish refuseniks or dissidents who had become too troublesome and were sent to concentration camps as a warning to others. The remarkable thing was the way in which these warnings did not seem to deter others who came forward to take their places.

The Yom Kippur War of 1973 did not affect the rate of Jewish emigration as much as the Jackson-Vannik amendment in the United States Congress tying Jewish emigration to the improvement in Soviet trade relations and to the granting of Most Favoured Nation status to the Soviet Union. The Russians seethed with rage at this, interpreting it as an unjustifiable interference in their internal affairs, an attempt to link two completely unrelated subjects, and a humiliating affront. They held their peace for some time, but in mid-December 1975 they denounced the trade bill as amended, in a letter from Gromyko to Kissinger and in a public statement.

While Russian reaction to the amendment was a key factor in the retreat from détente, it is not easy to judge its importance in terms of Jewish emigration. Certainly the number of exit visas in 1976, between thirteen and fourteen thousand, was marginally better than in 1975. From 1968 to the end of 1976, more than 150,000 were granted permission to leave, with a high in 1979 of 51,320. From then on, the numbers declined rapidly and in 1984 it was only 896. Of those leaving since 1975, a large number, perhaps 50 per cent, did not bother to go on to Israel before choosing another destination. The Soviets issued travel documents on the basis of 'repatriation' and were certainly aware of the drop-out rate. It did not seem to bother them that the actual destination was not Israel, although it greatly disturbed the Israeli authorities.

Figures differ about the size of the Jewish community remaining in the Soviet Union, but approximately three million is a fair guess. There seems little likelihood that the Soviets will be able to reconcile their hope of assimilating the Jews with their long-standing anti-semitism, or that they will be able to offer sufficient prospects of equality to the Soviet Jews to make them renounce their attachment to the international Jewish community and Israel. It is obvious, therefore, that the problem is going to preoccupy Western governments and their public as well as Israel for a long time.

Another important category of dissent consisted of the political activists who, while only a handful of individuals, alarmed the authorities because of the potential for opposition they represented. Almost every opponent of the regime had a different prescription for the Soviet Union, ranging from Solzhenitsyn who advocated a return to the purer forms of Russian Slav society as it existed in a kind of fantasy picture of nineteenth-century Russia, to Roy Medvedev who believed in communism but thought the system only needed structural and ideological improvements. In between existed every variety of political view from those who rejected the system totally such as Vladimir Bukovsky, Andrei Amalrik, Alexander Zinoviev and others, to Andrei Sinyavsky who remained a communist of sorts. But there was no 'movement,' since they were united only in wishing to change the present regime.

A kind of outgrowth of the political activists was represented by those Russians who seized on the Helsinki Act as a means of broadening the tolerance of the regime towards dissent in general. They formed a rather loose group intended to monitor the Soviet observance of human rights as spelled out in the Helsinki Document. Also associated with them were the *Chronicle of Current Events*, a *samizdat* (illegal) publication which tried to keep Russians and the outside world informed of Soviet political repression, and the Solzhenitsyn Fund, set up by Solzhenitsyn as a means of helping these groups financially.

Soviet attacks against all these dissidents were constant but the degree of pressure varied. Many of those who were arrested were subsequently exchanged for Soviet spies in the West or for Western communists – Bukovsky for Corvalan, the head of the Chilean Communist Party in 1976, for example. The more troublesome dissidents were simply physically dumped abroad. The Helsinki monitoring groups in Moscow and Kiev were nearly all arrested, as were all the members of the sub-group on psychiatric abuses. The

Ukrainian member, Oksan Mechko, was himself confined to a psychiatric prison. Other categories of dissent consisted of small and struggling groups such as SMOT, which attempted to defend trade union rights, another group protesting against the treatment of war invalids, and a fledgling feminist movement. The leading members of SMOT were soon arrested and three of the five women who contributed to an unofficial publication, 'Woman and Russia,' and who founded the Maria feminist club in March 1980, were expelled.

Another dissident group was composed of persons fighting for the right to practise their religion. Although article 52 of the Soviet constitution guarantees the 'right to profess any religion,' the ideology of Marxism-Leninism rejects religious beliefs and practices as incompatible with Soviet man. Since, however, it had proved impossible completely to destroy religious faith, there has been a very limited tolerance of religion, governed in part by the degree of internationalism involved, and the amount of foreign attention engendered. This means that religions with strong foreign ties (for example, the Roman Catholic Church and the Jewish temples) were subject to more severe attacks than the purely national Russian Orthodox Church, or the Lutherans, with fundamentalists such as the Baptists and Pentecostalists somewhere between. Islam presents a special case, which did not begin to preoccupy the Soviet authorities until the revival of fanatical Islamic fundamentalism in Iran, and the important politico-religious role it has played in the anti-Soviet anti-communist resistance in Afghanistan.

The persecution of the Catholic Church has been most severe in two areas: western Ukraine, where the Uniate Catholic Church has been almost destroyed; and in Lithuania. In both areas the religion was closely identified with Ukrainian and Lithuanian nationalism. Even so, we continued to receive information in the embassy about stubborn efforts in Lithuania to maintain the faith, and news of the arrest of active laymen and priests.

Protestant religious groups were also subject to persecution. The resistance of Pentecostalists has been publicized by the case of the Vashenko and Chemykhalov families who took refuge in the American embassy in 1978. Baptists also were under constant pressure and subject to sudden arrests; those who refused to comply with the officially state-sponsored church association were often harassed and many sought to emigrate.

The Orthodox Church continued to exist in a more flourishing way because, in line with Russian tradition, it is controlled by the government, with its head and priests chosen, and paid for, by the state. The three small seminaries allowed to function are state organizations. Priests who tried to infuse something more spiritual into their religious tasks invariably ran afoul not only of the KGB but of their own superiors. Under these difficult conditions a limited number of churches were open, and almost always full of worshippers or, increasingly, non-believers who were drawn to the beautiful Orthodox services out of curiosity or a feeling of identification with the Russian past.

Dissent from the official political line and freedom of religious thought were particularly difficult for Orthodox priests because of the identification of their religion with Russian nationalism. The case of Father Dudko illustrated the problem. An outspoken supporter of human rights and religious freedom, he was arrested in January 1980 for anti-Soviet agitation and propaganda. In June Dudko appeared on prime-time television to 'confess' his anti-Soviet activities, to repudiate his previous views, and to denounce his Western contacts who, he claimed, had first stimulated his activities and later directed them from abroad. In a very Russian xenophobic fashion, he portrayed himself as a classic example of a Soviet citizen falling into the trap of a Western agent through contact with foreigners. He cited among others Christopher Wren of the *New York Times* and members of the Swiss-based International Christian Movement for the Freedom of the Faith. Dudko's message was widely reproduced as a warning to Soviet citizens to avoid the thousands of foreigners who were about to descend on Moscow for the Olympics. We assumed his 'confession' was made under duress, realizing how difficult it would be for an Orthodox priest to resist the combined pressure of the KGB and his own superiors who were salaried appointees of the state.

With only approximately 53 per cent of the Soviet population of Russian origin, the Soviet leadership does not take lightly the problem of the lesser nationalities. Among the leaders themselves, all who occupied key positions by 1965 were Russians. The nationalities which gave the Russians the greatest difficulty were the Ukrainians, the Baltic peoples, and the Tartars. The three Baltic republics, incorporated in the Soviet Union by direct military intervention in 1940, and reincorporated in 1945 at the end of World War Two, constituted the most European part of the country. In spite of being subjected to persecution for four decades, they still resisted Russification, which was carried out in part by direct Russian immigration into the three republics, in part by various incentives to young people to accept the Soviet regime and to become assimilated culturally. It was remarkable that, in spite of the tremendous power of intimidation of the Soviet state, the small population, and the very feeble means of resistance of the Baltic peoples, the Soviets have not proved more successful. Resistance was strongest in Estonia, in part because of the proximity of their blood brothers, the Finns, just across the Gulf of Finland, and in Lithuania, where the Catholic Church, in spite of severe persecution, was a strong rallying point for Lithuanian nationalism.

The resistance of the Tartars is better known than that of other Asian nationalities because of their forced evacuation from the Crimea after the retreat of the Germans in 1944. Dispersed throughout Siberia, they persisted in their efforts to return to the Crimea, which in the meantime had been resettled by Russians and Ukrainians. In my visit to the old Tartar capital of Bakshisarai in 1978, I found no Tartars at all. Their principal defender, General Grigorenko, was finally silenced, first by incarceration in a psychiatric prison, then by a term of forced labour, and finally by expulsion from the Soviet Union.

The Moslem resistance to the Soviet forces in Afghanistan and the call to a return to primitive Moslem virtues by Ayatollah Khomeini in Iran have had little effect as yet, although it is something the Russians are watching with great care. The Armenians and Georgians occupied a fairly privileged place in the Soviet state, but there were rumblings of nationalist discontent in Georgia from time to time, usually related to the question of language rights. As I was frequently told in my several visits to Georgia, young Georgians were torn between choosing to make a career in the Soviet Union itself, which effectively meant living and working in Moscow, or confining their ambitions to the narrow confines of Georgia where they could resist assimilation and contribute to the preservation of Georgian culture.

However, it is Ukraine, the largest and richest of the lesser republics with a long and proud history of its own, that has always been regarded as a potential source of trouble by the Russians. It was a severe shock for Stalin when a sizeable number of Ukrainians welcomed the German invaders in 1941 and a fair number were recruited into a Ukrainian freedom army. The hatred of Stalin was turned against them after the Germans were driven out. The Ukrainians were cowed into silence, but news filtered through to us from time to time of the arrest of nationalists. The expulsion of the most active nationalist, Valentin Moroz, after many years in prison, meant the decapitation of active opposition. The Russians also used more subtle means to destroy Ukrainian nationalism. There was an active campaign to discourage the idea that Ukrainian was a distinct language and it was made materially profitable for Ukrainians to speak and use Russian. At the same time, there was considerable immigration of Russians into the larger cities so that by now Kiev, Odessa, and Kharkov are almost as much Russian as Ukrainian cities. At the same time the Ukrainians were encouraged to leave Ukraine and settle in the Baltic states and in the Virgin Lands of northern Kazakhstan.

A sign of what the attitude of the authorities towards the writers was to be came very early in the Brezhnev reign in the official reaction to some efforts to bypass the censorship. The novelist Valery Tarsis was expelled and the writers Andrei Sinyavsky and Yuri Daniel were condemned to harsh prison terms for publishing abroad books not particularly critical of the Soviet Union but without the prior authorization of the Soviet authorities. A number of writers expressed some reservations about the Soviet invasion of Czechoslovakia in 1968 and were severely persecuted. The fact that some intellectuals opposed the invasion reinforced the influence of the hard-liners in the establishment who saw a lesson for themselves in the Czech experiment. The result was a clamping down on every variety of dissent.

In 1972 the trial and condemnation of the writer Vladimir

Bukovsky took place, followed the next year by the expulsion of Solzhenitsyn and somewhat later of the great cellist Mstislav Rostropovich, who had had the courage to give Solzhenitsyn asylum in his house.

In 1979 some young writers tried to publish their works, mostly apolitical and inoffensive, in a journal called the *Almanac Metropole*, published outside the official system. They were nearly all hounded out of literary life and some, such as Aksionov and Voinovich, were expelled from the Soviet Union. The poets Andrei Voznesensky and Bella Akhmadulina were too famous and popular to be punished in this way, but they suffered almost total ostracism for some time for having contributed to the *Almanac*. In a petty act of revenge by the bureaucracy, the husband of Akhmadulina was expelled from his job as a leading choreographer of the Bolshoi Ballet. Both Voznesensky and Akhmadulina realized they had pushed the limits of tolerance of the rigid literary bureaucracy too far and they were saddened at the violent reaction. They had hoped to encourage younger writers who had no way of breaking into print and believed their prestige would help to cushion the official reaction. Akhmadulina, a lovely half-Tartar, half-Russian woman, tough and courageous under her fragile appearance, was shattered by the punishment administered to the less well-known writers and to her husband. It was clear that the Soviets would not tolerate any infraction of the rules and the harsh reaction was meant as a warning both to the younger writers and those in the establishment to toe the line.

It is hard for us to visualize the effect of ostracism on those intellectuals who had offended the bureaucracy, very often, as in the case of the *Metropole* writers, by what we would consider minor infractions. In the days of Stalin, the punishment would have been Siberia, so that mere ostracism was in a peculiarly Soviet way a vast improvement. For some artists it meant expulsion from the Writers' Union or the equivalent organizations of composers, musicians, actors, and so on. This involved the loss of any direct income and the inability to publish or perform. They managed to survive somehow through the generosity of friends, but the psychological effect of being treated as non-persons by the society in which they had played a not unimportant role was immense.

The hardier found ways of recovering. The poet Evtushenko, for example, who was ostracised in 1968 for criticizing the invasion of Czechoslovakia, remained out of sight for about a year and then gradually made his reappearance by writing some poems acceptable to the establishment. Akhmadulina, before the *Metropole* affair, had paid for political indiscretions by exile to Georgia, where she spent her time translating Georgian poetry into Russian. Voznesensky did not publish for a while after the *Metropole* and was not permitted to go abroad until he made amends. The possibility of depriving artists of foreign travel was in fact one of the more effective ways of keeping them in line.

The defection of Mikhail Baryshnikov in Toronto in June 1974 during a tour of the Bolshoi Ballet was a severe blow to Soviet pride and to the Russian theatrical world. Baryshnikov was just becoming recognized as the most promising dancer in the country and he had an impeccable Russian background. A year later when I was in Leningrad, where Baryshnikov had made his career, a ballet specialist told me that everyone in the Kirov Ballet had burst into tears when they heard that he had defected. Another told me in some awe that Baryshnikov had really fooled the KGB. He had bought a car and an apartment which he had lavishly furnished, and it was on the basis that no one would abandon such wealth that he had been permitted to join the Canadian tour.

The Soviet authorities were convinced that the Canadian government together with the Montreal impresario Nicholas Kudriavtsev had engineered the defection. I had several stormy interviews with Soviet officials without being able to convince them that we were not responsible nor would we force Baryshnikov to return against his will. They finally dropped the accusations against the government, concentrating their venom instead on Kudriavtsev who, in spite of having done a great deal to build up cultural exchanges with the Soviet Union, was nearly bankrupted by the cancellation of a number of contracts by the Soviets.

The most famous defection was that of Svetlana Alliluyeva, Stalin's daughter. The Egyptian ambassador, Murad Ghaleb, knew her well and used often to visit her and her Indian husband in their unpretentious flat in Moscow. As far as Ghaleb knew, he and his wife were the only foreign friends of Svetlana outside the Indian embassy. Ghaleb had been a doctor and therefore studied with interest the health of her husband, Pradesh Singh, and Svetlana's personality, which he said at the time showed all the symptoms of schizophrenia. He was convinced this grew out of her relationship with her father. As the only child Stalin was even vaguely fond of, she grew up adoring him to the extent that during the period of the Khrushchev revelations of Stalin's crimes she refused for a long time to accept them as true. When she finally came to believe them, she turned to a very Russian kind of spirituality which, after her marriage to Singh, was transformed into an Indian type of mysticism. This period was marked by long monologues about the horrors her father had committed, alternating with sessions of reminiscences of her life with Stalin when she would produce dozens of photos of herself in her father's arms.

According to Ghaleb, she was wildly, hysterically in love with Singh, who was small, very dark, ugly, visibly dying from a very difficult disease, but a 'sweet and intelligent man.' Svetlana's attitude towards him was strictly Dostoyevskian. She would throw herself on him and cover him with kisses, forgetting that he had a lung disease which made breathing very hard. He also suffered from a truly dreadful eczema of the feet and legs. In front of guests Svetlana would take off his shoes and socks and embrace and kiss his feet as if in some way she were expiating the sins of her father.

After Singh's death in 1966, Svetlana was enveloped in a state of total hysteria and religious mysticism. Once she terrified Mrs Ghaleb, who was visiting her in her flat, by seizing her and crying out wildly, 'Can't you see him? He is here with me now.' She then set about with determination the process of getting permission to take her husband's ashes to be buried in his native village in India. Ghaleb is certain she did not marry Singh for the purpose of escaping and he felt after her defection that this idea did not really come to her until she reached India. He was particularly irritated with what she said about Kosygin in her book since it was his personal intervention which secured her exit visa. Indeed, Ghaleb was in Svetlana's flat when Kosygin telephoned personally to tell her she could leave. Ghaleb was convinced she would return to Russia some day. She is happy now, he said, but if she enters a period of melancholy she could slip back into her true spirit of

Russian mysticism and heed the call of the motherland. He proved a true prophet.

Whether or not Svetlana prepared her defection in advance, she was successful in hiding her true feelings, something the Russians became highly skilled at doing. For a number of years a Soviet historian, Mikhail Voslensky, called on me regularly to discuss developments and to pass on the Soviet version of events. We considered him a classical example of a KGB disinformation agent. Never once in all the years I knew him did he depart even slightly from the official line. But, after carefully preparing his credentials and getting himself included in a delegation of scholars to West Germany, he seized the first possible opportunity to defect. He seemed to have everything to lose since he was a member of the class of privileged officials and a member of the intelligentsia known as the Nomenklatura. His book on the subject describes in detail the life of relative ease enjoyed by the communist upper class which he abandoned. The dissimulation required to reconcile over many years this outwardly conformist good life with seething inner dissent is hard to imagine.

What never ceased to astound me was the immense courage of the handful of people who stood up to be counted in the face of the enormous power of the state and the repressive machinery of the KGB, and the inability of the Soviets in spite of the feeble numbers and widely diverging aims of the dissidents to eliminate criticism completely. When the first major crackdown occurred in 1965, the Soviets must have thought it would be easy to crush or intimidate their critics. But every time the heads were cut off, new flowers appeared. By the end of the Brezhnev era, however, the garden had been decimated and the situation seemed desperate. Attacks on the opposition had eroded the quality of the leaders and their morale and popular standing. Only Sakharov remained in his brave and lonely exile in Gorki.

Opposition to the regime will never disappear completely. It seems to be a concomitant of the Russian character to seek to fight against hopeless odds, to welcome martyrdom, to oppose the strength of the spirit against the power of materialist forces. Nevertheless, the following points must be kept in mind. The active dissenters are very few in number and divided in their aims. The chances of their upsetting the system or even seriously modifying it are practically non-existent. The dissatisfaction of large numbers of people is directed at the low standard of living and irritants and frictions in everyday life; it is not politically oriented and the aims of most of the dissidents, even if they are widely known, would be incomprehensible, if not actually distasteful, to the bulk of the population. Only nationalist feelings on the part of the non-Russian peoples, above all the Balts, the Ukrainians, and eventually the Asians, have any degree of popular support. But religious feeling has not been stamped out and it is not likely to disappear.

The problem of dissent, of human rights, is not going to go away and will be a permanent object of friction between the West and the Soviet Union. We would like to apply our moral standards to Russia as part of a coherent overall concept of the kind of relationship that ideally should exist between us. But the Soviets are not going to change their aims or their society and will continue to exclude any place for human rights as we conceive them. The dilemma is therefore to fit our ideals into this brutal reality.

In September 1977 a formal session was organized in the Bolshoi Theatre, in the presence of all the Politburo and leading officials of the Party and, significantly, all the heads of East European diplomatic missions, to mark the one hundredth anniversary of Felix Dzjerzhinsky, the first security chief of the Soviet state. Yuri Andropov, at that time head of the KGB, gave the eulogy of his illustrious predecessor. He praised Dzjerzhinsky, the creator of the 'Red Terror' after the assassination attempt on Lenin's life, as a hero of the revolution and devoted to furthering communist ideals. The message was loud and clear. Sixty years before, in the midst of adversity, the Party relied on unity and the drastic measures of the 'security organs' to defend the revolution. Now, confronted with similar hostile forces, the same tools existed to do the job again.

And if we foreigners, or the average Russian, ever felt inclined to minimize the role of the KGB, we were constantly reminded of it by the huge statue of Dzjerzhinsky standing in front of the monumental building housing the Committee on State Security and flanked on the other side by Detski Mir, the Children's World department store. It is the kind of contrast which characterizes so much of life in Soviet Russia.

PART THREE

Russia's Problems

9

Internal Problems: The Flawed Giant

The economy of the Soviet Union is a mystery to most foreign observers. I once received a visit from a brilliant West European ambassador who had had no previous experience of the country but was a recognized economic expert. He had spent six months on a study of the Soviet economy and wished to discuss it with me. He outlined with great clarity and precise logic what was wrong with the economy and concluded that in a couple of years at the outside it was going to collapse. Each one of his reasons for the weakness of the system was flawlessly logical, but his conclusion was all wrong. As I said to him, it is impossible to apply the logic of Western economists to the Soviet Union. It can only be compared to the bumble bee which, according to the laws of aerodynamics, cannot fly. But somehow it does.

The contradictions in the Soviet economy which foreign observers find difficult to reconcile are primarily the difference between the relative success up to the 1970s in creating a solid base in heavy industry, including the industrial-military complex, and the dismal failures in the manufacturing and service industries, and in agriculture. When Khrushchev boasted of overtaking the United States economy in a decade, he was thinking in terms of the traditional indices of economic power: the production of coal, iron, steel, shipbuilding, oil and gas, electrical energy, and so on. And by the 1970s the Soviet Union had caught up and in some ways surpassed the West. But suddenly they realized that the rules of the game had changed. Kosygin once complained to me that just at the moment they had achieved pre-eminence in heavy industry, the computer revolution and the miniaturization of manufacturing had introduced a new element which he, at any rate, and certainly the technological experts in the Academy of Sciences, recognized put them at a vast disadvantage compared to the West and Japan.

It was simple enough for a highly centralized state to organize the leap forward permitting a great increase in the traditional heavy industries. The problem lay in light industry, distribution, and agriculture. It was easy to make provision for the production of a given number of tons of coal, or trucks, or tanks. But the problem became more complicated when the society became more urbanized, more sophisticated, more demanding. During my entire stay in Russia, the Soviets grappled with the problem of how to increase the quality and quantity of manufactured goods, given that this required greater flexibility in establishing a relationship between supply and demand, while maintaining total centralized control of economic production.

In the sixties Kosygin told me that one of the major problems in the economic system was to persuade managers to adjust to new situations created by an increasingly sophisticated society. He admitted that it was very difficult to convince managers who had been educated to be loyal and efficient executors of orders from Moscow that they were also expected to exercise initiative and imagination. He mused aloud that a school for management might be required.

On the eve of the Twenty-Fourth Congress of the CPSU in 1971, it appeared – an Institute of Economic Management. The new school was to study socio-economic sciences, economic and mathematical methods of planning and forecasting, automated systems of management, and psychological aspects of management. It was obviously not going to be a Soviet version of the Harvard Business School, nor did a description of it in *Socialist Industry* fill one with confidence that it would break the solid conservative mould of Soviet managers. 'The characteristic feature of the Institute,' it said, 'is that students (who were to include ministers and deputy ministers) will be taught not management in general but the application of scientific methods' (by which was meant Marxism-Leninism). In March of 1985 a member of the Soviet Academy of Sciences, writing in *Izvestia*, urged the need for a Western-type school of business administration the purpose of which seemed to be the same as the Institute of Economic Management. This would indicate that the latter had not proved very successful in drumming modern management methods into the heads of Soviet ministries and enterprises.

By the time of the Twenty-Fourth Congress the economic and social dysfunction of Soviet society was becoming clearer. When the results of the 1970 census were published they showed that 44 per cent of the population still lived on the land, approximately the same percentage as in Canada in 1917. The situation demonstrated that the standard of living was rising far too slowly even for the increasingly urban class of educated and technically advanced people, and the congress did little to convince them that early progress was likely. It was another masterpiece of ennui and, in view of the rapid increase in the proportion of youth (50 per cent under thirty years of age), it was remarkable that no effort was made to find an ideological theme which might have provided some inspiration for them, as indeed for the rest of the population. I concluded that somehow a policy of drift coincided with the wishes of the average Russian, who preferred to think that the uninspired and barely changing leadership was a guarantee that tough and unpopular measures would not be taken. Although the Russians respond to strong leadership, their experiences of it in the past probably led them in the seventies to prefer mediocrity.

The 1971 congress did, however, recognize the need to do something to raise living standards, to implement the technological revolution, to improve the system of economic management, and to increase agricultural productivity, and these goals were repeated in the new five-year plan. By the time of the next congress in 1976, it was apparent that they had remained empty words. Indeed, they had to, since the government was not prepared to tackle the questions of economic centralism, of financial incentives, or even of relating the cost of production to the price to the consumer.

What had been particularly noticeable between the two congresses was a small but visible increase in the urban standard of living, at least in the big cities. Big-city sprawl in the form of endless uniform apartment buildings marked the growth of Moscow and the other large cities, meeting, if rather shoddily, the enormous need for new housing. While the birthrate of Moscovites was very low, the population had increased to at least eight million by 1980 through immigration from the provinces. In the seventies the principle of condominium apartments was introduced. The struggle to acquire one's own apartment was intense and every conceivable bit of pull was exercised to be given the right to bid on one. The other most important sign of progress was the Zhiguli passenger car, known in the West as the Lada.

The Zhiguli was constructed by Fiat of Turin in a new plant in a new town on the Volga called Togliattigrad, after the Italian communist leader. The Zhiguli was based on the Italian original but with a more rugged interior and a heavier chassis to withstand the rigours of the Russian winter. A simple but useful car, it was far superior to anything then available on the Soviet market. Acquisition of a Zhiguli immediately became a status symbol and the factory could nowhere meet the local demand, particularly since a determined effort was made to sell them abroad for hard currency.

The Italian ambassador told me that Fiat had decided to seek the Soviet contract primarily to keep their communist-dominated trade unions happy, but the honeymoon lasted only a few months. At the beginning, the Italian communists were quick to volunteer to work in Togliattigrad, but a few months' exposure to Soviet working conditions was enough to diminish their enthusiasm. In the end, the Fiat experiment probably did the management no good at all with their workers, who strongly resented being sent to the Togliattigrad salt mines.

Togliattigrad lay in an area officially closed to foreign travel. For years, in spite of constant pressure, no one from the Italian embassy could get permission to go there, although there were hundreds of Fiat employees on the spot. The KGB could see no contradiction in this and argued that they could not make an exception in favour of one embassy. The reply that Togliattigrad could not have many secrets any more appeared to carry no weight with the KGB.

As part of the effort to raise living standards and modernize Moscow, the Soviets opened a number of hard-currency shops and restaurants, which were restricted to foreigners able to pay in hard currency, or Soviet citizens who were allowed the privilege of buying coupons for use in these shops or who were given coupons as a bonus for good behaviour. In 1965 a shop reserved for diplomats and foreign journalists was opened, the forerunner of the tourist Beriozka shops. The diplomatic store heralded its appearance by the issue of a glossy catalogue listing a few Soviet products such as wine, vodka, tinned goods, and a small assortment of imported fruits and vegetables that could be bought with hard currencies, at prices much lower than in Soviet shops. I at once bet that half the goods listed would be unavailable, and won easily. But I ordered vodka and was asked to pay in foreign currency, in bills. I pointed out that, according to Soviet law, it was illegal to import cash into the Soviet Union and they were therefore breaking the law. They finally agreed to take my cheque. A few days later I received at the embassy a small package of apples from the shop with the explanation that they had over-charged me by forty-four kopeks. They assured me that they were very fine Chinese apples. The following day the director phoned to apologize that they had made a mistake. The apples were Bulgarian, not Chinese. I said I had eaten all forty-four kopeks' worth without noticing the difference.

The hard currency restaurants caused so many problems I could never understand what advantage the Soviets saw in them. To start with, foreign 'comrades' found it difficult to find the right kind of ideological justification for this discrimination and visitors from East European countries were often infuriated. Shortly after the National Hotel hard-currency restaurant opened I saw two well-dressed men enter. The headwaiter asked in what currency they would pay: 'German marks,' they answered. 'East or West?' he asked. When they replied 'East,' they were unceremoniously shown the door.

The average Russian was equally irritated at these shops, where he imagined all sorts of unattainable goodies lay beyond his reach. He could justify special treatment for foreigners but not for Soviet citizens, and resentment against the special 'closed shops,' clinics, summer resorts, and other privileges accorded the better-off Soviets, though usually concealed, rankled deeply. Once we went on a picnic outside Moscow in the official car. Some Russians glared at us for some time and finally one, brave through drink, clearly thinking we were members of the privileged class, berated us for living like tsars while most Russians lived miserably. On another occasion, I had a conversation with a craftsman named Zhukov. I asked him if he was related ot the World War Two field marshal, to which he replied: 'Do you think I would be a worker if I were?' Slightly tipsy, he launched into a long harangue against the privileges of the upper class. He saw only two groups in the Soviet Union – the workers and the non-workers. The ambition of everyone was to get a job where one sat in an office and did nothing. No one wanted to work, he said, partly because of poor wages and lack of other incentives, partly because of working-class envy of the upper class.

This envy and distrust of authority was evident everywhere. It was kept under control partly by the Russian tendency to political apathy and fear of the state, and partly because, up to the late 1970s, workers and farmers had hoped that life would gradually get better and that their children would have better opportunities than they had had. But by the end of the decade the standard of living was not improving (in some areas it was actually declining) and the possibility that the average Russian worker's child could break into the upper class was fading. An unusually frank 1975 Soviet film illustrated the problem. It concerned a girl in a working-class family who completes high school and decides as a good communist she should work like her father in a factory. But like so many youths of her generation, she is better looking and more cultured than her parents. Thus, when she meets a young man in a café, he thinks she is 'one of us' (that is, a member of the elite), and starts to date her. When he eventually discovers that she is a factory worker, and therefore socially inferior, he drops her like a hot potato.

Resentment grew over the way in which this new class was becoming a closed and hereditary society. It was unheard of for a child of the Nomenklatura to drop down in the social scale, and almost as difficult for a working-class child, unless he had exceptional abilities, to rise above his family's status. Children of the communist upper class had certain obvious advantages to start with. They were better clothed, better fed and housed; they did not have to live in minuscule apartments without much opportunity or incentive to study; they had a better primary and secondary education so that their chances of getting into university were much greater. There were few institutes of higher education which would refuse admission to a child of the elite, no matter how unqualified he was.

Far from moving to eradicate these class distinctions, the government was tending towards formalizing them, actually abandoning the sacred concept that all citizens should have access to higher education. A new law in 1984 introduced the principle of selection, at a fairly early age, radically restricting entrance to universities. Since a state diploma is essential for a career in the Soviet Union, the measure was of immense importance.

In the past these privileges had been accepted as due compensation for the responsibilities of power, which most Russians would not have wanted. It was considered part of the austere period of communism which would disappear or at least decline as the standard of living of all the people rose. But in the late seventies, this expectation was clearly not being realized, while the number of people entitled to special treatment increased. It was one thing to accept privileges for a handful of men at the top; when this handful became many thousands, resentment was bound to increase, particularly against the way in which the Nomenklatura tended to form a new closed class into which access became very difficult except for the most talented.

The Russians are not at heart egalitarian. The idea of 'them' and 'us,' whether tsar or commissar, was accepted as the normal condition of things. But sixty years after the revolution the gap between the rich and powerful and the poor and defenceless was growing and becoming institutionalized. In many ways, the material and social differences were greater than in the West. The gap between a United Auto worker and a plant manager in the West is probably less than that of a Soviet factory worker or collective farm worker and his director. There is no way in which the average Russian can know this and he has no standard of comparison. One of the reasons for the Soviet leaders' uneasiness about liberal reforms in Poland and Czechoslovakia was the danger that workers' protests in so-called 'brotherly' lands might infiltrate to the Russians. There was not much likelihood of that during my time in the Soviet Union, but the Russians are an intelligent, if somewhat passive, people and the illusion of egalitarianism was beginning to disappear in the face of increasing evidence to the contrary.

It was always hard to convince casual tourists or official delegations of the real standard of living in the country, since they usually only saw Moscow and Leningrad, which are quite unrepresentative of the real Russia. They are great cities with a rich cultural life: dozens of theatres, opera, ballet, symphony orchestras, and a great concentration of artistic talent, even if stifled in the cocoon of socialist realism and the Soviet cultural bureaucracy. And they throb with the sensation of power. The limited resources of the state were lavished on these cities, and to a lesser extent on Kiev, Odessa, and Tbilisi, to make them reasonably modern as befitted a great power. But once one left these cities, or the well-known tourist centres such as Suzdal, Rostov Veliki, Zagorsk, or Novgorod, the picture changed completely, particularly in Old Russia. This whole vast region, of which Moscow was the centre, the heart and soul of Russia, was singularly neglected, apart from Moscow itself. Most of the roads were appalling, the villages not much changed since the nineteenth century, the communities usually without running water, and the towns decrepit, dilapidated, and depressing. After a visit in 1979 to the town of Mojaisk, I recorded my impressions. They give a picture of how most Russians live.

A city of about ten thousand inhabitants, one hundred and twenty kilometres west of Moscow just off the main highway to Smolensk, Minsk, and Warsaw, Mojaisk could be considered a typical provincial town of Old Russia, although in theory favoured by its closeness to the capital. Its principal claim to fame is its proximity to the battlefield of Borodino, the site of the 1812 battle between Napoleon and the Russians. The shopping centre in the middle of town – 'old' Mojaisk – comprised a few blocks of one- or two-storey ramshackle, plastered-brick buildings along a pair of wide intersecting main streets. The threadbare stores, as grubby inside as on the outside, offered the most meagre of consumer products: in the clothing shop, a rack or two of print dresses, a few cheap suits, a few East German overcoats. At mid-morning, a consignment of cotton kerchiefs was delivered which immediately attracted a crowd of women trying to get at them. Opposite the clothing shop was a large grey-windowed stand-up cafeteria patronized by truck drivers for a late breakfast or early lunch, a sprinkle of disconsolate-looking housewives who had given up on the clothing shop, and stout ruddy-faced women who were road or building labourers, in shapeless khaki pants and kerchiefs with yellow hard hats perched on top of them. Next to the cafeteria was a bread shop which sold only small, brick-like loaves that felt as if they could best be used to repair the crumbling buildings. Perhaps there had been some fresh bread earlier in the morning, but at eleven o'clock this was all that was available.

Behind these streets lay the main housing areas: narrow, unpaved streets lined with small dilapidated wooden houses, the style of which has not changed for centuries. From the tiny cultivated gardens surrounding each house, it was apparent that Mojaisk did not depend greatly on its state stores for produce. It was also clear its citizens did not depend much on state resources for municipal services. Water was available only at taps spaced out along the streets. The sewers and electricity appeared to be rudimentary. The condition of the unpaved side streets was appalling and driving down them even in dry weather was a matter of navigating from one pot-hole to another. There were two churches in Mojaisk, neither of them 'working,' as the Russians say. At the edge of town a rather pretty red-brick church seemed to be under restoration, though there was no discernible building activity under way. Its neighbouring outbuilding had been trans-formed into a kindergarten and part of the church grounds was occupied by the unused remains of a small fairground – a merry-go-round constructed out of pipe-metal, swings, and a boarded-up ticket kiosk. The other church, set among wooden houses off the main streets, had recently been repainted; but it was locked up and judging by its overgrown grounds did not appear to be in use. One very noticeable and clearly operating structure located not far from the church was a long two-storey building which served both as a small prison and police station. Labourers dressed in uniformly grey garb were unloading a truck at an entrance to the building and guarding them was an almost equal number of armed militia.

The 'new' Mojaisk consisted of its industrial outskirts ringing the town. These took the shape of a haphazard series of small factories whose activities enveloped the town with a constant cloud of smoke and dust, contributing to the sense of an unplanned maze of dug-up roads and miscellaneous construction. This jumble is typical of Soviet industrial suburbs and can be found even in certain parts of Moscow. Amid the disarray, typical Soviet apartment blocks were going up in the form of five- or six-storey precast concrete structures clustered together in a drab, permanently unfinished state, and exuding a sense of old age even before completion. However, in terms of warmth, running water, and other facilities, this type of housing probably represented a considerable improvement for its inhabitants.

What was so extraordinary about small towns like Mojaisk was the contrast not only between them and the capital but also between them and their equivalent in southern Ukraine and the Caucasus, and even in some parts of Central Asia. In view of the great stress being put on Great Russian nationalism, and taking into consideration the drastic drop in the Russian birthrate, it was hard to understand why a greater effort was not made to improve the conditions of life in the Russian heartland. There was indeed a great deal of resentment on the part of the Russians about the neglect of Russia itself in favour of investment in other areas and in other countries. This investment made economic sense since the first requirement of the state was to concentrate industry in areas where the natural resources lay, but it was at considerable cost to the people who make up the bulk of the Soviet population. A story current in the late seventies illustrates this: 'Did you hear that one of our planes carrying wheat to Africa was shot down?' 'No, where?' 'Over Ryazan' (a provincial town in central Russia).

Life in Mojaisk – indeed, life in most Russian cities – was hard and dull, with few chances of distraction or advancement. But it would be a mistake to think that the Russians wanted an alternative. They grumbled, they malingered, they opted out in any way they could, but they were assured of the basic necessities, even if primitive, from the cradle to the grave; and most of them were inclined to accept the mind-dulling propaganda which assured them that conditions were far worse in the capitalist world. They did not seem to be bothered by the contradiction by which nearly all assumed that Western goods had to be better than Soviet products.

This assumption was brought home to me vividly when we were preparing to leave the Soviet Union on my retirement. Most embassies had used a West German transport firm, but the experience of my secretary made me hesitant. She had been transferred from Moscow to Teheran and the Germans sent her effects to Jakarta. She eventually received them a few weeks before we had to close our mission in Iran. In any event, I decided to use the Soviet organization Sovtransauto to truck my goods to France, reasoning that they would be so happy to get the business (paid in dollars!) that they would make a special effort. In fact the shipment was delivered on time without any breakages. When I mentioned to a very senior Soviet official that I was using Sovtransauto, his immediate reaction was astonishment, disbelief, and then pity since he was sure I would never see my effects again.

Two results of this general economic malaise were a rapid decline in the birthrate among the Slavs, particularly the Russians and the Balts, and an extraordinary increase in health problems, above all alcoholism.

There was no secret about the decline in the birthrate in the Baltic states, Ukraine, Byelorussia, and the Russian Republic. In the large cities the rate dropped catastrophically; in Moscow in the 1970s it was less than 1.5 children per family. At the same time, the population of the Central Asian republics and Azerbaijan increased by leaps and bounds. In Uzbekistan, for example, the birthrate was 33.2 per thousand in 1972. The Russians still represent 53 per cent of the total population and together with the other Slavs, form about 70 per cent. But it is estimated that by the year 2000, out of an overall population of approximately 295 million, 62 million will be of Asian origin.

Increasingly the government recognized that the Russians were not only the dominant race but the most loyal and the only one they could thoroughly count on to provide the dynamism for the country. The proportional decline in the number of Russians clearly disturbed the leadership. But the appeal to Russian nationalism to offset the declining attraction of communist ideology was obviously enlarging the gap between Russians and non-Russians and the attempt to create a somewhat artificial loyalty to the idea of the Soviet citizen was not very credible.

The increase in Russianism and the sporadic efforts to impose more use of the Russian language on the non-Russian peoples occasionally provoked strong reactions in the other republics and indirectly increased the strength of local nationalism. Riots even took place in the streets of Tbilisi to protest against an attempt to downgrade Georgian in favour of Russian in the local schools. Paradoxically, the increased use of Russian was practically indispensable in a huge country like the Soviet Union, where no other language could take its place as a unifying force. It was absolutely necessary for service in the army and the administration, and impossible to replace in a complex industrial society. But every effort to increase its use in the education systems of the republics met with nationalist resistance. At the same time, outside the boundaries of the constituent republics no non-Russian schools were to be found. This was one of the reasons why Georgians, Uzbeks, and so on were reluctant to leave their own republics, because they would have to reconcile themselves to the fact that their children would become assimilated.

Unfortunately for the Russian leaders, the areas where the greatest pools of available labour will lie in the future are non-Russian and far from the present centres of industry or sources of energy. To invest heavily in creating new industries in Central Asia, which is the logical thing to do, will be strongly resisted by the Russians who already consider that too much of their money has gone to that area. Yet to move Central Asian workers to Russia will cause resentment among them and equal resentment among the Russians, who hardly bother to hide their dislike of the yellow race. According to Soviet contacts, admittedly prejudiced, the Central Asians had not proved very adept at mastering the complexities of modern industry, and their often rudimentary knowledge of Russian and their doubtful loyalty, as the war in Afghanistan later showed, were additional handicaps to using them to meet manpower shortages in the armed forces.

The fall of the Russian birthrate was accentuated by the continuing housing shortage and the need for young couples to live in cramped quarters with their parents. The rise in expectations also tended to make young couples prefer to have only one child, or none at all, because of the financial and material difficulties of raising a family. Abortion was cheap and no social stigma was attached to it, but the operations were performed so brutally that there was evidence it was having serious effect on the ability of women to bear children.

Every effort to change the situation seemed to prove fruitless. The state needed women in the labour forces, often in very menial jobs; but it also needed children and offered more money for large families and facilities for mothers, as well as the distribution of 'Heroine of Soviet Motherhood' awards. In practice, the status of women was far lower than in the West. No woman held any important political position and there were practically none in positions of authority in industry or management. The one exception for a few years was Ekaterina Furtseva, who was alleged to have been promoted because she was Khrushchev's mistress. She managed to survive his overthrow and became minister of culture, but when she was fired from this job, she committed suicide. There were many women doctors but almost all of them were in positions of secondary importance. The feeling of male dominance was so great that it was always the woman who, after a hard day's work, still had to queue up for food and do the household chores. It was hardly any wonder that they did not welcome the additional task of motherhood.

This lack of enthusiasm for parenthood was a reflection of a general feeling of boredom and indifference. Another manifestation was the bottle. In spite of periodic and astronomic increases in the cost of vodka, consumption was extremely high. The Russians drink to get drunk, not to enjoy themselves. Around Moscow, at suitable intervals, were situated sobering-up stations to which the police brought the Saturday-night drunks, often found lying in the gutters at twenty below. The stations themselves consisted of rooms where the drunks were expected to stay the night after a cold shower. There was a curious comprehension, almost tenderness, shown by the police and the average Russian to drunks. I once had to see someone off on the train to Kiev and just as the train was about to start, a man came weaving down the platform waving his ticket. The conductress told him he was too late and asked what was the matter with him. When he replied, 'I'm drunk, comrade,' she gave a great sigh, said 'Oh, well, in that case, come on,' and pushed him aboard.

In the mid-sixties health conditions in the Soviet Union started to deteriorate, and in particular a steady rise in infant mortality occurred. Studies based on Soviet statistics indicate that infant mortality increased by more than a third between 1970 and 1975. And mortality in every age category over twenty also increased by more than 10 per cent in the decade 1965–75, with the result that life expectancy in the Soviet Union became lower than it had been in the late fifties. This is in sharp contrast not only with developed countries but even in the poorer areas of the third world, where slow but steady progress is being made in providing better health services to the population. As far as child mortality is concerned, poor or defective drugs, alcoholism, and crude abortions all played a role. But it is hard to explain the rise in adult mortality. The health services, while extensive and comprehensive, were in practice poor and inefficient and the medical profession despised, except for the very best doctors, surgeons, and research specialists. Needless to say, the clinics available only to the elite had a much higher standard, and there were many extremely good specialists. Those who studied the phenomenon concluded tentatively that the decline in the life span of the average Russian was due at least in part to a general fall in expectations and a kind of dull fatalism which seemed to affect the population.

This malaise was understandable in workers in small towns and on the farms where the standard of living was dreadfully low and the isolation and lack of amenities could not be compensated for by the exhilaration of independent action. But it was also manifest in Moscow except, of course, among the privileged careerists. Its most obvious form was the absolute determination to do the minimum possible to survive within the system, total disinterest in the ideology, and cynicism about official propaganda. Among the youth, it took the form of a desperate search for the affluent society, Western-style if possible. It was curious that in the sixties and seventies when the youth in the West turned idealistic and impractical, the young Russians were crassly materialistic. They certainly seemed to show little sign of that toughness of body and spirit that their fathers and grandfathers had shown in two world wars.

In the late sixties I had a unique opportunity for a very frank discussion of the youth problem with an important former member of the Secretariat of the Communist Party, a Khrushchev appointee who had failed to see the writing on the wall and had lost his position with the downfall of his leader. Without any prompting from me, he expressed extreme disquiet about what was happening to the young people. He deplored their tendency to 'ape decadent Western ways' and shirk their responsibilities as Soviet citizens. Worse, he said, many of the bright young boys who should have been going automatically into the Party were not doing so, and many others were only joining because it was a way to the top. 'There are many things you cannot imagine that are going on – drug addiction, for example,' he said. The authorities didn't know how drugs were being smuggled into the country, but the government was ruthless with those caught taking drugs: they were sent to labour camps in Siberia. The leadership was also seriously worried about venereal disease, he said, and claimed it was being spread by Negro exchange students. It was a delicate matter and they did not know how to handle it.

Then he exclaimed that it was a shame the way the youth behaved. The young had never had it so good and his generation could not understand why they were not happy and hard-working. This would not have happened under Stalin, who was one of the most intelligent and clever men of this century and had made the Soviet Union a great country, he said. 'Stalin was a great man. I believe in him.'

He also expressed regret that the nature of the world communist movement was changing. In the time of the Comintern and indeed up to 1956, he said, to be a good communist you had to be a 'Soviet patriot.' This was no longer true: now the minimum requirement was that you must not be anti-Soviet. He put the major blame for this unfortunate development on China and called what was happening there a political sickness like McCarthyism in the United States. He was sure it would pass away, leaving a more healthy body politic in China after Mao. But Moscow would remain always the centre and soul of world communism.

His views undoubtedly reflected those of many of his generation in the Communist Party: disquiet about the present and the new generation, nostalgia for Stalin, and optimism about Moscow's future ascendancy. As for the educated classes, there was a suppressed but evident longing for innovation, particularly when the post-Stalin decade of Khrushchev permitted some exciting developments in poetry, literature, theatre, ballet, music, and science. The return in the 1970s to rigid conformity with socialist realism brought back a mind-shattering dullness. It was this as much as politics which drove so many Soviet intellectuals and artists to defect to the West.

The insistence on uniformity in all the arts reflected not only the ideological conservatism of the leadership but its philistine attachment to Victorian standards and its fear of innovation on any front. And even those intellectuals who had a lively mind, who knew the West, were extraordinarily attached to the mould in which Russia was set in 1917. The Moscow apartment of Lili Brik, the mistress of Vladimir Mayakovsky (the most popular poet of the revolution who committed suicide in 1930), was almost exactly what you would expect an early twentieth-century apartment in St Petersburg to have been. Tea with a Soviet writer in a cottage in the writers' colony in Peredelkino seemed almost copied movement by movement out of Chekhov.

This insistence on uniformity and tradition had more serious effects on the economy. In the field of research and development, except in the armaments industry, there was a tendency to concentrate on the safe and abstract. Even when the undoubtedly able Soviet scientists came up with a new invention, the dead weight of the bureaucracy made its exploitation extremely difficult. It was always so much easier to lumber along with an existing system which had been approved from the top down years before. This explains much of the attraction of importing entire factories from abroad since they could be fitted into the existing system without too great a dislocation. The scientists in research and development tended to go into the military-industrial complex because there they could see a new invention implemented and applied within a short time. But because of the compartmentalization of the system, there was practically no spillover from military research into the civilian economy.

If the Soviet leaders were concerned by the problems of youth, alcoholism, morale, infant and adult mortality, and a decline in the birthrate of the Russian population, it was seldom apparent. They were content to issue sporadic appeals to the young, a constant barrage of communist propaganda and expressions of alarm about heavy drinking, and a constant call to patriotic unity, reinforced by an unending reminder through films, novels, and the celebration of anniversaries of battles, of the sacrifices made in repulsing the enemy in World War Two. Slogans, usually in the simplest form, plastered on every available wall, advertised the material achievements of the regime as compared to the alleged backwardness of the Western world.

No doubt all this had some effect on the average Russian, sceptical and cynical though most of them tended to be, but the contrast between vainglorious claims and the obvious reality had an unsettling effect on the educated part of the population. This contrast between propaganda and reality tended to provoke among them what Arthur Koestler once called the collapse of synapses. There was one slogan which almost provoked it in me: 'The basis for peace is the peaceful character of Soviet intentions.'

If the Soviets seemed almost unaware of so many of their social problems, this was not the case with regard to the economy and agriculture, to which the Twenty-Fifth Congress in 1976 devoted a great deal of attention. The five years since the previous congress had seen the great hopes of maintaining and even increasing agricultural production, shattered, partly because of two years in which drought devastated the grain-producing lands. Investment in agriculture had risen by 60 per cent while overall output increased only 13 per cent and the crucial goal of increasing the average annual grain production to 195 million tons was way off. In addition, sugarbeet and potato production actually declined. In

1974 the grain harvest was only one hundred and forty million tons, necessitating huge grain purchases abroad and the slaughter of livestock to conserve feed. The repercussions were obvious in the targets set for the next five-year plan, although the figures the Soviets hoped to achieve still seemed highly unrealistic.

Brezhnev could hardly fail to acknowledge the setbacks and the fact they were not solely due to poor weather. But as usual he had no solution to the perennial problem of agriculture. He claimed that the 'extremely difficult struggle against the elements would not prevent the continued advance of agricultural production,' although he admitted that the output of farm products and certain consumer goods, and the rate of growth of the national income, would be affected by bad weather conditions. But there was absolutely no indication that the basic defects in the agricultural system were going to be tackled.

Neither Brezhnev nor Kosygin nor anyone else in their official speeches referred to the role of the private plots. But the final draft of the next five-year plan added for the first time a significant phrase urging the 'collective and state farms to supply all the necessary assistance to people in management of private farming.' This was an important change since the productivity of the private plots in comparison with that of the collective and state farms was a constant source of embarrassment to the Soviet leaders. But the government contented itself by repeating its emphasis on planned discipline, better management, better quality, more efficiency, the elimination of waste, coupled with higher capital investment. Without tackling the basic problem of incentives, this meant that agriculture would remain the weakest sector of the Soviet economy, and the production targets, particularly for grain, largely unattainable.

In spite of the great agricultural potential of the Soviet Union, it is likely to continue to be incapable of meeting its own needs for a very long time. It is true that a good deal of northern Russia is not particularly productive agriculturally, but neither is much of Canada. On the other hand, Ukraine, the lower Volga basin, the Don valley, the Kuban and the Virgin Lands of northern Kazakhstan are very rich grain-growing areas, richer in many ways than the Canadian prairies, since the land of European Russia can be sown to fall wheat whereas in the Canadian prairies one must rely exclusively on spring wheat. There is no doubt that the weather is more erratic in Russia. Nevertheless, the contrast between Canadian or American grain production and that of Russia cannot be laid solely at the door of the weather.

The waste and inefficiency of Soviet agriculture is incredible. The mismanagement of machinery was proverbial and, except in showcase farms, as much as 50 per cent of the equipment was frequently unusable. The unavailability of spare parts, the lack of skill of the machinists, and the slowness of distribution all contributed to low productivity. Once at an international agricultural fair in Moscow the Canadian exhibitors of some farm machinery noticed a group of Russians who came to examine and stare at a certain piece of equipment every day for almost a week. On the last day they finally broke down and approached the stand to explain that their collective farm had been provided with a similar piece of Canadian equipment five years before. They had never been able to make it work and they wondered if the Canadians could show them how. This was typical of the mismanagement of resources.

Internal distribution of agricultural products was so poor that the semi-tropical fruits grown in Central Asia and in the Caucasus seldom reached the markets of Moscow and Leningrad; if they did, they were half rotten because of the lack of refrigerated transport. Enterprising Uzbeks and Armenians could make a great deal of money by filling up suitcases with oranges or lemons, flying to Moscow, and selling them on the black market. But during the entire time I was in the Soviet Union, no effort was ever made to bring the products of these areas to the major markets in an organized system of distribution.

The Soviet economy had many formidable strengths – in particular, great natural resources and a malleable population easily controlled and directed – which gave the government an uncontested ability to rally the entire economy behind the build-up of heavy industry and the creation of an immense military machine. By the mid-seventies, however, the deficiencies and weaknesses of the system, already very apparent in 1964, were becoming even more clear to the outside observer and, evidence showed, to many of the more informed Soviet officials. This was most obvious in the inability of the system to adjust to the exigencies of a complex and sophisticated economy.

In the last half of the decade, the economic prospects were further clouded by manpower shortages, a decline in productivity, and problems involved in the supply of energy, particularly oil. After three decades in which the pool of labour available for industrial expansion seemed inexhaustible, the Soviets were beginning to face up to the possibility that this had come to an end. Much of the expansion had been due to the siphoning off of labour from the farms, but this was no longer possible without adversely affecting agricultural production ever further. The Russian birthrate had dropped drastically, but the government was reluctant to utilize the only available pool of manpower – that of the Central Asian republics – and unable to reduce the huge size of the armed forces, estimated at about three and a half million.

The low productivity of labour was a constant source of complaint on the part of the authorities, and no amount of gimmicks or exhortations seemed able to increase it. Low pay, little opportunity for advancement, poor housing, few consumer goods, and constant food shortages all provided no incentive to work any harder than was absolutely necessary. The introduction of high technology from the West was supposed to increase productivity but it proved an illusion and in the more visible forms – the Lada car, or condominium apartments, for example – it affected primarily the better-off and tended to increase dissatisfaction at a lower level.

While estimates of an energy crisis were exaggerated, the Soviet leadership took the problem of oil production very seriously. With the decline of the Baku and more easily accessible Western Siberian oilfields, a very great effort in capital investment, research, and technology was being devoted to the development of the vast oil deposits that existed in the country. The bigger fields lay in marshy soil which in summer was almost impassable and smothered in black flies, and in winter frozen solid with an average temperature of twenty or thirty below. The deficiencies in the system became apparent through stories which reached us of the stratagems used by the local managers to meet impossible production demands laid down in Moscow.

Nevertheless, there was not the slightest sign during the last five years I spent in Moscow that the Russians were prepared to do more than tinker with the system. The eleventh five-year plan (1981–5) did produce more realistic growth-rate goals, accompanied by some disciplinary moves which included a crackdown on corruption and inefficiency and the execution or removal of the more notoriously corrupt or inefficient managers. But the fundamental problem of reconciling economic reform and some decentralization with political control had not been resolved, and by the very nature of the system seems almost insoluble.

As one Russian writer once put it to me: 'How can you reconcile modern technology with mediaeval autocracy? We need computers, but then control slips out of the hands of human beings into machines. We need such a simple thing as direct-dial telephones, but then the police find it more difficult to control our thoughts. Project this into almost any field and you will realize the extent of the problem.'

During all the years I was in Moscow there was never any sign that the leadership intended to modify the strictest orthodoxy in the arts, communist theology, or political control. The only area in which there was clearly some questioning of the official line was over the basic issue of guns or butter. The leadership claimed that providing a better life for the people was the principal way by which the system justified itself. In practical terms, an increase in the standard of living, even if very small, was the easiest way to deflect criticism. And the Soviets were constantly preoccupied with the unpalatable fact that the standard of living in Eastern Europe was generally higher than in the Soviet Union itself. The usual reaction of Russians visiting Prague or Budapest for the first time was: *Eto bratskaya strana!* (This is a brotherly country!) It was a reaction of both surprise and resentment.

But during all this period no serious effort was ever made to re-examine and modernize the basic tenets of Marxist-Leninist theory. This left three other possible means of improving the faltering economy: more discipline; détente and a search for technology from the West; and a decrease in the defence budget. The first two have not worked, and can never prove more than temporary palliatives. The third posed, and continues to pose, immense problems, with the military, with security, with the superpower relationship, and with the potential threat from China. The demands of the civilian economy are the most potent arguments for a reduction in the burden of armaments. But they can only prove acceptable to the military and security forces if the international situation appears to be less menacing.

Soviet society and the Soviet economy, judged by our standards, are in deep trouble; they are the strongest reasons that exist in favour of more normal relations with Russia. It is almost the only way the Kremlin can be convinced that the risk could be taken of reducing the arms race while preserving Soviet security and superpower status. Since Western economics and Western societies can compete very favourably with the Soviet model, it is undeniably to our advantage to move the competition from the military, where the Soviets can contend on the basis of equality, to the civilian. And let us not fear to help improve the Soviet standard of living. It will be decades before it can approach the level of ours, let us hope decades of respite, in which the system might be given a chance to mature and mellow.

10

The Dilemma of Eastern Europe

For the decade after the brutal crushing of the Hungarian revolt in 1956, Moscow had few visible problems with its East European empire, except for Romania which, by a strictly orthodox internal policy, 'paid' for some deviations from Moscow in foreign affairs. The people of Eastern Europe seemed to have learned the lesson of Hungary and accepted the reality that there was no apparent alternative. Hungary was in the intelligent but firm hands of Janos Kadar, who never departed from the Soviet line in foreign affairs, while quietly and pragmatically introducing a measure of economic change and liberalism in internal affairs, all strictly in accordance with official Marxist-Leninist doctrine. Poland was quiescent, and East Germany, with a large Soviet military presence, was in no danger of questioning the existing system.

Czechoslovakia under the control of the Stalinist Antonin Novotny seemed the last of the East European countries likely to cause trouble for Moscow. But immediately after the celebrations of the fiftieth anniversary of the revolution it began to emerge as a potential crisis area. Novotny's failure to adjust to the post-Stalin period, the administrative incompetence of his regime, and failure to control the ancient quarrels between Czechs and Slovaks came to a head in the fall of 1967. In December, faced with a revolt by a majority of the Party Presidium, he called on Brezhnev to intervene personally on his behalf. Brezhnev had already done so once before, in 1963, when Khrushchev had sent him to Prague on a rescue operation. Unfortunately for Novotny, the Czech leader expressed his gratitude to Khrushchev by supporting the latter against Brezhnev in 1964.

Brezhnev did go to Prague on 8 December, but only to decide that Novotny was finished and that it was up to the Czechs to solve what seemed an internal problem. After his departure the crisis erupted. On 5 January 1968, Alexander Dubček, who had been the Slovak Party leader, replaced Novotny as first secretary of the Czechoslovak Communist Party. On the face of it, the Russians had no cause for alarm. Dubček had an impeccable proletarian background, had been brought up in Moscow, and was a graduate of the Higher Party School. In March, Ludvik Svoboda, who had served with Brezhnev in the Red Army at the liberation of Czechoslovakia in 1945, succeeded Novotny as president.

But Soviet disillusionment soon set in. About a month after Dubček came to power, he used the occasion of the celebrations in Prague of the twentieth anniversary of the communist takeover in February 1948 to begin sketching out the general lines of 'communism with a human face.' Although he was careful to underline Czech loyalty to Moscow, the reform program included changes which were ipso facto anathema to the Soviets: a socialist market economy; the abolition of censorship; freedom of the press and movement; liberalization of the world of culture; and a degree of democracy in the Party apparatus.

From talks I had with Russians in Moscow, it was clear that the leadership was deeply worried by the proposals for democratizing the Czech Party, the planned economic reforms which would undermine the authority of the Party and its policy of control from the centre, the introduction of a greater degree of federalism between the Czech and Slovak regions, and the prospect of a possible military gap in the defences of Eastern Europe. The weakening of the Czech Communist Party and the economic reform concerned the entire Soviet Party. We had reports that local Party bosses around the country were expressing alarm that the Czech developments, if permitted to continue, could have an insidious effect inside the Soviet Union and seriously undermine their authority. And the military, of course, looked askance at the possible weakening of the Western front. No doubt they had in mind the dictum of Bismarck: whoever controls the Bohemian bastion controls Europe.

There were clear signs at that time that military intervention was a possible option and Warsaw Pact manoeuvres were held in and around Czechoslovakia. At the United Nations, statements by Soviet representatives and leaks to the press seemed to be preparing the way for the use of force. Privately, the Soviets spread the word that the Soviet Union would have the moral and legal right to intervene militarily in certain circumstances, such as the establishment of an anti-socialist or bourgeois government in Prague. But the leaders hesitated. They were hoping for some plausible pretext, such as a decision to leave the Warsaw Pact (but Dubček kept repeating Czech loyalty to the alliance), the disintegration of the Czech Party (but it seemed to have rallied behind Dubček), or a civil war (but the peaceful removal of Novotny and the total lack of popularity of the Moscovite wing of the Party made this implausible). The Soviet leaders, therefore, uncharacteristically, dithered.

It was hard to read the signals in Moscow. In Prague, Dubček appeared to interpret the dismay and indecision in the Kremlin as tacit consent to the Czech reforms. Meanwhile the Soviets huddled with their hard-core allies in the Eastern bloc and became increasingly alarmed over the possibility that the Czech Party would lose its dominant role in the country and Czechoslovakia would leave the Warsaw Pact.

All the efforts by Dubček to explain what the Czech Party was trying to do and why it believed the process was controllable and compatible with the leading role of the Communist Party failed to carry conviction with the Russians. Perhaps the Czechs did believe that with their history and their integration in Western culture, it was possible to combine the leading role of the Communist Party and a recognizably democratic state. But nothing in their background would permit the Russians to understand this. They obviously considered that such phenomena as a free mass media and limited activities by other political parties would be totally incompatible with communism as they understood it. Therefore the Russians concluded that the Czech attempts to argue otherwise were double-talk concealing a return to bourgeois democracy.

But still the Soviets hesitated. Tito, Kadar, Ceausescu, and the Italian communists expressed their reservations about intervention, and there were strong rumours of a division in the Politburo. Those who hesitated were aware that control of the Czechoslovak situation had to be carried out smoothly to avoid further loss of Soviet international prestige. They were also aware that intervention would be a disastrous prelude to the conference of world communist parties which they hoped to convene in November, and they were uncertain how third world leaders would react.

Finally, the Soviets had difficulty in setting the stage for intervention. No matter how implausible in substance, the Russians had always been careful to preserve the legal fiction that their troops were in allied countries by agreement. The principle was reaffirmed many times. Obsessed by their need to maintain some kind of legal form, the Soviets were faced in July 1968 by the dilemma of Dubček: how to get him to invite Soviet troops into Czechoslovakia on the basis of events which could be represented as uncontrollable, counter-revolutionary violence; or, if he proved intransigent, how to replace him with someone who would welcome Russian tanks.

From the middle of July on, the tone of the Soviet press became vitriolic, with several commentators calling for intervention. The avalanche of accusations against the Czech government and party and the elaborate inventions about u.s., NATO, reactionary, imperialist, counter-revolutionary activities in Czechoslovakia succeeded in gaining credence with the average citizen. The intelligentsia, no doubt reasonably aware of the true situation in Prague, had been put on the defensive in the preceding few months and certainly did not speak their minds, with one or two notable exceptions, such as the poet Evtushenko. But most Russians came to accept that there was a serious danger of Czechoslovakia escaping from Russian control and the reaction was a patriotic one. They were angry that a brother Slav people, liberated by the Russians from the German yoke, and helped economically at their expense, should ungratefully reject all this and choose an independent course. Our own soundings indicated that Soviet military intervention would generally be approved by the Russians, provided it did not bring a risk of war; equally that Soviet acceptance of an unsatisfactory compromise with Dubček would lead to misunderstanding on the part of the Soviet public precisely because of the Russian nationalist instincts the leadership had aroused.

What seemed at the time like a turning point came at a meeting 29 July to 1 August at Cierna-nad-Tissou between Brezhnev and nine of the eleven members of the Soviet Politburo and the entire Czech Presidium, followed by a six-power communist conference at Bratislava. The Cierna meeting was stormy, but the communiqué issued after Bratislava and the smile on Brezhnev's face seemed to indicate that Dubček had made sufficient concessions to satisfy Moscow. The communiqué stressed the duty of every communist country and party to do its duty to protect and strengthen communism in each country and throughout the world, and it particularly emphasized the duty of the participants in the meeting to maintain the leading role of the Communist Party: 'In doing so, each brotherly party, creatively resolving the questions of further socialist development, should take into consideration national characteristics and conditions.'

This sounded like a significant back-tracking on the part of the Soviets – an indication that they, too, had made some concessions at Bratislava. But after a brief pause, the vitriolic attacks on Dubček in the Moscow press began again. Whatever Dubček promised at Cierna he either could not or would not carry out. Soviet anger mounted.

Then finally, the night of 20 August, in a lightning military move, the Russians occupied Prague and all the major Czech centres. In accordance with their mania for 'legality,' *Pravda* went up on wallboards early on 21 August with a statement that:

The Party and Government leaders of the Czechoslovak Socialist Republic have asked the USSR and other allied states to render the fraternal Czechoslovak people urgent assistance including assistance with armed force. This request was brought about by the threat which has arisen to the socialist system existing in Czechoslovakia ... and by the threat emanating from counter-revolutionary forces which entered into collusion with foreign forces hostile to socialism.

The situation in Czechoslovakia, *Pravda* asserted, affected the vital interests of the Soviet Union and other socialist states and constituted a threat to European peace. The statement claimed the decision was fully in accordance with the right of states to individual and collective self-defence as envisaged in the treaties of alliance concluded between socialist countries. It promised that the armed forces would be immediately withdrawn from Czechoslovakia as soon as the threats to socialism and to the security of the socialist community were eliminated. The final sentence of the communiqué affirmed: 'Nobody will ever be allowed to wrest a single link from the community of socialist states.'

What finally decided the Soviets to intervene was probably the conclusion they had reached that Dubček was unable or unwilling to stop or control the reform process which was sweeping Czechoslovakia in a wave of popularity and that a real danger to the communist system existed. A Czech journalist in Moscow told me the reason for the timing of the invasion was information the Soviets had received that Dubček was starting to take measures to weight the September congress of the Czech Party so heavily in favour of the reformists that pro-Moscow elements would have been totally eliminated. But, most important, the Soviets clearly could not tolerate the nightmare of a communist party formally within the bloc, but practising totally heretical ideas and threatening contamination of the other countries of Eastern Europe and eventually the Soviet Union itself.

The military also played an important role in arguing that it was not possible to leave a weak spot in the defence of Eastern Europe. Shortly after the invasion, I had a conversation with a very senior party functionary who argued that it was intolerable to leave a gap in Bohemia between their forces in East Germany and in Hungary. When I queried the validity of this kind of military thinking in the days of nuclear weapons, he shrugged his shoulders and said, 'I can assure you that is what the military think.'

The military operation (which included troops from other communist countries to spread the responsibility) was a complete success from the Soviet point of view. But almost immediately the political end of the operation ran into trouble. Dubček, Prime Minister Oldrich Cernik, and National Assembly Chairman Josef

Smrkovsky were seized and flown to Moscow and great pressure put on them to resign so that a pro-Moscow leadership could be installed and a form of legitimacy given to the invasion. To give the process some tint of legality, the Russians also brought in President Svoboda on 23 August. To maintain the fiction of normal relations, Brezhnev went through the farce of receiving him at the airport with all the usual panoply of honours. For four days of negotiations and threats by the Soviets, the Czechs held out and, thanks to the courage of Svoboda, the Russians were forced to return them to Prague on the basis of a compromise which on the surface looked hardly more satisfactory than the Bratislava communiqué. Again, they were seeking a way out of the political impasse which would save some Soviet prestige through a Hungarian-type solution in which the Party would be run by Czechs, with Soviet troops remaining in the background as a powerful reminder not to get very far out of line. Vasil Bilak, the toughest of the pro-Moscow Czech communists, remained in Moscow.

Few observers expected that the return of Dubček and his reforming ministers to Prague could be more that a temporizing measure, but until 28 March 1969 the situation was calm on the surface. Soviet troops remained in Czechoslovakia, but in their barracks; Dubček was on a very short rein and the reforms had been halted. There seemed little doubt that accounts between the hard-liners and Dubček would be settled as soon as the occasion presented itself. The pretext was a victory by the Czech hockey team over the Russians, followed by spontaneous anti-Soviet demonstrations throughout the country. The response was immediate. The Soviet minister of defence, Marshal Andrei Grechko, arrived with a letter from Brezhnev accusing Dubček of inability to maintain order. Ten days later Dubček gave in to the intolerable pressure and the hardly veiled threat from Moscow to reoccupy Prague and form a military government. He and his reformists were replaced by Gustav Husak, Bilak, Lubomir Strougal, and others more amenable to the Kremlin. Communism with a human face was finished and Czechoslovakia returned to orthodoxy and complete loyalty to Moscow.

From the point of view of plugging the military gap, restoring an orthodox pro-Moscow communist leadership in Prague, and snuffing out any liberalizing reforms which might have infected other communist countries, the Soviet operation was successful and the price Moscow paid not very high. Every effort was made to convince Washington and other Western capitals that it was strictly an internal, defensive affair. It did have an effect on relations with the West and postponed the development of détente by perhaps a year. The stationing of Soviet troops in Bohemia altered slightly the military balance, but it was as clear in 1968 as it had been in 1956 that there was nothing the West could do about it.

Western reaction was not so emotional, anguished, and universal as in 1956. In the case of Hungary, the crisis was short but vivid and the desperate battle in the streets of Budapest left a stark impression on the Western public. In the case of Czechoslovakia, the crisis stretched out over eight months, interest waxed and waned, and when intervention took place, it was organized with such brutal skill that the Czechs had no chance to put up a fight.

The reaction in Europe, particularly Britain, was stronger than in the United States or in Canada, partly because of a guilt complex over the abandonment of Czechoslovakia in 1938, partly because the events were closer to home. There was always in Washington's attitude the superpower factor, an effort to prevent Czechoslovakia from destroying President Johnson's hopes for an improvement in Soviet-American relations. The beginning of arms limitation talks, and the war in Vietnam, were very much in his mind. Shortly after the invasion, Johnson made it clear in public and private that he still earnestly desired that arms negotiations should begin, and that a planned meeting with Kosygin take place. And a year later, the Canadian government invited Gromyko to visit Canada. Thus the Soviet calculation that the Czech operation would not permanently damage East-West relations was correct.

The price the Soviets paid in the form of economic stagnation in what should be one of the most industrialized and technologically advanced countries in Eastern Europe only became apparent later, and in Soviet terms it was not high in view of what they gained. I doubt that economic reform in the Soviet Union would have advanced very much even without the events in Czechoslovakia. The Soviet leaders were already deeply disturbed by experiments in economic reform, first in Yugoslavia and more importantly in

Czechoslovakia, because they originated with communist parties and were advanced as a legitimate development in Marxist ideology. They saw that economic reform led inevitably to demands for political reform, intellectual freedom, and a weakening of the Communist Party monopoly on power. The lesson of Czechoslovakia was not lost on the Russian communists and the whole idea of reform in the Soviet Union or any tampering with the system was shelved.

It was not long after the Czech invasion that the next step was taken in the development of its ultimate justification. What came to be known as the Brezhnev doctrine was basically not a new concept and the main tenet had been incorporated into the Bratislava communiqué. But it was put in a more sophisticated form in a major article in *Pravda* on 25 September 1968. The doctrine stated that the sovereignty of any member of the 'socialist community' was subject to the 'higher law of socialist or proletarian internationalism' which must take precedence over the usual norms of international behaviour applicable to all states. These communist norms were said to rise above narrower questions of national independence and self-determination. The other members of the community were justified in using any measures, including force and military intervention, to re-establish 'solidarity.' Even when only liberalizing reforms were involved, the threat of 'imperialist encroachment' could be invoked.

In a speech on 13 November 1968 Brezhnev put it succinctly:

There are common natural laws of socialist construction, deviation from which could lead to deviations from socialism as such. And when external and internal forces hostile to socialism try to turn the development of a given socialist country in the direction of restoration of the capitalist system, when a threat arises to the cause of socialism in that country – a threat to the security of the socialist commonwealth as a whole – this is no longer merely a problem for that country's people, but a common problem, the concern of all socialist countries.

This doctrine subsequently became one of the key elements in Soviet foreign policy and was formally restated with minor refinements by Brezhnev in his opening address on 30 March 1971 to the Twenty-Fourth Congress of the CPSU. Claiming that intervention in Czechoslovakia in 1968 had been made imperative because of the extraordinary conditions 'created by imperialists and counter-revolutionaries,' he said: 'We were bound to do so by our class duty, loyalty to socialist internationalism, and concern for the interests of our states and the future of socialism and peace in Europe.' Although the nod the Soviets had previously given in favour of 'socialist sovereignty and independence' had been little more than an exercise in semantics, in 1971 Brezhnev did not even bother to mention non-interference or national sovereignty. On the contrary, his whole emphasis was on the establishment of the new, socialist type of inter-state relations. 'We want,' he said, 'the world socialist system to be a well-knit family of nations, building and defending the new society together.' And to underline the point, the Czech leader, Gustav Husak, stated categorically: 'The abstract notion of the sovereignty of the socialist state does not exist. The real expression of this sovereignty is the power of the working class, the realization of the leading role of the Communist Party.'

After the invasion of Afghanistan, the Brezhnev doctrine was revived and given a new exegesis, a highly disturbing development since, for the first time, it was applied to a country outside the Soviet bloc. The Soviet magazine *New Times* of 18 January 1980 asserted that 'imperialist' intervention against 'revolutionary' movements is aggressive, while socialist intervention to combat 'imperialist' machinations is morally and politically right. The international solidarity of revolutionaries, it said, could not consist only of moral support, but 'under justified extraordinary conditions' could involve 'rendering material aid, including military aid. To refuse the potential which the socialist states possess would mean, in fact, avoiding an international duty.'

After the invasion of Czechoslovakia, the extrapolation of the Brezhnev doctrine gave many communist parties reason to pause. It was a catalyst in launching what later became known as Euro-communism and in pushing Yugoslavia, China, and Albania even further away from Moscow. When the Soviets started to realize the implication of justifying the invasion of Afghanistan through the doctrine of the solidarity of the communist community, they suddenly stopped mentioning 'revolutionary solidarity' as a justification for the intervention. Moscow's help to the Afghan communists became not a defence of the gains of socialism but 'a means of aiding the Afghans to rebuff external aggression,' to cite Foreign Minister Gromyko on 18 February 1980.

It is superfluous to say that Poland has been a major preoccupation for Russia for a thousand years. It is hardly surprising, therefore, that it has been the most difficult to handle of all the communist states in Eastern Europe. From the beginning of communist rule, Moscow felt obliged in Poland to permit a degree of tolerance of political activity outside the Party, acceptance of the Catholic Church, a more liberal attitude to the arts, and collectivization of only a small portion of the agricultural land. The Soviets treated Poland with special care because of its size, its deep-seated anti-Russian feelings, the intense individuality of the Poles, and their passionate attachment to their own culture and to their religion, the two being almost synonymous. In 1951, when I spent a few days in Warsaw on my way to Moscow, I asked the Polish driver of the embassy why I had received rather off-hand treatment in the hotel. 'Because you spoke Russian to them,' he immediately replied. 'You would have done better to speak German!' Twenty-five years later a Soviet official expressed extreme disquiet to me on learning that Zbigniew Brzezinski had been appointed President Jimmy Carter's national security adviser. His reasoning, very well justified, was that Brzezinski was Polish, Catholic, and upper class and therefore inevitably anti-Soviet.

In spite of the care the Russians took with the Poles, there was nothing much they could do to make the communist system work any better in Poland than in the Soviet Union. The standard of living therefore remained abysmally low, particularly outside the bigger cities, although it always seemed to be considerably higher than in Russia itself. The riots in Warsaw in 1956 which preceded the Hungarian revolt and which the Russians were quick to suppress, brought Wladislaw Gomulka to power. In December 1970 a similar outbreak, starting in Gdansk, was put down with considerable bloodshed. Again food shortages sparked the disturbances, although they were only the manifestation of general malaise. A Soviet show of force was sufficient to back up Gomulka, but there was no doubt that the Soviets had prepared contingency plans for all-out military intervention if that had proved necessary. Gomulka paid the price for his inability to keep his house in order and in 1971 was replaced by Edward Gierek.

For the following years the Soviets looked on complacently as Gierek attempted to follow Moscow's policies of détente by seeking technology and capital aid from the West to improve the competitiveness of Polish industry and the standard of living. He failed on both accounts and once again, in 1980, Gdansk became the focus for the workers' revolt. This time the unrest led to the creation of Solidarity, a truly independent and representative trade union movement; a wave of protest swept the country, almost destroying the Polish Communist Party, eventually leading to the establishment of rule by military junta, albeit a communist one.

The Polish situation caused as much concern to the Soviet leaders as Czechoslovakia had twelve years before, but military intervention to reverse events was both more and less necessary. Czechoslovakia stood in an exposed position facing West Germany and Austria and highly vulnerable to Western military pressure and culture and political penetration. Poland lay firmly wedged between East Germany and the Soviet Union and two Soviet divisions were stationed on Polish soil to assure the lines of communication between the two. Poland, therefore, was important militarily but not exposed or highly vulnerable. The East Germans, as the rump of old Prussia, considered the Poles their traditional enemy in spite of sharing superficially the same ideology. They were nervous about the disintegration of the Polish Communist Party and would have been delighted to join with the Russians in a military intervention.

There were a number of developments in Poland which from the Soviet point of view threatened the very base of a true communist regime. The first was the defiance of the Communist Party and the government by an unauthorized group, Solidarity, especially when it belonged to the proletariat and was supported by the Catholic Church and identified with Polish nationalism, both of which are almost by definition anti-communist and anti-Russian. In Solidarity the Russians perceived a revolt of the working class. According to Marxism-Leninism, the dictatorship of the proletariat must be exercised by the small inner group of the Communist Party. It was unheard of to think in terms of the proletariat itself pretending to exercise this power: it was a left-wing deviation. The trade union revolt in Poland appalled the Russians because it was the first time that workers in a communist country had actually and successfully challenged the doctrine that a small group of men can monopolize power in the name of the workers.

The next factor which worried the Russians was the inability of the Polish government and Party to solve the country's economic, political, and social problems, or to suppress a revolt which sprang largely from the disastrous situation created by the inefficiency of the communist system. The Russians never liked weak and inefficient communist leadership, even if it was loyal to the orthodox line. From Moscow's point of view, the Polish party was completely unsatisfactory since it was both inefficient and unable to prevent the spread of dangerous liberal trends within its own ranks. Above all, the success of unauthorized groups in enforcing the removal of unpopular communist officials was particularly disturbing for the Soviets. The proposal for secret elections to the Polish Party Congress and Central Committee was a clear threat to the concept and security of the closed, privileged, communist governing class. This was clearly unacceptable to Moscow, especially as free elections would almost certainly have resulted in a 'liberal' party prepared to introduce sweeping economic and political reforms.

And yet in the face of these vital considerations, the Russians demonstrated considerable prudence. They were clearly able to handle Poland militarily in spite of the fact that at the same time they had on their hands a civil war in Afghanistan. But they knew that the Poles would resist and that Western reaction to an invasion of Poland would be strong and prolonged. It would have meant the end for some time of any possibility of preserving elements important to them in their relations with the West and, in view of the election of a conservative hard-liner and proclaimed anti-Soviet president in the person of Ronald Reagan, it could have fostered outright confrontation. Finally, a military takeover would have created yet another crisis of confidence and loyalty in the communist parties of Europe, particularly as the Polish Communist Party had been so demoralized that no pro-Moscow elements seemed capable of taking over, even with the help of Russian bayonets.

There were other, strictly Polish, factors. The Russians had no illusions that practically all of Poland's thirty-seven million inhabitants would be hostile, the army's attitude uncertain, and the reaction of the workers unpredictable. The Soviets had had no experience in dealing with enraged and determined workers, and while they would not hesitate to shoot as many as necessary, it would have been a novel and unpalatable situation for them because, unlike the Hungarian and Czech revolts, the opposition in Poland came unmistakably from the working class. And then, having stamped out opposition, they would have been faced with the problem of persuading the workers to work harder than ever, for less – a necessary prerequisite for getting the Polish economy functioning properly. Secondly, the Soviets preferred to have a reliable group in the Polish Party invite Soviet assistance than have to repeat the Czechoslovak experience of moving in to depose the leadership of an allegedly fraternal communist party and impose their own puppets.

The Soviets were also far from enchanted with the prospect of assuming responsibility directly for the Polish economy. By 1980 it was already in a catastrophic state and it would have deteriorated even further in the aftermath of a Soviet takeover. Western aid would have dried up and Poland would either have had to default on its foreign loans or the Soviets would have had to take over its debts. And finally, the Soviet economy itself was in trouble and suffering from the decline in East-West trade. One almost had the impression that the Soviets were coming to the same conclusion as Western observers – that there was no cure under the Polish communist system for the economic maladies of the country.

The situation continued to deteriorate during 1981. The Polish United Workers' Party (Polish Communist Party) meeting in July did nothing to satisfy the Soviets. It decided on freely elected delegates to the congress, a freely elected Central Committee, a popularly elected first secretary, and the rejection of a majority of the Politburo. These innovations ran entirely contrary to everything the CPSU stood for. The Polish concept that people in positions of responsibility must be freely elected and then judged by their performances was clearly anathema to the elite of the Soviet party.

The process of democratization in Poland was confined to the Communist Party itself and there seemed to be no question of it being extended to the rest of the population. The Polish party was well aware that any extension of democracy beyond the party would be unacceptable to Moscow, since one of the major requirements of the Soviet system has always been 'all power to the Soviets.' At the same time, the Poles did not question membership in the Warsaw Pact or loyalty to Moscow or the principle of the solidarity of the 'socialist community.'

For the next few months the Russians watched very carefully for any signs of side effects of these Polish developments in other East European parties, or anything that might seem to affect the security of the Soviet Union or its lines of communication with East Germany and Czechoslovakia. There was never any chance, however, that the events in Poland could be repeated in the Soviet Union, even though the standard of living was much lower than in Poland, and it was living conditions that had provoked the 1970 and 1980 revolts by the Poles. The Russians are very different from their Slav cousins. While they have many admirable qualities, they seem condemned to political apathy and the acceptance of authority. The trade unions in the Soviet Union are nothing more than government tools for the control of the workers. Even if a gifted organizer like Lech Walesa had appeared in, say, Khabarovsk or Odessa, and by some miracle succeeded in raising a workers' revolt, it would almost certainly have been crushed locally before news of it spread to other unions, thousands of kilometres away. Word of food riots in a Siberian city in the 1970s, for example, was only received in the capital a year later.

While the Polish experiments seemed to have little immediate effect on other parties in Eastern Europe, they undoubtedly introduced an element of envy and uncertainty. The very existence of a different, liberal system in another neighbouring communist party made the Soviet leaders uneasy. And finally, there was the spectacle of a people assumed to have been cowed into submission standing up both to their own pro-Moscow leaders and to the threat of Soviet intervention.

The eventual solution, if it can be called that, was the imposition of martial law in December 1981, the dissolution of the government, and the takeover by General Wojciech Jaruzelski and a military junta. This temporarily solved the problem for the Russians and made it possible for them to avoid a military intervention. But all the problems remained: the contradiction of having a dictatorship of the proletariat exercised by the army, the continuation of the economic problems with no prospect of a long-term solution, the strengthening of the Catholic Church and its appeal to most Poles, and the lingering example of Solidarity and the revolt of the proletariat.

The Russians claim to need Eastern Europe for their security. This in turn depends on the acceptability of a Soviet-imposed system. It is unlikely that this alien rule will ever be truly popular in Eastern Europe, especially since the regimes cannot even provide a reasonable standard of living. The events in Poland have proved without a shadow of doubt that communism does not work. Nor will the Soviets permit the changes that might make it at least slightly more productive because of the fear of infecting their own rigid society. Thus the Kremlin needs Eastern Europe but can do nothing to make the peoples of the region dependable allies. They have the military force to maintain their rule, and they know that the West is not going to challenge this. But they cannot expect the West to be indifferent.

11

Russia and Asia: The Preoccupation with China

Russia and Asia. Many political observers would say 'Russia *is* Asia,' as two-thirds or more of the country lies beyond the artificial line of the Urals by which geographers divided Europe from Asia. In fact, much of European Russia was under Mongol rule for centuries and the Crimea, the Kazan Khanate, and Azerbaijan were as Asian as Turkey. The personality of the Russians has been (and still is in many ways) more oriental than some races which are of Asian origin – the Finns and the Hungarians, for example. Race notwithstanding, the Russians were deeply influenced by their long and frequently bloody contacts with Asia, and their Asian future can hardly be contested since the bulk of the vast natural resources of the country lie in Siberia. The political and economic exploitation of these resources depends to a certain extent on their own Central Asian peoples, only now awakening from centuries of torpor.

Soviet aims in Asia under Brezhnev were fourfold: to secure the Soviet hold on Central Asia, which in practice meant maintaining the dominant presence in Afghanistan; to protect Siberia and its increasingly important natural resources, which meant containing China and Japan; to exclude Chinese communism from the mainstream of Marxist-Leninist doctrine; and to expand Soviet influence in the rest of the continent, particularly India. Support for North Vietnam was considered a necessary but not very welcome concomitant to the theory of support for national liberation movements. The ideological passion which dictated the goal of 'setting the East ablaze' in the 1920s had died away in the light of more realistic objectives.

The Soviets were obsessed with the idea of a unified world communist movement, and Brezhnev made an effort when he came to power to heal the rift between the two biggest communist parties in the world. But, like Khrushchev before him, he was not prepared to accept the claim of Mao Tse-tung, as leader of the largest party numerically and the senior communist in power, to be head of world communism. For the Soviets this had to be the Soviet leader. Hence Brezhnev's attempt to heal the rift was doomed to failure and the Soviets knew it. Their efforts at reconciliation were intended primarily to improve their posture before the world communist conference held in 1969.

Ideological conflicts always tend to accentuate differences based on national and material interests. The dispute with China would have occurred even without the struggle of the two communist giants to dominate world communism. The Soviets dismissed Chinese rejection of the 'unequal treaties' of tsarist times and opposed Chinese claims on territory alleged to have been stolen from them. The Russians were determined not to give an inch, reinforced by an almost visceral hatred. Passionate dislike of the Mongols, Turks, and Tartars dates back a very long time: it was only in the late sixteenth century that the Mongol Horde was reduced to impotence and European Russia freed, and it was the late eighteenth century before the Crimean Tartars were finally conquered.

These victories led to the extraordinary outburst of energy by which the Russians spread across Siberia to the Pacific in a mass movement not unlike the American and Canadian conquests of the West. But there was one major difference. There were no rich prairies ready for tilling. The climate was as harsh or harsher than northern Canada and between the acres of arable land stood vast extents of forest, rock, and swamp. The gold, diamonds, tungsten, oil, gas, iron, and coal were to be discovered later. In spite of its richness and vast size, larger than Canada, Siberia has a population not bigger than that of Chinese Manchuria, about thirty million inhabitants.

Until the Chinese communists came to power, China had never represented any real threat to Russia in Siberia. There had been practically no opposition to Russian expansion into an area largely unoccupied and for the most part despised by the civilized Chinese. In any case, China was primarily preoccupied in defending itself first against European imperial powers and then Japan. Thus it was paradoxical that Russian rule in Siberia was only seriously challenged when another communist party came to power in Peking. (The Russo-Japanese War of 1905 and clashes in the thirties had little to do with the substance of Russian control of Siberia.)

In March 1969 fighting broke out between the Chinese and Russians on the disputed island of Damansky in the Ussuri River, which constitutes part of the Sino-Soviet frontier in the Far East. Two weeks later another even bloodier clash took place. The fierce war of words had been replaced by arms, or so it first appeared from Moscow.

Since the invasion of Czechoslovakia eight months earlier, the tone of the Sino-Soviet dispute had become increasingly vitriolic. The Soviets, worried that the Chinese might take advantage of their preoccupation with Eastern Europe, had increased the number of troops, normally ten divisions, stationed in Siberia and the Far Eastern provinces. The Chinese appeared to think that if the Russians could intervene to preserve the leading role of communist orthodoxy in Czechoslovakia, they might do so in China. While it seemed highly unlikely that the Soviets ever seriously considered this, there were persistent rumours that the military were in favour of a quick surgical strike to destroy the incipient Chinese nuclear forces.

I made a visit to Siberia and the Soviet Far East two years before and was able to judge for myself how tense relations were. The city of Khabarovsk, for example, with a Russian population of about half a million, is situated seven thousand kilometres from Moscow, on the Amur River near the junction with the Ussuri, less than twenty kilometres from the Chinese border. Nervousness about Chinese intentions was palpable, as palpable as the frosty air at thirty-five below. City officials took us to a site where we could peer across the frozen river to the Chinese side, but reassured us that the Chinese would be sternly rebuffed if they attempted to invade. When I suggested that the Chinese did not have the equipment to take on the Soviet army, the deputy mayor replied that what they feared was that millions of Chinese would just start moving into Russia. 'We would shoot half of them, but that would still leave an awful lot.' This idea seemed somewhat fanciful, but it illustrated the panicky feeling of the European, more or less isolated, face to face with what seemed like the yellow hordes.

The Soviet leadership reacted immediately and strongly to the Ussuri River incidents, accusing the Chinese of every crime in the communist book. The general public rallied behind the government in a unanimous outburst of Russian patriotism, including the launching of several new nationalistic songs and a poem by Evgenny Evtushenko about Russian blood on the snow of the Ussuri. The Chinese responded by labelling the Russians neo-colonialist revisionists and therefore traitors to communism.

Passions soon calmed down as it became evident that the incident was not the beginning of something more serious, and both sides made it clear that they did not want an escalation of the border clashes. The Soviets categorically reaffirmed that their borders were 'sacred and inviolable,' and that the clauses on territorial issues recorded in the various Sino-Russian treaties were legally fixed and valid. Nevertheless they proposed direct talks on all border and river navigation issues at the assistant deputy minister level. The Chinese accepted and talks have continued regularly ever since. While they have produced little of substance, they have helped to prevent any further clashes.

The Soviet government in its public presentation of the quarrel began to play down the ideological factors in favour of a frank and emotional appeal to Russian patriotism, coupled with a crude campaign not only against the 'traitorous Mao clique' but also against the Chinese people, evoking the spectre of the yellow peril and thus creating an atmosphere which played an important role in the development of Sino-Soviet relations in the following decade. The Soviets still professed that the removal of Mao and his associates would permit the return of true communism to Peking and ensure friendly relations between the two powers. I detected little conviction in these assertions and it was apparent that a return of an orthodox, pro-Moscow leadership in China would have posed great difficulties for the Soviets. The average Russian cared very little about the charges of ideological deviation on the part of the Chinese Party. But he responded viscerally and enthusiastically to the call for unity against the Chinese menace.

The leadership used this as one means of getting volunteers to go to Siberia to help implant a Slav, mostly Russian and Ukrainian, population in the vast and largely empty land. The Chinese coveted this area not because of some rather nebulous claims to sovereignty over parts of it, but because it contained all the natural resources of which China itself was deprived. The Russians were intent on peopling a comparatively narrow strip along the Chinese border from Chita to Vladivostok, an area as austere as northern Ontario or Quebec. Most of the arable land had already been taken up and it could sustain only a relatively small population. As in Canada, there was a limit to the number of people who could be absorbed by mineral and forest industries. While energy resources were great, even the Soviet planners recognized that there was little point in developing industry in areas far removed from the major centres of population.

One of the answers was an effort to push population and industry farther north. The Russians had always worried about the vulnerability of the Trans-Siberian Railway. Although it had been largely double-tracked, it was insufficient to bear the immense civilian and military traffic of a vast empire, and much of it ran parallel to the Chinese frontier. They therefore launched a project to build another line some five hundred kilometres farther north from Baikal to the Pacific and the mouth of the Amur River. BAM, as it came to be called (Baikal-Amur-Magistral), was a major engineering feat, but it also became a kind of national challenge and every effort was made to persuade young people to volunteer to work on it. While there was no doubt a good deal of arm-twisting, there were thousands of genuine volunteers and the motivation was quite clearly that of helping to protect Russian Siberia from the Chinese.

Shortly after the Ussuri River clash I had a conversation with a leading member of the Politburo, Kyrill Mazurov, in which I mentioned that I had just read André Malraux's *Anti-mémoires* in which he discussed the future of China. 'We have great respect for Malraux,' he replied. 'What does he say about the Chinese?' I answered that he thought China would become a great power in twenty-five years and a superpower in fifty. Mazurov burst out: 'I thought Malraux was an intelligent man, but he is a fool.' And he went on to declare that it was totally impossible for China to become a great power because the weight of its population was too huge, an incubus which would prevent it ever becoming technologically efficient or organized. And for good measure he criticized Canada for negotiating to establish diplomatic relations with Peking.

From the many talks I had with Soviet officials, it was evident that they were not seriously worried about China as a possible military threat. Indeed they had no reason to do so since the Chinese army, while huge in numbers, was very badly equipped and demoralized by the various twists and turns of Chinese policies. What did worry them, however, was the long-term prospect of a China associated in some form with Japan and/or the United States, acquiring Western capital and technology and eventually transforming itself into a modern state. In spite of their anti-Chinese propaganda they had considerable respect for Chinese ability. They were perfectly aware of what Chinese in Taiwan and Hong Kong could accomplish when given the proper political atmosphere, capital, and Western know-how. Indeed, the ubiquitous Victor Louis, the long-time Moscow correspondent for the *London Evening News* but also a very useful agent of the Soviet government, went on at least one mission to Taiwan, although there were no relations between it and the Soviet Union. One senior Soviet official told me they regretted the error of the Taiwanese in failing to proclaim the Republic of Taiwan; the Soviet Union would have been the second country, after the United States, to recognize it.

One of the mysteries of Soviet diplomacy was the failure to establish a close relationship with Japan when they had identified the main enemy in the east as China. Shortly after the Ussuri River incidents, they did make an effort to rectify the situation. The rather heavy-handed Soviet diplomatic campaign had three aims.

The first was the prevention of a rapprochement between China and Japan, or at least in a period of Sino-Soviet tension to keep Japan friendly. The second was to try to detach Japan from its American alliance, or at least loosen it. The third was the need to develop the resources of eastern Siberia by utilizing Japanese capital and technology. All three were perfectly legitimate objectives. The Soviet Union on its own did not have the capital or the technological resources to exploit this vast area; and the only logical market for the products of eastern Siberia, particularly the oil, gas, coal, and forest products, was Japan. Negotiations spread over a fairly lengthy period, but the Japanese eventually abandoned all the projected joint ventures because of the intransigence of the Russians on two issues: they insisted on the Japanese paying for all the costs of building oil and gas pipelines and the railway which was necessary to permit access to the fields; and they flatly refused to permit Japanese experts to verify for themselves that these fields did contain the reserves of oil and gas claimed by the Russians. Without independent verification, the Japanese felt they could not accept the Russian word or make the huge capital, and political, investments required.

Thus the Russians lost an opportunity to exploit eastern Siberia, and the Japanese turned to China as the alternative country in which they could invest their capital and technology. The Russians saw looming on their eastern horizon the threat of Japanese-Chinese co-operation of which they were most afraid. To compound this short-sighted policy, they decided to stick stubbornly to their position on the four small uninhabited islands lying between southern Sakhalin and Hokkaido. When Sakhalin was given to Russia in 1945, they interpreted this as including these islands which the Japanese had always considered integral parts of their homeland. I am not in a position to judge the military worth of the islands to the Soviets. In unfriendly hands they might have the potential to block access to the Sea of Japan and the very important naval base of Vladivostok. Probably the main reason for refusing even to discuss the status of the islands was the fear of creating a precedent which could be used by the Chinese to press their own territorial claims on the Soviet Union. For the Japanese it was a question of national honour, and the refusal of the Russians even to consider the return of any of these islands put a political frost on Soviet-Japanese relations.

The Soviets had more success in turning events to their advantage in India and Pakistan. Historically, the Indian subcontinent had had an important place in Russian strategic thinking because of the British imperial presence. After the the revolution, the Bolsheviks entertained the illusion that the Indian people could easily be aroused to revolt against their alien masters, an illusion spread in the 1920s by fanatical Indian communists such as M.N. Roy. After independence in 1947 they again turned their attention to India, cultivating Prime Minister Nehru and the Congress Party on the one hand, and the Indian Communist Party on the other. Indian diplomats and politicians saw this as a means of creating a balance in Indian non-alignment, and later of securing arms cheaply to counter the alleged threat from Pakistan. But the Soviets, while favouring India, did not adopt policies which would so weaken Pakistan as to remove it as a counter-balance to India.

Thus Kosygin played an important conciliatory role in ending the 1966 hostilities between the two countries, creating what the Soviets were delighted to call the 'Spirit of Tashkent,' although the soul of it evaporated rather quickly. Prime Minister Pearson, who followed developments in the Soviet Union closely and was preparing the improvement in Canadian-Soviet relations described in chapter five, believed the constructive role played by Moscow in preventing war between India and Pakistan needed encouragement and recognition. I was therefore instructed to see Kosygin and present a message of congratulations from Pearson for the Soviet contribution to ending the fighting and bringing the two opponents together. As I explained to Kosygin, the Canadian interest in developments on the subcontinent stemmed from our friendship with both countries in the Commonwealth and the considerable aid we had given to each. The insularity of the Soviets was evident in Kosygin's incredulity that a country so far away as Canada could have any real interests at stake.

The Russians had very great political and commercial investments in both countries, but inevitably they had to take sides when passions became too great. In August 1971 they abandoned any effort to treat the two countries even-handedly by signing a twenty-year Treaty of Peace, Friendship and Co-operation with India. In this way they drew a more clear-cut line between friend and foe and helped to polarize the sub-continent, with the Soviet Union and China lined up behind the two opposing factions and the United States in an uneasy position in the background.

The possibility of conflict had been building up for some time, localized in the growth of Bengali resentment in East Pakistan against the federal government and the policies of Yahya Khan. But in addition, border problems with India caused by the exodus of refugees from East Pakistan, the growing Chinese support for Pakistan, and possibly the visit of Henry Kissinger to Islamabad added to the tensions and made it easier for Moscow to persuade India of the need for the treaty of friendship. An Indian friend told me later that the initiative for a treaty came from Delhi in 1968 to counter what they thought was a Soviet rapprochement with Pakistan after the latter had sought and secured a considerable arms shipment from the Soviet Union. The Soviets expressed interest and drew up a draft treaty which was ready for signature in 1969. But Indira Gandhi's defeat at the polls made it impossible for the new government to risk a revolt of the right wing of the Congress Party by introducing a controversial Soviet-Indian treaty into a delicate parliamentary situation. It remained in abeyance until the elections in 1971 once again gave Mrs Gandhi a clear parliamentary majority. Shortly afterwards she revived the idea of the treaty, feeling that developments in East Pakistan and the Kissinger visit to Islamabad and Peking made the treaty necessary as a form of reassurance. My friend said it might be difficult for a foreigner to understand, but the Indians had felt very deeply that Kissinger had misled them by using his visit to India as a cover for his eventual trip to China, that he had shown total indifference to the problem of the refugees from East Pakistan, and that he favoured Pakistan over India because it was essential as a spring-board for Nixon's Chinese venture.

Some time later I was told by a Pakistani confidant that the Russians and Indians had been right up to a point in accusing Pakistan of lending itself to a 'Sino-American conspiracy.' According to him, President Nixon on his visit to Lahore in 1969 had broached the subject of a rapprochement with China. Yahya Khan had naturally welcomed the idea and offered his services. He mentioned it to Mao Tse-tung during an official visit to Peking later that year and within a few months Yahya received word from Mao that he was prepared to receive an American envoy. The rest is well known.

In any event, by the fall of 1971 the situation in East Pakistan had become impossible to control and the Soviets had decided that its separation from Pakistan proper was only a matter of time. The only question that remained was whether it would happen without a major conflict. It was clear that Pakistan could not defend both East Pakistan and West Pakistan and in the crunch the latter was the first priority.

When war broke out in December, the Soviet policy became clear: to condemn and isolate China for allegedly encouraging Pakistan against India, which the debates in the United Nations showed was only partially successful; to see East Pakistan emerge as an independent state susceptible to Soviet influence; to avoid too great a defeat for Pakistan in order to preserve it as a counter to India, thus making the latter more likely to look to Moscow for support; and to avoid direct involvement in the military conflict. Apart from some temporary setbacks in the United Nations, the Soviet Union emerged from the brief but nasty war successful on all counts. Certainly it served Soviet interests to have a weakened Pakistan and a struggling new country, Bangladesh, to deal with, and to expose China as incapable of giving its allies military help. And in the years that followed the dismemberment of Pakistan, Soviet ambitions in the whole area south of their Central Asian republics were whetted.

An integral part of the Sino-Soviet dispute is Outer Mongolia, or rather the Peoples' Republic of Mongolia. Canada had been one of the main actors in securing the admission of Mongolia to the United Nations in 1956 through a compromise which permitted Spain to join the world organization. Most NATO countries had established diplomatic relations with Mongolia and exchanged ambassadors, but it was only in 1974 that the Canadian government decided to follow suit and accredited me to Ulan Bator as well as Moscow. The news of the appointment as it appeared in the press gave the impression that I had been transferred to Ulan Bator, and I received several letters asking what sin I had committed to be consigned to the back of beyond.

Canada had no particular interest in Mongolia. The establishment of diplomatic relations with China and the opening of an embassy in Peking had attracted attention to the northern Pacific area. So the government decided it was logical to complete the process by formal relations with Mongolia, a step already taken by most NATO countries except the United States. While External Affairs did not share the view put forward by Harrison Salisbury that Mongolia could become the cockpit of World War Three, it was interested in knowing more about a country that occupied a strategic position between the two largest countries in the world, and was a constant bone of contention between them.

In May 1974 I travelled to this odd country to present my letters of credence, which I did in the middle of a snowstorm. I thought snow in mid-May was a bit too much. In fact, although the weather is very cold, there is usually not much snow, and lack of adequate precipitation is one of the many problems of Mongolia, creating desert conditions in the Gobi, which occupies the southern half of the country.

We approached Mongolia from China by a train which traverses the Great Wall and the Gobi desert. It was a wise decision since if we had come directly from Moscow, Ulan Bator would have seemed much like just another Soviet Central Asian city. Coming from China, the contrast between Asia and Soviet Asia was much more apparent. Most of the city is built strictly on modern Soviet utilitarian lines, but at least half the population still lives in felt yurts, or gers, to use the Mongolian name for the traditional tents. Unlike Peking, where practically the entire population seemed dressed in the ubiquitous Mao jacket, most of the inhabitants of Ulan Bator wore European clothes and those who did not were dressed in the rather beautiful traditional Mongolian costumes. Apart from the complex housing the Grand Lhama, Ulan Bator was as much a Soviet city as Tashkent or Samarkand. In fact, our official visit included a Russian-type rock concert (early Beatles songs) and a performance of the ballet 'Don Quixote,' staged exactly as in the classical Russian production, although it was slightly distracting to see the little Mongolians dressed in Spanish costume.

We paid a formal call on the Grand Lhama in his elaborately decorated ger, which looked singularly like a small circus tent. Here, drinking fermented mare's milk treated with salt, we were momentarily transported into the past, although not the past of those redoubtable warriors who, under Genghis Khan, Kublai Khan, and Batu the Terrible, conquered half the known world. In Ulan Bator, or riding in a land rover across the desolate plateau, or up to the fringes of the Gobi, it was difficult to imagine how a handful of people in this almost completely nomadic land seven centuries ago could subdue China, all of Central Asia, Afghanistan, Persia, most of Russia, and only turn back at the gates of Vienna. Their secret was mystery and the ruthless use of terror. Perhaps Stalin, in his study of history at the Orthodox seminary in the Caucasus, learned something from this remarkable people.

Mongolia, with a territory of 1,565,000 square kilometres, a population of about 1,600,000 and locked in between the two biggest countries in the world, had little choice but to adopt the Soviet model if it was not to give up the unequal struggle to maintain its identity. The country had stagnated for two hundred years during the reign of the Manchus, its people were almost totally illiterate, and were under the control of an idiotic form of Tibetan Buddhism by which 45 per cent of the male population were in monasteries and gradually dying out. It was clear in the 1920s that a drastic effort was necessary to drag the country into the modern world.

The Mongolians had only two choices: Soviet or Chinese tutelage. Previous Chinese rule had left very bad memories; the Chinese had attempted to hold on to Mongolia, not recognizing its independence until 1945, in contrast to instantaneous Soviet recognition in 1921. The Manchus had introduced Tibetan Buddhism into Mongolia in order to emasculate the Mongols and turn the society into one which was tranquil and unlikely to challenge its Chinese rulers. Buddhism had also opposed any kind of development and it had been a clever Chinese policy to colonize

Mongolia without bloodshed and to pacify a potentially aggressive people.

The Chinese communists were no different, according to Prime Minister Yumjagiyn Tsendenbal. He quoted Mao as saying in 1936 that China would annex Mongolia, and the Chinese had continued constantly since then to harass the country with frequent incursions into Mongolian territory. At the same time, the Chinese treatment of Inner Mongolia and the practical disappearance of Mongolians in China as a cultural or political unit indicated the true intentions of the Chinese communists toward the Mongolian race. Anyway, he concluded, the Chinese were never in a position to give the Mongolians the massive economic and technical aid they required and which the Soviets made available.

The Soviets were hardly disinterested since Mongolia was of enormous value to them as an advertisement of a 'benevolent' colonial policy in Asia and as a buffer between China and Siberia. Its huge and difficult territory, with forty-seven hundred kilometres bordering on China, clearly reduced the risk for the Russians of Chinese pressure against the central portion of Siberia. And Mongolia has considerable mineral riches, including copper, coal, iron, titanium, bauxite, and uranium. To make this treasure trove secure, the Soviets maintained a force of several divisions on Mongolian soil, and other forces in the Chita and Irkutsk areas of Siberia were deployed so that they could come to their aid if necessary. The Mongolian armed forces and police were formed along the lines of the Soviet forces, even to identical uniforms. In 1974 there were as many as ten thousand Soviet technicians and instructors in the economic enterprises, and advisers in all the important ministries, including that of foreign affairs.

Unlike the countries of Eastern Europe under Soviet control, however, it was clear that this was not resented by the Mongolians. The educated classes had been brought up entirely on the communist pattern, many of them trained in Moscow, and they recognized that the survival of Mongolia and the increase in the standard of living were the result of following the Soviet pattern in both internal and foreign affairs. Since the Chinese followed a policy of constant cultural and political threats to Mongolia, they had indeed very little choice. It seems extraordinary that the

Chinese did not recognize that their policies simply reinforced the Soviet position in Mongolia. There were certainly signs of an incipient Mongolian nationalism, including occasional incidents between young Mongols and Russians in the streets and shops. But on the whole, the Mongolians seemed satisfied with their position and much better off than the Soviet Asian republics, particularly Kazakhstan, Uzbekistan, or Kirgizia, all of which were at one time part of the Mongol empire. Effectively, the Mongolians have no more independence than the Soviet Asian republics, but the trappings of independence, including the presence of foreign diplomats, helps them maintain their feeling of national pride.

The diplomatic corps in Ulan Bator must be one of the oddest in the world. The huge Soviet embassy to all intents and purposes has a proconsular function and of course effectively supervises all activities in the country. There are in addition small missions from the East European countries, and from Yugoslavia, China, Japan, India, Great Britain and France. All other countries that have diplomatic relations with Mongolia accredit their ambassadors from Moscow or Peking, and when in Ulan Bator they are lodged in the one Soviet-type hotel.

The style of the British and French missions was curiously illustrative of the national character of these countries. Recognizing that living permanently in Ulan Bator would be for most Westerners a fate worse than death, the British always selected someone with some eccentricity that made it possible to survive the isolation of the capital. For example, one ambassador was an expert in Confucian culture and Chinese art. Regularly every two months he would go to Peking by train, spend a week looking at Tang and Ming porcelain, and return to Ulan Bator spiritually refreshed. Another British ambassador was a fanatic hunter and every Friday would take off in a land rover equipped with tent and guns to shoot gazelle.

The French solution was to appoint an ambassador who spent three months in Ulan Bator, after which time the mission was completely closed down and he returned to Paris for three months; after the respite back home, he could then return to Ulan Bator for another spell of duty. This seemed to work out well enough, but when on a visit to Mongolia in 1979 I called on the ambassador, he was in a state of total despair. He had just been informed that this system was coming to an end and he would have to make arrangements to live permanently in Ulan Bator.

On this occasion, a diplomatic 'incident' worthy of Evelyn Waugh was in the making. The new British ambassador had arrived six weeks before and I had met him at a performance of the Mongolian ballet. The French ambassador on whom I called the following day regretted that he could not invite our British colleague to a lunch he proposed to give for me because the man from London had not called on him officially. It seemed slightly absurd in a place as small as Ulan Bator with only two Western ambassadors on the spot that diplomatic niceties would prevent their talking to each other. No doubt they eventually worked out a satisfactory compromise.

During the many years I spent in the Soviet Union I was constantly amazed by the Soviet frustration over China and their inability to grapple with a subtlely elusive opponent. They feared and despised but at the same time respected the ability of the Chinese. It was rare to receive a dispassionate assessment of the country. When the Japanese rapprochement with China was beginning to take shape in 1972, I was subjected to a highly emotional discourse on the subject by one of the deputy foreign ministers. He was alarmed by the dangers inherent in an alliance of Japanese technology with nine hundred million Chinese. Nine hundred million, he repeated, a figure difficult to envisage, especially when you cannot understand how their minds work. Thinking out loud, he said: 'Just imagine if the Japanese, in some innocent-appearing electronics factory, might not be manufacturing some new secret weapon. And that's another risk in a Sino-Japanese alliance.'

I suggested that in the long run the Chinese fact would oblige the Soviet Union to turn to the European world. He responded without hesitation: 'That's beginning already and to start with we have agreed with the Americans that there can never be a war between us. That is definite and final.' And then, rather revealingly, he spoke of the need for understanding between the 'white people,' although he added that he could never come to like or trust the Germans who would try to change Europe again if they were reunited, adding emphatically and violently: 'But that will never happen. We will never permit it.'

As the situation evolved in China away from Maoism in internal affairs and toward a closer relationship with the United States and other Western countries, Soviet concern grew. In February 1979 I had a long talk with Leonid Zamyatin, head of the international information department of the Communist Party Secretariat, which was devoted almost exclusively to the subject of China. The points he made repeatedly were: that China was not a military threat to the Soviet Union by itself, but it had the resources and the potential to become a major military power. What worried the Soviets in the short run was the clearly outlined aim of Peking to form an anti-Soviet alliance in a large circle around the Soviet Union. China planned to make up for its military weakness by trying to ally itself with the United States, Western Europe, and Japan, and this was not only against the interests of the Soviet Union, but in the long run against that of the United States as well.

One of the tragedies of American policy in Vietnam was the failure to understand this rivalry between China and the Soviet Union. In February 1966 I found it depressing to realize that the official American assessment of the Chinese threat had scarcely changed from the very first days of the communist victory in Peking. It was based on the simple proposition that China, having adopted the ideology of the Soviet Union, had also adopted the foreign policy aims of Moscow. The possibility that these did not necessarily coincide, or that the national aims of these two vast and historically hostile countries could differ did not seem to enter into official calculations, although of course many American experts disagreed with Washington's perspective. And the Chinese did not make it easy to understand them.

I was frequently impressed by the similarity of the propaganda line taken by Mao in the 1960s and that of Stalin in 1951–2. The outlandish Chinese statements on foreign and domestic affairs were no less credible than those that had emanated from the Kremlin. The 'Little Red Book of Mao' was no more ridiculous than the 'Short Course' of Stalin; and the adulation of the latter no less absurd than that of Mao.

Faced with the implacable hostility of the United States, Mao had little choice but to follow the policy that Stalin adopted in 1945: the rejection of collaboration with the West in favour of a policy of autarchy and hostility which he considered necessary to conserve the ideological base of the regime and to bring the Soviet Union through the period of privation needed to rebuild its economy and acquire the military means to achieve equality with the United States.

Having served in Belgrade, I was sensitive to the ideological and national differences which made a split between China and the Soviet Union inevitable. And in my first talk with Marshal Tito in early 1959, it was clear that he foresaw the likelihood of Sino-Soviet rivalry, even though he also deeply resented the way in which Mao continued to consider him as a heretic from Marxism. Thus it was hard to accept the United States' conviction that China and the Soviet Union had similar aims in Southeast Asia. Early in 1963 President John F. Kennedy dismissed the Sino-Soviet dispute as a mere quarrel over tactics, whereas by the summer of that year the seriousness of the break was unmistakable. In the end, of course, it was the North Vietnamese who decided the fate of Indo-China, and a more accurate appreciation of Sino-Soviet relations and Chinese foreign goals on the part of the Americans would probably not have changed things very much, since Kennedy and Johnson had pledged the United States to defend the free world in every circumstance.

However, the Americans were not alone in failing to understand what was happening in China. The Soviets misjudged the situation from the very beginning. They did not understand the strength and determination of the communists under Mao and Chou En-lai. As the war with Japan ended in 1945, Stalin calculated that the communists would only be able to control a part of China, therefore he planned on the assumption that the Nationalists would remain in power. Certainly relations with Chiang Kai-shek were cordial right up to the final collapse of his government. There is plausibility in the argument of some experts that Stalin would have preferred a divided China and that he underestimated the weakness and corruption of the Nationalists.

The Russians are not adept at judging other people, and they are at heart racists. Their attitude to the Chinese was often overbearing and neo-colonialist, and it was complicated by ideological differences, the quarrel over leadership of world communism, and conflicting national ambitions. The Chinese were prepared to accept Stalin as the dominant communist figure but they would not do the same for Khrushchev or Brezhnev, nor will they ever accept a relationship with the CPSU except on a basis of equality.

The Russian fear and dislike of the Chinese is understandable in emotional terms and in strategic geopolitical terms – that is, of a China allied to the United States and Japan. But in considering China, the Russians find it difficult to be rational. They constantly either underrate or overrate it, rationalizing that the danger to the Soviet Union consists in China being 'used' by the United States. The danger to Moscow exists more likely in China 'using' the United States to promote its national interests at the expense of the Soviet Union. It is too great a country to be anyone's pawn.

It seemed to me that the Russians analysed Chinese developments in the light of their own experience. Theoretically, a disciplined communist leadership was destined to build up a modern military machine that would permit it to claim great power status even without a modern economic base. Political vagaries and upheavals inside the Chinese Communist Party kept reassuring the Russians that this could not happen in their time. And then the unpredictable happened in the rise of a great leader, Deng Xiao-ping, capable of reversing the direction of internal affairs and reconciling China with the West.

I do not think the Russians have any idea what will happen in a decade's time. More normal relations between Moscow and Peking may well be established. It would be unusual if this did not take place. But whatever does occur, the Chinese will act in their own self-interest, which is unlikely to coincide with that of the Soviets. For the Kremlin, Soviet relations with China, and China's growing role in world affairs, will become only slightly less important a foreign policy problem than that of the relationship with the United States.

12

The Afghan Blunder and the Southern Approaches

It was not only China and Japan that the Russians misunderstood and misjudged. Even in Afghanistan, the key country on their Asian border, they failed to comprehend what was happening. Their dramatic and brutal invasion late in December 1979 compounded one of the major errors in Soviet foreign policy since Stalin's decision in 1950 that the time was ripe for taking over South Korea. But the blood spilled in that war was not Russian, as it was to be in Afghanistan.

The invasion took most people by surprise, including Jimmy Carter, who confessed it had finally revealed to him the true nature of the Soviet system. Yet Moscow's decision to commit armed forces in Afghanistan, although unwise, was consistent with the overriding strategic and political importance the Russians attached to the country and to the whole of the Soviet Union's soft underbelly.

The Russians had succeeded in creating a buffer zone between themselves and Western Europe by the forcible incorporation of Eastern Europe into the Soviet bloc and by neutralizing Finland after World War Two. The creation of an 'independent' Mongolian state and the stationing of a large Soviet standing army there helped cushion their vulnerable possessions in Siberia from China. The relative isolation of Sinkiang made the Chinese presence on the frontier with Kazakhstan and Kirgizia easy to contain. But the frontier in the south abutted directly on Turkey, Iran, and Afghanistan, and the neighbouring regions of the Soviet Union were largely inhabited by non-Slavic races whose loyalty to the Soviet system imposed by Russia was uncertain. The Caucasus consists of three republics – Georgia, Armenia, and Azerbaijan – and a number of smaller autonomous regions speaking a bewildering variety of languages. The inhabitants of the area are nationalist and proud of their history, culture, and traditions. Yet although they are uneasy in their attitude to Moscow, their Turkish and Iranian neighbours exert palpably less attraction. Except for the Moslem Azerbaijanians and Dagastanians, they share a Christian tradition with the Russians. Part of Russia since the late eighteenth century, the Caucasian peoples consider themselves European even if determined to maintain their own cultural and national identities. Small, mountainous, easily defensible, this ethnically non-Russian region of the Soviet Union, while strategically important, gives Moscow little cause for concern. Armenian nationalist demonstrations are directed primarily against their Moslem neighbours, not the Russians. After all, they are reminded every day by the sight of Mount Ararat across the frontier in Turkey and the heart of their ancient kingdom, that there is no other secure homeland for them.

The same cannot be said of the five republics of Central Asia which are largely populated by people of Asian descent, with an ancient warlike tradition, an alien culture and, in spite of Soviet efforts to stamp it out, the heritage of Islam. Russian expansion into the area in the nineteenth century was inevitable. Colonization spread across Siberia, due partly to the inexorable surge outwards of a dynamic people against the backward, decaying, and weak remnants of the empires of Genghis Khan and Tamerlaine, and partly due to the drive to protect their lines of communication to the north across Siberia. The conquest of the local emirates, above all those of Bokhara, Khiva, and Kokand, stretched out over most of the last century. As soon as the emirates fell, the Russians' perception of security inevitably required the extension of their area of conquest as far as possible, particularly as many of the conquered peoples, especially the Uzbeks and Tadjhiks, had racial, religious, and occasionally dynastic ties with their fellow Moslems across the frontier in Afghanistan.

This aroused the fears of the British in India who were occupied in doing exactly the same thing south of the Hindu Kush – that is, in expanding their area of conquest, they were seeking to incorporate or neutralize the peoples of Afghanistan for security reasons. Again, many of the tribes of the North West Frontier, particularly the Baluchis and Pathans, occupied territory on both sides of the loosely defined border.

The result was the 'Great Game,' in which the two most important imperial powers of the time skirmished and feinted in Afghanistan in an effort to keep the other side out. The British, in particular, could never forget that Baber, the Mongol conqueror of India, had departed from Kokand, first for Afghanistan and then, wisely for him, the more amenable lands and peoples of northern India. Both powers learned the hard way that the Afghans were best left to themselves. It is salutary to recall that the British occupied Kabul in 1840 and established a puppet regime. The Afghans rose in revolt, and when the only surviving member of the British expeditionary force staggered into Jalalabad, his first remark was that he only wished that it had been the Russians who had tried to impose themselves on the Afghans. The subsequent Afghan wars did not end in British conquest, but they did keep the Russians out. The Anglo-Russian agreement of 1907, guaranteeing Afghanistan independence under British influence, in turn provoked anti-British feeling and the third Anglo-Afghan war of 1919.

In the light of events in the last decade in Iran, it is also worth recalling that King Amanullah, who changed the Afghan emirate to a kingdom in 1926, was deposed in 1929 by fanatical Moslems who opposed his mild efforts to modernize the country; and his successor, Mohamad Nodei, was assassinated in 1933 for trying to revive the program of modernization.

During this period the Soviet regime was engaged in a difficult battle to bring the various Central Asian tribes and emirates into the communist framework. Since this involved the destruction of the existing feudal society and the suppression of the Moslem religion, it encountered fierce opposition which continued sporadically up to World War Two. Tens of thousands of Uzbeks, who speak a variant of Turkish, and Tadjhiks, who speak Persian of a form similar to that of the dominant Afghan tribes, fled to Afghanistan, where they settled permanently and maintained suspicion of and hostility to the Soviet system. In fact, the estimated four million Tadjhiks in Afghanistan now outnumber those in the Tadjhik Soviet Republic by about one million.

British activities in Central Asia in support of anti-Bolshevik forces after 1918, although extremely limited, were interpreted by the communists in Moscow as an effort to establish independent countries in Central Asia which would permit Britain to extend its influence. The fact that the British consulate general in Kashgar, the capital of Sinkiang, was used as the base of operations and that it was organized from New Delhi only increased Soviet suspicions and made them more determined to incorporate the Asian republics into the Soviet Union. Suspicions on the British side were in turn increased as the activities of two Indian communists, Mahendra Pratep and M.N. Roy, became known. Their objective, hardly disguised and fully endorsed by Lenin, was to 'liberate' the Indian subcontinent.

Thus it was inevitable from the start of the Bolshevik regime that the Soviets would maintain an intense interest in whatever happened in Afghanistan. As their rule was consolidated in Central Asia, they came to regard Afghanistan primarily as a hostile pole of attraction for their own Asian peoples, not as a tool of British imperialism, the threat of which was clearly eroding in the years between the two world wars.

The Soviets were not at that time in a strong enough position to do much about Afghanistan. They did remind the Afghan monarchy frequently and without much subtlety of the overwhelming Soviet presence on its northern frontier; and they continued to stress their legitimate interest in seeing that subsequent Afghan governments maintained neutrality in world affairs and did not permit refugees to create trouble in Soviet Central Asia. In return the Soviet leaders, while tolerating the existence of the monarchy, exerted increasing pressure, as a consequence of which Afghan neutrality slanted more and more in the direction of Moscow.

The peoples of the Soviet Central Asian republics became slowly adjusted to life under Soviet control. The younger people, who quickly became a majority because of the fecundity of the population, seemed not greatly to miss the Moslem religion nor the mullahs, who decreased rapidly in number. Today there are almost as few mullahs as there are functioning mosques, and only one seminary, in Tashkent, under close Russian supervision. What they got in return for becoming in effect Uzbek, Turkomen, Tadjhik, Kirgiz, or Kazakh Soviet citizens was a rapid increase in their standard of living and almost universal education. These things together made the attraction exerted from across the frontier almost minimal. Indeed, the Soviets believed the influence ran the other way, from the Soviet Union to the backward tribes of Afghanistan.

The Russians had every reason to be satisfied with their relations with the Afghan monarchy, and with the Shah of Iran, particularly since 1962 when, in spite of the shah's clever military, political, and economic involvement with the West, the Soviets established friendly, even benevolent, relations with Teheran. There seemed nothing for the Soviets to fear from a somewhat ineffective Afghan monarchy dedicated to a slow program of modernization, often with Soviet help, inside the country, and pro-Moscow neutrality in foreign affairs.

This Soviet policy of neutrality, with varying degrees of benevolence, was extended to all countries in the area – Pakistan, India, Nepal, Burma, and later Bangladesh – no matter what the nature of the regime or its ideology. The main aim seemed to be to maintain a measure of stability in the region and above all to neutralize any effort by China to extend its influence. This relative moderation and pragmatism in Soviet policy was at the same time accompanied by a determined and aggressive effort to extend Soviet influence by the rapid expansion, modernization, and deployment of Soviet naval forces in the Indian Ocean. At the same time, Russia was contributing to the creation of conditions in Afghanistan bound to lead to the demand for the abolition of the monarchy, in particular the training of thousands of Afghan students in Soviet universities and technical institutes.

In 1973 King Mohamed Zakir Shah was overthrown and a

moderate republic under Mohamad Daoud Khan established. While it is tempting to think that this was the work of the Russians, I have seen no overwhelming evidence to this effect. Afghan friends, not pro-Soviet, have told me that the king was deposed almost entirely for internal reasons because he had been unable to reconcile the constantly warring tribes or fit the younger and better educated people into what was still basically a feudal system. An Afghan confidant in a position to know claimed it was the result primarily of the ambitions of Daoud Khan, a bitter, revengeful man and a Pushtu who despised all the northern tribes whom he considered had been favoured by the king. He also loathed the British, a feeling that dated from what he considered a personal humiliation when he was foreign minister. Not only had he failed in his great ambition to get the frontiers between Afghanistan and Pakistan revised, he was not even received by the British foreign minister when he went to London for the frontier talks. He had vowed revenge on the king because of the monarch's alleged pro-British sentiments.

The democratic republic set up by Daoud was on the whole Western-oriented, but the Russians seemed to find it easy to maintain with it much the same kind of mutually profitable relations as with the monarchy. Moscow seemed satisfied with both internal developments in the country and the continuation of its neutralist foreign policy – satisfied, that is, until the sudden emergence of China as a more active force in southwest Asia. For differing reasons, Pakistan, Bangladesh, and India all began to respond in varying ways to Chinese overtures, as Peking demonstrated a new interest in the area. Only Afghanistan seemed conscious of Soviet preoccupations with the Chinese diplomatic offensive and remained ostensibly pro-Soviet, although by 1977 Moscow was becoming suspicious that Daoud was contemplating a shift toward the West.

By April 1978 the democratic republic was in turn overthrown and replaced by a communist government under Nur Mohamad Taraki. While the Soviets appeared likely to gain by the establishment of a regime openly communist and pro-Moscow, my Afghan informant claimed the Soviets did not have a long-term plan to bring Kabul into their orbit. The immediate reasons for the overthrow of Daoud were internal. He had been unable to cope with growing economic problems and he had alienated the powerful northern tribes by trying to impose Pushtus in all important posts. The Soviets nevertheless had made preparations for the eventuality of a communist coup, and this was touched off when Moscow learned that Daoud was abandoning the traditional line of pro-Soviet neutrality. The Soviets decided to support the coup when the Soviet embassy learned that Daoud was planning a visit to Saudi Arabia to seek Saudi money and Western support.

The communist seizure of power resulted in a significant advance of Soviet influence in the whole area, including the increased ability to exert pressure on Iran and Pakistan, and the subsequent setback to China. It seemed too favourable to Soviet interests to be pure coincidence. The Soviets had also become disturbed by signs of growing instability in Pakistan and India and destabilization in Iran, and the opportunity this seemed to give to a newly dynamic China, already turning toward the United States, to stir up trouble along their enormously long southern frontier. In Soviet eyes, a regime in Kabul drifting out of their orbit could only have further contributed to the danger.

The moment Taraki took power, his government proclaimed its aims: to create a modern socialist society modelled on the Soviet Union and with Soviet aid. Taraki began immediately to implement this program by agrarian reform and the break-up of big estates, and by reform of a number of Moslem social customs, including the total abolition of the dowry, the emancipation of woman, and the right of divorce. In an almost illiterate population, devoted to the Moslem way of life, this provoked an immediate reaction. Taraki responded by bombarding recalcitrant villages, brutal repression of any who opposed the forces of modernization, and sweeping purges in the army and administration. To survive he needed to rely totally on Soviet support and Soviet advisers in large numbers.

For the Soviet Union this was not its first experience in sending military and civilian consultants abroad: to Guinée and Mali, Egypt and, of course, to already established communist regimes in Cuba and Vietnam. But the advisers in those countries generally remained external to the societies in which they operated. In

Afghanistan, on the other hand, they moved into every government department; and since the bulk of them were from Soviet
Central Asia, they were able to penetrate the Afghan administration effectively. Indeed, in many ways it was the opposite of what
many observers had thought was the Soviet fear: that is, the
infiltration of Islamic ideas into Soviet Central Asia. In this case it
was the Soviets who tried to spread their propaganda as an Asian
power in Afghanistan. In any event, the Soviet presence became
massive, somewhat like their domination of the administration of
the Mongolian Republic, where every government department
had a Soviet deputy and dozens of advisers.

The Afghan Communist Party had first become a force in the
country when various leftist elements united to form the Popular
Democratic Party in 1965. In 1968, a schism in the party took place
between the Khalq and Parchem factions; it was to be finally
reunited in 1977. The two factions, the Khalq under Taraki and
the Parchem under Babrak Karmal, joined to stage the coup which
destroyed Daoud. Taraki became prime minister and Karmal
vice-premier until July, when the union fell apart. Karmal was sent
into exile as ambassador to Czechoslovakia and Taraki and the
Khalq held power until the Soviet invasion eliminated him and
installed Karmal in Kabul. The Khalq officially supported the
Karmal government, but only as the result of strong Soviet
pressure. In fact, it was largely excluded from any role in the
administration.

Although dedicated to a Soviet brand of socialism, the two
factions found their basis of popular support in the countryside
and the Pushtu tribes in the case of Khalq, and in the Tadjhiks and
the urban classes in the case of Parchem. But Taraki's victory,
primarily of the Khalq, led to a confrontation with the very
elements on which his popular support depended, because the
unlimited and immediate application of Soviet-type socialism ran
contrary to the traditions and wishes of his supporters. Taraki also
faced a confrontation with the Parchem and the Tadjhiks who in
turn were confronted with the double hostility of the Khalq and of
the Soviet advisers, often of Tadjhik origin. Hence Taraki had
increasingly to fall back on Soviet aid, and increasingly the

Parchem were driven into a position of hostility to the Soviet advisers.

Thus we see that the problems which led to the Soviet armed intervention were apparent very soon after the advent of the communist government under Taraki. In principle, the Soviets had a better chance of installing communism in Afghanistan by relying on the Parchem, drawing its support from the educated urban classes and allied to the Tadjhiks, than by allying themselves with the Khalq, but the policies of the latter drove the Parchem and their supporters into opposition.

The Russians, no matter what doubts they might have held about Taraki, were committed to him. In December 1978 they signed a Treaty of Friendship, Good Neighbourliness and Co-operation with his government, somewhat along the line of one they had just negotiated with Ethiopia. It seemed to dispel any lingering doubts about Afghanistan's future path, and Brezhnev called it a demonstration of 'not simply good neighbourliness but profound, sincere and durable friendship permeated by the spirit of comradeship and revolutionary solidarity.'

I had a chance to talk to Taraki when he visited the Kremlin. I found him a handsome, elegantly groomed gentleman who went out of his way to try to convince me that the communist government in Kabul, and the treaty of friendship, did not mean any lessening of Afghan interest in good and productive relations with Western countries. He said he hoped we would not lose interest in his country.

After his return to Kabul, the smouldering hatred between Taraki and his foreign minister, Hafizullah Amin, burst into the open, complicated by a rebellion by the Resistance Front and the Moslem Brotherhood representing as much as 80 per cent of the population. On 19 September 1979, Amin had Taraki murdered – only a few days after Taraki, on his return from a non-aligned summit in Havana, had been received in Moscow by Brezhnev and Gromyko in a public display of Soviet support. Amin maintained that it had been necessary to eliminate Taraki in order to unify the country and end the rebellion. But he made no attempt to change the Khalq policy and reverted increasingly to severe repression to crush the revolt, and to put down Khalq elements determined to revenge the death of Taraki. The Soviets showed increasing concern that his brutal policies would undermine all possibility of a stable government and would lead to a lessening of Kabul's dependence on Moscow.

The revolt against the communists had introduced a new volitility on the southern Soviet frontier, and added the totally new factor of a resurgence of Islamic feeling. The more the rebellion in Afghanistan took on a fanatical Moslem slant and was identified as well with anti-Russian sentiment, the more the Soviets became alarmed at this new development across their long southern frontier. I doubt they had much reason to fear that this intense Islamic feeling would touch very many of the contiguous and ethnically related groups in Soviet Central Asia, but they were worried about the possible revival of national feeling on the part of Azerbaijanians, Uzbeks, Turkomen, Tadjhiks, Kazakhs, Kirgiz, and others. Above all, they worried that the Asian Soviet peoples might begin to question the desirability of fusing their national background into one great Homen Sovieticus at the expense of their own ethnic origins. Such sentiments had been kept in the background until then, but they might be resurrected out of sympathy for the Islamic outburst in Iran and Afghanistan.

In Moscow events began to develop rapidly. We were dismayed by the failure of the Carter administration to react strongly to the kidnapping and murder of Adolph ('Spike') Dubs, the American ambassador to Kabul, and by the chaotic situation that was evolving. The Soviets began secretly to plan for the overthrow of Amin, the imposition of their man Karmal, still banished to his diplomatic posting in Prague, and the use of armed force to make sure this was the definitive decision. The humiliation of having Taraki murdered one week after being endorsed in the Kremlin by Brezhnev was also an important factor in the Soviet decision to act. The unpopularity of Amin and his brutal regime must have helped persuade the Soviets that they had a unique opportunity to fulfill the ambitions of a century and a half and establish themselves militarily and politically in an area they had always considered of vital importance to them. But the primary reason for the decision to intervene and to impose their puppet on the Afghan Communist

Party was the imminent prospect of the overthrow of the communist regime, the substitution of an anti-Soviet government in its
place, and the elimination of Soviet influence in this key area.

On 27 December the Soviet ambassador in Ottawa informed the
Canadian government that the 'democratic regime' in Afghanistan
was under threat from outside interference and under these
circumstances the Afghan leadership had 'appealed to the USSR for
assistance and co-operation in the struggle against outside aggression.' Moscow had agreed 'to send limited military contingents to
Afghanistan.' The Canadian deputy under-secretary to whom this
statement was given immediately replied that our government
would be deeply concerned at the Soviet move. No evidence existed
to support Moscow's claim that Afghanistan was subject to external
aggression – the Russian move was clearly intervention in a civil
conflict in a neighbouring country.

A day later the Soviets moved with a force of eighty thousand
troops which met little initial resistance. But on the political side the
intervention was badly mishandled. It was presumably intended
that Amin should have been taken into custody and replaced by the
Soviet puppet, Karmal, and that the latter would then call for
military assistance. I received information that the military had
persuaded the defence minister, Dmitri Ustinov, that the security
situation was at the point of total breakdown, and that the Soviet
army could take over and reduce the rebellion in short order
without major repercussions. Ustinov in turn had persuaded
Brezhnev. My source said that the plot went wrong because of the
precipitate action of the senior KGB representative in Kabul, who
jumped the gun and sent a signal for the military to move before
Amin was actually arrested and before Karmal had been returned
to Kabul. In the confusion Amin was assassinated. Because of the
mistiming, the Soviets were put in the position of alleging that they
had been invited to intervene in Afghanistan by a government
headed by a man who was at the time flying from Prague to Kabul
via Tashkent in a Soviet plane. Thus at the time of this 'invitation'
the actual head of the government in Kabul was being murdered by
the KGB or its Afghan agents.

I had come to know the Afghanistan ambassador in Moscow
fairly well. He was a young man, a member of the Afghan

Communist Party, who had spent fourteen years as a student in the Soviet Union. He struck me as a typical example of the immense effort the Russians must have put into training the young generation in Afghanistan. He professed to be an atheist and ambitious to help turn Afghanistan into a modern society. One week before the murder of Amin, he asked to see me urgently to say that he had been recalled to Kabul and was leaving, obviously in great distress. I subsequently learned that the Russians took him off the flight from Moscow to Kabul at Tashkent and kept him there in order that he could join Babrak Karmal and return with him in triumph to the Afghan capital. When the new government was formed, he became minister of agriculture.

Canada, together with most other Western countries that had received the flimsy 'explanation' for the Soviet invasion, protested strongly, contesting the Soviet version, and expressing alarm at the effect of this action on East-West relations. The Canadian government of Joe Clark reacted strongly but fell shortly afterward. When the Liberals returned to office Pierre Trudeau also saw the need to protest the Soviet action and wrote a letter to Brezhnev underlining Canadian concern at the implications of the Soviet invasion of a peaceful neighbour. When I transmitted the missive through Deputy Foreign Minister Igor Zemskov, I received from him a revealing, highly emotional version of events as seen by the Soviets.

It became apparent from Zemskov that the Soviets had made up their minds that the United States, which by then had reacted strongly, was deliberately adopting a more confrontational policy with the Soviet Union. The deputy minister insisted that at the root of the current problems in the world was the American effort to encircle his country. Under the shah, the Americans had stationed forty thousand troops in Iran, and this was a continual threat. The Americans had been forced to get out of Iran, but the situation was still fluid there and the Soviet Union could not permit another neighbouring country to be a threat to its security. He claimed the CIA was behind the 'counter-revolutionaries' in Afghanistan and that the build-up of u.s. naval forces in the Indian Ocean and the Persion Gulf, and plans to train a rapid deployment military force, were fresh evidence of American intentions to intervene militarily anywhere it considered its interests were threatened. It was impossible for Moscow to ignore American actions when they were close to Soviet borders. The Soviet Union, Zemskov said, simply could not remain idle during u.s. military action vis-à-vis Afghanistan and their threats to the regime of Ayatollah Khomeini in Iran.

In spite of the mishandling of the installation of Karmal, the Russians must have thought that the operation would be relatively easy. They were mistaken on two counts: the strong reaction from the Western countries and the third world; and the Afghan nationalist resistance which appeared almost as soon as the initial shock of the Soviet invasion had worn off. The Soviets completely misjudged Western reaction to Afghanistan. To draw the proper conclusions from history, they should have returned to the brutal communist takeover of Czechoslovakia in 1948, even though it was accomplished without overt military intervention. The Russian actions in Hungary in 1956 and in Czechoslovakia in 1968, while a revolting display of naked power, did not alter the military or political balance in Europe. The 1948 coup, however, did represent a radical change in the balance of power in central Europe by incorporating a benevolently neutral country into a member of the Soviet bloc and by bringing Soviet power within striking distance of Munich and Vienna. Western reaction was strong enough to lead to the creation of NATO, to bring American and Canadian military forces back to Europe, and to put the stamp of the cold war on East-West relations for the following decade. Even if Soviet motives in Czechoslovakia had been defensive, it was almost universally interpreted in the West as an aggressive move to extend the area of direct Soviet control, carrying with it the threat of further expansion into an almost defenceless and fractured Western Europe.

The Russians clearly made another historic miscalculation in the invasion of Afghanistan. Since the West had not reacted to the downfall of the monarchy, nor to the overthrow of the democratic republic and the installation of a communist regime, nor to the murder of the American ambassador, the Soviets believed they were safe in concluding that the United States did not consider Afghanistan of vital security importance. They assumed there would be protests, but that this would pass with time. They failed to see the difference between military moves within the Soviet sphere in Eastern Europe and the invasion of a neighbouring country outside the existing Soviet bloc. In addition, they believed that the timing was right: both American preoccupation with the Iranian situation and internal political problems in the United States, and the souring of American relations with the Soviet Union made it seem likely that Moscow had little more to lose. Furthermore, their past experiences with the third world showed that they could get away with almost any crime, particularly at a time when the Arab and Islamic states were concentrating their wrath on the United States.

However, the Soviets would almost certainly have used military force in Afghanistan even if they had correctly anticipated Western reaction, since it was inconceivable that they would permit the erosion of a communist regime in a neighbouring country of vital importance to them. Whether they would have done so if their military advisers had properly calculated the length and effectiveness of Afghan nationalist resistance is another question.

But their move into Afghanistan was taken almost entirely for local reasons. It was not, as the American administration and some other observers in the West concluded, the first move in a thrust toward the Indian Ocean. This may be a very long-term Soviet aim, but the Russians are highly realistic and their ambitions in 1979 were limited to preserving a Marxist, pro-Soviet regime in Afghanistan and protecting Soviet security in Central Asia. The situation in Iran was probably an important subsidiary consideration. Internal instability there affected Soviet security interests, and trouble in Iranian Azerbaijan, contiguous to the Soviet republic of Azerbaijan, made this problem especially important to the Russians.

It was clear from the moment Soviet troops invaded Afghanistan that Western countries had to react, and discussions among NATO and other Western countries commenced immediately. Few of us had any illusions that we could force the Russians out of Afghanistan. The objective of any reprisals had to be, first, to make the Russians pay a price for their action, and second, to make it clear that with the invasion of Afghanistan the limits of tolerance had been reached and that any further Soviet expansion would finally destroy the chances of reviving détente. Nevertheless, we had to make sure doors were not completely closed; in due course means had to be found to live with the Soviet Union in spite of actions which often passed beyond acceptable international conduct.

The most obvious options for reprisal were a boycott of the Olympic Games and an embargo on grain shipments. The grain trade between Canada and the Soviet Union was of immense importance to Canada and particularly the Western farmer. If we had followed the American lead, not only would we have suffered at least as much as the Russians, but the very special and enduring relationship between the Canadian Wheat Board and the Soviet organization Exportkhleb would have been seriously damaged. So we chose not to go the embargo route. In any case, the American action was short-lived, was opposed from the beginning by Ronald Reagan, and did not seriously damage the Soviet economy.

The boycott of the Olympic Games, however, hit at Soviet pride. This, the first major international sporting event in Moscow, was to be an enormous demonstration of Soviet efficiency and organization. Above all, it was to show the triumph of Soviet communism. The boycott was intended to make every Russian aware of the price they had to pay for the invasion of Afghanistan, and in that sense it was successful. But at the same time, so much effort had been involved by so many Russians in the Games, the boycott came to be resented by the average Russian as a further example of Western, and especially American, hatred of their country. As in the case of most efforts to 'punish' a great power by secondary means, the reprisals against the Soviet Union were limited in duration and certainly limited in their effect. Nevertheless, the main point was made: it will not be easy for the Soviets to repeat their Afghan adventure without risking a major confrontation with the West.

From the time of Ivan the Terrible, the Russian tsars had a primordial interest in pushing back the Tartars and Mongols who had occupied ancient Russian lands. It was a slow and difficult process and only at the end of the seventeenth century did Peter the Great succeed in destroying the power of the Volga Tartars and reaching an outlet on the southern seas at Taganrog on the Sea of Azov. In fact, he planned to make this his window on the outside world and laid out Taganrog as the new imperial capital; even today in this rather sleepy provincial town one can see the architectural layout for a great city. In the park overlooking the harbour stands a statue of Peter the Great pointing to the sea. The plans, of course, were abandoned when Peter drove the Swedes out of the south-eastern corner of the Gulf of Finland, permitting him to establish in St Petersburg his real window on the West.

The Crimea was still a Tartar khanate and it only came under Russian control in the middle of the eighteenth century. At the same time the Russians pressed into the Caucasus, in part to occupy the fertile lands lying between the River Don and the Caspian, and in part as a response to the dynamic surge of the Russian peoples and the requests for help from the Christian kingdoms and tribes in Georgia, Armenia, and smaller areas of the Caucasus. Armenia spread across the frontier into Turkey, and the boundary was not established permanently until well after the Russian revolution. In 1946 it took a threat of force on the part of Britain and the United States to persuade the Soviets to evacuate Persian Azerbaijan which they had occupied as part of a wartime agreement.

Memories of the Mongol invasion and occupation of a large part of Russia in the thirteenth century, and the constant Tartar raids out of the Crimea up until the eighteenth, are still part of the vivid memories and folklore of Russia and it takes very little to revive the spectre of the yellow menace. In 1951-2, for example, some loose talk in Turkey of Greater Turkistan, which would include Azerbaijan and the Central Asian Turkish-speaking republics of Turkmenistan and Uzbekistan, evoked a violent response from the Russians.

The preoccupation of the Russians, therefore, with their porous southern frontier is not new and is understandable. For a long time Iran was not considered a menace as long as it remained more or less stable, backward, and free of British (and later American) influence. The Soviets had a player in Iran, the Iranian Communist Party, Tudeh, but I doubt whether before the Khomeini uprising they ever really believed it could seize power. But it was a useful instrument for reminding the royal house of Iran of the potential for mischief controlled by Moscow.

The Soviet Union made a very special effort to cultivate the shah in spite of his pro-American leanings. He was received at regular intervals in Moscow and in 1974 with some pomp. I had a conversation with him then and was astounded at his pretensions. He said his ambition was to turn Iran into the Japan of the Middle East, and that within a few years his country would transform the whole area. He said that he had no particular reason for coming to Russia except to maintain relations with the Soviet Union on an even keel and alleviate any anxieties the Russians might have about Iran's close relations with the United States. He obviously considered himself and his country on a par of importance with Russia. Certainly he gave not the slightest indication of preoccupation with the internal situation in Iran. But as far as that goes, neither did the Russians, who treated him on this and other occasions with extreme deference. And yet at the same time they were carefully maintaining contacts with the remnants of the Tudeh and building up Iraq as their counter to Iran. In fact, Brezhnev warned the shah in 1974 to avoid a conflict with Iraq as such a confrontation would not be in the interests of either country or of the Soviet Union.

It is a constant mystery how neither the shah nor first-hand Western observers understood what was happening prior to the revolution. In the summer of 1978 my wife and a Canadian friend made a month's tour of Iran. They came back appalled at what they had seen and certain that the regime of the shah would not last very long. When they expressed their views in Teheran, however, to the Canadian and American ambassadors, these were dismissed with gales of laughter as the foolish inventions of mere amateurs.

In any event, the Khomeini revolution was as great a surprise to the Russians as it was to the West. They were delighted with the blow to American influence, but unwilling to believe that the Americans would abandon the shah or their position in Iran without a struggle. The creation of the u.s. rapid deployment force strengthened these suspicions and they began gradually to increase the anti-American tone of their comments on Iran, and to express qualified support for Khomeini. But they were equally dubious of Khomeini and found it very, very difficult to make an accurate assessment of the forces which he had released. They were uneasy about the possible impact of fundamentalist Moslem ideas on their own Central Asians, and unsure of the direction in which Khomeini would go. But a non-Khomeini supporter in the Iranian embassy in Moscow told me that almost immediately after the ayatollah took power, the Soviets put into action a long-term plan of support for all of the leftist elements, particularly the Tudeh Party, which they had begun to believe would eventually take power.

The seizure of the American embassy in Teheran in 1980 and the holding of the staff as hostages caused the Russians some concern; but they were still smarting from the American reprisals over Afghanistan and the failure to ratify SALT II and were in no mood to help the Americans out of their dilemma. In my capacity as dean of the diplomatic corps, I tried on several occasions to persuade the Russians that this was an intolerable infraction of diplomatic immunity and civilized international practice and that, no matter what the state of U.S.-Soviet relations, they should join in international pressure on the Iranians. On one occasion, I spoke to Foreign Minister Gromyko about it, starting out by saying that they should feel sympathetic since their great ambassador and poet Griboyedov had been murdered in the Russian embassy in Teheran by a fanatical Moslem mob one hundred and fifty years earlier. He looked at me with his steely grey eyes and said: 'Please don't give me lessons in Russian history.'

However, more important for the Russians was the persecution of the left-wing parties, and particularly the Tudeh, by Khomeini's followers. Moscow's reaction was interesting and an example of the way in which the Russians can control their emotions and practise patient diplomacy with long-term aims in view. Although they protested, they swallowed the affront and settled down to the long wait for Khomeini's demise. After he is gone, they expect to increase their influence in the chaotic situation likely to result and to promote their long-term aims. This can be summed up as primarily to prevent events in Iran from influencing their own Asian populations; to advance their own influence and that of the Iranian Communist Party in order to have a southern neighbour amenable to Moscow; and to prevent the return of the United States as the dominant power in Iran.

The Russians can afford to sit and wait in Iran, and they must calculate that the extravagances of the regime of the mullahs and the destructiveness of the war with Iraq will prevent Iran from becoming a danger for a long time to come. Afghanistan, however, is another story. Early in 1980, a Soviet official, irritated by my criticism of the invasion, burst out that we would one day forget Afghanistan as we had forgotten Czechoslovakia and that they would never leave. This might have been the case if there had not been a determined resistance to the Soviets by most of the Afghan population. Probably many in the Soviet leadership, even before the arrival of Mikhail Gorbachev, regretted the decision to commit armed forces, but in 1979 the alternative must have seemed unacceptable. It has taken nine years of war, increasingly heavy Soviet casualties, little likelihood of crushing the guerrilla fighters, and a new and more realistic leadership to lead Moscow to contemplate a military and almost certainly a political withdrawal from Afghanistan and a proportionate decrease in its power to influence developments in the Indian subcontinent.

We in the West and certainly in North America tend very often to be insensitive to genuine Soviet security concerns. The same can be said of the Russian lack of concern for Western security interests. Nevertheless, we should not overlook the fact that the strategically important zones of Russia in the Caucasus and Central Asia are inhabited in overwhelming majority by non-Russians whose loyalty the Russians suspect, and whose integration into Soviet Russian society can never be totally successful. And beyond this soft underbelly of the Soviet Union lie the volatile and difficult countries of Afghanistan and Iran, both of whom for more than one hundred and fifty years have been key players in the 'Great Game.' The problem would be somewhat similar if Texas and Louisiana were largely populated by Mexicans and that Mexico was a country in a state of constant turmoil. From the Soviet point of view, American preoccupation with El Salvador, Nicaragua, and Cuba seems like child's play compared with the problems they face on their own southern frontiers.

Theoretically, Soviet Central Asia and the southern frontier would be much more secure if the Soviets had left the situation alone in Afghanistan. But the constant search for total security and the temptation easily to extend the communist domain were too much for the Soviet leaders. Now they are faced with problems which seem unlikely to be solved and are certain to become more acute in the decades to come.

Our Man in Moscow

Prime Minister Trudeau's visit to the Soviet Union in 1971: Mr Trudeau with General Secretary Brezhnev and Foreign Minister Gromyko. The author is second from the left.

Pierre and Margaret Trudeau share a social moment
with Prime Minister Kosygin

A study in concentration during the Canada-Soviet hockey series,
Moscow, 1974

Margaret Trudeau and Thereza at the Young Pioneers Palace,
Moscow

A handshake from the Soviet president, Nikolai Podgorny

Exchanging a few words with Brezhnev

A Politboro chorus line at the Kremlin, July 1977: Brezhnev becomes president
of the Soviet Union

Ambassador to Mongolia: reviewing the guard of honour in a snowstorm,
Ulan Bator, May 1974

Winter in Moscow, with the gilded towers of the Kremlin in the background

A rare compliment: a signed portrait of Brezhnev presented to the author

Dean of the diplomatic corps in Moscow:
the author in a reflective mood

Presentation of the medal of Companion of the Order of Canada by Governor General Roland Michener, Ottawa, 1972

Leaving Moscow for the last time, September 1980; in front of the Canadian embassy with the usual contingent of police in the background

Canadian representative on the Independent Commission on Disarmament and Security Issues, headed by Olof Palme of Sweden, 1982

With Prime Minister Trudeau at Parliament Buildings, Ottawa, on the occasion of the presentation of the Palme report

PART FOUR

The Rise and Fall of Détente

13

The Superpower Relationship: Vietnam and the Nixon Initiative

Although the United States and the Soviet Union are vastly different, they have a relationship which is not shared by any two other countries. It goes beyond their huge nuclear and conventional arsenals, although obviously that is the basis for the superpower designation. China may eventually achieve the military strength to be included in this category, but for the foreseeable future it is restricted to the United States and the Soviet Union.

On the part of the Russians there exists a curious love-hate relationship. They have never been at war with the Americans and there is no historical enmity. There is jealousy and envy of American technological and industrial skill, fear or uneasiness about the military and economic strength of the United States, and admiration for its almost Russian-like open spaces. There is a certain rapport between Russians and Americans which exists rarely between Russians and Europeans. They are the two races which share immense territories and immense strength. Each in its own way is fascinated with power and this simultaneously draws them together and repulses, enhanced by the awesome nuclear arms they each hold.

Hence, as soon as the obstacle represented by Stalin disappeared, it was almost inevitable that American and Soviet leaders should try to meet in an effort to regulate the relations between their countries. Although the first post-Stalin meeting was on a four-power basis in 1956 in Geneva, all succeeding encounters between American presidents and Soviet leaders have been bilateral and have taken total precedence, in the Soviet Union at any rate, over any other form of international diplomacy. Since the Eisenhower-Khrushchev meeting in 1959, all Soviet leaders have considered summitry an essential part of their relations with the United States, even though some of these meetings were hardly productive.

The decade after 1962 saw no meeting between a u.s. president and a Soviet leader, and the obstacle was almost entirely Vietnam. But this did not prevent an obsessive concentration by the Soviets on the question of their relations with the United States. While striving to catch up with the United States economically, and accepting tacitly the enormous gap between the two superpowers, Brezhnev seemed to long for acceptance in world affairs on a basis of political and economic equality with the United States, and to entertain the impossible hope that the two giants could divide up the world between them. Being realists, the Soviet leaders after Khrushchev were fully aware that Russia's title of superpower rested largely on its military strength. Economic equality was a long way off, but political equality seemed attainable provided there was at least the appearance of acceptance by the other superpower. Summit meetings appealed to the Soviet leaders as the simplest way to achieve not only the appearance of equality, but the international 'respectability' they so ardently sought.

Better relations between the United States and the Soviet Union began to take shape in 1963 after the re-examination by both sides of the implications of the Cuban missile crisis. This was followed by the signing of the non-proliferation treaty and the anti-ballistic missile accords. But they did not develop further after the assassination of President John Kennedy and the ouster of Nikita Khrushchev, primarily because of increasing American involvement in Vietnam. It was ironic that President Johnson and Leonid Brezhnev had the same political priorities: each was in his own way intent on improving his people's standard of living, with the parallel aim of reducing tensions between the superpowers. And both were frustrated by the basically marginal issue of Vietnam.

In January 1967 the principal concern of the Kremlin was China. The Soviets had returned to the position of Khrushchev: in other words, no business on a national or communist party level could be carried on with Mao, and the time was propitious for a showdown with Peking. The Russians would clearly have liked cordial relations with the United States so as to free their hands to deal with China, but this had proved impossible because of the intensification of the Vietnam war. The Russians resented particularly the bombing of their ally, North Vietnam, which they thought went beyond the limits of understanding between the superpowers. It embarrassed and humiliated them; it carried risks of escalation of the war; and it seemed to herald a new and more aggressive phase in u.s. foreign policy.

But the question was more complicated than that. The Russians seemed not entirely unhappy to see American prestige suffer from the Vietnam war and American attention almost exclusively riveted on this area, particularly as a means of countering the supposed Chinese threat to Soviet East Asia. At the same time, the Russians considered the u.s. military presence in Southeast Asia of some advantage since it provided a counter-balance to China and kept the latter preoccupied on its southern flank. The Soviets made it fairly clear that a return to a policy of good relations with the United States was impossible as long as the bombing of North Vietnam continued; but they were equally determined not to permit a major deterioration of relations, and above all not to sacrifice the possibility of agreements on some issues of practical interest to Moscow.

At various times in 1966 and in the first half of 1967, Soviet contacts approached me to try to find out what American war aims really were in Vietnam. One source told me that there were undoubtedly a number of what he called 'coincidental parallel aims' of the United States and the Soviet Union in Vietnam, of which the most obvious was the need to prevent a vacuum in Southeast Asia which would result if u.s. forces were withdrawn abruptly. It was clear, he said, that a vacuum would not last very long and it was essential to do something to keep South Vietnam neutral and viable. He said the Soviets were sceptical that the Americans intended to leave South Vietnam, but they were ready to be convinced. At that time a member of the Politburo, A.N. Shelepin, was on a mission to Hanoi and my source said his task had been complicated because of the Soviets' inability to give an assurance to North Vietnam that the Americans did not want to establish a permanent military presence in the south and would withdraw if the integrity of South Vietnam were assured.

This source was clearly aware that this crucial point was hardly something that the Americans were likely to disclose, and I expressed my scepticism about any assurances passed to the North Vietnamese by the Russians. In fact, a few days later at a Kremlin reception, I was talking to First Deputy Prime Minister Kyrill Mazurov when he spontaneously came out with a statement that the North Vietnamese were the most difficult people they had ever had to deal with. Several times in succeeding years I heard similar complaints from Russians about the problem of trying to control their tough and prickly allies.

In a long talk with President Podgorny in September 1966, which was intended to be about Canadian-Soviet relations but which turned into a discussion of Vietnam, the Soviet puzzlement (or professed puzzlement) about American aims was repeated. The president made one prophetic remark: the only absolute certainty was that the Americans would leave Vietnam, though only time would tell as to whether it would be accomplished with great damage to their prestige in the world and to the prejudice of many of their legitimate foreign policy objectives. He called on Canada to use its influence to persuade the United States to recognize this. I said it would be more practical for the Soviet Union to convince North Vietnam to end hostilities. The Americans would then negotiate without risking humiliation. His reply was revealing: 'How can a country as big as the United States, a superpower, be humiliated?'

At times I had some sympathy with the Russian effort to understand President Johnson. In the summer of 1965 I had been called back to Ottawa for a few months to act as assistant under-secretary (political) for External Affairs and I recall a letter addressed from President Johnson to Prime Minister Pearson giving Canada advance notice of the u.s. decision to increase its aid to South Vietnam by committing a maximum of twenty-five thousand ground troops, and asking for Canadian understanding of the reasons for the decision. The prime minister asked me to lunch at Sussex Drive to discuss a reply which we had drafted. Just before I arrived, it was announced from the White House that fifty thousand troops had landed in Vietnam. Relations between the president and the prime minister were never good, and had been exacerbated by Pearson's recent Temple University speech in which he had questioned the wisdom of some aspects of American policy in Vietnam. But it was this kind of senseless pinprick by Johnson that made it difficult for friends of the United States to support them unreservedly.

The Soviets clearly could not believe that the Americans really considered that China was the main enemy in Southeast Asia. If that was really so, they reasoned that logically the Americans should exploit to the full the Sino-Soviet split and accentuate common u.s.-Soviet interests in the face of the Chinese threat, and as a corollary to work towards a community of interests with those Asian countries capable of resisting the expansion of Chinese influence, primarily India. But on the contrary, American policy was seen in Moscow as being predicated on a military plus political effort in Vietnam which increasingly alienated the strongest Asian countries and assumed the nature of an American war in Asia, not related to the aim of containing China.

Scepticism about American intentions was manifest in October 1966, in the cool Soviet response to various American overtures, including negotiations on a direct air-link between Moscow and New York, and the appointment of Llewelyn Thompson as ambassador. Thompson was one of the last of the brilliant group of Russian experts the State Department had developed in the thirties, had served previously as ambassador to Moscow from 1957 to 1963, and was highly regarded by the Soviets for his expertise and his balanced view of u.s.-Soviet relations. But the Russians were not impressed.

To me it seemed obvious that the Soviets could not modify their position so long as North Vietnam was being bombed. But even if the bombing had stopped, there seemed little hope of a real change in the Soviet position. They were committed to Hanoi and Hanoi was committed to the conquest of South Vietnam. They felt their credibility was at stake, much as the Americans felt that their friends and allies in Southeast Asia were watching to see if they would meet their obligations and promises of support. I think the Russians were unhappy to be forced to squander so much of their political reserves on an ally they could not control. But they had reached the point where they had no choice.

In October 1966 Johnson made a number of overtures to Moscow, including economic concessions to the East Europeans, indications that the United States were ready to conclude the non-proliferation treaty, and an offer by the president to meet with the Soviet leaders. Brezhnev said flatly that the United States laboured under a 'strange and persistent delusion' if it believed that relations could be improved while the war in Vietnam continued, making him in fact the father of the linkage theory. In an interview I had with Kosygin at that same time he made it perfectly clear that any American initiatives toward an improvement in bilateral relations without regard to Vietnam he considered a deliberate cover for Johnson's real intentions, which in his view were to convince the Soviet Union to reduce its aid to North Vietnam and abandon its objectives in Indo-China. I presented the Canadian view, which was a plea to seek an early solution to the Vietnam problem so that East-West relations could return to normal; but he would not alter in any way the Soviet position that the bombing of the North had to stop and that the Soviet program for Vietnam was identical with that of Hanoi.

In fact Soviet diplomacy had become to all intents and purposes a hostage to Hanoi's rigidity. The Soviet Union had undertaken an open-ended commitment to aid North Vietnam which clearly irked the Russians since the war did not touch their vital interests. They seemed to be impatient to rid themselves of an incubus which limited their diplomatic freedom of action and drained their resources. Gromyko even told George Brown, the British foreign secretary, that the West would be amazed how quickly things would move once Vietnam was out of the way.

As the war escalated in the spring of 1968, there was a good deal of speculation that it had become a sort of Soviet war by proxy. I found it difficult to agree with this. The Russians, like the Americans, had been gradually drawn into a situation from which they could not easily withdraw, and no matter what position of influence the Russians had been able to buy in Hanoi through their support, they were much more captives of the relationship than masters of it. The degree to which the Vietnamese were acting independently of the Soviets was clearly demonstrated at the World Communist Conference in June 1969, where Vietnam was to have served as the leading example of the 'struggle against imperialism.' To the chagrin of the Kremlin, the supposed victim of imperialism failed to turn up, in spite of considerable Soviet pressure on Hanoi.

During 1968, in spite of the increased intensity of the war and the Tet offensive, United States–North Vietnam negotiations finally got under way in Paris. The Russian attitude was constantly ambivalent. It was certain they preferred a negotiated settlement but at the same time they kept on reaffirming their support for the Viet Cong program. But at the back of their minds was the lingering doubt as to why the United States showed no signs of seeking a means of withdrawing in face-saving circumstances. Their conclusion was that the United States would not commit such huge military resources in Vietnam only to withdraw them again, and therefore the American objective was to establish a permanent footing in South Vietnam. And the constant reiteration by President Johnson and senior figures of his administration that South Vietnam was vital to U.S. national security interests reinforced their suspicions about Washington's intentions.

On 25 November 1968 the Russians signed another military and economic aid agreement with North Vietnam, envisaging massive Soviet shipments of foodstuffs, petroleum products, transportation equipment, machinery, chemical fertilizer, military equipment, and so on. They thus committed themselves to aiding Hanoi on such a scale as to imply a substantial Soviet presence for the foreseeable future. Yet in private talks it was clear the Russians viewed the future of Vietnam in relation to their quarrel with the Chinese. Southeast Asia was remote from their direct interests. Eastern Europe and the Middle East inevitably loomed much larger in their calculations. Since they had problems in Eastern Europe and the Middle East, they clearly hoped to see the Vietnam war disposed of peacefully. But once the risk of escalation was reduced, they saw no particular hurry about negotiations. Certainly they believed they would not have got away with their intervention in Czechoslovakia so easily had the United States not been proccupied with the Indo-Chinese problem. As long as Vietnam was in a state which did not involve them in the risk of a serious confrontation with the United States, but distracted the United States and sapped American strength, Soviet interests were well served.

Superpower relations started to change with the election of Richard Nixon as president of the United States. In his first State of the Union message in 1969 he put out a signal to the Russians that he wished to move from a policy of confrontation to co-operation. The Soviet experts, who are in the habit of studying every word of important Western statements, were well versed in Nixon's history of anti-Sovietism. They were therefore highly sceptical that the real Nixon had changed. But further declarations by Nixon of a willingness to seek a solution of American problems with the Soviet Union, and new policies in Vietnam, gradually led the Soviets to believe that there was a new Nixon, which even his visit to Romania and the irritation this caused in Moscow did not dispel.

By the end of the year the Soviets seemed sufficiently satisfied with the international situation and the favourable 'correlation of forces' to move toward renewing the dialogue with the Americans, above all the tentative start of SALT talks in Helsinki. In view of speculation two decades and a half later concerning Soviet motives in u.s.-Soviet arms talks, it is worth recalling that in 1969 I wrote that SALT was of great importance for the Soviets because they considered it the key element in evolving a working relationship between the superpowers, and because it was related to the vital economic questions bedevilling the Russians: releasing very scarce, technically competent workers from the military sector into the backward civilian economy and freeing up capital for investment in the more obviously lagging civilian industries, particularly consumer goods and agriculture. SALT seemed of sufficient importance to the Soviet Union that negotiations could proceed in spite of Vietnam.

Nevertheless, there was no public or official response to President Nixon's second State of the Union message in January 1970, when he mentioned the possibility of a new relationship developing between the United States and the Soviet Union. While Nixon was ignored, the Soviet press soundly attacked Vice-President Spiro Agnew and Secretary of State William Rogers, accusing them of policies in Asia which amounted to getting Asians themselves to do the dirty work of suppressing national liberation movements, which *Pravda* claimed was what 'Vietnamization' really meant.

Llewelyn Thompson had been replaced as American ambassador in 1969. He left Moscow not bitter but frustrated by the way in which the Soviets had failed to utilize his considerable expertise and recognize his patient, balanced appreciation of u.s.-Soviet relations. He was replaced by Jacob Beam, another of the old school of Soviet specialists. In February 1970 Beam returned from consultations in Washington and told me of the increasing exasperation there at continued public attacks on the United States and the failure of the Soviets to do anything to help toward a solution of the Vietnam problem. Beam was particularly annoyed by the gall of the Soviet ambassador, Anatoly Dobrynin, in asking the State Department to avoid attacking Lenin during the centenary celebrations of his birth in April.

The developments in Cambodia and the renewed bombing of North Vietnam in the spring of 1970 led to an unusual direct attack on Nixon by Kosygin. Soviet and third world officials told me that distrust of Nixon and suspicion that the 'old Nixon' had reasserted himself had been revived. One official said that on the whole they preferred Johnson to Nixon. They had understood Johnson, although they disliked what he had tried to do in Vietnam, and they were not at all sure what Nixon was up to. And then, he said, they recognized that Johnson had played a statesmanlike role during the Middle East crisis of June 1967, and had genuinely tried to seek a reasonable solution of the Arab-Israeli dispute in 1968. They saw no sign that Nixon was interested in peace in the Middle East if it meant concessions by Israel. Nor had they yet decided what were Nixon's intentions with regard to the Soviet Union.

In the fall of 1970 the Soviet Communist Party could look back on sixty-three years in power with considerable satisfaction, even complacency. The leaders had finally signed a treaty with West Germany which legitimized the existence of the East German regime, the West appeared to have accepted their intervention in Czechoslovakia, frontier talks with China were proceeding, the strategic arms limitation talks with the United States had started, discussion had begun on the Soviet initiative for a conference on security and disarmament in Europe, and tensions in Vietnam and the Middle East had eased. Most important, the Soviets seemed to have reached the conclusion that their principal opponent, the chief obstacle to the achievement of Soviet goals in the world, the United States, was in the throes of a moral and economic crisis which would gradually alter the relative positions of the two countries in their favour. The Russians constantly misinterpreted domestic developments in the United States. They were by no means alone in this, as I found most of my European colleagues in Moscow equally unable to understand events in America. The Institute of American Studies, headed by Georgi Arbatov, had a reasonably accurate idea of what was happening in the United States, but their reports normally had to pass through the American department of the Central Committee Secretariat. This was staffed primarily by bureaucrats highly influenced by ideology, with little first-hand knowledge of the United States and interested in presenting analyses which were ideologically sound and satisfying to the leaders. Except for Gromyko himself, most of the Politburo knew next to nothing of the United States, and the distorted reports reaching them undoubtedly helped to create an unreal perception of what was happening.

The Politburo had a picture of the United States as a country rotten with drug-taking and perversions of every sort, ripe for revolt by the youth, beset by social troubles, on the eve of a major economic recession as a result of the Vietnam war, torn between military-economic pressures and the anti-war movement, with a troubled middle class and a 'ruling class' incapable of decision. They probably projected a gradual withdrawal of u.s. power back to the continent and a growing paralysis which would leave Washington unable to face up to further major military adventures abroad. The Soviets therefore assumed that they could prepare gradually to move into certain areas without risk of serious confrontation with the Americans.

In step with this decline of the United States, as they saw it, the Soviet leaders took considerable satisfaction in the evolving climate of the post-war world: the disintegration of the great colonial empires, the emergence of the new states from colonial and feudal pasts, and the growing attraction in these new countries of one-party regimes looking more and more to the communist example as being relevant to their problems, in contrast to the sophisticated democracies of the West. At the same time, in the first six years of the Brezhnev regime, the Soviet Union had rapidly evolved into a world power in the traditional sense of the term. By 1970 there was no development in any part of the world which did not evoke a reaction in Moscow, and Soviet economic, political, and military influence was being felt everywhere, supported by the rapid expansion of Soviet naval power in every ocean. The Russians were avid disciples of Admiral Mahan and his theories on the close relationship between political and naval power.

To reinforce the concept that the Soviet Union was now a real world power, at the Twenty-Fourth Congress of the CPSU in 1971 Gromyko claimed that 'there is not a single significant question of any order which today would be decided without the Soviet Union or against it. If anyone attempted to show that the USSR could be bypassed in the decision of any such questions, he would be looked upon as an anomaly.' Then, after a long attack on American foreign policy, he deemed an improvement in Soviet-American relations possible, provided Washington's statements in favour of negotiations were reinforced by practical deeds.

To many, these vague, almost Manichaean statements promised very little. But I thought at the time that the Soviets seemed to be trying to convey a message of sorts, and that it was an old Russian practice to place generalities on the table and encourage the other side to come forward with specific proposals to which they need only react. Ambassador Beam was of the same opinion and, indeed, in an effort to find out more, he saw Gromyko on 30 April. Although the foreign minister proposed nothing concrete, he made it clear that an increase in trade was essential and implied that they were waiting for a positive reaction from Washington. In a talk with Beam later I said I thought the Soviet assumptions about the United States were probably being adjusted in favour of a more realistic analysis of American strength, and that this was important if an improvement in relations were to take place.

In November 1971 I visited Washington in a private capacity but saw unofficially some senior State Department people. I knew nothing at the time of the secret pour-parlers between Henry Kissinger and the Russians. Nor did Beam as far as that goes. But to the questions asked by my American colleagues concerning Soviet interest in improving relations with the United States, I replied that the relationship with Washington, good or bad, was the principal preoccupation of the Soviets, and everything else took second place. I thought there were significant signs that Moscow wanted to break the stalemate imposed by Vietnam. As it seemed unlikely that Hanoi would be defeated, that probably made it easier for the Soviets to reconcile their ideological and practical commitments to the Vietnamese communists with a rapprochement with the United States. They should interpret the Canadian-Soviet rapprochement that year as an indication of what they wanted on a bigger scale.

During the winter of 1971–2, negotiations were in progress between the United States and the Soviet Union. None of us was aware of this at the time, but by March it appeared that a u.s.-Soviet summit was in the offing. It became almost immediately compromised by military developments in Vietnam and Cambodia which led to the intensified bombing of North Vietnam. In mid-April I talked to Kosygin, who started the conversation by referring to the forthcoming visit of Nixon to Canada, adding that 'the English radio' had stated that the talks would primarily cover economic matters. He was clearly amused by Nixon's statement that in spite of the differences between the two countries the discussions would be carried out in a friendly spirit.

Kosygin then referred to the probability of a Nixon visit to Moscow. He said they proposed to talk with him about economic relations, SALT and other related disarmament matters, and European problems. But the issue of Vietnam would inevitably hang heavily over the conversations unless there had been a notable change in the situation between then and 22 May, the planned date of the visit. He wondered if it was too late to get a message to Prime Minister Trudeau while Nixon was still in Ottawa. When I said it was possible, he asked if I could transmit to Trudeau an expression of his worries about the bombing of North Vietnam and a suggestion that the prime minister, if he felt it desirable, might mention this to Nixon. He did not ask us to use our influence to end the bombing, but simply to pass on his opinion that the bombing was 'extremely dangerous.' The message was transmitted to Trudeau, who mentioned it to Nixon. Shortly afterward, Kissinger came to Moscow on very short notice at the invitation of the Soviets. There is some slight evidence that the message transmitted to Nixon in Ottawa may have helped in the Soviet decision to invite Kissinger to Moscow.

The American embassy was extremely discreet about the visit of Kissinger. At the time it looked as if the Americans were simply being very uncommunicative, but in the light of subsequent information, it is clear that the American representatives in Moscow were only partly aware of the direct talks between Kissinger and Brezhnev. The day after Kissinger left Moscow, a high-level Soviet delegation headed by K.F. Katushev, one of the leading members of the party Secretariat, went to Hanoi, and the Paris talks between the Americans and the North Vietnamese recommenced. All of this pointed to Russian anxiety to have the summit take place. The other indication of Soviet eagerness for the summit was the unprecedented decision of Brezhnev to devote so much of his time personally to talks with a u.s. presidential aide, talks at which neither President Podgorny nor Prime Minister Kosygin participated. Brezhnev thus became identified almost exclusively with a policy of improving relations with Washington.

The American decision to blockade North Vietnam and bomb Hanoi only a fortnight before the presidential visit created an acute dilemma for the Soviets, but they took the agonizing decision to go ahead with the summit and President Nixon arrived in Moscow as planned on 22 May 1972. The reservations and hesitations of the Russians quickly disappeared in the glow of a superpower summit. The tone was set at the Kremlin banquet by Nixon's speech and that of Podgorny, who stressed the need to find mutual aims between the two biggest powers in the world and for them to 'act in such a way as to ward off the danger of a global war.' The Soviet press and television also passed from reserve to enthusiasm in coverage of the visit, including the inauguration of news broadcasts in colour TV.

Richard Nixon was no stranger to the Russians. He had already engaged Khrushchev in the famous 'kitchen debate' in 1959, as vice-president representing President Eisenhower at an industrial exhibition in Moscow, and he had made a private visit to Moscow in 1965 when he was out of politics. He had been on the Soviet list of 'anti-communist fanatics' since the days of the McCarthy hearings and it was only very slowly that the Russians had accepted him as a convert to détente. Hence there was great curiosity about this enigmatic figure. Nixon was under great strain when he arrived, knowing the political risk he was running of a rebuff and humiliation at the hands of the Russians. But he seemed to sense that the outcome would be favourable and, after the first difficult session with Brezhnev, he appeared sure of himself, but somewhat diffident, characteristics which appealed to Brezhnev and made for a congenial personal relationship.

I think he enjoyed the pomp and circumstance with which the Russians surrounded his visit. As if to underline the significance of the first official visit to the Soviet Union of an American president (if one excepts the Yalta conference in 1945 attended by Franklin Roosevelt), he was lodged in the Kremlin, like General de Gaulle eight years earlier, with the difference that the private apartments of the tsar were restored with meticulous care and opened for the first time on this occasion. The Kremlin, with its completely walled enclosure, its fantastic semi-oriental air, particularly noticeable in the Granoviti Palace of Ivan the Terrible and its beautiful Orthodox churches, gives off an aura of mystery and power which impresses even the casual visitor. To *live* inside those walls was a unique experience which could hardly fail to impress. In addition, the rich but slightly barbaric beauty of the newly refurbished imperial apartments and the stunning grandeur of St George's Hall, vast, startlingly white, ablaze with magnificent chandeliers and still decorated with the names, engagements, and victories of the old imperial regiments, were quite overwhelming.

A lavish reception given by the Soviet leadership in St George's Hall was the only time when the diplomatic corps had an opportunity to meet the president. My first encounter with him was confined to cordial comments on what he described as his most successful and pleasant trip to Ottawa and the useful talks he had had with Prime Minister Trudeau. Later, the president called me over to say how satisfied he was with the negotiations in Moscow and expressed the hope that they would be recognized throughout the world as a serious effort to reduce tensions and to make the world an easier place to live in. Kosygin, who was standing by, added much the same comment to me after the president had moved on.

As he was leaving the reception, President Nixon caught sight of me and to the surprise of those present came across once again to express his warm feelings about Canada. I mentioned to him that in 1958 when I had been ambassador in Colombia, I had admired the courageous way in which he had behaved at the Bogotá airport during a mass demonstration against him when he was vice-president, and that I had gone to the airport to support my American colleague. Nixon glowed and his remarks indicated he remembered every detail of the experience. Subsequently I was bombarded with questions about my conversation with Nixon. It was hard to convince my diplomatic colleagues that we had talked about Bogotá.

Later at the same reception, I had a talk with the first deputy prime minister, Dmitri Polyansky, who said the summit would start the two superpowers on a new path, a development which could only be opposed by one country; obviously he was thinking of China. He suggested that in many ways we together had started this whole process: it was the invitation to Polyansky to visit Canada in 1966 that had broken the ice and gradually built up an atmosphere of co-operation and made the breakthrough in Soviet-American relations possible. At this point we were joined by Kissinger, to whom Polyansky repeated his last comment. Kissinger looked puzzled and I explained to him what Polyansky meant. Kissinger retorted 'nonsense,' and said this had nothing to do with the president's visit. After Kissinger had moved off, Polyansky repeated to me that he was positive he was right. I am not sure that this was the case, but it was obvious that Kissinger would never acknowledge the contribution of anyone else to the development of détente.

Some years later I was discussing the Nixon visit with Georgi Arbatov, head of what had by then become the Institute of American and Canadian Studies, and mentioned this story. Arbatov said he had encountered in Kissinger the same lack of recognition for the role of Willy Brandt's Ostpolitik in setting the stage for an improved climate in u.s.-Soviet relations. He believed that Nixon would have adopted similar policies even without Kissinger, simply because the political temper of the country called for them. He characterized Nixon as 'a small man elevated beyond his natural abilities by the office he had held and who later sunk to his true level.' Arbatov also recalled how nervous Kissinger was at the beginning of the 1972 visit, particularly prior to the first dinner in the Kremlin, which immediately followed news of the mining of Haiphong harbour. Nixon had been invited into a private apartment alone with Brezhnev and his advisers. Kissinger was extremely tense, obviously fearing that Brezhnev would not go ahead with the negotiations and the result would be a humiliation for Nixon. When he caught sight of Arbatov, Kissinger rushed over to him and asked anxiously, 'Just tell me one thing. Is it going to be alright?' At that moment, Brezhnev and Nixon appeared, smiling, and the mood turned from apprehension to jubilation.

The political Nixon could never be obliterated, no matter what the setting. At the conclusion of the official performance of 'Swan Lake' at the Bolshoi Theatre, Nixon, reaching the bottom of the staircase, caught sight of what he took to be a representative of the Russian younger generation – a bearded, long-haired young man in far-out clothes. Nixon broke away from his escorts, strode up to the young man, grasped his hand saying: 'This is a memorable night. When I am back in the White House, I shall constantly remember this superb performance.' He continued on his way, having, he believed, made contact with Soviet youth. Since the young man had been struck dumb by this unexpected encounter, the president had no way of knowing whom he had addressed. The performance that night had been restricted to Soviet invitees and

Americans. In the u.s. embassy, a draw had been made for tickets and one of the lucky ones was Nixon's victim. He was an American student who, to be near his fiancée, who worked in the embassy, was staying with a master-sergeant of the u.s. Marines and his wife as a male baby-sitter.

But the most bizarre aspect of the visit was the way in which Nixon and Kissinger treated their own secretary of state and the American ambassador. It was only later that we learned through the Kissinger memoirs the extraordinary steps taken to keep the State Department team ignorant of the negotiations with the Russians. I doubt if there is another case in history in which the head of one negotiating team asked the head of the other, particularly the leader of the Soviet Union, not to let his secretary of state know about a planned agreement, in this case the Declaration of Principles, the key document in the talks, which in fact had been worked out without the knowledge of William Rogers or Ambassador Beam. Apart from the discourtesy to loyal collaborators, the suspicion placed on them by the president and Kissinger inevitably weakened the American bargaining position and comforted the opponent. The effect of this was obvious in the follow-up period when the American embassy was constantly bypassed by both its own government and the Soviets, who utilized what Kissinger called 'the Channel' (that is, his direct contact with Ambassador Dobrynin in Washington).

Almost two years later I had lunch with a senior Soviet official who remarked on the extraordinary way in which Kissinger operated. He was clearly intrigued by the role of the American embassy and Ambassador Walter Stoessel, for whom the Soviets had great respect. He commented that he hoped Kissinger would permit Stoessel to function properly, without prejudicing the 'enormously valuable' Kissinger-Dobrynin channel. He mentioned how surprised the Soviets were at the way Kissinger seemed to have gone out of his way 'to kill the American embassy in Moscow' and he doubted that Kissinger would give Stoessel much leeway. It was at the time, and still is, a mystery shrouded in the complex personalities of Nixon and Kissinger why affairs were conducted in such a way that the enemy seemed to be the professional American diplomats rather than the Kremlin.

The visit resulted in an enormous number of agreements on such things as environmental protection, co-operation in medical science and public health, science and technology, exploration and use of outer space for peaceful purposes, trade and so on. These were all important steps toward what Kissinger considered the aim of creating a 'network of interests' between the two countries. They also reflected the enthusiasm of the Russians, on any high-level visit, to be seen signing agreements. More important than these technical accords, however, was the oral understanding to proceed with the conference on European security in 1973 and the mutual balanced-force reduction talks. Equally important were the breaking of the logjam on SALT and the signature of the ABM treaty; a protocol on ballistic missile submarines; and an interim executive agreement on a missile freeze.

In light of the debate in recent times over 'Star Wars,' radar defences, and other esoteric elements of the arms race, it is perhaps worth while outlining what these agreements constituted. Essentially, the ABM treaty gave the Soviets the option of modernizing their defences around Moscow and neighbouring missile sites, or of building a second protected site beyond the Urals (that is, out of range of the radars around Moscow). The crux of the problem was that the radar strength should be such that the Russians could cover only what each side was permitted to cover. The United States had the option of covering the Washington area and in addition one of two midwestern missile concentrations for which it was preparing defences.

The interim executive agreement on a missile freeze made sense only in terms of the situation which would have existed without it. At that precise moment, the so-called missile imbalance was largely cosmetic, since by putting multiple re-entry warheads (known as MIRV) on its missiles the United States had twice as many deliverable warheads as the Soviet Union and expected to have three times as many at the end of the next five-year period. At that moment, the American experts estimated that Russia could not improve its MIRV technology sufficiently to reach equality, let alone superiority, with the United States in that five-year period.

The protocol on submarines missiles had some sensitivity for the Soviets, since it admitted that they would be permitted more submarines than the United States, although because of the overall missile freeze included in SALT, the Soviet Union had to retire other missiles if it constructed the maximum number of submarines permitted under the protocol. Article 12 of the ABM treaty and article 5 of the executive agreement were of considerable interest in that they prohibited interference in 'national technical means of verification' (that is, orbital satellites), as well as barring new systems of concealment. This meant, for example, that one side was not permitted to hollow out a mountain in order to build up a stock of weapons unobserved by orbital satellites. The Soviets argued the need for compensation because of advanced American experience with submarine-launched missiles (SLMs) and other missile technology, as well as the advanced technology of its allies such as Britain and France and the advantage the Americans had in forward bases such as Loch Ness. The United States successfully resisted these arguments and seemed to believe the freeze had been made at the best level its negotiators could obtain.

The trade agreement was mainly important psychologically in giving the highest official blessing of both sides to get on with the job of increasing trade. It was given a particular boost through the American decision that financing could be made available for Soviet purchases. But it aroused quite unreasonable expectations in U.S. business circles of an untapped trade bonanza. The disillusionment that followed contributed in no little way to the general retreat from détente.

Politically the most important agreement signed by Nixon and Brezhnev was the 'Basic Principles of Relations between the USA and the USSR.' Discussions on it had begun in April, without the knowledge of the secretary of state or the embassy, so it was not surprising that neither Canada nor any of America's principal allies had any advance word of an accord which had all the earmarks of an agreement intended to establish a special if not exclusive superpower relationship. Certainly it went far beyond the French-Soviet and Canadian-Soviet agreements of the previous year. I remarked at the time that it went so far toward underlining a desire by both countries to establish friendly working relations that if Canada or France had signed such an agreement, it would have evoked a sharp outcry in Washington. Kissinger, in a press conference in Moscow, claimed that it did not impinge on the rights of other states or change alliances. He said that its purpose was primarily to avoid nuclear confrontation between the superpowers.

Before Nixon arrived in Moscow the principles were discussed only in fairly abstract terms, and had to be worked out in intensive sessions. Some of the articles, as a result, were not only abstract but highly unrealistic. One stated that the two powers 'will always exercise restraint in their mutual relations.' This commendable aim could hardly be applied to the propaganda of Radio Moscow, or the activities of the KGB (or of the American press as far as that went). Article 2, defining the superpower relationship in terms of the need to prevent or peacefully settle situations that could bring on confrontation and nuclear war, called for a spirit of reciprocity, mutual accommodation, and mutual benefit, and decried efforts to obtain unilateral advantages. And one formulation sounded like the elements of a non-aggression pact: 'Prerequisites for maintaining and strengthening peaceful relations between the USA and the USSR are the recognition of the security interests of the parties, based on the principle of equality and the renunciation of the use of threat of force.'

But in a press conference on 19 May Kissinger outlined the limitations which the Americans realized the document contained:

We have no illusions. We recognize that Soviet ideology still proclaims considerable hostility to some of our most basic values. We also recognize that if any of these principles is flouted, we will not be able to wave a piece of paper and insist that the illegality of the procedure will in itself prevent its being carried out. This document indicates an aspiration and an attitude ... We assume Soviet leaders are serious people and would not sign such a document in a rather solemn ceremony unless they had some serious intention. If this judgment should turn out to be incorrect, we can always return to patterns well tried in the last twenty years.

Kosygin, in an interview with me later, gave his own assessment. The new definition of relations was a major step, he said, but it was not going to help find an end to the Vietnam war or settle the Middle East problem. The Soviets had agreed with the Americans to seek an improvement by tackling the key problem, that of nuclear armaments. 'We had reached parity,' he said. 'We knew what they were working on. They knew what we were working on. Sputniks can see everything. We were both faced with the prospect of new developments which would have cost tens of billions of roubles. This had to be contained and limited and we proceeded to make concessions on a one-for-one basis. Neither side tried to squeeze unilateral advantages from the other.'

Kosygin was mildly optimistic about the various technical agreements but had some reservations about trade. He mentioned particularly divergences in relation to lend-lease, u.s. import levies, and the need for the Soviet Union to obtain most-favoured-nation treatment. He said he realized that Nixon could not settle these issues by himself in Moscow since Congress alone could give its approval. He found it difficult to envisage good prospectives for trade without major changes in the present situation.

I conveyed Canada's first reactions to the summit. As neighbours and friends of both parties we were delighted, and also relieved, that the summit had succeeded, since a failure would have had an adverse effect on the entire international atmosphere. Kosygin mentioned that the Canadian-Soviet exchange of visits the year before had fostered the process at the big-power level. He claimed that Canadian-Soviet relations never had been conflictual, had developed in the direction of strengthening peace and co-operation, and had thus showed the way for the Soviet-American rapprochement. I remarked that in developing good relations with the Soviet Union, the Canadian government had two goals in mind: to improve bilateral relations because they appeared to be of practical, useful interest, and to contribute in some way to improving relations between the Soviet Union and the West as a whole.

President Nixon called his week in China one that changed the world. In retrospect, its importance was more as an event that made his visit to Moscow possible. The week in Moscow, although it did not change the world, radically changed the course of international relations for the next half-decade. What made both visits remarkable was that, on the American side, they represented initiatives which even a year or two earlier would have seemed totally out of the question, and on the Soviet and Chinese sides, almost equally impossible in view of the dilemma of negotiating with the 'imperialist aggressor' which was at that very moment bombing their communist ally. As one observer put it, it almost looked as if the war against Vietnam were being conducted from the Kremlin.

The average Russian was more than a little bewildered by the sudden shift in the Soviet propaganda line and at the same time filled with considerable pride and elation at what he considered a recognition by the world's greatest power of the Soviet Union as its equal. The press treatment must have continued to confuse the Soviet public, however. The illustrated weekly *Ogonyok*, for example, entitled its fulsome article 'USSR-USA: The Triumph of Reason and Goodwill,' and *Pravda* implied that it was a triumph for the Russian 'peace program adopted by the 24th Congress,' implying that Nixon had merely rallied to a cause championed by the Soviet Union practically since Lenin. The joint agreements had become 'the great victory of our Party, of all the people, in the cause of détente.' The fact that they were reached with the chief imperialist power was not deemed inconsistent with *Pravda*'s call for the 'continuing irreconcilable struggle against aggressive imperialist forces and against any and all opponents of peace and security.'

The average Soviet citizen was well accustomed to digesting such gobbledegook, but it was quite apparent from talks I and other foreign observers had that the Russian people were confused. Imperialism had certainly lost a good deal of its identifiably American features. America as Enemy Number One had never been very credible to the average Russian and now seemed even more abstract. Between the lines of everything that was written, however, could be seen the shape of the new enemy. China was not talked about very much, but it was felt as a ghost in the background. At the same time, the Vietnamese question, while discussed in often rather bitter terms, was not permitted to interfere with the good atmosphere. If the temporary losers seemed the North Vietnamese, it provided an ideal opportunity for the Chinese to attack the Russians for collusion with the enemy.

Apart from the slight astonishment with which the Russians

greeted the sight of their leaders embracing The Enemy, there was a tendency to jump to the conclusion, on the basis of the series of agreements and other manifestations of friendship with the Americans, that a new era of prosperity was in sight and that the cold war was over. Since the propaganda machine operated on the basic assumption that the Russians could be persuaded to accept a low standard of living, hard work, and discipline because of the threat of an external enemy, the question immediately arose as to how they were going to do this now that they had made peace with the Americans. My conclusion at the time was that the government would probably tighten rather than relax discipline in the country in order to counter any illusions on the part of the population. But it was clearly going to be more difficult than in a period of tension.

The policy of improving relations with the United States appeared popular with the bulk of the population and certainly with the intelligentsia. But in the ranks of the Party the attitude was more divided. There were some, like the Ukrainian Party leader Pyotr Shelest, who had been hostile from the beginning, but there were many more who were doubtful of the wisdom of this rapid change of tack. As at the time of the Czechoslovak crisis, it was the mass of little Stalins in the Party organizations around the country who were afraid that détente would make their disciplinary problems more acute. The ideologists also had difficulty in reconciling the rapprochement with the United States, the continuing war in Vietnam, and the ideological imperatives of the struggle against the class enemy. There was no evidence, however, that Brezhnev's hold on power was threatened.

In many ways it would have been impossible for the Moscow summit to take place if the Nixon-Kissinger strategy of first establishing relations with China had not taken place. Once the Chinese factor had been added to the equation, however, it became nearly impossible for the Russians to abandon the field to the Chinese. The Russians certainly believed that they had strengthened their position vis-à-vis China by creating a working superpower relationship with the United States, and a very practical one in the form of numerous ongoing agreements in addition to the Declaration of Principles. The Soviets were confident that they were well on their way to achieving a stabilization of the situation in

Europe so that they no longer needed to fear trouble on the Western front if disputes with China broke out.

Access to American technology developed more rapidly in the following year, but in 1972, from Moscow's perspective, it seemed that the most important result of the visit was the public recognition for all the world to see that the United States accepted the Soviet Union as a power of equal strength. It did not matter if the United States had already tacitly admitted this. The Soviet inferiority complex was still so strong that they wanted this to be said by the Americans, in Moscow, and written down on a piece of paper. This was probably the most important achievement for Brezhnev. No matter what his critics thought of the wisdom of relaxation of tensions, all of them as good Russians were proud and pleased at the diplomatic success of appearing to be accepted on an equal basis in the most exclusive club in the world.

The allies of the United States watched the American-Soviet rapprochement with a mixture of relief and slight anxiety – relief that the dangers of a nuclear clash seemed likely to be reduced, anxiety because of uncertainty of its implications for the smaller powers. It seemed obvious that the 'special relationship' which had been building up between the Soviet Union and countries such as Canada and France would become less special. At the same time Nixon and Brezhnev were correct in avoiding anything which might smack of spheres of influence or superpower deals at the expense of others, even though there was inevitably some trace of this in their agreement to exercise restraints with regard to the vital interests of one another. Such pledges of restraint were praiseworthy in principle – until those interests had to be defined.

14

Peaceful Coexistence

One of the major defects in détente as elaborated in the first Nixon visit to Moscow was the hyperbole which accompanied it and by the vast expectations which it aroused. The new relationship between the United States and the Soviet Union was spelled out, even in the Declaration of Principles, in the light of 'peaceful coexistence.' There was never any doubt what the Soviets meant by this phrase and they assumed that the Americans understood it as well since it was incorporated into the joint statement.

Peaceful coexistence for the Soviets meant that the struggle between the two systems would continue, but without recourse to war; the ideological battle would go on undiminished, and the Soviets would support national liberation movements throughout the world. This had been spelt out in numerous articles and speeches, often in great detail, so there could hardly be any misunderstanding of what it meant. The Soviets usually act with a high degree of pragmatism, but their hold on power depends to a considerable extent on justifying this by proving their ideological credentials. The ideological confrontation is one way, and in foreign affairs support for leftist movements is another – provided, of course, that it advanced Russians national interests and did not carry the risk of a clash with the United States. It seems likely that the Soviets believed the Americans understood what the doctrine of peaceful coexistence meant and therefore that they had freedom of action to support pro-Soviet governments in such places as Angola, Mozambique, and Ethiopia, particularly as they considered these countries were not vital to American security.

A year earlier, in working out the terms of the Canadian-Soviet Protocol on Consultations, I advised Pierre Trudeau, and he agreed, not to accept reference to 'peaceful coexistence' as the Soviets wished, because this apparently innocuous phrase carried a very specific meaning for the Soviets. The inclusion of the term in the Principles for the Conduct of United States–Soviet Relations signed in 1972 seemed to me therefore highly unwise and likely to lead to misunderstanding on the part of the Soviets. This view was confirmed in 1985 by Arkady Schevchenko, until his defection one of Gromyko's closest collaborators. He states in *Breaking with Moscow* (page 206) that the principles were 'not just words to the Soviet leadership. They represented a fundamental change in Washington's policy towards the Soviet Union. The declaration was considered judicial recognition by the United States of the Leninist idea of peaceful coexistence, a great triumph for Soviet foreign policy.'

The return visit of Brezhnev to the United States in June 1973 was conducted on much the same premises as that of Nixon to the Soviet Union. This time the hyperbole was Russian. The Soviet public was startled by the picture of America that accompanied the visit, particularly as it had become accustomed to seeing the United States mainly in terms of slums and race riots. But the most extraordinary feature was the hour-long broadcast on Soviet television of Brezhnev's address on American TV. Not only did his effusive remarks on the new U.S.-Soviet relationship run contrary to everything the average Russian had been taught to believe, but for the first time Brezhnev admitted that the Soviet Union had 'many problems, many shortcomings,' a far cry from Khrushchev's boasting of a decade earlier. Even more curious was his outlining of 'great plans for the future,' which included raising the standard of living of the Soviet people, and linking this to a vision of prosperity as a result of a vast increase in U.S.-Soviet trade. The implication was that a great new era of prosperity was about to open up for the Soviet people.

This prediction raised quite unjustifiable hopes in the Russian people and uneasiness among officials, who knew perfectly well that there could be no huge increase in trade even if détente continued, and that whatever commerce took place had to be concentrated primarily in the essential industries. This unease was especially evident in the security organs, and shortly after the visit a marked tightening of the screws on dissidents and potential liberals took place. Pressure on dissidents of every persuasion had been evident since the invasion of Czechoslovakia and gradually increased even further after the Nixon visit. After the Brezhnev visit to the United States, further arrests were made and considerable publicity given to the trials of two Jewish dissidents, clearly with the aim of warning the people not to expect that détente with the West meant that there would be internal détente as well. At the same time, Sakharov and Solzhenitsyn, both still in Moscow, spoke up against détente, arguing that it simply strengthened the position of the repressive regime in Russia.

Détente only became possible for the Soviet leaders when they had convinced themselves that they could adopt a more forward policy towards the West without endangering their control of Eastern Europe and their own people. The elimination of the Czech cancer and the tightening of discipline inside Russia seemed to have persuaded the Soviet leaders that they could proceed with détente. Hence they were clearly shocked to discover that there were still pockets of resistance among various dissident groups. They were equally surprised at the strength of Western reactions to Soviet internal measures, since they had clearly believed it would be possible to absorb or offset the effects of détente with tighter domestic control. And as usual, the leadership misunderstood or misinterpreted events abroad, equating Nixon's declarations during the Watergate scandal that congressional opposition to the White House was the equivalent of treason with their own attitude towards dissent.

There was considerable speculation in Moscow as to why Brezhnev took the risk of going to Washington in June at the height of the Watergate scandal. It was rumoured in Moscow that Nixon had sent a personal message to Brezhnev assuring him that there would be no problem and that the visit would help Nixon personally. It seemed likely also that Brezhnev was misled by Nixon as to the importance of the commercial exchanges and that congressional approval was not essential. The German ambassador was convinced that Brezhnev was simply naive about Western political procedures, and that he did not have a realistic view either of the way Western capitalism worked or of economic realities. I was inclined to think that most of the ideologically motivated Russians, including Brezhnev, were strongly influenced by Marxist theories concerning the thirst of Western capitalists to do business with the Soviet Union. Certainly the Americans did little at the beginning to dispel this illusion, and they were busy developing trade projects and assuring the Soviets of the American government's determination to implement the Nixon-Brezhnev accords.

I had information, however, that some Soviet experts had queried the advisability of placing too much reliance upon the United States as a supplier of raw materials. In addition, those in the Party who seemed to think that Brezhnev was going too far and too fast were reinforced in their hesitations when economic relations with the United States began to be complicated by political factors. The sceptics clearly accepted the basic thesis that the Soviet Union needed technology and credits from the West, provided the internal price was not high. But they were beginning to think that the results would not be brilliant and the price excessive.

The strongest argument that was produced in favour of Brezhnev's policy of détente was the lack of an appealing alternative. The Soviet hierarchy and Party were probably divided roughly into three groups in their attitude to détente: those who were totally opposed to it because of the dangers it carried for the predominant role of the Party and internal discipline (this group was headed by the Ukrainian first secretary, Shelest, who was dismissed for his pains); those who were totally committed to détente because it seemed the only hope of modernizing the Soviet economy and society without endangering the existing political structures; and those who accepted détente half-heartedly, recognizing the arguments in its favour but worrying at the same time about the potential effects on Party control. For all three groups, the paradox certainly existed that Moscow continued to preach the need for the anti-imperialist struggle while embracing the major element in it. It called for policies which would logically result in closer co-operation on every front between the United States and the Soviet Union, yet it underlined the dangers of the convergence of the two societies. It adopted policies of friendship with a major capitalist enemy at the same time that it espoused internal policies intended to make impossible the expression of any deviation from the communist line.

By the fall of 1973 American businessmen also were beginning to realize that neither the big co-operative deals for oil and gas nor many of the lesser projects were likely to be consummated in the near future; that the returns were likely to be minimal, the political risks considerable, and the credit terms unpalatable. And for the first time Western financiers had begun to question seriously some of the assumptions previously held that the Soviet Union was a good credit risk, on the basis that an unacceptably high proportion of its available hard currency and gold would have to be committed to servicing and repaying its debts. And the wheat deal of 1972, when the Soviets very cannily moved to conclude a contract for large quantities of grain at a very favourable price before the extent of Russian needs was known, left a bad taste with American businessmen and officials who, while admiring the Soviets' bargaining skill, felt that they had been deliberately misled.

The Soviets had in the mean time moved to consolidate their relations, both political and economic, with West Germany and France. To their surprise they had discovered that u.s.-Soviet détente was not universally popular and that countries as different as Iraq and France showed some suspicion, obviously for different reaons. The meeting between the French president, Georges Pompidou, and Brezhnev in a hunting lodge in Byelorussia in January 1973 was intended to reassure the French that the superpower relationship should not damage French-Soviet relations. It was only partly successful and the French continued to remain suspicious.

The odd man out in the effort at détente was Britain. The expulsion of 105 Soviet diplomats and officials from the United

Kingdom in September 1971, while long overdue and highly salutary, had put a deep chill on British-Soviet relations, and little effort was made on either side to improve the situation. The foreign secretary, Sir Alec Douglas-Home, had told me in June 1970 that he considered the Soviet Union lay outside the real interests of Britain, and the development of relations with Moscow remained a very low priority of the Conservative government of Edward Heath. In fact, the only visitors of mark in those years were Peter Walker, for the Mixed Trade Commission, and Prince Philip, who came solely as chairman of the International Riding Association and was received as such.

By the fall of 1973 the Soviets were beginning to have second thoughts about Nixon, about the wisdom of getting so deeply involved with and reliant on someone of whom they still had a lingering suspicion. They were not worried about the implications of Watergate, but simply the personality of Nixon himself. At the beginning of November the Soviet press for the first time began publishing reports on the internal problems of Nixon. A Soviet contact told me he thought Nixon might indeed be forced to go. A few weeks earlier he had dismissed this as a very remote possibility. He considered it disastrous for the Soviet Union if he was forced to resign because there would be no one able to carry on energetically the policy of rapprochement with Moscow. When I suggested that Kissinger would presumably continue under a new president and try to implement détente, he said this was possible but it would not be the same thing.

During the winter of 1973–4 the Soviets grappled with two related problems: how to dissociate themselves from any stigma which might be attached to too close an association with an impeached and disgraced president; and how to make sure that the loss of Nixon would not mean the loss of détente. Nevertheless, détente was still very much the official line and it was summed up in a speech by Brezhnev to the World Congress of Peace Forces in Moscow in October, when he spoke of the receding danger of nuclear war, reasserted his belief in peaceful coexistence, and stressed in particular the significant changes in relations not only with the United States but also with Western European nations.

The Watergate affair baffled most Europeans, but probably the most mystified of all were the Russians. At times I felt almost sorry for them in their desperate effort to understand what it was all about. They started, of course, from the difficult position of trying to judge an apparently all-powerful president in terms of Soviet power. It was only gradually that they came to realize that no analogy could be drawn and that there were strict limits on what an American president could do. Nevertheless, the actual charges against Nixon – the Watergate break-in and the subsequent cover-up – seemed to them totally trivial and inexplicable. Even the experts on the United States had problems with Watergate; they usually came up with the right evaluation about six months after some development in the affair and were then frustrated to find out the situation had changed again and they had to go back to square one. Then after another six months they would come up with a reasonably correct analysis only to find it quickly outdated.

In the winter and early spring of 1974, Soviet preoccupations and worries about détente became more evident. The most important development was the sudden removal of two of the three main pillars of Brezhnev's détente policy through the death of Georges Pompidou of France, and the resignation of Willy Brandt, chancellor of the Federal Republic of Germany, as the result of a scandal involving his personal assistant, Gunter Guillaume, who was revealed to have been a communist agent during the entire period Brandt was in office. In the case of both countries there was uncertainty about the succession; in the case of Germany it also meant the departure of the main architect of the Ostpolitik which Brezhnev clearly considered the base for European détente. The complicity of the KGB in the penetration of Brandt's office made the future of West German–Soviet relations suddenly murky.

At the same time, Soviet mystification about the position of Nixon increased. In early February a senior official told me that they were starting to have new doubts about American intentions, based in part on declarations made by James Schlesinger, then secretary of defense, concerning new targeting of u.s. missiles on the Soviet Union and the need to increase the u.s. budget for defence because of the 'alleged Soviet military threat.' The official speculated about American intentions. He thought there might be three explanations. First, Nixon's ability to maintain control of his government might have evaporated, thus allowing the 'hard-liners' to develop views at variance with the policy of détente. Secondly, Nixon might have been losing interest in détente and be trying to find out where public opinion stood about it. (Approximately a year before, public opinion polls had showed an overwhelming majority of Americans in favour of better relations with the Soviet Union and this was an important factor in Soviet political calculations.) Thirdly, it was possible that the American government wanted to increase the defence budget and the best way to get it through Congress was by reviving the Soviet threat. He said they inclined to the third theory but it was clear that they could not understand exactly what was going on, nor calculate precisely why, in view of the popularity of détente, it seemed to be under pressure.

The Soviet official particularly mentioned the rejection of most-favoured-nation treatment by Congress, tied to the question of Jewish emigration delays in getting on with SALT II, and a lag in developing trade. When I pointed out that there were major contradictions in Soviet policy, particularly toward Latin America, because of Soviet efforts to encourage revolutionary forces and yet cultivate good relations with Latin American governments, he admitted there was a contradiction but said they were not worried about Latin American governments. He hoped there would be no connection made between this and East-West détente.

When he expressed disappointment at delays at the European security conference, I said they understood very little about the Western world if they did not think that the question of human rights and the fate of men such as Solzhenitsyn and Sakharov were very important to us. He ignored Sakharov, but said that Solzhenitsyn was trying to convert Soviet youth to his reactionary views, but he had badly miscalculated. Some were curious, most were indifferent, and all were indignant because of his defence of General Vlasov (the Russian officer who had defected to the Germans and raised a division to fight on the Nazi side). He said he was totally baffled because even someone as out of touch as Solzhenitsyn was with Soviet realities should have realized how strong Russian patriotism remained. 'He has proved he is really just an internal immigrant,' he said. 'And a very bad writer at that.' I asked him if he had read *The Gulag Archipelago*. He admitted he had not. I offered to lend him my copy in Russian, but he hastily declined.

Things changed somewhat for the better in April when a large number of American public figures, including Senators Scott, Kennedy, and Roth, David Rockefeller and Headly Donovan, editor-in-chief of *Time*, came to the Soviet Union for a seminar on u.s.-Soviet relations. The Russians plied them with innumerable questions about Watergate, impeachment, the American political system in general; the main Soviet concern seemed to be to determine what would happen to détente if Nixon were impeached or resigned. By this time it had been agreed in principle that Nixon would come again to Moscow in July. The general opinion of the members of the American delegation with whom I talked seemed to be that the judiciary committee would find grounds for impeachment, that the lower house would follow its recommendations, and that Nixon would then resign. The Republicans thought this would of course make it impossible for the visit to take place, but Vice-President Gerald Ford, as president, would be able to move u.s.-Soviet relations ahead faster than Nixon because much of the congressional opposition to détente, and specifically to ratification of the economic agreements with the Soviet Union, stemmed from personal objections to Nixon.

Nevertheless, the Jewish element in this was very important. The American politicians seemed to believe that Jewish leaders at home were not happy at having the problem of Jewish emigration appear to be the main stumbling block to détente and were anxious for a compromise. But Senator Edward Kennedy decided to play a provocative role by visiting a number of Jewish dissident leaders at midnight in the apartment of Lenner, a leading Jewish scientist who had been refused permission to emigrate on security grounds. The visit was permitted by the Soviet authorities with great reluctance and only if a Soviet official were present. One of the questions posed by Kennedy was, 'What can we do to help?' Lenner replied it was necessary to keep up the pressure, but if a compromise agreement about trade and emigration became necessary, to make sure every word in it was examined with the greatest of care. The Russians were clearly not happy with Kennedy's performance with the Jewish dissidents, but as proof of the Soviet desire to maintain good relations, the press ignored all this and played up his favourable remarks on détente after he was received by Brezhnev, which in itself was rather remarkable.

In spite of the developments in Washington and continuing doubts in Moscow about his future, Nixon's second visit took place as scheduled at the end of June 1974. The reception accorded him by the Russians was as warm as in 1972 and was given a more relaxed tone by alternating the venue between the Kremlin and Oreanda, a Crimean resort near Yalta. As in 1972, a number of agreements were signed, most of minor importance. But the ten-year agreement on economic, industrial, and technical co-operation, as well as three agreements on strategic arms, were of considerable significance.

No headway was made on SALT II. All that could be agreed was that there should be a new accord covering the period up to 1985 and dealing with both quantitative and qualitative limitations. It seemed strange to me that the Russians, knowing that the position of Nixon and Kissinger was fragile and that their successors might be in a less favourable position to complete SALT II, failed to seize the opportunity to conclude the agreement. Americans close to Kissinger told me the latter was puzzled and frustrated on the issue. They felt the explanation may have been that the Russians were attempting to build up their missile system to equality before embarking on stage two of SALT. It was my opinion that an important element of the Soviet military opposed an early conclusion of SALT II, and many Russians had doubts as to whether any agreements signed by Nixon could be made to stick.

I was told by a good source close to Kissinger that he expressed his bitterness with 'the bureaucracy' on his own side, who were continually bringing up what he called piddling details such as that of diesel submarines. My source said that Kissinger had declared: 'You have to believe that the Russians are as determined as the U.S. to stop the arms race and avoid war. If you do, then you have to accept the likelihood that the Russians will not cheat on the agreement since the U.S. would quickly find out and that would tear it.' I thought the Soviets would probably not cheat once they had signed an agreement, but it was unwise to tempt the Soviet military with ambiguous clauses. It seemed to me that SALT was one area in which the Russians were deadly serious, where they knew there was no real advantage to be gained in seeking cheap, temporary victories, and that a special effort had to be made to get a full strategic arms limitation agreement as fast as possible, having in mind that it was not only Nixon that was about to go, but that Brezhnev could also fade away, and with his departure the chances of an early agreement.

In their joint communiqué and in the speeches by both Nixon and Brezhnev at the end of the visit, it would have been hard to guess Nixon was on the point of being ousted. Brezhnev concluded the visit by a huge reception in the Kremlin on 3 July. The atmosphere, however, was rather subdued; and, unlike the 1972 reception, it was organized in such a way that there was a human wall of security people between the American and Soviet leaders on the one hand and the rest of us on the other. Nevertheless, as dean of the diplomatic corps I had a brief conversation with Nixon, who looked tired and strained – as did Kissinger, who was hovering in the background. The president wanted to know what I thought of the visit and how it would be received in Canada. I said that the Russians had gone out of their way to make it successful and to stress its importance. I personally thought everyone should be grateful to him for continuing the process of détente and improving relations between the superpowers. This was important not only to the United States, but to Canada and the whole world. He thanked me and added that he thought they had made progress and that the visit would be helpful to the cause of peace.

Undoubtedly one of the main aims of the Soviets in the summit meeting was to determine if the Nixon policies could survive his departure, which they assumed would also include that of Kissinger. For the Russians, this was not just academic. They were in the process of completing their next five-year plan and their general economic forecasts for the following decade, which depended to an important extent on their calculation of American policies. If the United States continued to develop friendly relations with them in the next five to ten years, it would have an important influence on long-range Soviet economic planning, defence spending, and in their calculation of the amount of foreign credits and technology they could count on.

What the Soviet conclusions were at the end of the meeting was almost impossible to guess. Watergate clearly weighed heavily in their thinking and the American journalists in Moscow were subjected to an almost continuous barrage of questions about the political situation in Washington. One correspondent told me the Russians had an almost hysterical interest in finding out what effect impeachment would have on the administration's policies towards the Soviet Union. Many of the American journalists themselves contributed to Soviet doubts by the outspoken and critical way they referred to Nixon. One journalist even told his Soviet hosts that Nixon was a criminal and should have been in jail, not in the Kremlin.

The visit certainly did not clear up Soviet doubts or confusion about the state of affairs in Washington, even though most of the journalists reassured their Soviet hosts that it would be almost impossible for an American administration to retreat from détente unless there were a spectacular development in the Soviet Union which made it difficult to continue with good relations. It is not hard to understand the Soviet confusion since there were signs of differing policies inside the presidential party. In the middle of the visit, the columnist William Safire came out with an 'inside' report of an alleged struggle between Nixon and Kissinger. The Soviets began to conclude that Nixon was no longer strong enough to mediate between Kissinger and what they thought of as the hard-liners in Washington – those in the Pentagon and Congress who had their doubts about SALT and Soviet intentions, and preferred a return of hostility and a strengthening of NATO.

It seemed to me that the Russians very badly wanted to believe that the Nixon-Kissinger policies would continue, no matter what happened to this duo. For example, a month earlier Brezhnev had gone out of his way to receive the former New York governor, Averell Harriman, in order to ascertain the thinking of the Democratic party. Harriman told me that the Russians did not fully trust what they heard from Senator Kennedy and wished to check it out against an elder statesman of the party. At any rate,

Harriman told Brezhnev that the Democrats fully supported the Nixon policy of détente and any Democratic candidate would continue it.

While the third summit was unable to lay to rest the last doubts of the Soviet sceptics about the continuity of American policy, my guess was that they concluded that détente would continue with or without Nixon, although probably with more ups and downs, and that the Americans had no real alternative to that policy. While the Soviets probably did not agree with the American goal of 'institutionalizing relations,' Brezhnev clearly aimed at making the process of détente irreversible.

It was, therefore, no surprise to the Soviet leaders when in August Nixon resigned and Gerald Ford was installed as president. The reaction in Moscow was cautiously but firmly positive, with accent on the formal statements from Washington affirming that détente and co-operation with the Soviet Union would be maintained. The Soviet public had been prepared for Nixon's removal through coverage of the proceedings of the House judicial committee, with brief explanations of the ensuing process in the House and eventually in the Senate if impeachment were recommended. But no explanation was given to the Soviet public of why Nixon resigned. I talked to a number of Russians from various walks of life and all confessed total bafflement at the resignation, relief at the ease of transition to the new leadership, and curiosity about the new president. Almost immediately on Ford's installation as president, Podgorny sent him a congratulatory message, expressing confidence that relations between their two countries would continue to improve.

Ford replied in a friendly message which the American ambassador, Walter Stoessel, transmitted to Andrei Kirilenko, the senior Politburo member available, since Brezhnev and most of his colleagues were holidaying in the Crimea; he stressed his intention to do all in his power to carry on the Nixon policies and to strengthen and widen relations with the Soviet Union. He referred to the importance of personal contacts and renewed Nixon's invitation to Brezhnev to come to Washington. At this point, Brezhnev phoned from the Crimea and asked Kirilenko to make sure Stroessel transmitted his personal good wishes to Ford. There was no mention of Nixon, nor did Kirilenko refer to him in transmitting Soviet assurances to Ford of their desire to continue the policy of détente.

The Russians seemed reassured about the desire for continuity in Washington, but they were watching very carefully to see if the new president could dominate the government and Congress enough to prevent the growth of what they considered anti-détente forces. The Russians seemed ready to give Ford some help, such as progress on SALT – help which our information indicated they had previously decided not to extend to Nixon at the June summit because they were afraid he would be unable to extract comparable concessions 'from his military.'

Kissinger came again to Moscow in October and was given unusual treatment in that the talks with the Soviets were almost all conducted by Brezhnev. The concern of the latter was to ensure that the meeting with Ford should take place in the Soviet Far East, as previously agreed. The Soviet motives in holding another summit with an American president within five months were clear: to sum up Ford, to ensure the continuity of détente, and to give a final push to an agreement on SALT II. What the Americans hoped to gain from the concessions they made for this second meeting on Soviet soil in such a brief period was not so clear. And concessions they made, apart from meeting in an inaccessible spot fifty minutes by helicopter from Vladivostok. For example, the Soviets insisted and the Americans agreed – mistakenly, I think – that Ford could not fly directly from South Korea, which was his last stop before Vladivostok, but had to return to Tokyo and fly from there. The impression this gave the Soviets was of a president in a weak position seeking through the confirmation of détente to strengthen his internal position.

The Soviet reaction to the summit was one of complete satisfaction at an historic and successful confirmation of détente, imparting new momentum to the development of u.s.-Soviet co-operation. Out of this summit came a major new understanding on the draft of a revised ten-year SALT II; a renewed commitment to implement previous agreements, in particular the declaration on basic principles, the agreement on the prevention of a nuclear war and SALT I; an understanding on co-operation in resolving political problems; and an agreement to hold regular summit meetings and to increase trade and economic exchanges.

These hopes were soon clouded by a public dispute between the two countries over Jewish emigration. In October 1972 Senator Henry Jackson had introduced his amendment to the u.s.-Soviet trade bill, making ratification of the trade agreement and the granting of most-favoured-nation treatment dependent on freedom of emigration. This amendment, jointly sponsored by Congressman Vannik, had been accepted by Congress, but in view of its effect on u.s.-Soviet trade (since it was clearly directed against the Soviet Union), a compromise had been worked out in 1974 permitting the president to decide if the countries concerned were respecting human rights, including freedom of movement. In December this question became more acute with the publication by the Soviets of a letter from Gromyko to Kissinger which was sent eight days after the release of an exchange of letters between Kissinger and Jackson, which had implied that Soviet concessions had been made. Gromyko stated categorically that the u.s.-Soviet understanding on the issue of emigration involved no change in Soviet policy or additional obligations on the Soviet part.

I had it on good authority that the leadership felt it had been pushed too far on this issue and that it was stung by the idea of outsiders monitoring their good behaviour. Local Party bosses were disturbed at the effect on Party control of liberalized emigration, and many Arab countries, already uneasy about the u.s.-Soviet rapprochement, were worried about apparent Soviet concessions to the United States over Jewish emigration. The Algerian ambassador confirmed this to me and said several Arab governments had persistently prodded the Soviets to refuse to give in to 'Zionist pressure.'

The trade bill called for a review of the issue of emigration at the end of eighteen months, which the Soviets quickly calculated meant at the start of the 1976 presidential campaign. After the Senate refused to made trade credits available, and probably to take this issue out of the impasse into which it had fallen, the Soviets unilaterally revoked the trade agreement in January 1975.

The denunciation of the 1972 trade agreement by the Soviets

marked the beginning of the decline of détente. Soviet doubts first became apparent in their thinking about relations with the West in the light of what they considered the incipient crisis of capitalism. In October the ideological aspects of this problem were raised in speeches by Brezhnev and Mikhail Suslov. It was not surprising that Suslov, as the chief ideologue of the Party, should regale his audience with a picture of the disastrous economic and social situation in the West. That Brezhnev also did so was the first indication that the Party leaders were beginning to consider seriously the implications for the Soviet Union of a depression in the capitalist world. Brezhnev spoke of 'deep crisis phenomena ... affecting all spheres of life of bourgeois society: galloping inflation, monetary-financial unheavals, an acute energy crisis, a slump in production, the growth of unemployment,' not to mention the ideological and moral crisis of modern capitalist society which inevitably was leading to an aggravation of the economic and political contradictions between capitalist states, to an arms drive, and to new elements of tension in international relations. Suslov spoke in almost classical Marxist-Leninist terms of a disastrous situation in the capitalist world and assured his audience that 'the world revolutionary process is irreversible' and would triumph throughout the world.

While both leaders ended with the conclusion that the Soviet Union wanted peace and peaceful co-operation, and was a strong bulwark against the forces opposed to détente, the question had obviously been raised in the their minds as to the desirability of seeking co-operation with the major capitalist powers if they were in fact on the point of collapse. It seemed to me that the Soviet leadership was working out a compromise assessment by which it recognized economic difficulties in the capitalist world, but figured Moscow would be advised to forego any possible opportunities to advance the cause of communism in favour of a national policy which would give greater advantages to the Soviet Union. At the same time, the Soviets believed that their détente policy would enable communism and other forces of the left in the West to exploit the new possibilities offered by growing Western economic, social, and political difficulties.

It was odd therefore to read the comments by Kissinger in an interview with columnist James Reston on 23 October.

If we do not get a recognition of our interdepedence, the Western civilization that we now have is almost certain to disintegrate because it will first lead to a series of rivalries in which each region will try to maximize its own special advantages. That inevitably will lead to tests of strength of one sort or another. These will magnify domestic crises in many countries, and they will then move more and more to authoritarian models. I would expect then that we will certainly have crises which no leadership is able to deal with, and probably military confrontations. But even if you don't have military confrontation, you will certainly, in my view, have systematic crises similar to those of the twenties and thirties, but under conditions when world consciousness has become global.

Kissinger was obviously no Marxist, but his analysis of the ultimate crisis of capitalism must certainly have sounded familiar to the Soviets. The day after the interview was published, I asked the editor of *Moscow News* what he thought of Kissinger's interview and his reply was that it proved the interests of the leadership of both the United States and the Soviet Union lay in co-operation in order to avoid troubles in the West, complicating peaceful coexistence. He added the intriguing comment that Kissinger, during his recently concluded visit to Moscow, had remarked with apparent envy that the Soviet Union had a 'scientific political philosophy.'

Kissinger's concept of détente seemed to be based on the assumption that the main aim of the West had to be the development of a set of relations with the Soviet Union – formal, practical, and mutually acceptable – which would make nuclear war impossible. Few people would disagree, but what was questionable was whether elaborate supplementary relations in the political and economic fields were needed to achieve that primary goal. A thaw in the cold war was certainly necessary and the establishment of more normal relations; but long before the signature of the u.s.-Soviet documents in June 1972, a kind of tacit agreement about the limits which each of the superpowers would impose on its behaviour was already in existence.

Institutionalizing the superpower relationship was important, but Kissinger seemed to pass over in silence the other Soviet aims in détente: to complete their control over Eastern Europe; to separate the European allies from the United States; to free their hands to be able more easily to deal with China; and to obtain the Western capital and technology urgently needed to compete successfully with the West. These were all legitimate aims of a great power, but Kissinger appeared to present the equation as if it were either/or. For example, either the Soviet Union would seek to further isolate Soviet society and reinforce autarchic policies within a closed communist bloc, which would make peaceful coexistence more difficult; or it would seek aid from the West and move much further along the path of co-operation and interdependence.

At that time a former member of Kissinger's think tank told me he had asked for a transfer to another position because he could not accept the basic Kissinger concept that détente was fragile, could easily evaporate, and that the West had to pay a heavy price for it. The alternative for Moscow, he thought, was no more attractive than for Washington, perhaps even less so. While it was perhaps unwise to make the Soviets pay a price for détente, as Senator Jackson wanted, it was equally unwise for the United States to appear on the defensive.

I recommended at the time that a very strong case could be made to complement the strategic/political dimensions of détente with a drive for intensified co-operation in the economic, political, scientific, and cultural areas. But the justification had to be more sophisticated and detailed, with clear assessments of Western and Soviet goals, of the risks and limits. It was not good enough to consider this interrelationship simply the 'indispensable' complement to strategic/political understanding, which meant basically the establishment of foolproof means of avoiding conflict.

In April 1975 a plenum of the Central Committee took place, the main aim of which was the endorsement at the highest level of Brezhnev's policy of détente. The very tough language which was used seemed to be a warning to the West that détente had its limits from the Soviet standpoint; it was also a reflection of growing Soviet confidence on the international scene.

I had been fairly certain that there were many in the Soviet Party who were biding their time to see if détente was going to work. Among them I included the military and their civilian supporters, worried about the implications of SALT II and cuts in the defence budget; the dogmatists who were not sure that as Marxists they should be embracing capitalist-imperialism; Party bureaucrats who were worried about the eroding effects of détente on the Soviet public and especially Soviet youth; the economists who were becoming dubious about the economic benefits; and finally those who were worried about the increase of American influence in such areas as the Middle East at the expense of the Soviet Union.

Still, in the summer of 1975 the policy of détente seemed still flourishing and was taking on a more bilateral U.S.-Soviet nature. Early in August the Apollo-Soyuz space spectacular took place and the Soviet press and media gave extraordinary coverage to an event which was called a 'symbol of détente' and which inevitably created an image in the mind of the average Soviet citizen of a new, friendly co-operation between the United States and the Soviet Union. The Soviet government went far beyond what was required in stressing this new relationship. Soviet television showed American films, including a series starring Brezhnev's favourite cowboy, Chuck Connors. And a new brand of cigarettes called Apollo-Soyuz, produced jointly by Philip Morris and Glavtabak Trust, went on sale. Around this time, the Bolshoi ballet and opera toured the United States, an American exhibition came to Russia, and a visit by some American senators was given top billing in the Soviet media.

All of this seemed almost deliberately arranged as a build-up to the grand finale, the signing in August 1975 of the Final Act of the European security conference in Helsinki, pictured as the crowning achievement of détente. The Helsinki Final Act was presented as a great accomplishment of Soviet policy and something for which the world should be grateful. All stops were pulled out to reinforce this tune, and Soviet television showed meetings in factories from the Amur to the Dnieper in which ordinary workers voiced their pride in this Soviet accomplishment, their gratitude to Brezhnev, and their happiness that war had been eliminated from the European horizon.

The NATO countries had agreed to participate in the Conference on Security and Co-operation in Europe with considerable reluctance and worked with remarkable unanimity to produce from it a balanced document, primarily in the sense of satisfying Soviet requirements for language which seemed to accept the post-war boundaries in return for comprehensive agreements on human rights. Since European boundaries had already been tacitly accepted, the Helsinki agreement was a victory for the West, as the Soviets agreed to human rights provisions which they could not possibly respect without a total revision of their system. At the same time, expectations by the Western public for an improvement in the situation in the Soviet Union were greatly increased. No doubt the human rights issue would have continued to bedevil East-West relations in the following decade, but the Helsinki document sharpened western perception of the issue and made it an even more rancorous cause of dispute than it might otherwise have been. How the Soviets failed to foresee this in signing the act is difficult to fathom.

I was certain that the excessive emphasis on Soviet-American friendship by the Soviet government and the euphoria over the Helsinki Final Act were likely to raise questions among those in the Soviet governing class who were at the least unenthusiastic supporters of the policy of détente. The problems that this was likely to create became evident to me a few days later at a luncheon I had with a group of Soviet writers and poets. Gathering around the embassy dining-room table, happily smoking Apollo-Soyuz cigarettes, they waxed enthusiastic about the joint space program and thought that it, far more than the Washington agreements, ruled out the possibility of war between the two superpowers, and indeed that it heralded the beginning of an important new era in relations between the Soviet Union and the West. Several were amazed at the extent of TV coverage of Apollo-Soyuz and one said that during the space flight Kirilenko, who was the Politburo man in charge in Moscow at the time, became very angry with the producers of the programs for showing American technology in too favourable a light and demanded that they show the Soviet Union on a par with the United States in space technology. As a result, a series of deadly boring interviews with Russian scientists was put on the air.

The writers told me that the publication of the full text of the Helsinki Final Act was a bombshell. None of them had previously known what it was going to contain. When it was produced, they all concentrated on the section guaranteeing basic human rights such as freedom of speech and movement. They were certain it would result in new and freer cultural exchanges, how so-and-so could now finally get his visa to visit Italy, and so on. Not all of them were totally optimistic, but the discussion reflected a genuine hope for better things to come.

15

The Fading of Détente

The Russians are obsessed by the United States, whether relations are good, bad, or indifferent. Arkady Schevchenko, in his book *Breaking with Moscow*, describes Gromyko's fixation on the United States and how difficult it was to get ahead in the Foreign Ministry or to have access to him unless you were an American specialist. While I seldom had difficulty in seeing Gromyko, the ambassadors of most of the smaller countries constantly complained to me about his inaccessibility. There were many representatives of smaller West European countries who never were received by him, and as for the Africans and Latin Americans, there was no question of his wasting time on them unless something horrendous had happened in their countries.

This concentration on relations with the United States inevitably led to excessive euphoria on the part of the Soviets when détente seemed to be working, but as it began to fade, it led to continuous and often agonizing efforts in Moscow to understand what was happening. And when it eventually disappeared in the aftermath of Afghanistan and the election of Ronald Reagan, it was replaced by excessive concentration on confrontation.

The glow generated by the Helsinki summit began to dissipate almost immediately. The first trouble point was the failure to make any progress on SALT II, which the Russians ascribed to the alleged anti-détente views of James Schlesinger, the American secretary of defense. His replacement in November 1975 by Donald Rumsfeldt gave the Soviets some hope that the American administration would be more favourably disposed to reaching an agreement on SALT. But an American proposal in the United Nations advocating freedom for political prisoners was interpreted by the Russians as being anti-Soviet. It still seemed to me that the Soviets had as great an interest in SALT II as the United States because it lay at the heart of the U.S.-Soviet attempt to limit and control the danger of a nuclear conflict, and because the cost of increasingly complicated nuclear weapons was becoming a heavy burden on the Soviet economy.

I had a long conversation about that time with a senior Soviet official who had access to the Politburo. He insisted that the leadership was committed to détente and there were no basic differences between 'the politicians, the ideologues and the technicians,' although curiously enough, there was a problem with the rank and file of Party workers and older people. He said they received a remarkably large number of letters on the subject from across the country, almost all of which expressed suspicion of détente. Their theme was primarily that one should not forget the betrayal of Stalin by Hitler in 1941 and that the capitalists were not to be trusted. He said this kind of reaction on the part of the public could not be ignored and that the Secretariat of the Party kept a kind of chart of public opinion. He found it curious that the more educated people, members of the intelligentsia, academicians, scientists and so on, were 100 per cent in favour of détente.

In 1975 the installation of a pro-Soviet government in Angola, supported by Cuban troops, put another dent in détente. The same Soviet official, shortly before the coup in Angola, had complained to me that the Soviets wished the United States would not try to draw some African nations into its orbit because then the Soviet Union had to try to balance this. He claimed were it not for this element of competition, there was nothing Moscow would have liked better than to forget the whole of the Dark Continent.

Soviet support for the new regime in Angola looked like a classic example of the wedding of two elements: the ideological imperative of aid for a so-called national liberation movement, and the opportunity to establish a position of influence in a potentially rich southern African country. Since they had not detected any American interest in Angola and had concluded it was not in an area of vital security interest for the United States, they decided they could proceed without major damage to détente. But they badly miscalculated on two scores: they showed complete insensitivity to the American preoccupation with Cuba, and they overestimated American 'understanding' of Soviet commitment to support for any national liberation movement that did not risk a direct confrontation with the United States.

Two aspects of the Soviet interpretation of peaceful coexistence were of particular relevance in the case of Angola: rejection of the idea of détente in the sphere of ideology and the class struggle, and the nature of national liberation movements. The Soviet position on the ideological struggle really boiled down to the simple doctrine that Marxist ideology demanded the continuation of class war, but that any effort on the Western side to spread Western ideas was contrary to the spirit of détente. Similarly, Soviet support of national liberation movements had to be excluded from peaceful coexistence, whereas Western support for any movements in former colonial territories considered opposed to 'progressive forces' was deemed to be imperialist and contrary to Helsinki. Just as the Soviets found it impossible to continue to pose as the leaders of a world communist movement if they renounced the ideological confrontation with non-communist forces, they found it hard to abandon the myth of Soviet leadership of the leftist forces in the third world. Certainly the Russians never made any mystery about this or the nature of détente. They never intended it to create a stable world order on the basis of the status quo. They therefore considered that an effort to support revolutionary forces in Angola was entirely justified and part of the natural order of things.

The Soviets were therefore surprised that the Americans considered the Soviet intervention in Angola contrary to détente. They clearly underestimated the reaction to the use of Cuban troops in installing a pro-Soviet regime in Luanda. It also looked as if they might be deliberately using Angola to test the American will to resist and they had some cause for rejoicing when Congress questioned American aid to the forces in Angola opposed to the pro-Soviet government.

Détente between the United States and the Soviet Union was beginning to look troubled by the end of 1975. The Russians themselves were beginning to realize that President Ford was seriously threatened on the Republican right and that one of his administration's policies which was most vulnerable was détente. Nevertheless, many practical agreements signed during the previous three years were being implemented and the grain accord that was so important to both sides was working satisfactorily. Both countries seemed to have practical reasons to want a good relationship to continue. On the Russian side there was a clear hope to have another summit meeting in Washington in order for Brezhnev to be able to present his détente policy as a total success to the Twenty-Fifth Congress coming up in 1976.

Kissinger returned to Moscow in mid-January 1976 to try to keep the momentum going and again had as many talks with Brezhnev as with his opposite number, Gromyko. Brezhnev made it clear that he wanted to return to Washington, even remarking that he hoped there would be fewer official functions and more time at Camp David, for which he confessed great fondness. The atmosphere was generally good, but slightly soured by Kissinger's insistence on linking SALT II and Angola, which was obviously essential for the Republican administration with presidential elections coming up. He told Brezhnev flatly that the Cuban-Soviet intervention in Angola could seriously affect détente and might lead to pressure to cut off grain shipments to Russia. Brezhnev reproached the Americans for distracting both powers from the main issues, to which Kissinger responded that one of the main issues was adherence to the 1972 agreement on guidelines in the conduct of u.s.-Soviet relations. In spite of this decidedly unpromising reaction, Kissinger concluded that the Americans had to separate SALT and Angola because of the overriding importance of reaching an agreement to limit the nuclear arms race.

There was a sigh of relief in Moscow when Ford was chosen over Reagan as Republican candidate, since the former had attempted to continue the Nixon-Kissinger policy. Jimmy Carter was a puzzle to them, but they were encouraged by the fact that he seemed to be in favour of détente.

During the final stages of the electoral campaign the Soviet government adopted a fairly relaxed attitude and showed a much more sophisticated and understanding view than in the past of the complexities of American political campaigning. There was no doubt the Soviet leaders would have preferred to see Ford continue as president, but they quickly adapted to the victory of Jimmy Carter. During the first few weeks they were notably cautious in making an appreciation of the new president, clearly waiting to see what kind of a team he chose and an indication of the way in which he planned to develop relations with Moscow. They made no secret, however, of their disquiet over the heavy input of national security adviser Zbigniew Brzezinski into the formation of Carter's foreign policy.

In the mean time, a curious dispute took place over the appointment of a new American ambassador and the refusal of a re-entry visa for the senior political counsellor in the Embassy, apparently in retaliation for the expulsion of a very junior Soviet diplomat from the Soviet mission to the United Nations in New York. The American government's handling of the matter of the Ambassador was difficult to understand. Kissinger withdrew Walter Stoessel just on the eve of the elections and then nominated as ambassador Malcolm Toon, who had already been rejected by the Russians three years before. Toon was an experienced Russian-speaking career diplomat, highly qualified for the job although known by the Russians to be hard-nosed and outspoken. It was a mistake on the part of Kissinger to accept the rejection of Toon on his first nomination but then to appoint him again. Toon was finally accepted by the Russians with great reluctance, probably not to prejudice relations with the new Carter administration, but it did not facilitate the ambassador's task.

Early in December relations began to return to normal and the Soviets were delighted with a visit by the outgoing secretary of the treasury, William Simon, and a delegation of 350 businessmen. Indeed, the Russians were so pleased to see this demonstration of interest in détente on the part of the Americans that Brezhnev himself had a private meeting with Simon and gave a dinner for him and the more important businessmen. He used the occasion to convey to Carter the Soviet intention to avoid any crisis or test of the new president during the initial stage of his administration. Brezhnev, possibly having learnt something of American public relations, made it a point to shake hands with every American businessman at the Kremlin banquet, which was repaid in a rather absurd scene in which the 'capitalist exploiters' rose and sang together 'Happy Birthday, dear Leonid.' His anniversary fell on 19 December.

But Soviet officials were already becoming nervous about the views of Carter's foreign policy advisers and his support for dissidents in the Soviet Union. Several Russians commented to me just after the election that they hoped it would be possible to forget the campaign rhetoric and get down to business. They clearly did not believe that Carter meant every word he said, particularly about dissent.

Perhaps to test this, the Soviets arrested the dissidents Vladimir Ginsberg and Yuri Orlov early in February 1977, and they were surprised at the strong reaction from Washington. When I had a talk with a senior official on this question, I stressed the fact that human rights was an integral part of Carter's program and that it evoked a very strong emotional response in the United States, as well as in Canada and other Western countries. The official's reponse was that we should not underestimate the importance of the emotional reaction in the Soviet Union to foreign support of opposition elements. The so-called dissidents, he said, were of absolutely no political importance and they operated entirely outside the political structure of the country. American support for them, he claimed, would be comparable to Soviet support for the Weathermen in the United States.

On the question of the direction of Democratic foreign policy, several officials remarked that they were certain they could do business with such able and experienced people as Cyrus Vance and Paul Warnke. But almost all of them expressed extreme suspicions of Brzezinski, who had been appointed national security adviser. But what the Soviets were hoping for was a severance of any linkage between the question of dissent and other bilateral issues such as SALT.

Even though the Soviets were prepared for a tough time over dissent, the exchange of letters between Carter and Andrei Sakharov in mid-February came as an unpleasant shock. It is hard to tell if Carter understood the full implications of the president of the United States writing personally to the most prominent dissident in the Soviet Union, or if he decided deliberately to provoke the Soviets on an issue which they considered strictly an internal affair, and a highly delicate one at that. Ambassador Toon attempted to dissuade the President from provoking the Russians to this extent at the very beginning of his administration, but he was overruled and ordered to deliver the letter. The exchange of letters and their subsequent publication were indeed unusual in relations between states. Soviet irritation was further aroused by a well-publicized meeting in the White House between Carter and the dissident Vladimir Bukovsky, described by *Pravda* as a criminal emigré.

It had been the axiom of dissidents in the Soviet Union that expressions of support from the West served an important protective function for those engaged in the struggle to humanize the communist regime, or the Jewish activists trying to emigrate. This theory was badly shaken by the arrest of a number of dissidents, including Anatoli Shcharansky, on charges of espionage. They had written a collective letter to Carter warning that the Kremlin was moving back to the Stalinist practice of staged trials, and that the gravity of the situation should not be underestimated. In information that we collected at the time, it was clear that there was confusion in the ranks of the dissidents as to the wisdom of seeking Western support, since almost all of them were agreed that indeed there was a distinct tightening of the screws. The intention of the Soviet government to confront the Carter administration head-on on this issue was illustrated by the fact that Shcharansky was arrested just two weeks before a visit by the new secretary of state, Cyrus Vance, and that he was accused of espionage on behalf of the American embassy. But what was remarkable was that none of the dissidents, from Sakharov on down to the less well-known Ukrainian and Tartar nationalists, appeared at all cowed.

As the dissidents expected, in the succeeding months the Soviets chose to stage public trials of Orlov, Shcharansky, and Ginsberg.

All three were given severe sentences in spite of strong protests from the United States, Canada, and other countries. The trial and sentencing of Orlov was particularly repugnant since he was chairman of the committee to observe Soviet compliance with the Helsinki agreement. The case of Shcharansky was also disturbing since for the first time a Jewish activist on behalf of human rights was charged and convicted of espionage on behalf of the American embassy. The State Department accused the Soviets of a 'gross distortion of internationally accepted standards of human rights,' a statement Carter fully endorsed. On their side, the Soviets showed no sign of contrition, or even worry about the effect on U.S.-Soviet exchanges or the possibility of a Carter-Brezhnev summit, even though Moscow still badly wanted a meeting.

The arrest and harassment of dissidents continued through the entire Carter administration, occasionally tempered by gestures to appease visiting American delegations and, in 1979, a sudden spurt of Jewish emigration. In the same year there occurred the curious exchange of an arrested and condemned Soviet spy in the United States, Colonel Abel, for the release of a number of Soviet dissidents, including Ginsberg, Kuznetsov, and the Ukrainian nationalists Moroz and Vina. But the Soviets stubbornly refused to release either Orlov or Shcharansky.

One odd departure from this depressing routine was the sudden eruption into the American embassy on 27 June 1978 of a family of seven Pentecostalists from Siberia. The eighth member of the group, the leader's seventeen-year-old son, was detained by the police, badly beaten up and returned to his home in Chemogorsk. The Americans refused to force them to leave and the Soviets refused to agree to the Pentecostalists' demand for assurances that they would not suffer retaliation for entering the embassy and that their applications to emigrate would be processed 'normally.' This impasse lasted for a number of years and bedevilled U.S.-Soviet relations as well as making life difficult for the personnel of the American embassy, who had to accommodate these seven extra persons in already badly overcrowded space.

The two main planks of Carter's foreign policy appeared in his first four months in office to be disarmament, accompanied by the maintenance of good relations with the Soviet Union, and the defence of human rights. The Soviets, even those with expert knowledge of the United States, confessed bafflement at Carter. They began to believe that his interest in the dissidents looked more like a plot, manipulated at the highest level, to use them to destabilize the internal policies of the Soviet Union. They tied the increase in the financial allocations to Radio Liberty and Radio Free Europe to this alleged plot, concluding that Carter's support of the dissidents had nothing to do with his belief in human rights.

But the Soviets were prepared to believe in Carter's conviction that détente had to be continued and SALT II completed. They were in for a rude shock, therefore, when Cyrus Vance visited Moscow in March 1977 and proposed a radical departure from the Vladivostok accords, involving deep cuts in strategic weapons, while excluding the cruise missile from discussions. Apart from the fact that this created serious problems for the Soviet negotiators with their military, they do not like sudden surprises, and the importance and complexity of the proposals put them at a disadvantage. They concluded that the Americans were trying to gain a tactical advantage by a surprise move which represented a retreat from what had already been agreed through slow and painful bargaining.

The Russians were gradually becoming convinced that the personal commitment by President Carter to the issue of human rights in the Soviet Union could not be simply dismissed. They were completely confused by the casual way in which Carter responded to each Soviet warning about interference in Soviet internal affairs.

To respond to this and to what they considered the unjustified American position over SALT, Gromyko called an unprecedented press conference after Vance had left Moscow. This was the first time that most Russians and all foreigners had been able to see Gromyko at his best. His command of the subject-matter, his skill in putting across the Soviet point of view and deflecting unpleasant questions, and his almost total imperturbability added up to a brilliant performance, which no doubt helped him in his eventual accession to the Politburo. What came through was Soviet fear of the cruise missile and of American attempts to increase nuclear superiority over the Soviet Union and therefore endanger Soviet security. Gromyko made it quite specific that if Carter intended, as he had claimed, to develop the cruise missile if no progress were made in the Geneva talks, full responsibility for the subsequent situation would fall on the United States; and that the Soviet Union would not sign a treaty based on the Vladivostok agreement without including the cruise missile. The Soviet leaders had patience, he said, but not infinite patience. Through the whole interview, which concentrated on the nuclear arms issue, there was a very noticeable, barely suppressed anger at the Americans, which at times was reflected in what was, for Gromyko, intemperate language.

To a certain extent Gromyko was right about the question of exercising patience. Georgi Arbatov, a short time later in a talk with me, went to considerable pains to show how the Soviet leaders had gone to extraordinary lengths to exhibit patience and understanding in dealing with a new and inexperienced administration in 'a nation which only recently had emerged from the traumas of Vietnam and Watergate.' The Soviet leaders had also shown patience during the first two years of the Kennedy administration, and indeed almost through the entire first term of Nixon, and it had taken considerable restraint, he said, to agree to receive Nixon in Moscow when Hanoi was being bombarded and Haiphong blockaded. But he continued to express puzzlement about Carter's foreign policy aims, as did Gromyko in a talk I had with him a few weeks later. Gromyko was genuinely preoccupied over the stalemate in arms talks, expressed some disquiet again over the influence of Brzezinski on the White House, and real puzzlement about what he regarded as the clear contradictions in Carter's attitude toward the Soviet Union.

The American administration seemed intent on baffling not only the Russians, but its friends as well. In July 1978 the administration grandiosely announced that future sales of oil technology would be subject to more stringent review in reprisal for the latest convictions of Soviet dissidents. Exactly one month later, Dresser Industries of Dallas was given the green light to proceed with the sale to the Soviet Union of a plant producing oil-well drilling bits. Not only was the approval for the sale inconsistent with the announced policy, but the Soviets concluded that inclusion of oil production equipment in the future was unlikely to pose any problems. The Dresser deal was an important test case since it included a highly sophisticated computer operated electron beam welding machine. Since Canada was directly affected as a competitor for the Soviet market, we had detailed but fruitless talks with the Americans, who claimed it was actually in the interests of the United States to enable the Soviet Union to develop its oil-drilling capabilities; otherwise, the Soviets could have ended up as competitors with the West in the much more restricted oil market projected for the 1980s.

The growing anti-American feeling among the Soviet leaders and their difficulty in understanding the situation in the United States can be illustrated by a long conversation I had with the deputy foreign minister in mid-August. Igor Zemskov was more than willing to sound off on U.S. policy. He found it impossible to believe that a responsible government could flippantly dismiss a serious agreement entered into by its predecessor; there had to be other reasons for Carter's refusal to accept the Vladivostok accord. It was his opinion that the Democrats were closely allied to the industrial-military complex and committed to altering the policy of the Republican party because it was too friendly to the Soviet Union. He believed that the human rights issue was the ideological arm of the new policy of Carter, basically determined by the CIA, aimed at establishing American superiority. Having put Watergate and Vietnam behind them, the Americans felt it possible to reassert a dominant role in the world.

I suggested that this was a highly simplistic, if not dangerously simple, explanation of Carter's policy. I asked him if they had ever considered Carter's background as a Southern fundamentalist Baptist who believed very seriously in certain moral principles which he had tried to apply to foreign affairs. Zemskov dismissed this out of hand. 'If Carter really believed in his principles,' he said, 'why not apply them first to the numerous social and economic problems of the United States? Why try them out on the Soviet Union unless this was simply part of a CIA plot?' There seemed no point in continuing this line of argument so I tried to convince him that the Americans did have serious proposals for the limitation and control of strategic nuclear arms, even if they might have presented them unwisely. He reacted strongly, saying that the proposals aimed only at establishing permanent American nuclear superiority. 'They not only want superiority in strategic weapons, but they want to exclude tactical weapons and air bases which encircle the Soviet Union and this is something we cannot accept.'

In a talk a few days later, Georgi Arbatov was equally emotional about American efforts to play the 'Chinese card,' orchestrated by Brzezinski. I suggested American overtures to China were a normal part of the great power relationship, although possibly also intended to remind Moscow of the possibilities inherent in Sino-American co-operation. Arbatov said on the contrary this was a very dangerous gambit and the West simply failed to understand that the qualitative improvement in Soviet weaponry – he would not call it an arms build-up – was linked to Soviet defence needs in face of a huge, hostile, and unpredictable neighbour who laid claims to large parts of Soviet territory. Both he and Zemskov suggested the West should consider what would be the implications of helping to modernize and arm China.

Despite the strains, both sides seemed determined to try to improve relations, above all in trade and disarmament. As far as trade was concerned, another American spectacular took place with, among other things, a visit by the secretary of commerce accompanied by a number of senators and a cast of more than three hundred businessmen. In return, the Soviets pulled out most of the stops, including meetings with Brezhnev, Kosygin, and other senior leaders, a Kremlin dinner, and so on. Nevertheless, very little forward movement was apparent in commercial terms.

During the winter and spring of 1979 there was on the surface a feeling of immobilism in the Soviet Union, but the patient negotiations in Geneva had paid off and the basis for the SALT II agreement was reached. It was a skilful compromise between the Soviet determination to retain the basic elements of the Vladivostok accord and the American desire to see greater reductions and qualitative constraints on the limits agreed by Brezhnev and Ford. SALT II consisted of a treaty based on the Vladivostok understanding to last through 1985; a protocol of three years' duration to cover certain issues such as cruise missile constraints, mobile ICBM limits, and qualitative limits on ICBMs, while deferring further negotiations on these issues to SALT III. The negotiations were supposed to start as soon as SALT II was ratified and be guided by a joint statement of principles.

When the negotiators reached an agreement on SALT II, the question arose of its signature and both sides quickly agreed that the importance of the document needed to be underlined by the presence of the leaders of the two superpowers. While Brezhnev would probably have preferred another summit in Washington, the political atmosphere in the United States made this a doubtful proposition and Vienna was chosen for the purpose. On 19 June the two leaders signed the elusive agreement and it immediately became clear in Moscow that the Soviets were confident that a new international atmosphere would emerge and that in bilateral terms there would be an across-the-board improvement in relations with the United States.

The Soviets hoped that SALT II would mean a more open American acceptance of Soviet credentials as a superpower and an end to American attempts, as they saw it, to put them in a humiliating secondary position through emphasis on highly subjective moral values, particularly the question of human rights. Although almost certainly unjustified by anything that happened in Vienna, the Soviets also appeared to hope that this new understanding would deter Carter from pursuing his flirtation with China and preserve the status quo, with the United States and the Soviet Union sharing world power on a basis of rough equality, keeping China limited in its potential, and restoring the special relationship which Brezhnev believed should exist between the world's two strongest countries.

Equally important for the Soviets was the hope that the meeting in Vienna marked the beginning of a new economic and commercial relationship. Above all, they looked forward to an end to the hated Jackson-Vannik amendment, which they still interpreted as an unwarranted interference in their internal affairs, and the establishment of a new impetus for the rapid development of enhanced commercial and scientific exchanges. Knowledgeable Soviets realized that the path of American-Soviet relations was bound to be rocky and uncertain with the coming struggle for the ratification of SALT II in Congress, followed closely by a presidential election. But they seemed to believe that a major breakthrough had been achieved creating a new relationship between the superpowers.

One of the aims of the Russians in seeking the Vienna meeting was to demonstrate to Soviet public opinion that Brezhnev was in reasonable health and in full command of the Party and state apparatus, and to impress Carter and Western opinion that there was no reason to believe that he would be abandoning power in the near future. The presentation of the talks in the Soviet media was carefully calculated to show a healthy, confident Brezhnev dealing directly with the American president. But the American participants were less impressed by a Soviet leader who had difficulty concentrating on complicated subject-matters for more than an hour at a time and who was visibly suffering from some unidentified disease. Some kind of rapport between Brezhnev and Carter was established, but the scene of the two of them embracing did neither a very great service politically in the long run.

In retrospect, it is interesting to note that I suggested in a dispatch before the encounter that Brezhnev might raise the subject of Soviet interests in Afghanistan and Vietnam. I thought he would try to make the case that both countries should be seen as part of the Soviet sphere of interest and that American policies should be amended accordingly. While the question of Vietnam was perhaps too delicate for the Soviets, particularly if they intended to establish a permanent base at Cam Rahn Bay, I thought, mistakenly as it turned out, that the strategic and political importance of Afghanistan to them might prompt the Soviets to try to reach an understanding with the Americans about these concerns.

The optimism which the Vienna meeting engendered on both sides began to evaporate almost immediately. In the United States opposition in Congress to SALT II made it apparent that ratification was going to be difficult. Equally important, a majority in Congress was determined to stick to the Jackson-Vannik amendment tying Jewish emigration to the U.S.-Soviet trade agreement. Although the number of Jews leaving the Soviet Union increased considerably in 1979, the continued persecution of dissidents and the publicity attached to their harassment made it difficult for the administration to argue very persuasively in favour of abandonment of the amendment. Two other events also increased opposition to détente: reports of the presence of a Soviet brigade in Cuba and, far more important, the gradual realization of the extent of the modernization of the Soviet nuclear forces and the deployment of the new intermediate-range and very accurate nuclear missile, the ss–20.

American charges of the formation of a Soviet combat brigade in Cuba were flatly rejected by the Soviets on the grounds that Soviet troops had been in Cuba for seventeen years to train the Cuban defence forces and that neither the function nor the numbers of Soviet personnel had changed in that time. As seen from Moscow, the uproar made over these forces by Washington seemed excessive and inept, particularly the concentration on a minor issue which could only exacerbate NATO-Soviet relations at the expense of really serious issues. The Soviets showed equal ineptitude in their inability to understand the sensitivity of Americans to the issue of Cuba, at a time when the presence of Cuban forces in Angola was a major issue in the United States. The question of the Soviet troops in Cuba was eventually passed over when it became apparent that the Soviets had not broken the informal understanding about Cuba or that the presence of a small number of ground forces did not seriously change the strategic balance in the Caribbean.

The ss-20s were another matter. Their range prevented them from being included as intercontinental ballistic missiles, but permitted them to hit almost any target in central and Western Europe from bases in western Russia. Thus they altered radically the strategic situation, since they were far superior to any intermediate-range or tactical nuclear weapon then in place in central Europe.

It was the West Germans who first became alarmed at the implications of the ss-20s and it appears that the American administration was dragged rather reluctantly into what turned out to be a major confrontation with the Soviets. There has been a great deal of speculation about the political reasons for the Soviet move. However, when one considers that it normally takes from ten to twelve years from the beginning of research on a new weapon to its production, testing, and deployment, one has to reach the conclusion that work on the ss-20 must have begun about 1967–9. This was a period when u.s.-Soviet relations were tense and complicated by a near-military confrontation in the Middle East, a very large American military offensive in Vietnam, and the crisis over Czechoslovakia. One can well imagine that the Soviet leaders at that period saw good reason to proceed with the development of a new weapon, apart from the fact that the continued qualitative improvement of weapons is an integral part of the superpower game plan.

By 1977, therefore, the Russians probably had produced and tested their first ss-20s. The question then arose as to what to do with them. It seems inconceivable that the military would forgo using this formidable new weapon, and, knowing the Russian mind, it is hard to believe that the civilian leaders would either want to waste all the money that had gone into the ss-20 or abandon the political option of deploying the weapon in order to increase their political leverage in Europe. Therefore a few missiles were deployed and there was no reaction from the West. A few more were deployed, and it was not until at least twenty had been sited on targets in Western Europe that the West reacted. I can envisualize the delight in the Kremlin as the ss-20 was first deployed without provoking anger in the West. But it is hard to understand how the Soviet leaders could not have realized that eventually, as the implications of the ss-20 grew, there would not be some sort of riposte.

In mid-September, Soviet officials began demonstrating some awareness that they had a problem. They began pushing for the rapid ratification of salt ii, start of work on salt iii and other measures of military détente, in particular breaking the logjam at the mutual balanced force reduction talks in Vienna, and putting a halt to nato Tactical Nuclear Force (tnf) modernization.

From talks I had with various Soviet officials, the growing concern about the international military situation was evident. They pointed to such things as an increased defence budget in the United States, the decision to turn the British-owned island of

Diego Garcia in the Indian Ocean into an American base, the decision to proceed with deployment of the MX system, and a strengthening of American global military capability simultaneously with a growing Sino-American rapprochement.

There was a good deal of ambivalence in the Soviet thinking. On the one hand they had consistently sought to separate the United States from Europe, while on the other they clearly did not want the emergence of a strong independent European military structure. At that time, it seemed to me, the Soviets were tending to believe that it would be better for them if the Europeans left their defence to the United States. In the long run this might permit them to strike a military accord with the United States that would simultaneously meet their security concerns and offer the prospect of expanding their political influence in Europe.

The Soviets hoped to secure a global strategic military modus vivendi with the United States through SALT III while promoting political opposition to a strong European strategic force as a counterweight to Soviet power in the European theatre. They did proceed with the gesture of withdrawing twenty thousand troops from East Germany, but it was quite clear that this unilateral move, taken outside the context of the Vienna talks, would never have been proposed if NATO had not made it clear that it was inclined to the modernization of its tactical nuclear forces. If such a move had been made a few years earlier, it could have had a devastating effect on Western public opinion. Probably the military in the Soviet Union were able to frustrate any move to reduce forces unilaterally until they were actually faced with the prospect of meaningful Western improvements.

As the meeting of the NATO foreign and defence ministers approached, the Soviet attitude on TNF hardened. Although public statements and articles were ambivalent about the results of a positive NATO decision, in private Soviet officials were threatening dire consequences. In talks I had with Foreign Minister Gromyko, he declared flatly that a NATO decision to proceed with its plan for TNF modernization 'would destroy the basis for negotiations.' Negotiations, Gromyko claimed, were possible only on the basis of the military situation as it then existed. I argued that the problem was a misunderstanding of intentions and that Soviet policy had seemed in the West designed not to promote arms talks but to dissuade Western efforts to achieve parity. The principle of equal security depended on assessments of military balance and NATO judged that the Soviet military build-up in recent years did not offer promising grounds for negotiations on the basis of equal security. The NATO proposal for TNF modernization was intended simply to keep up with the Soviets, not to seek military superiority. To this Gromyko replied with unusual acerbity and rigidity that this was a policy of negotiating from strength which the Soviets rejected – a policy line from which the Soviets hardly departed for the next four years, and which became the official attitude after NATO did approve the program.

As the year 1979 ended, the hopes for a new and fruitful relationship between the Soviets and the Americans were fading rapidly. One Soviet official said he had had little real expectation that the Vienna meeting between Carter and Brezhnev would set things right, but the 'right-wing reactionaries' in the United States were determined to prevent a revival of détente. He cited the failure of Congress to ratify SALT II, the fuss over 'Russian military advisers in Cuba,' and the NATO decision on TNF as evidence. He would not admit one iota of Soviet responsibility for the situation.

Détente was clearly in serious trouble, and the increasing tendency in the United States for it to become a major issue in the forthcoming presidential election did not augur well for the prospects of a reversal of this trend. The invasion of Afghanistan at the end of December, therefore, came as the culmination of a process of disintegration that was already well advanced. It was an event which would have wrecked détente in any event, but it alone was not responsible for its demise.

16

The End of the
Brezhnev Era

The prospects for East-West relations at the beginning of 1980 looked grim. Talks I had over the weekend of the Russian new year with a number of Russian writers and artists, all of them respectable members of the Soviet cultural establishment, revealed a reaction of alarm, surprise, and disapproval over the invasion of Afghanistan. They were worried about the effect on relations with the West and a probable reduction of cultural exchanges. An economist said that the bureaucracy had been upset because of the need to rethink totally the new five-year plan, since the invasion seemed likely to affect imports of technology from the West and certainly access to the world grain market. Although the average Russian accepted the Soviet version of events, he seemed more worried about the prospects of Sino-American encirclement and a serious deterioration in relations with the United States.

It was obviously necessary to get across to the Soviets the extent of the damage they had inflicted on détente, and to prevent developments in Afghanistan from spreading to other areas. One of the problems in talking to the Russians was the tendency, which had been developing in the previous years, for an ailing leadership to retreat behind the walls of the Kremlin and to avoid contact with westerners except on very special occasions. It was made even more difficult in 1980 by the limitations placed on Brezhnev's activities by increasing illness, and by a sudden malady that was shortly to lead to the death of Prime Minister Kosygin. The American ambassador, Thomas Watson, Jr, managed to see Gromyko early in February, but the results were sterile, and Soviet Ambassador Dobrynin in Washington was apparently under instruction to do no more than repeat *Pravda*'s official line.

On 18 February Gromyko made an 'election' speech (for elections to the Supreme Soviet) in which he asserted the Soviet Union's determination to maintain its achieved strategic parity with the United States and its status as a global power commensurate with its interests and influence. Equal status with the United States was linked to the Soviet need not to have to yield in areas where they judged their vital interests were affected. Afghanistan was an example of this and Gromyko issued a stern warning to Washington to 'keep control of itself,' and curb those who preferred to deal with the Soviet Union in an 'invariably cocky manner.'

Discussions with Soviet officials became increasingly difficult and at times emotional. Gromyko was suddenly unavailable, but Deputy Foreign Minister Igor Zemskov was prepared to argue over developments. Blame for everything was passionately laid at the door of Washington, whereas the Soviet actions in Afghanistan, for example, were clear-cut and above suspicion of any ulterior motive. They had dispatched troops only after fourteen requests by three Afghani governments. They had agreed only when it became absolutely clear that covert American intervention in Afghanistan was seriously threatening to destroy the Kabul government. He claimed the Soviets had specific concrete evidence of American involvement in the training and arming of Afghan rebels in Pakistan long before the Soviet intervention. Without their counter action the United States would have created in Afghanistan a bridgehead for aggression against the Soviet Union. A declaration by Carter in his State of the Union message that the United States had vital interests in the Persian Gulf region, he said, was comparable to the Soviet Union declaring it had vital interests in Mexico or Canada.

The subsequent effort I made to rebut this extreme view of the situation and a plea to recognize the legitimate interest, not only of the United States and its allies but of most of the non-aligned countries, failed to budge him. In every subsequent conversation I had with him, he stuck doggedly to the same line. And in fact this still continued until well into the Gorbachev era.

Since the decision by the International Olympic Committee to hold the 1980 Olympic Summer Games in Moscow, the staging of this event had become a major preoccupation of the Soviets. They hoped to demonstrate to the whole world the achievements of the Soviet regime and, by cornering the largest number of medals, show the superiority of Soviet athletes. To accomplish the latter goal was well within possibilities since the Russians are a hardy race capable, by the intensive help and training afforded by the state, of producing superb sportsmen. The achievement of the first aim was a more doubtful proposition. The stadiums, swimming pools, and all the other sites for the various disciplines were already built, or could be built with little difficulty, and Lenin Stadium was easily capable of staging the gala opening and closing ceremonies. But a number of problems remained.

The Soviets wished to show their country to as many Western tourists as possible, the inflow of foreign currency being, of course, an added incentive. Adequate hotel accommodation posed one problem which they partially solved by building a new hotel put up by the French Meridien chain in Moscow, and another built by the Swedes in Leningrad. The other major problem was security – not of the tourists and athletes, but of preventing their contact with the Soviet people. This was met by plans to remove a fair portion of the population out of Moscow and by elaborate devices to insulate those who remained from contamination. Since more than eight thousand Canadians alone were planning to attend the Games, the extent of the dilemma facing the Soviets was apparent.

Another serious problem was how to feed this huge influx of presumably hungry and demanding foreigners. The solution suddenly dawned on them: fast food. They had neither the experience, the ingredients, nor the know-how to handle this on their own, though they tried hard before turning to the inevitable source – McDonald's. For reasons I never quite fathomed, when the head office of McDonald's divided up the world for future conquest, the Soviet Union and Eastern Europe fell to the Canadian branch. Hence it was the Toronto-based executives of McDonalds who were invited to negotiate a deal with the Soviets.

For over six months George Cohon, president of McDonald's Canada, negotiated with the Soviet Olympic Committee to provide a mobile restaurant capable of serving fifteen thousand meals a day near the main Olympic site, the Lenin Stadium. At the end of October 1979, after negotiations almost as difficult as the Helsinki treaty, McDonald's signed a forty-four-page contract with the Olympic Committee. McDonald's was jubilant and anticipated that this would lead to the establishment of a chain of restaurants throughout the Soviet Union after the Games. Two days later, their hopes were dashed by the news that the deal was off.

From talks I subsequently had with various members of the Soviet Olympic Committee, who were visibly shattered at the cancellation and the appalling prospect of themselves having to service thousands of spectators, it appeared that the ideologues in the Party had vetoed the scheme. The vision of the Big Mac, this highly visible symbol of the capitalist system, providing food which the Soviets could not produce, in front of *Lenin*'s stadium was too much for them. I tried to convince the committee that this would discourage Canadian businessmen from trying to trade with Russia in the future, but to no avail: ideology was stronger than the Big Mac. The one positive side of this sad story was the propaganda the Canadian embassy was able to make out of the thousands of Big Mac pins, shopping bags, and other items printed in Russian that Cohon and his delegation left behind in disgust.

The seriousness with which the Soviets took the Games was evident in the appointment of Ignaty Novikov, one of the deputy prime ministers and head of Gosstroi, the vast organization overseeing all major construction work in the Soviet Union, as president of the Olympic Committee. As dean of the diplomatic corps and ambassador of the country which had played host to the 1976 Games, I had a good deal to do with him. He was extremely competent and the whole logistical part of the Games, except for the services for the tourists, was a model of efficiency. Even he, at times, showed slight signs of panic over the prospect of feeding and surveying the flood of tourists. I once suggested to him that the

320 / Our Man in Moscow

North American concept of fast food was the most efficient, utilitarian, and proletarian way of feeding large numbers of people and ought to be ideal for a communist country. He firmly denied this, but I heard later that he had been intrigued by my remark.

The decision by the major Western countries to boycott the Games as a result of the invasion of Afghanistan came as a distinct shock to the Russians. I am quite certain that they had not taken this form of reaction into account. Nor did they believe at first that Western unity could be maintained on the issue, or that Western governments would be able to persuade or prevent their athletes from attending.

Early in the morning after the invasion, Tom Watson, the American ambassador, had telephoned to ask if he could see me urgently. Watson was the retired chairman of IBM and a close friend of Carter. He had made no secret of the fact that he had been appointed because the president believed the United States and the Soviet Union were about to move into a period of closer co-operation in which trade would be very important and that Watson was the ideal man for the job. He might well have been, but he confessed to me that 30 December that he had no background to meet the kind of situation presented by the invasion of Afghanistan.

We talked over the reasons the Soviets had decided to take the plunge, the implications, and the need for the West to demonstrate its anger without risking a military confrontation. I suggested that there were two ways to register disapproval: by a selective economic boycott, which had never proved very effective in the past and usually hurt us as much as the country targetted, or by a boycott of the Olympic Games. Watson at once agreed and very shortly afterwards Carter announced that the u.s. government would boycott the Games unless the Soviets withdrew from Afghanistan by 20 February. The Conservative government of Joe Clark also announced Canada's intention to boycott the Games, as did the United Kingdom and West Germany, among others.

I was unable to find out why the American government made the boycott dependent on a Soviet withdrawal, nor why 20 February was fixed as the deadline. Using the boycott to force Soviet troops out of Afghanistan was unrealistic and should never have been presented as its aim. The Canadian government made it clear, when the decision was confirmed by the Liberal government after it returned to office following the elections of February 1980, that our boycott was a price the Soviets had to pay for an inadmissible departure from accepted international behaviour.

The insensitivity of the Soviets to outside opinion was demonstrated by their arrest of Andrei Sakharov in mid-January, a development that made it even more difficult for Western governments to modify their stand on the Olympics. It probably helped a number of governments which had been wavering to join in the boycott.

The new Liberal government in Canada had been reluctant to endorse a Conservative decision without a careful re-examination of it, a reluctance reinforced by Pierre Trudeau's tendency to try to find an intermediary line between the United States and the Soviet Union, and by those official and unofficial bodies which had spent a great deal of money and effort in preparing for Canadian participation in the Games. But there was never really any alternative for the government. No matter what the objective merits of participation or boycott, the fact was simply that no self-respecting Western government could ignore what was happening in Afghanistan by taking part in the Games. The decision to endorse the boycott was taken with curious ineptitude, on the eve of the visit to Ottawa of the American secretary of state, Cyrus Vance, thus giving the impression to the Russians that Canada had succumbed to American pressure – which may, of course, have been the government's intention.

The Canadian role would have been important if the Games had proceeded normally. Apart from a very large number of athletes and tourists, Canada had a special position as host of the previous Games and it was the duty of the city of Montreal, which held the official Olympic flag, to transmit it formally to the city of Moscow. Mayor Jean Drapeau had been planning to do this himself, but declined after the boycott was announced. Indeed, at one point it looked as if he might hold on to the flag and refuse to transfer it to Moscow. He relented in the end and sent it with two young Montreal athletes and their parents. The Olympic attaché at the embassy met them and escorted them to their hotel, the flag safely in his custody. At the hotel entrance, he was refused admittance. He then said flatly that if he could not see his charges safely ensconced in their rooms, the flag would not be handed over. This brought frantic consultations and he was finally admitted. The young people did carry the flag at the official opening and behaved with great aplomb and dignity in transmitting it to two young Soviets.

As it became apparent that the Western countries, Japan, China, and many third world countries were determined to boycott the Games, resentment grew among Soviet officials at what they considered this underhanded way of responding to the Afghan adventure, and they spent a considerable amount of money and political capital to persuade non-aligned countries to participate. The Olympics did take place as scheduled with all the pomp and circumstance that the Russians are capable of producing for such a formal event as this. But without the participation of so many major powers, and the resulting downgrading of the athletic competition, the heart went out of it.

The boycott did not affect Soviet policy in Afghanistan nor reduce their military hold on the country. Nor did it prevent the Soviets from proclaiming the Olympics a success, but it did reduce the Games to a controversy-ridden event of relatively limited athletic scope and political impact. The elite was undoubtedly stung by the boycott and deeply resentful at what they considered an attempt to humiliate their country. Resentment, belligerence, scorn, and anger seemed the main reaction. At the same time they were defensive and aggressive, providing the best indication that the boycott had the impact the West intended.

The boycott cost the Soviets more than just prestige. While no figures were ever produced, it was estimated that the Olympic operation amounted to the equivalent of approximately three billion dollars, of which half a billion was in foreign currency. While the Soviets recovered some of this prior to the Games in licensing and contract fees, TV rights, sale of coins, and so on, they had counted on making up the remaining $250 million through tourist expenditures. In the event, this only amounted to less than $100 million. Given the chronic need for hard currency, this was a serious setback.

Another of the East-West friction points was Poland. The grounds-well of resentment in that country against the Gierek government, and against Russia, had been growing imperceptibly during the summer of 1980 but had been partly obscured by the Olympic Games and the continuing war in Afghanistan. When its actual proportions became apparent to the Soviets, particularly in the form of a true revolt of the proletariat, something which theoretically could never happen in a communist state, it quickly became the major concern of the Kremlin. Soon afterwards, with the election of Ronald Reagan as president, it assumed an additional importance as a major element in u.s.-Soviet relations.

Soviet disquiet over the prospect of a Reagan presidency began to grow during the election campaign. However, in their usual pragmatic fashion, the Soviets quickly adjusted to his election, and indicated they were prepared to work with him. Almost immediately they began trying to assess the views on the Soviet Union expressed by Reagan during his electoral campaign. What they were trying to decide was whether he was going to be another Nixon. They had a very vivid recollection of the way in which the latter switched from a particularly virulent form of anti-communism to constructive co-operation. But there remained the question of the Reagan counsellors. As in the case of Carter and Brzezinski, they were disturbed that another person of Polish origin, Richard Pipes, and the right-wing California think-tank group, might be able to exert a major influence on the views of a president who was obviously already determined to adopt a tough stance towards Moscow.

Nevertheless, they made an effort to establish normal relations with the new administration, and their effort to woo Reagan came sooner and more effusively than could have been expected from the Kremlin. They obviously thought, on the basis of previous experience, that conservative Republican administrations were in the long run more likely to do business with Moscow than liberal Democrats. It therefore behoved them to make this clear to the new administration. But the speed and eagerness with which the signals were being sent to Washington indicated in addition a genuine alarm over the possibility of a new American arms build-up. This in turn would necessitate a Soviet effort to keep pace, a tougher response by the United States to Soviet policies around the world, and a greater willingness to risk a confrontation. In addition, there remained in the Kremlin a certain nostalgia for u.s.-Soviet détente.

It was not long before disillusionment set in. Statements by Reagan and by his new secretary of state, Alexander Haig, attacked the Soviet Union for, among other things, support for international terrorism, and in effect rejected the olive branch from Moscow. The blow to the Soviets was severe. The rebuff came at a particularly complicated moment for the Soviet leadership: it was deeply preoccupied with the Afghan situation and baffled as to how to handle the developments in Poland; two of its leading figures in the government, Brezhnev and Kosygin, were in poor health; and the Twenty-Sixth Congress of the Communist Party was imminent. In private talks I had with Soviet officials their concerns became very clear. I was told that the reaction at the top to the Reagan 'insults' at first was one of absolute fury and indignation. One Soviet described Reagan to me as 'stupid, uneducated, misinformed, primitive, a neanderthal man,' surrounded by people of low intellectual calibre. He regarded Richard Pipes, for example, the counsellor on Soviet affairs in the National Security Council, as being far worse than Brzezinski and a 'tragic appointment.'

It seemed to outsiders in the West totally unrealistic for the Soviets not to have expected that the Reagan administration would react against a Carter policy which appeared to the American public as weak and indecisive. They were being naive if they expected that the invasion of Afghanistan and the revolt in Poland would make normal relations between a right-wing Republican administration and Moscow possible. Relations were complicated even further in February 1981, when Brzezinski revealed that Carter had effectively stopped the invasion of Poland the previous December by threatening Moscow with dire consequences. Since this warning had been passed by the top secret hotline, it convinced the Soviets that this device for diffusing potentially dangerous situations would prove less effective in future crises as the Russians would not wish to appear publicly to have given in to American threats.

At the same time, there was no indication that Brezhnev was prepared to accept that the Soviet Union had any responsibility for the deterioration of these relations. There was no sign that he considered the continuing Soviet military presence in Afghanistan a problem, or had any intention of discussing it seriously or admitting that the invasion could be considered a breach of the rules of international conduct or was in flagrant contradiction to the 1972 U.S.-Soviet code of conduct. Nevertheless, for Brezhnev there was probably no political alternative for him but to seek a meeting with Reagan since he was personally identified with the policy of détente. He could hardly have described the achievements of détente as a great victory nor could he have admitted the failure of détente without producing an alternative.

A month later I had a long talk with Arbatov. He found that the prospects for U.S.-Soviet relations were even worse than he had imagined, and the appointment of Eugene Rostow as a member of the White House staff in charge of disarmament and Caspar Weinberger as secretary of defense made the prospects even more daunting. I found it hard to believe that Eugene Rostow would alarm the Soviets, but Arbatov claimed Rostow was an advocate of a limited nuclear war which the United States could win, even if it might cost three million American lives. I strongly contested this assessment of Rostow whom I had always found a conservative and reasonable man. But at that point the Soviets were prepared to believe the worst.

It was odd that the Soviets did not realize that the fate of Poland was of immense political and psychological importance to the West and that if the United States reacted strongly to the invasion of Afghanistan, the mere threat of intervention in Poland was enough to strain Soviet relations with the West. In any event, it soon became clear during 1981, and vividly so after the establishment of a military-communist government in Poland in December 1981, that the Reagan administration was prepared to challenge Soviet assumptions about what was permissible in Eastern Europe. It was ready to endure differences with its European allies if necessary to get across to the Soviet Union the basic message that the United States intended to substitute the spirit of the Helsinki agreement for the reality of Yalta in Eastern Europe and was ready to react strongly if provoked.

The Soviet worries about the influence on Reagan of the California think-tank group, and particularly Richard Pipes, were reinforced in the year and a half following Reagan's inauguration by the increasingly ideological tone given to the president's pronouncements on the Soviet Union and by statements of Pipes, Haig, Richard Allen, and other members of the inner circle. The Soviets were puzzled that two successive American administrations had chosen men of Polish origin as advisers on Soviet affairs. Curiously enough, they respected both Brzezinski and Pipes as historians and indeed Pipes's book, *Russia Under the Old Régime*, is a highly perceptive study of tsarist Russia. But his views on what policies the United States should follow toward the Soviet Union were exaggerated, unrealistic, and often highly emotional.

In June of 1982 I had a long talk with Pipes in the White House and later over dinner. He was convinced of the coming collapse of the Soviet economy and social system and certain that a little push on the part of the West was all that was needed to hasten that day. I argued that an economy the size of the Soviet, backed up by vast, even though poorly exploited, natural resources could not collapse in the classic Western sense. And in any case total Soviet control of the economy made it possible for the country to survive outside pressure, particularly since economic boycotts and other such measures could never be universally applied. Pipes was badly misinformed about the Soviet leadership, but when I proposed that a u.s.-Soviet summit could be useful to try to assess the Soviet leaders, he rejected it on the grounds that the Soviets were even more puzzled about the nature of the American leadership and it was time that they be forced to engage in a bit of guessing. I suggested that a policy of trying to destroy the Soviet system was not only unrealistic but unwise unless we had a clear idea of what was going to take its place. I could think of terrifying scenarios in which the Soviet system disintegrated and rival groups fought over possession of the biggest nuclear armoury in the world. It was surely less dangerous for the outside world to have the nuclear weaponry under tight control than at the mercy of warring factions or some totally unknown and unpredictable quantity. I had the impression that Pipes had not really thought through the implications of such a policy.

The Soviets were relieved when Pipes left the White House to return to Harvard in the fall of 1982. I am not certain that Pipes had that much influence on the president's concept of Russia. Certainly, his departure, and that of Alexander Haig shortly before, did not make much initial change in the wilder statements out of the White House on u.s.-Soviet relations. The Soviets were particularly disturbed by three things: first, the apparent determination to strengthen American military might in order to negotiate from a 'position of strength'; second, the constant statements from Secretary of Defense Weinberger which the Soviets interpreted as meaning that the United States were intent on seeking military superiority; and lastly, the statements by the president himself concerning the 'evil empire' and the determination of the United States to see the Soviet Union cast into the dustbin of history.

In September 1982 I had a long session with the new secretary of state, George Shultz, in Washington and he queried me as to why it seemed acceptable for the Russians to repeat ad nauseam their Marxist dogmas about the end of capitalism, and to heap insulting epithets on the United States, whereas they were outraged when the United States responded in kind. I replied that the reasons for the Soviet reaction were complex. In the first place, they had never before had to deal with an American president who seemed to be genuinely ideologically motivated. They had become accustomed to hard-headed but pragmatic American leaders who were prepared to adjust their political views as required if it appeared to be in the interests of the United States. But, like Carter and his passionate attachment to the one issue of human rights, they now had to deal with a new president who had an unswerving attachment to a capitalist anti-Soviet ideology. This unnerved the Soviets and they were having difficulty adjusting to it.

The second factor was that the head of state or government of the Party in the Soviet Union had never personally attacked the president of the United States. They expected, therefore, that this unspoken rule would be respected. They did not like having their leaders attacked by the lower echelon of American officialdom, but they accepted this as inevitable. But the personal attacks and the moralistic view of the Soviet Union advanced by the president himself gave this a completely new depth. In addition, the Russians suffered from a deep sense of inferiority and they felt they had been ridiculed and humiliated in front of the world by the president's remarks.

Finally, since most of the Soviets paid no attention whatsoever to the constant stream of dogmatic propaganda ground out by the Soviet ideological journals day in and day out, they assumed we paid no attention to it either. When they predicted the imminent end of capitalism, they did not take it seriously. But when the president of the most powerful country in the world predicted the collapse of the Soviet system, they interpreted this as meaning the American administration was intending to embark on efforts to make the forecast come true. Therefore they took it very seriously and reacted accordingly.

I was impressed by the seriousness with which Shultz was approaching what he had at once recognized as likely to be the toughest part of his assignment, relations with the Soviets. He had asked to see me as part of a series of consultations with other Soviet specialists. From the hour-long talk with him I came away convinced that he would make an effort to modify the president's Manichaean view of the world and to try to find some basis for eventual compromise with the Russians. After our talk, the deputy under-secretary of state, Lawrence Eagleburger, took me aside and said that he agreed with my explanation of why it was unwise of the president to insult the Russians. But there was a serious problem inherent in this: Reagan really believed in the concept of the 'empire of evil.'

Reagan did a good deal in his first term to awaken American national pride and rebuild American military strength. Both were salutary initiatives. But they were accompanied by a misunderstanding in the White House of Soviet aims and psychology, and of the real facts of the superpower relationship and its limits. The Soviets for their part contributed to the misunderstanding, by pushing geopolitical advantages beyond acceptable limits during the Carter years, by the intervention in Afghanistan, by the bullying of Poland, and by deploying the ss-20. All these actions were bound to generate a strong reaction in a strong government. The situation was never as dangerously confrontational as some critics thought. But it resulted in four largely wasted years in which the immobilism of the last months of Brezhnev's reign, and of the following brief Andropov and Chernenko interregnum, spread over into the international field.

On 10 November 1982 Brezhnev died. As was the almost invariable custom, he had made his obligatory appearance three days before at the annual parade to mark the anniversary of the revolution, standing for several hours in sub-zero weather, and in the afternoon hosting the traditional reception in the Kremlin for the high dignitaries of the Party and government, foreign guests, and the heads of diplomatic missions. These two events proved too much for his already failing health.

There was relief on the part of most of the younger members of the hierarchy and the intelligentsia. They had become increasingly embarrassed in the preceding years by the image Brezhnev presented abroad of a dull, semi-incapacitated leader unable to hold his own with his foreign counterparts. The Nomenklatura was uneasy because they did not like change. During the entire period of Brezhnev's illness the gerontocracy in the leadership had succeeded in propping him up in order to avoid change. The average Russian was relatively indifferent. The death of Stalin, who had been the awesome tyrant for more than twenty-five years, brought fear of what the future might hold. The passing of Brezhnev the average Russian thought was unlikely to alter life very much.

Leonid Brezhnev was not an intellectual, nor probably a great brain, but he had the qualities of a supreme politician which permitted him to survive in one of the most cutthroat political systems in the world for longer than any other Soviet leader except Stalin. While he never succeeded in establishing any real popularity or prestige with the people, who on the contrary often made fun of his alleged limited mental capacities and his vainglory, he did bring a strong element of stability and order to the country. There is in the Russian character a contradictory element. The Russians are constantly dissatisfied with their leaders and yet at the same time their history has created in them a longing for order which they realize means respect for authority. The Brezhnev era lacked the excitement and uncertainty of Stalin, and the brilliant innovations of Khrushchev. But it gave most people a sense of stability and continuity and, at least up until the late 1970s, a feeling that things were gradually getting better within a system about which they constantly grumbled but which unconsciously suited them. And at the same time Brezhnev managed to instil a feeling of national pride in most Russians for the achievements of their country in world affairs without any of the dangerous risk-taking which characterized so much of the Khrushchev period. Although the policy of détente he fathered had many elements and was intended to further Soviet national interests, which is hardly surprising, he impressed me as being genuinely desirous of seeking a means to avoid armed confrontation and to develop mutually profitable relations between the two major blocs and especially between the superpowers.

Brezhnev's failing health had turned him from a vital, self-assured, and well-informed leader into a wooden figure presiding over but not ruling the country. In spite of his physical decline, however, his hold on power remained secure. Brezhnev was a ruthless political operator. This was demonstrated in foreign affairs in the way in which he dealt with Dubček and the other Czechoslovak leaders in the 1968 crisis, and in advising and supporting the ouster of Wladislaw Gomulka as Party leader in Poland in 1970, and his successor Edward Gierek a decade later. But it was in his handling of his rivals within the Soviet hierarchy that the steel in Brezhnev was most apparent. Although by previous standards his treatment of Khrushchev was lenient, he refused to contemplate the latter's rehabilitation and Nikita Sergeivitch remained a non-person. When the Ukrainian Party boss, Pyotr Shelest, contested Brezhnev's policy of détente with the United States, he was dismissed. The two capable, industrious, and intelligent younger men in the Politburo in the sixties and seventies, Dmitri Polyansky and Alexander Shelepin, were eased out of office in order to maintain the Brezhnev clique's hold on power. Polyansky was blamed for the failures in agriculture and was demoted, first to be minister of agriculture, then ambassador to Japan, and later to Norway. Shelepin opposed Brezhnev's Middle East policy in 1967 and was demoted to head the trade union movement, an organization totally devoid of power, influence, or significance, and then into the obscurity which encompasses anyone who loses his position in the Soviet Union.

Brezhnev never completely forgave Podgorny for his ambivalent attitude in the 1964 coup which ousted Khrushchev. He was moved from the far more influential position as a senior member of the Secretariat in December 1975 to the largely ceremonial position of chairman of the Presidium of the Supreme Soviet, the equivalent of head of state. He was retired from this job in May 1977 and replaced by Brezhnev, in spite of the 1964 Politburo resolution that the three principal positions of power – secretary general of the party, prime minister, and president – would henceforth be kept separate. Khrushchev had been prime minister as well as secretary of the Party.

This rule was respected in a sense when Brezhnev assumed the presidency while remaining secretary general, since the other position of real power was that of prime minister. There were strong rumours in 1970 and again in 1971 that Brezhnev had attempted to secure the key position but had been thwarted. Podgorny performed his duties as head of state punctiliously and with dignity. It was obvious that Brezhnev's health would prevent him from fulfilling most of the ceremonial obligations inherent in the job, and in fact he only carried out those of great importance or those which interested him. For the rest, a new position of first vice-president was created and the veteran diplomat Vasily Kuznetsov was appointed to it.

There were two reasons for combining these positions. In the first place, there was a need to give the most powerful man in the country some constitutional right to treat on the same level with such foreign leaders as the president of the United States, and it had always rankled with Brezhnev that when President Nixon came to the Soviet Union he was outranked by Podgorny. This constitutional anomaly had nevertheless not prevented Brezhnev from being given head-of-state treatment in the United States and other countries he visited. Brezhnev had already been president from 1960 to 1964 and had liked the job. One of Khrushchev's major blunders lay in transferring Brezhnev from the presidency to the Secretariat, where he was in a position to play the key role in building support among the Party faithful for the overthrow of

Khrushchev. Brezhnev made no such mistake. When Podgorny was removed he went into carefully controlled retirement.

The other reason for assuming the presidency was the immense, almost childish, vanity with which Brezhnev liked to accumulate honours. The development of a cult of personality around Brezhnev had started only two years after the coup against Khrushchev. On his sixtieth birthday in 1966, he was made a Hero of the Soviet Union and, wearing his brand new medal, was given a standing ovation by the Supreme Soviet.

Brezhnev, like nearly all the others of his generation, was an anti-intellectual without much of an education. Khrushchev, with even less intellectual background than Brezhnev, nevertheless had an instinctive sense of the value of the arts, even if he often treated the artists with a bewildering eccentricity. But Brezhnev had a highly conservative approach and his attachment to socialist realism was genuine. Art had to do its share in the construction of communism; otherwise it was superfluous or even subversive. He had no scruples, therefore, in ordering the crackdown on writers and artists which developed after his arrival at the summit of power.

When Brezhnev became president in 1977, he asserted that the reason for combining this position with that of general secretary of the Party was to assert the absolute pre-eminence of the Party in Soviet life. His aim, he said, was to incarnate 'the indivisibility of the authority of the Party and the State.' Like his predecessor before him, and indeed his younger successor Mikhail Gorbachev, for Brezhnev the Party was what mattered and there could never be any conflict between its interests and the interests of the nation.

In the mid-seventies, a debilitating disease, the nature of which we are not certain, struck Brezhnev. As the years progressed, it became increasingly difficult for him to stand the pace of work and he disappeared from sight for longer and longer periods. These rest periods were either at his dacha some forty to fifty kilometres from Moscow, or at his villa in the Crimea. Increasingly he tended to spend the entire summer there and members of the Politburo and important foreign guests from the Soviet bloc would gather at the villa. There were times when it seemed almost certain that Brezhnev could not continue very much longer. At one ceremonial meeting of the Supreme Soviet, he had almost to be carried to his seat by two aides and he remained throughout the session almost completely motionless. Yet two days later he turned up at a Canada-Soviet hockey game looking full of life. It was almost impossible to judge the state of his health because on some occasions in official talks he seemed reasonably alert and a few weeks later almost incapable of doing more than repeating the brief in front of him. His memory was failing and towards the end of my time in Moscow it was clear he could never quite remember names and persons. After the resignation of Brezhnev's old friend, Urho Kekkonen, the long-time president of Finland, his successor Koivisto attended the 7 November ceremonies. When Koivisto approached Brezhnev, the chief of protocol whispered in his ear 'the President of Finland,' Brezhnev took him in his arms saying 'My dear old friend Kekkonen, thank you for coming.'

During his bouts of illness there were frequent resorts to extreme measures, by Western standards, to preserve his health, including consultations with American and French medical specialists in conditions of complete discretion. His advisers in 1979 even called on the powers of a Georgian faith-healer. This lady had established a considerable reputation in Tbilisi. A French psychologist friend of mine who spoke good Russian was given permission to visit her in 1978 and told me that she undoubtedly possessed some extraordinary psychic powers. She was rapidly becoming a rouble millionaire in Tbilisi when she was summoned to Moscow and established in a comfortable flat where she could exercise her hypnotic ability on Brezhnev. The summons of this faith-healer caused excitement in a population not so far removed from the fantastic episode of the efforts of the last tsar to cure his son's hemophilia through the faith-healing of Rasputin.

The illness of Brezhnev and his often prolonged absences from the public scene inevitably provoked speculative stories in the West. On one occasion a senior Soviet official, Leonid Zamyatin, complained to me about the foreign press. I said it was only natural that the outside world should be interested in the health of one of the most powerful men in the world. He replied that he could assure me that Brezhnev had recovered from his (unspecified) illness and that he would be back at work within a fortnight. I said in that case why not say so, or publish a photo of him and his wife strolling in the woods at his dacha. After hesitating, Zamyatin replied that they had actually suggested this and the answer had been: 'What for? In a short time the world will know it was all lies.' Zamyatin spread his hands as if to say: 'You see. They don't really understand the problem.'

The two last years of Brezhnev's life must have been difficult, with the deaths of Alexei Kosygin and of Mikhail Suslov, the member of the Politburo in charge of ideology and the high priest of the Communist Party. These two had formed with Brezhnev the triad which dominated the Politburo for more than sixteen years. Their deaths and the illness of Brezhnev seriously weakened the capacity of the government to take any kind of imaginative action in the last two years, years in which, in addition, Brezhnev's cherished dream of a new world condominium of the two superpowers was rapidly unravelling.

The Gorbachev Generation

At the end of September 1980 I left the Soviet Union after sixteen and a half years, eight of them as dean of the diplomatic corps. The Soviets had no reason to love me since I had defended Canadian and Western interests vigorously, but correctly, and had prevented the KGB from penetrating the defences of the embassy. But I had worked equally hard to develop East-West and Canadian-Soviet relations on a basis of mutual interest, and as dean I had helped the one hundred and six embassies representing very different and often antagonistic regimes work together in some form of co-operation and restraint. The Soviets chose to ignore all this. I was received by no official of any importance and the traditional farewell lunch was given only by Deputy Foreign Minister Kornienko. The Soviets admitted frankly that the tense state of East-West relations had dictated their 'boycott' of my departure.

Leaving Moscow did not mean leaving Soviet affairs, as I was appointed special adviser on East-West relations to the Canadian government and Canadian representative on the Independent Commission on Disarmament and Security Issues, headed by Olof Palme. It was on this commission that I found again my old Moscow acquaintance, Georgi Arbatov. Hence until the death of Brezhnev in November 1982, and the prolongation of his era through the brief leadership of Yuri Andropov and Konstantin Chernenko, I remained constantly occupied with the problems of the Soviet Union and the West.

The Brezhnev era wound down slowly. Even after his death, his elderly associates managed to maintain their hold on power by blocking the ascendancy of the younger generation. Yuri Andropov might have started the process of revitalizing the Soviet Union, but his rule lasted only briefly, and he was incapacitated for the nine months preceding his death in February 1984.

The hierarchy still could not bring itself to abandon power, and chose as secretary general Konstantin Chernenko, a member of the Dnepropetrovsk mafia, Brezhnev's closest friend, and quite literally his alter ego. Incompetent, unimaginative, unwell, he lacked even the semblance of charisma that Brezhnev possessed. But the effort to prevent change was futile. Chernenko's rule ended with his death in March 1985. At this point it was simply no longer possible to find a valid candidate among the older men in the Politburo. The Brezhnev era came effectively to an end with the choice of Mikhail Gorbachev as secretary general.

The appointment of Mikhail Gorbachev marked the coming to power not only of a new leader but of a new generation of Party officials and administrators. This has already created a radically different situation in Moscow as they courageously attempt to confront the manifold economic, social, and political problems of the country, to return to better relations with the West and China, and to undo some of Brezhnev's foreign misadventures, such as the intervention in Afghanistan. The intelligence and ability of the new leaders should not be underestimated, or at the same time the obstacles to transforming Soviet society.

The generation gap is more evident in the difference between Gorbachev and his associates and the gerontocracy which they replaced than would normally be expected because of the elimination from power by Brezhnev of nearly all the younger members of the inner circle until his last few years, when the exigencies of administration made it impossible for the elderly clique to do without the help of younger and more energetic people like Gorbachev. But he only came to Moscow from Stravopol in late 1978. In June 1980, of the fourteen members of the Politburo, only two were under seventy. Two of them, Kosygin and Suslov, were dying, the prime minister, Nikolai Tikhonov, was seventy-five and in frail health, and one member, Arvid Pelshe, was well over eighty. I once asked a member of the Secretariat why Pelshe was still in the Politburo as he seemed to serve no particular purpose. The answer was a surprised: 'But he is the only one who knew Lenin.' This illustrates vividly the importance of tradition and continuity in Soviet thinking.

The gerontocracy was not confined to the Party hierarchy. An extraordinary number of ministers and deputy ministers and heads of major enterprises had been in the same position for twenty or twenty-five years. Many of them were competent and honest but committed to a way of operating which had been overtaken by developments in the Soviet economy, not to mention the economic and technological revolution in the West. Most ministries had no intercom system. Nor did any kind of up-to-date equipment such as even photocopiers exist. There was, of course, a strong aversion to the latter; it represented a means of easily circulating material and was therefore potentially dangerous. But the lack of modern equipment was the result in part of inertia, in part of the establishment of priorities. If it was not possible to produce both sophisticated telephone interchanges and high-tech listening devices, then 'bugging' equipment had to come first.

Underneath the surface of the calm and order that reigned in Moscow one sensed the quiet dissatisfaction and impatience of the generation of Gorbachevs. They knew the degree of inefficiency, nepotism, and often bribery and corruption that existed at the top and indeed at every level of society. And one of the first acts, anticipating Gorbachev, was to remove some of the more notably inefficient ministers and to try to eliminate corruption and bribery.

It was highly unusual for a relatively young unknown from the provinces to move directly into the Politburo, especially to a key position bearing responsibility for economic and agricultural questions. Gorbachev therefore attracted my attention and I identified him in 1979 as a probable candidate for the succession. And a discreet word from Alexander Yakovlev, then ambassador to Canada, that Gorbachev was the coming man helped to reinforce my conviction. His visit to Canada in 1983 under the auspices of Yakovlev strengthened this impression later, since he talked and behaved with the authority and frankness of someone already sure of himself. The trip assured the rapid ascendancy of Yakovlev to a top job in the Politburo, and may also have helped convince Gorbachev of the need for economic reforms to catch up with the West.

The personality of Gorbachev, since his accession to power, has become familiar to most people in the West. The contrast with Brezhnev and Chernenko was obvious because of their failing health and age. But the important difference lies not in the energy and ease with which Gorbachev handles himself. Khrushchev in his time made the same impression on both the Soviet people and world opinion. It is what he represents which is important, and above all the fact that he is typical of the large number of Soviet politicians and administrators in their forties and fifties who must become the dominant force in Soviet ruling circles in the decades to come.

These are a new breed. None of them saw the revolution or the civil war and their recollections of the Second World War are those of children. They therefore differ radically from the Brezhnev generation who grew up in revolution and civil war and participated in some capacity or other in the Great Patriotic War, as the Russians call it. The hardship, bloodshed, actrocities, and near defeat at the hands of the Germans left a lasting imprint on them. Gorbachev and his colleagues are less emotional about the war, less influenced by the events of the past, and readier to find new solutions to their country's problems.

The Brezhnev generation had on the whole only very limited education, usually in technical schools, and was pushed ahead quickly in the 1930s to replace the older communists purged by Stalin. These men had at the same time a feeling of gratitude to the Communist Party for their advancement up the ladder of power and a vivid awareness of the precariousness of their positions, based on the arbitrary use of terror by Stalin. Even though many of them were Stalinists at heart, they did not disagree with Khrushchev's fundamental proposition that no future leader be permitted to use Stalin's methods. It was not that they had any moral scruples about maintaining order and discipline, but they were aware that

Stalin's personal use of terror had been turned against the Communist Party itself.

The new generation is largely urban in background, better educated, usually with university degrees, much more sophisticated, with a greater knowledge of the realities of the outside world and the problems of cohabitation. They also have a greater awareness of the new technology and the electronic revolution. They are self-confident, tough, and able. And above all, they are for the most part Russians, proud of their Russian history, their Russian achievements, and determined to defend the dominance of the Russians in the Soviet Union and to advance Russian national interests in the world.

Nevertheless, there is one thing these new leaders have in common with their predecessors and it is all-important; all of them, and those treading on their heels, came up through the Party apparatus. They owe their personal success to the Party and their collective survival to the communist system and ideology. Thus, while acting normally in a practical, pragmatic way in both foreign and internal affairs, there are certain ideological imperatives which will continue to impinge on their general behaviour. In other words, they will not act in accordance with Marxist doctrine if this endangers the Soviet Union or the security of the hierarchy and Nomenklatura. But there are some things they will be unable to do because they would undermine their credentials as Marxists-Leninists.

No matter how different superficially the newer generation, their basic aim is identical with that of their predecessors. A ruling class has been formed representing the elite of the Communist Party in the hands of which total power is concentrated and which enjoys immense privileges, prestige, and influence. To hold onto this is their overriding goal. They also legitimately hope to make the Soviet Union a strong and prosperous country. But for them this aim and that of preserving power are indistinguishable.

There are three ways this can be done. The first is by maintaining the status quo and concentrating the country's resources on creating a powerful military machine to assert Russia's place in the world, and an equally powerful police system to sustain the

Communist Party as the sole recipient and dispenser of power inside the country. This was the formula up to the end of the Brezhnev era. And it did achieve stability and assured the CPSU of its undisputed leadership. But it ignored changes in the world, the immense cost of nuclear weapons which often proved of little use, as in Afghanistan, the increasing gap between Soviet industry and technology and the West, and the declining standard of living in the country as a whole. Perhaps even more important, it did not take into consideration the ability of the Soviet Union to compete with the industrialized world and China on the economic plane. The nightmare of the Russians is the prospect of one billion Chinese organized into a modern and efficient society with the help of Western and Japanese capital and technology. And the progress toward economic reform in China, while maintaining its communist credentials, greatly disturbs the Soviets.

The second formula is to lower tensions with the developed countries of the Western world and Japan in order to be able to reduce the enormous proportion of GNP devoted to the armed forces, and to acquire Western technology and capital to modernize the Soviet economy, improve its competitiveness internationally, and increase the standard of living above its present dismally low level. In the first decade of his long rule Brezhnev did toy with this formula as a means of alleviating the country's problems. He made a genuine effort to reduce tensions with Western countries, which did have some political advantages for the Soviets. But the effort to solve the economic problems through the importation of whole factories did little to improve the basic situation. It was, in fact, not much more than tinkering with the system. And, in any case, it was obviously exposed to the vagaries of Soviet foreign policy, as the collapse of the Brezhnev-Nixon efforts at peaceful coexistence and the invasion of Afghanistan demonstrated.

The third formula is radical economic reform. Some changes were attempted by Khrushchev, and others by Kosygin in the early years of the Brezhnev era. But they were too timid to accomplish anything substantial on the economic front, and they were abandoned outright when economic reforms in Czechoslovakia led almost immediately to demands for political reform.

Gorbachev has recognized that there must be an alternative to the Brezhnev formula inasmuch as economic stagnation, while tolerable with a people as passive as the Russians, threatens in the long run the leadership's hold on power and the position of the Soviet Union in the world. He is therefore introducing reforms and changes the aim of which is to make the Marxist-Leninist state more efficient internally and its image abroad more attractive. Both these goals, if achieved, would at the same time strengthen the position of the Communist Party and its leadership.

The Soviet Union could probably continue to lumber along without change – that is, with immensely powerful military might but with a stagnant economy at a level approaching that of an under-developed country. It can match American military improvements, but at a cost. And this cost is the continuing concentration of Russian technology and innovation in the military sector, leaving the civilian economy increasingly backward. A further arms race and a decline in the standard of living, and an increasing technological gap between the Soviet Union and the West are things Gorbachev recognizes cannot continue. This is clear from the introduction of measures to revitalize Soviet society, invigorate the economy, present a more civilized face to the outside world, and attempt to negotiate political agreements which would permit Russia to achieve its internal and foreign aims more successfully and at a reduced cost. In the two latter aims he has made remarkable progress.

But what really counts in the long run, both for the survival of the Soviet system and for the emergence of Russia as a superpower in any but the military sense, is going to be Gorbachev's ability to modernize the economy.

The key is central planning which is essential for ideological and administrative reasons, and, equally important, as a means of maintaining the power and authority of its elite. This is exercised through five-year plans which determine down to the last detail and for the whole country what is to be produced and how it is to be done. Making a profit for an enterprise has been desirable but not essential. All that has been required of managers and workers was to follow the directives of the plan as laid down by Moscow. Nearly all knowledgeable Russians, from Gorbachev down, are aware of the problems of central control of the economy, and of the deficiencies of collectivized agriculture, and they are trying to find solutions. But there is vast opposition to real reform.

This is closely linked to the fear of the thousands of little Stalins all over the country that they will lose their power and privileges; and that they will have to think and take decisions. This fear is not limited to the Party and administrative bureaucracy. It is shared to an extent by the majority of the people. They want things to be better, but deep down most of them are afraid of change, of the fatal step into the unknown. So there is a curious kind of convergence of lethargy about reform between the conservative Party people and much of the population.

The dilemma for Gorbachev is that truly reforming the system carries the risk of the whole structure coming unstuck, even if it were possible to convince his conservative partners of the need to reform. But without major changes the situation is bound to get worse, which in turn would endanger the Communist Party's hold on power. In other words, to maintain a centrally controlled command economy undermines one of Gorbachev's basic aims – to force managers of local enterprises to take decisions and to make a profit. Yet to relax central planning risks losing control, both of the economy and eventually even of political power.

At the time of writing this in July 1988, Gorbachev has made a number of spectacular gestures towards opening up Soviet society and introduced changes which would have been unthinkable only a short time ago. He seems to be trying to shake the population and the Communist Party out of its torpor and, like Peter the Great, thrust Russia willy-nilly into the modern world. Some of his proposals for political changes are inchoate and probably impractical, and nowhere is there any hint of toying with democracy outside the limits of the Communist Party itself. Gorbachev in fact has described his view of democracy as 'conscious discipline and an understanding for everybody to participate ... in the building of socialism.'

Nevertheless, some of his political overtures, above all the proposals to create a presidential form of government, are of immense potential importance. These administrative changes would leave the country still firmly in the hands of communists, but would end the duplications that exist at present of departments in the Party apparatus corresponding to and supervising the day-to-day operations of ministries and enterprises. As Gorbachev put it clearly, the intention was to streamline the administration while permitting the Party to carry out its policies 'through communists working in governmental organs.'

To justify their claim to govern the Soviet leaders need not only to improve the economy and living standards of the people but to demonstrate that they are able to make the Soviet Union a great power able to defend itself against any foe and to project an image of the country of which all its citizens can be proud. In this they have partially succeeded. The armed forces are vastly greater than needed for an adequate defence of the country against any and all foes. But it is difficult to eliminate centuries of fear of invasion and the memories of the near defeat of 1941. The leadership, while boasting of the invincible strength of the country, at the same time insists on the constant 'imperialist' threat, in part to justify the huge proportion of the GNP devoted to the armed forces, in part to keep the population in a continual state of alert. On the whole, however, the average Russian is satisfied that the leadership has made their country militarily strong.

He is proud also of the way in which Russia has become a superpower and is accepted as such by the rest of the world. When this is questioned, as it has been occasionally by the United States or China, it provokes a feeling of deep resentment on the part of the leaders and the intelligentsia and to a lesser extent the people. Brezhnev was meeting a deep-felt need on the part of all Russians when he sought and believed he had secured formal acceptance by the United States of political parity. Rejection of this assumption affects the prestige of the leaders, but most Russians resent this as an insult to the whole nation.

More and more the average Russian expects or at least hopes that the Soviet leaders will be able to present an image of Russia consonant with its power and its role as part of the Western world. The new look of Gorbachev reflects this expectation and it has an internal domestic aim as well as an international one: to be seen both by the Russians and the outside world as sophisticated, cultured, modern Europeans. And on this score there can be little doubt that Gorbachev has displayed an uncanny aptitude for foreign affairs. In an fairly short time he has improved the image and the position of the Soviet Union not only vis-à-vis the other superpower but throughout the world.

No matter what happens to Gorbachev and his experiments, he has introduced the first breath of fresh air into the Soviet Union since Khrushchev revealed the crimes of Stalin. He has offered some genuine competition of factions and interest groups within the Communist Party elite, a tiny but important step for the future, although it can only continue so long as the monolithic dominance of the elite is not seriously threatened. Any semblance of competition or democracy beyond the Party itself seems, at least for the time being, out of the question.

Gorbachev may suffer Khrushchev's fate eventually, but what he is doing cannot easily be reversed completely. Nor will the younger, educated Russians, whether committed communists or not, accept for very long an attempt to reimpose the antiquated economic and political immobilism of the Brezhnev era.

Gorbachev is a refreshing change from the past. He will not alter the basic nature of the Soviet system; but his aims in disarmament and arms control, while badly needed for domestic Soviet purposes, coincide broadly with aspirations long cherished in the West. He is a skilful, imaginative leader who wants to make his country the fully great power it is not at present. And he seems to recognize that security today for any country, no matter how strong, must rest on a concept of common security and a degree of mutual interest in spite of immense and continuing ideological differences.

The new leaders and those coming up through the ranks must not be underestimated. They are competent, realistic, tough, prickly, and determined to defend and advance Russian national interests in the light of Marxist-Leninist doctrine. They will insist on the right of the Soviet Union to be treated as an equal superpower, and not only in the military sphere where Soviet strength is indisputable. They want political equality as well. It still rankles with them that the equality they thought they had achieved through the series of American-Soviet agreements of 1972–5 evaporated, unjustifiably denied to them, as they passionately believe.

There is hope that the new generation of Soviet leaders, increasingly preoccupied by their economic, social, and political problems, will be prepared to return to a realistic relationship with the West. But they will have to be accepted as political equals and convinced that the aim of the West is cohabitation and not destruction of their system. They themselves will have to recognize the realities of the Western world and be prepared for the compromises necessary for coexistence. They have almost certainly rejected as unrealistic nonsense Khrushchev's program of 1961 which vowed 'to sweep imperialism away and bury it.' But it must be formally scrapped if they expect the West to forget its hyperbole. Compromise will not be easy. The Soviets will not facilitate the task and an almost excessive amount of patience will be required. But it is the first priority of politics, diplomacy, and common sense, and I think it can be done.

The great Russian poet and diplomat Fyodor Tyutchev over one hundred and fifty years ago wrote:

> Russia cannot be understood
> Only with the mind – no normal
> Standard can judge her
> Greatness. She stands alone, unique.
> In Russia one must only believe.

While a debatable proposition then and now, these lines still sum up succinctly the problem for any Westerner in assessing Russia. One can describe the facts as they appear to us, one can try to penetrate the Russian, and the communist, mind, and one can only hope that some slight flicker of illumination may result.

INDEX